OXFORD MONOGRAPHS IN INTERNATIONAL HUMANITARIAN AND CRIMINAL LAW

Series Editors

SALVATORE ZAPPALÀ
Professor of International Law at the University of Catania

PHILIPPA WEBB
Professor of Public International Law, The Dickson Poon School of Law, King's College London

Proving International Crimes

OXFORD MONOGRAPHS IN INTERNATIONAL HUMANITARIAN AND CRIMINAL LAW

This series emerged through the vision of the late Antonio Cassese. Since then the series has published original and innovative works on challenging issues in international humanitarian law and international criminal justice, primarily by emerging authors. Given the ever-growing intersection of these areas with other fields of international law such as the *jus ad bellum*, and disciplines such as criminology, sociology, and history, the scope of the series also incorporates these perspectives. Fresh approaches and new ideas for improving conceptual and practical challenges are welcomed. The series editors encourage submissions from around the world, and will consider edited collections, although the primary focus is on authored works.

ALSO PUBLISHED IN THIS SERIES

International Criminal Tribunals and Domestic Accountability
In the Court's Shadow
Patryk I. Labuda

The Morality of the Laws of War
War, Law, and Murder
Marcela Prieto Rudolphy

Accountability for Mass Starvation
Testing the Limits of the Law
Bridget Conley, Alex de Waal, Catriona Murdoch, Wayne Jordash KC

The Defence of Mistake of Law in International Criminal Law
A Study on Ignorance and Blame
Antonio Coco

The Use of Force against Individuals in War under International Law
A Social Ontological Approach
Ka Lok Yip

Proving International Crimes

YVONNE McDERMOTT

OXFORD
UNIVERSITY PRESS

OXFORD
UNIVERSITY PRESS

Great Clarendon Street, Oxford, OX2 6DP,
United Kingdom

Oxford University Press is a department of the University of Oxford.
It furthers the University's objective of excellence in research, scholarship,
and education by publishing worldwide. Oxford is a registered trade mark of
Oxford University Press in the UK and in certain other countries

Published in the United States of America by Oxford University Press
198 Madison Avenue, New York, NY 10016, United States of America

British Library Cataloguing in Publication Data

Data available

Library of Congress Control Number: 2024939136

ISBN 978–0–19–884297–2

DOI: 10.1093/oso/9780198842972.001.0001

Printed and bound by
CPI Group (UK) Ltd, Croydon, CR0 4YY

MIX
Paper | Supporting
responsible forestry
FSC® C013604

The manufacturer's authorised representative in the EU for product safety is
Oxford University Press España S.A. of El Parque Empresarial San Fernando de Henares, Avenida
de Castilla, 2 – 28830 Madrid (www.oup.es/en or
product.safety@oup.com). OUP España S.A. also acts as importer into Spain
of products made by the manufacturer.

To Cormac

Foreword

I first encountered the complexities of international crimes in 1999, when I joined the International Criminal Tribunal for the former Yugoslavia (ICTY) as a senior prosecuting trial lawyer. At that time jurisprudence from ICTY—and the even more recent Rwanda Tribunal (ICTR)—was in its infancy. The crime of genocide post-dated the Second World War military tribunals and had never been prosecuted. The nature of the evidence required to establish that those accused of international crimes, in particular the leaders (far removed from the actual commission of those crimes), was endlessly discussed by the judges, lawyers, and academics as the trials progressed. Each judgment led to further discussion, often producing wholly divergent opinions. For a lawyer used to practice in a domestic jurisdiction (where the law either was long settled or, if in development, the doctrine of 'precedent' prevailed), the uncertainty and the 'hybrid' nature of procedural matters at ICTY proved to be both fascinating and frustrating.

The International Criminal Court (ICC) came into existence, during this period, with a statute that differed in many major respects from those of ICTY and ICTR. Whilst its sources of applicable law (Article 27) do not mention the jurisprudence of the ad hoc tribunals, nonetheless it provided a basis for early ICC judgments. Since the first trial judgment in the case of *Lubanga* (2012), the ICC has developed a substantial body of its own jurisprudence. However, numerous academic commentators have pointed to a lack of consistency by all the divisions (most importantly the Appeals Chamber) in their approach to what may be considered basic principles of law and procedure. This was highlighted by the Independent Expert Review (September 2020) which in one of its recommendations (217) stated: 'Recognising the importance of legal certainty and consistency, the Court should depart from established practice or jurisprudence only where that is justified on grounds precisely articulated in the decision/judgment.'

It is no exaggeration to say that this Report acted as a 'wake-up call' to all the organs of the court. Many of the recommendations have already resulted in amendments being made to the Statute, Rules of Procedure and Evidence, Regulations of the Court and the Chambers Practice Manual. Judicial discussions continue in respect of finding a resolution to other issues highlighted in the report.

In the light of the background and current developments, this book by Professor McDermott could not be timelier. As she points out, in her chapter on the 'Principles of International Criminal Law', [T]he procedural flexibility inherent in the legal frameworks of all international criminal tribunals means that international criminal evidence cannot be viewed as a fixed and immutable construct but one that constantly evolves and changes.' Thereafter, in a chronological manner, she sets out the—sometimes contradictory—aspects of the law, the nature of the evidence, and the procedures which presently prevail during proceedings involving international crimes.

Professor McDermott's overall argument (as set out in full in Chapter 2) is that the future development of the law and practice of proving international crimes must be underpinned by two key principles: rectitude of decision and the highest standards of fairness. The latter principle might be thought to be self-evident but bears repetition. The former, as she explains, is more controversial but is one for which she makes what may be considered to be a compelling case.

While the list of crimes defined as international continues to be augmented, the standards required for proof thereof remain constant. This book should have the effect of reminding all judges and practitioners of the need to ensure that those standards are both consistent and compliant with the ultimate goal of delivering justice to the victims of these egregious crimes by means of a fair trial process.

Joanna Korner
December 2023

Series Editors' Preface

Yvonne McDermott's book *Proving International Crimes* is an important addition to the Oxford Monographs in International Humanitarian and Criminal Law series. It is important due to the rigour of its analysis, but also because it tackles an issue at the heart of efforts to end impunity: can the reality of international criminal justice live up to its promise?

The author explains that the book aims to examine how international criminal courts and tribunals have handled the 'immense and complex task' of proving international crimes. It does this not just by studying the legal framework but also by analysing how the law is applied in practice through judgments, decisions, motions, and transcripts. The book moves beyond the scholarly debate on whether international criminal procedure is characterised by adversarial or inquisitorial features and advances an argument for a coherent legal framework driven by two principles: rectitude of decision and the highest standards of fairness. The book also advances the scholarship on evidence beyond the well-trodden questions surrounding admissibility to the question on what happens once the evidence is admitted.

Prosecuting a case involving international crimes is not for the faint-hearted. As the author observes, every aspect of such a case is challenging: there will inevitably be a mountain of evidence, but that evidence may relate to events of years earlier or, indeed, to events unfolding in real time. The reliability of the evidence will vary, and fears for the safety of witnesses can inhibit access to vital evidence. Cases may form part of situations that are political flashpoints, bringing tensions, pressure, and intense criticism to bear on the Office of the Prosecutor or the judges. At the time of writing, the ICC Prosecutor is seeking arrest warrants against the leadership of Hamas and the Israeli government, provoking strong reactions from many sides of the political spectrum. If warrants are approved by the Pre-Trial Chamber, the author's principles of rectitude of decision and the highest standards of fairness provide a beacon in the political storms to come.

The author rightly notes that right to a fair trial (a right owed primarily to the accused individual) requires a system for the admission and evaluation of evidence that does not jeopardise the multiple components that make up the right to a fair trial—including equality of arms, the right to a defence, the right to examine witnesses, the presumption of innocence, and the right to appeal. She identifies three implications for future practice in international prosecutions better to secure fair trial rights. First, the author urges a more systematic and coherent approach to international criminal procedure, including the treatment of evidence. Second, she highlights the need to rigorously link fact-finding to just legal outcomes at every stage, rising above the false dichotomy of the atomistic/holistic debate. Technology could play a useful role in this process. Third, and relatedly, the quality of evidence must be ensured.

This book by Professor McDermott is a timely and welcome contribution to the literature on international criminal law. She follows in the great tradition of Mirjan Damaška in seeing developments in their historical context, drawing out themes, and urging improvements for the future.

The Editors

Acknowledgements

This book has been many years in the making and would not have been possible without the encouragement of many dear friends, family members, and colleagues. Special thanks to Xabier Agirre Aranburu, Michelle Coleman, Matt Cross, Simon De Smet, the late and much-missed Megan Fairlie, Jonathan Hak, John Jackson, Alexa Koenig, David Lagnado, Alice Liefgreen, Manuel Sanchez Miranda, HHJ Keith Raynor, Barrie Sander, Gheorghe Tecuci, and Eric Tully, who provided feedback on draft chapters of this work, and especially Konstantina Stavrou, who meticulously reviewed the complete final manuscript. My friend and mentor William Twining, who has inspired so much of my thinking about evidence and proof, generously gave rigorous and thoughtful feedback on several drafts of the entire manuscript as it developed. The book is immeasurably better thanks to his comments and encouragement. I am truly honoured that Her Excellency Judge Joanna Korner CMG KC kindly agreed to write the foreword, and I am very grateful for her insightful comments on the manuscript.

Thanks to the entire team at Oxford University Press, especially my editor Kate Plunkett, for going a million miles beyond what any author could hope for. The cover image shows the mimeograph room in the Palace of Justice during the Nuremberg trials and is reproduced here with the kind permission of Stadtarchiv Nürnberg. Special thanks to Douglas Guilfoyle for suggesting this very fitting image and for hosting me as a visiting researcher at Monash University School of Law in 2018.

This book has particularly benefited from feedback on lectures delivered at the Honourable Society of the Inner Temple; Oxford University's Public International Law discussion group; the Siracusa International Institute for Criminal Justice and Human Rights, and the North Sea Group. Thank you to Master Hughes, the Rt Hon Lord Hughes of Ombersley; Talita de Souza Dias, Miles Jackson, and Antonio Coco; the wonderful William Schabas; and Anne-Ruth Mackor and Christian Dahlman for the invites, and to students and colleagues for their thought-provoking questions and comments.

For moral support and a lot of laughs along the way, thanks to my colleagues at Swansea and all the usual suspects, especially Aoife Daly, Michelle Farrell, Dimitrios Giannoulopoulos, Niamh Hayes, David Keane, Helen McDermott, Daragh Murray, Joe Powderly, Evelyne Schmid, and Tara Smith. I would like to thank the entire McDermott and Rees clans, particularly my parents, for their unwavering love and encouragement, and Osian and Cormac, for everything.

Swansea
October 2023

Contents

Table of Cases

EUROPEAN COURT OF HUMAN RIGHTS

EXTRAORDINARY CHAMBERS IN THE COURTS OF CAMBODIA

INTER-AMERICAN COURT OF HUMAN RIGHTS

INTERNATIONAL CRIMINAL COURT

Situation in the Central African Republic (ICC-01/05)

Prosecutor v. Bemba

Prosecutor v. Gbagbo and Blé Goudé

Situation in Darfur, Sudan (ICC-02/05)

Situation in the Democratic Republic of the Congo (ICC-01/04)

Situation in Kenya (ICC-01/09)

Prosecutor v. Gicheru and Bett

Prosecutor v. Muthaura et al.

Prosecutor v. Ruto et al.

Situation in Uganda (ICC-02/04)

Prosecutor v. Ongwen

International Criminal Tribunal for the former Yugoslavia

International Criminal Tribunal for Rwanda

International Military Tribunal at Nuremberg

International Military Tribunal for the Far East

International Residual Mechanism for Criminal Tribunals

Kosovo Specialist Chambers

Special Court for Sierra Leone

Special Tribunal for Lebanon

National Courts

CANADA

UNITED STATES OF AMERICA

UNITED STATES MILITARY TRIBUNAL AT NUREMBERG

Table of Legislation

INTERNATIONAL CRIMINAL TRIBUNAL FOR THE FORMER YUGOSLAVIA

INTERNATIONAL CRIMINAL TRIBUNAL FOR RWANDA

INTERNATIONAL MILITARY TRIBUNAL (NUREMBERG)

INTERNATIONAL MILITARY TRIBUNAL FOR THE FAR EAST

KOSOVO SPECIALIST CHAMBERS

INTERNATIONAL RESIDUAL MECHANISM FOR CRIMINAL TRIBUNALS

SPECIAL TRIBUNAL FOR LEBANON

SPECIAL COURT FOR SIERRA LEONE

AFRICAN UNION

UN GENERAL ASSEMBLY

UN HUMAN RIGHTS COUNCIL

UN SECRETARY GENERAL

UN SECURITY COUNCIL

UN PREPARATORY COMMITTEE ON THE ESTABLISHMENT OF AN INTERNATIONAL CRIMINAL COURT

DOMESTIC LEGISLATION

Abbreviations

DC-Cam	Documentation Center of Cambodia
DRC	Democratic Republic of Congo
ECCC	Extraordinary Chambers in the Courts of Cambodia
ECHR	European Convention of Human Rights
ECtHR	European Court of Human Rights
EU	European Union
ICC	International Criminal Court
ICTR	International Criminal Tribunal for Rwanda
ICTY	International Criminal Tribunal for the former Yugoslavia
IDP	internally displaced persons
IER	Independent Expert Review
IIIM	International, Impartial and Independent Mechanism
IIMM	Independent Investigative Mechanism for Myanmar
IMT	International Military Tribunal
IMTFE	International Military Tribunal for the Far East
IRMCT	International Residual Mechanism for Criminal Tribunals
KSC	Kosovo Specialist Chambers
NGO	non-governmental organisation
OTP	Office of the Prosecutor
RPE	Rules of Procedure and Evidence
SCSL	Special Court for Sierra Leone
STL	Special Tribunal for Lebanon
UN	United Nations
UNGA	United Nations General Assembly

1
Introduction

A. Introduction

> Despite the fact that public opinion already condemns their acts, we agree that here they must be given a presumption of innocence, and we accept the burden of proving criminal acts and the responsibility of these defendants for their commission ... [W]e do not ask for convictions unless we prove crime.[1]

United States Chief Prosecutor Robert Jackson, in his opening statement at Nuremberg, recognised what is surely a truism of any legal process: judgments must tell a story that is accountable to the evidence.[2] Without sufficient evidence to prove both the contextual and specific elements of the crimes alleged, and the requisite mode(s) of liability, accountability for international crimes cannot be established.

Yet, the International Criminal Court (ICC) has an 'evidence problem'.[3] Several cases have been dismissed at the confirmation of charges stage, with the Pre-Trial Chamber determining that the low standard of proof required at that stage ('substantial grounds to believe') had not been met.[4] High-profile acquittals such as

[1] R.H. Jackson, Opening Statement before the International Military Tribunal, Second Day, 21 November 1945, in *Trial of the Major War Criminals before the International Military Tribunal: Volume II*.

[2] Jill Lapore similarly wrote that 'history is the art of making an argument about the past by telling a story that is accountable to the evidence': J. Lapore, *The Story of America: Essays on Origins* (Princeton University Press, 2013), 15.

[3] C. De Vos, 'Investigating from Afar: The ICC's Evidence Problem' (2013) 26 *Leiden Journal of International Law* 1009; P Labuda, 'The ICC's "Evidence Problem"' (*Völkerrechtsblog*, 18 January 2019). See further, D. Groome, 'No Witness, No Case: An Assessment of the Conduct and Quality of ICC Investigations' (2014) 3 *Penn State Journal of Law & International Affairs* 1; Independent Expert Review of the International Criminal Court and the Rome Statute System. Final Report, 30 September 2020, paras 785–801; D. Guilfoyle, 'Part I—This Is Not Fine: The International Criminal Court In Trouble' (*EJIL:Talk!*, 21 March 2019); D. Guilfoyle, 'Lacking Conviction: Is the International Criminal Court Broken? An Organisational Failure Analysis' (2019) 20 *Melbourne Journal of International Law* 401.

[4] *Prosecutor v Abu Garda*, Decision on the Confirmation of Charges, ICC-02/05-02/09-243, 8 February 2010; *Prosecutor v Mbarushimana*, Decision on the Confirmation of Charges, ICC-01/04-01/10-465, 16 December 2011; *Prosecutor v Ruto et al.*, Decision on the Confirmation of Charges Pursuant to Article 61(7)(a) and (b) of the Rome Statute, ICC-01/09-01/11-373, 23 January 2012, and *Prosecutor v Muthaura et al.*, Decision on the Confirmation of Charges Pursuant to Article 61(7)(a) and (b) of the Rome Statute, ICC-01/09-02/11-382, 23 January 2012. See further W.A. Schabas, 'Thoughts on the Kenya Confirmation Decisions' (*PhD Studies in Human Rights*, 30 January 2012), depicting this as

Proving International Crimes. Yvonne McDermott, Oxford University Press. © Yvonne McDermott 2024.
DOI: 10.1093/oso/9780198842972.003.0001

those of Laurent Gbagbo and Charles Blé Goudé at the 'no case to answer' stage of proceedings,[5] and that of Jean-Pierre Bemba Gombo on appeal,[6] included criticisms of the Office of the Prosecutor for bringing cases that were, in the view of the Chamber, insufficiently supported by the evidence.[7] The *Bemba* Appeal Judgment, and its accompanying dissenting and separate opinions, provided a fascinating insight into some of the key tensions, disputes, and uncertainties that have plagued the ICC since its inception. It showed that fundamental questions, such as the extent to which Trial Chambers should underscore which evidence supports a factual finding and how that evidence led the Chamber to its conclusions, are answered differently by different judges.[8] It also demonstrated a sharp dispute in interpretation on the standard of appeal for findings of fact,[9] and the

a 'failure rate of 29%', or 4 out of 14 cases at that point. In October 2023, the Prosecutor withdrew the charges against defendant Maxime Mokom prior to the Pre-Trial Chamber's issuance of its confirmation decision on the grounds that the Office of the Prosecutor had insufficient evidence to proceed with its case: *Prosecutor v Mokom*, Order in Relation to the Prosecution's 'Notice of Withdrawal of the Charges against Maxime Jeoffroy Eli Mokom Gawaka', ICC-01/14-01/22-276, 17 October 2023.

[5] *Prosecutor v Gbagbo and Blé Goudé*, Reasons for oral decision of 15 January 2019 on the Requête de la Défense de Laurent Gbagbo afin qu'un jugement d'acquittement portant sur toutes les charges soit prononcé en faveur de Laurent Gbagbo et que sa mise en liberté immédiate soit ordonnée, and on the Blé Goudé Defence no case to answer motion, ICC-02/11-01/15-1263, 16 July 2019 ('*Gbagbo* Reasons').

[6] The academic community was quick to respond to this judgment, with some reactions suggesting that the Appeals Chamber had gone too far (if such a thing were possible) in its rigorous evaluation of the Trial Chamber's judgment and the evidence (or lack thereof) underpinning its findings: See e.g. D.M. Amann, 'In Bemba and Beyond, Crimes Adjudged to Commit Themselves' (*EJIL Talk!*, 13 June 2018); L.N. Sadat, 'Fiddling While Rome Burns? The Appeals Chamber's Curious Decision in *Prosecutor v. Jean-Pierre Bemba Gombo*' (*EJIL Talk!*, 12 June 2018); N. Hayes and J. Powderly, 'The Bemba Appeal: A Fragmented Appeals Chamber Destabilises the Law and Practice of the ICC' (*PhD Studies in Human Rights*, 26 June 2018); A. Whiting, 'Appeals Judges Turn the ICC on Its Head with Bemba Decision' (*Just Security*, 14 June 2018); S. Sácouto and P. Sellers, 'The Bemba Appeals Chamber Judgment: Impunity for Sexual and Gender-Based Crimes?' (2019) 27 *William & Mary Bill of Rights Journal* 599; cf. A. Heinze, 'Some Reflections on the *Bemba* Appeals Chamber Judgment' (*Opinio Juris*, 18 June 2018).

[7] *Gbagbo* Reasons, n 5, Reasons of Judge Henderson, ICC-02/11-01/15-1263-AnxB-Red, 16 July 2019, paras 2038 and 2041; *Gbagbo* Reasons, n 5, Opinion of Judge Tarfusser, ICC-02/11-01/15-1263-AnxA, 16 July 2019, paras 3–5; *Prosecutor v Bemba*, Judgment on the appeal of Mr Jean-Pierre Bemba Gombo against Trial Chamber III's 'Judgment pursuant to Article 74 of the Statute', ICC-01/05-01/08-3636-Red, 8 June 2018 ('*Bemba* Appeal Judgment'), para. 183; *Bemba* Appeal Judgment, Separate Opinion of Judge Van den Wyngaert and Judge Morrison, ICC-01/05-01/08-3636-Anx2, 8 June 2018, paras 3–18; *Bemba* Appeal Judgment, Concurring Separate Opinion of Judge Eboe-Osuji, ICC-01/05-01/08-3636-Anx3, 14 June 2018, paras 7–11.

[8] *Bemba* Appeal Judgment, Separate Opinion of Judge Van den Wyngaert and Judge Morrison, n 7, para. 4.

[9] The Majority held that, where a Trial Chamber fails to make clear the evidentiary basis for a finding and the Chamber's analysis of that evidence, 'the Appeals Chamber has no choice but to set aside the affected finding, since the lack of adequate reasoning renders the finding unreviewable, thereby constituting a serious procedural error': *Bemba* Appeal Judgment, n 7, para. 66. On the other hand, the two dissenting judges argued that their colleagues had erroneously substituted their own analysis of the evidence for the Trial Chamber's, thereby breaching the principle of appellate deference to findings of fact (*Bemba* Appeal Judgment, n 7, Dissenting Opinion of Judge Monageng and Judge Hofmański, ICC-01/05-01/08-3636-Anx1, 8 June 2018, para. 13).

role of the confirmation of the charges stage of proceedings in shaping the later trial proceedings.[10]

Outside of the ICC, other international criminal tribunals have grappled with similar issues of evidence and proof, including the admissibility of, and the weight to be given to, certain forms of evidence;[11] the meaning of the standard of proof;[12] the standard of review for alleged errors of fact,[13] and the manner in which evidence should be evaluated and marshalled towards findings of fact.[14] As shall be seen throughout this book, these issues have been beset by a lack of certainty on how they should be interpreted, and practice between tribunals (or, on occasion, different chambers of the same tribunal) has been inconsistent.

These controversies come at a time when our ways of knowing about atrocity crimes have been transformed by the digital era, and the advent of so-called user-generated evidence in particular.[15] Around the world today, eyewitnesses to international crimes—and, often, perpetrators themselves or their allies—are recording and sharing videos and images that could be used as evidence in proving international crimes.[16] The landscape of international criminal investigations, more broadly, has changed fundamentally in recent years, with United Nations-mandated human rights investigations, fact-finding missions, and commissions of

[10] *Bemba* Appeal Judgment, n 7, paras 98–119.

[11] For example, on written witness statements not subjected to cross-examination: *Prosecutor v Martić*, Judgment, IT-95-11-A, 8 October 2008 ('*Martić* Appeal Judgment'), para. 193. On the weight to be afforded to hearsay evidence, see *Prosecutor v Prlić et al.*, Decision on Admission of Transcript, IT-04-74-AR73.6, 23 November 2007, para. 53; *KAING Guek Eav* alias *Duch ('Case 001')*, Judgment, 001/18-07-2007/ECCC/TC (E188), 26 July 2010, para. 43. On expert evidence, compare *Prosecutor v Popović et al.*, Decision on Joint Defence Interlocutory Appeal concerning the Status of Richard Butler as an Expert Witness, IT-05–88-AR73.2, 30 January 2008, paras 29–31 with *Prosecutor v Milošević*, Decision on Admissibility of Prosecution Investigator Evidence, IT-02-54-AR73.2, 30 September 2002, para. 17. See further Chapter 5.

[12] *Martić* Appeal Judgment, n 11, paras 55–63; *Prosecutor v Tadić*, Judgment, IT-94-1-A, 15 July 1999 ('*Tadić* Appeal Judgment'), paras 181–3; *Prosecutor v Ngirabatware*, Judgment, IRMCT-12-29-A, 18 December 2014, para. 20. See further Chapter 4.

[13] *Tadić* Appeal Judgment, n 12, para. 64; *Prosecutor v Akayesu*, Judgment, ICTR-96-4-A, 1 June 2001, para. 178; *Prosecutor v Musema*, Judgment, ICTR-96-13-A, 16 November 2001, para. 204. See further Chapter 7.

[14] Judgments commonly note that even if a piece of evidence has not been expressly cited, it will nevertheless have been considered: see, for example, *Prosecutor v Popović et al.*, Judgment, IT-05-88-A, 30 January 2015, para. 375; *Prosecutor v Perišić*, Judgment, IT-04-81-T, 6 September 2011, para. 23; *Prosecutor v Bikindi*, Judgment, ICTR-01-72-T, 2 December 2008, para. 29; *Prosecutor v Stanišić and Simatović*, Judgment, IT-03-69, 30 May 2013, para. 34; *Prosecutor v Gotovina*, Judgment, IT-06-90-T, 15 April 2011, para. 47. See further Chapter 6.

[15] R. Hamilton, 'User-Generated Evidence' (2018) 57 *Columbia Journal of Transnational Law* 1; S. Dubberley et al. (eds), *Digital Witness: Using Open Source Information for Human Rights Investigation, Documentation, and Accountability* (OUP, 2020); D. Murray et al., 'Mapping the Use of Open Source Research in UN Human Rights Investigations' (2022) 14 *Journal of Human Rights Practice* 554; Y. McDermott et al., 'Open Source Information's Blind Spot: Human and Machine Bias in International Criminal Investigations' (2021) 19 *Journal of International Criminal Justice* 85; L. Freeman, 'Digital Evidence and War Crimes Prosecutions: The Impact of Digital Technologies on International Criminal Investigations and Trials' (2018) 41 *Fordham International Law Journal* 283.

[16] In addition to those cited in n 15, see Special Issue, 'New Technologies and the Investigation of International Crimes' (2021) 19 *Journal of International Criminal Justice* 1–233.

inquiry increasingly conducting their enquiries in a manner that recognises the potential for future criminal accountability processes.[17] Meanwhile, specific international mechanisms have been established to preserve evidence explicitly for the purpose of supporting criminal trials in domestic and international fora.[18] Civil society and international organizations working on the collection, preservation, and verification of information that could be used as evidence in international criminal trials often look to the ICC, in particular, for guidance on the applicable legal and procedural standards,[19] only to find that practice on many key issues is still evolving, and as such is unpredictable and uncertain.

This book also comes at a time of resurgence in the domestic prosecutions of international crimes,[20] as well as increasing calls for the creation of new international criminal tribunals.[21] These initiatives may seek to draw on the experience of the ICC and other international criminal tribunals in conducting international criminal trials. Meanwhile, as the ICC enters its third decade, some commentators have remarked that it is leaving its difficult adolescent years and entering full

[17] F. D'Alessandra, 'The Accountability Turn in Third Wave Human Rights Fact-Finding' (2017) 33 *Utrecht Journal of International and European Law* 59; C. Henderson (ed.), *Commissions of Inquiry: Problems and Prospects* (Hart, 2017); P.G. Alston and S. Knuckey (eds), *The Transformation of Human Rights Fact-Finding* (OUP, 2016); M. Aksenova and M. Bergsmo, 'Non-Criminal Justice Fact-Work in the Age of Accountability' in M. Bergsmo (ed.), *Quality Control in Fact-Finding* (TOAEP, 2013), 1; D. Jacobs and C. Harwood, 'International Criminal Law Outside the Courtroom: The Impact of Focusing on International Crimes for the Quality of Fact-Finding' in M. Bergsmo (ed.), *Quality Control in Fact-Finding* (TOAEP, 2013), 325.

[18] UNGA, Resolution adopted by the Human Rights Council on 27 September 2018, Situation of human rights of Rohingya Muslims and other minorities in Myanmar, UN Doc A/HRC/RES/39/2, 3 October 2018, para. 22, establishing the Independent Investigative Mechanism for Myanmar (IIMM); UNGA, Resolution adopted by the General Assembly on 21 December 2016, International, Impartial and Independent Mechanism to Assist in the Investigation and Prosecution of Persons Responsible for the Most Serious Crimes under International Law Committed in the Syrian Arab Republic since March 2011, UN Doc A/Res/71/248, 11 January 2017.

[19] For example, the International Nuremberg Principles Academy's 'Digital Evidence' project, and *The Leiden Guidelines on the Use of Digitally Derived Evidence in International Criminal Courts and Tribunals*, online at https://leiden-guidelines.com (last accessed 2 October 2023). In September 2022, the ICC Office of the Prosecutor (OTP), Eurojust, and the EU Genocide Network launched a set of guidelines entitled, *Documenting International Crimes and Human Rights Violations for Accountability Purposes: Guidelines for Civil Society Organisations*, which 'set out a series of proposed "do's" and "don'ts" from the perspective and advice of national investigative and prosecuting authorities and the Office of the Prosecutor of the ICC'. The OTP/Eurojust guidelines are not derived from the case law of the Court, but rather on best practices for civil society investigations.

[20] For a detailed overview of recent cases, see B. McGonigle Leyh, 'Using Strategic Litigation and Universal Jurisdiction to Advance Accountability for Serious International Crimes' (2022) 16 *International Journal of Transitional Justice* 363; M. Langer and M. Eason, 'The Quiet Expansion of Universal Jurisdiction' (2019) 30 *European Journal of International Law* 779; K. Aksamitowska, *Justice at Home, Justice Abroad: The Accountability Efforts Relating to the Conflicts in Eastern Ukraine, Northern Iraq, and Syria* (PhD thesis, Swansea University, 2023); P. Labuda, *International Criminal Tribunals and Domestic Accountability: In the Court's Shadow* (OUP, 2023); M.L. Fremuth, A. Sauermoser, and K. Stavrou (eds), *International Criminal Law before Domestic Courts* (MANZ Verlag Vien, 2024).

[21] Such as the idea of an international criminal tribunal for crimes committed in Ukraine, with jurisdiction over the crime of aggression: see O. Corten and V. Koutroulis, *Tribunal for the Crime of Aggression against Ukraine—A Legal Assessment* (Policy Department, Directorate-General for External Policies, European Parliament), December 2022.

maturity.[22] The Court's third Prosecutor, commencing his term of office in 2021, asked all senior trial attorneys to certify whether the cases they were leading gave rise to a realistic prospect of conviction,[23] showing a commitment to proceed only with the cases with the strongest evidentiary foundations. There could be no better time to reflect upon and consider whether international criminal evidence, as a body of law and practice, is fit for purpose in meeting the well-documented challenges of proving international crimes.

This book aims to elucidate how international criminal tribunals have tackled the immense and complex task of proving international crimes. In undertaking this task, it particularly examines the legal framework, judgments, decisions, motions, and transcripts of the ICC, in light of its permanent nature and centrality in international criminal law today. It also examines the legal frameworks, judgments, decisions, and procedures of other international and hybrid criminal tribunals,[24] to contextualise the law and practice of the ICC.[25] It argues that, because of the flexibility built into the legal and procedural frameworks of international criminal courts and tribunals, international criminal evidence is still evolving and cannot yet be said to have developed into a coherent body of law. The lack of a 'normative corpus' is not unique to matters of evidence and proof in international criminal trials and is in many ways emblematic of the international criminal procedure more generally;[26] but, as a burgeoning body of literature has shown, it is possible today to extract common practices, principles, and standards of international criminal procedure.[27]

[22] L. Smith van Lin, Remarks at *International Criminal Court at 20: Reflections on the Past, Present and the Future* conference, The Hague, 1 July 2022.

[23] *Prosecutor v Said*, Confirmation of Charges Hearing, Transcript, ICC-01/04-01/21-T-004-Red2-ENG, 12 October 2021, 18. See also *Prosecutor v Mokom*, Notice of Withdrawal of the Charges against Maxime Jeoffrey Eli Mokom Gawaka, ICC-01/14-01/22-275, 16 October 2023, para. 1.

[24] Namely the International Military Tribunal at Nuremberg (IMT); the International Military Tribunal for the Far East (IMTFE); the International Criminal Tribunal for the Former Yugoslavia (ICTY); the International Criminal Tribunal for Rwanda (ICTR); the Special Court for Sierra Leone (SCSL); the Special Tribunal for Lebanon (STL); the International Residual Mechanism for Criminal Tribunals (IRMCT); the Extraordinary Chambers in the Courts of Cambodia (ECCC); and the Kosovo Specialist Chambers (KSC).

[25] E. van Sliedregt and S. Vasiliev, 'Pluralism: A New Framework for International Criminal Justice' in E. van Sliedregt and S. Vasiliev, *Pluralism in International Criminal Law* (OUP, 2014), 3, at 4 similarly note that ICL is 'unlikely ever to become a monopoly field. The lasting presence of the "phantom limbs" in the system will be keenly felt as the International Criminal Court (ICC) and other courts continue building upon the more persuasive parts of their predecessors' jurisprudence and best practices.'

[26] S. Vasiliev et al., 'Introduction' in G. Sluiter et al. (eds), *International Criminal Procedure: Principles and Rules* (OUP, 2013), 8; C. Stahn and L. van den Herik, '"Fragmentation", Diversification and "3D" Legal Pluralism: International Criminal Law as the Jack-in-the-Box?', in L. van den Herik and C. Stahn (eds), *The Diversification and Fragmentation of International Criminal Law* (Martinus Nijhoff, 2012), 21; van Sliedregt and Vasiliev, n 25, 23–4; J.D. Jackson and Y.M. Brunger, 'Fragmentation and Harmonization in the Development of Evidentiary Practices in International Criminal Tribunals' in van Sliedregt and Vasiliev, n 25, 159, 162–6.

[27] See e.g. Sluiter et al., n 26; C. Safferling, *International Criminal Procedure* (OUP, 2012); K. Ambos, *Treatise on International Criminal Law: Vol. III* (OUP, 2016).

A good deal of scholarship relating to international criminal evidence to date has focused more on questions of admissibility than on what happens to that evidence once it is admitted.[28] Leading reference works in the field investigate such issues as the various types of evidence that can be presented, the collection and disclosure of evidence, the presentation of evidence, and the evolution of rules of evidence in international criminal law.[29] These works provide an excellent overview of how legal gaps have been resolved in the creation of a body of rules governing evidence in international criminal law. However, evidence is about more than the formal rules on admissibility and disclosure.[30] Following a recent scholarly turn to the examination of 'epistemological controversies' and the evaluation of evidence in international criminal law,[31] this book conceptualises international criminal evidence as stretching beyond the rules of evidence presentation in trials, to incorporate practices on the evaluation of evidence, the interpretation of the burden and standards of proof, and principles such as appellate deference to Trial Chambers' factual findings.[32] It argues that, rather than resorting to old debates

[28] E.g. P. Murphy, 'No Free Lunch, No Free Proof: The Indiscriminate Admission of Evidence Is a Serious Flaw in International Criminal Trials' (2010) 8 *Journal of International Criminal Justice* 539; S. Kay, 'The Move from Oral Evidence to Written Evidence: "The Law Is Always Too Short and Too Tight for Growing Humankind"' (2004) 2 *Journal of International Criminal Justice* 495; E. O'Sullivan and D. Montgomery, 'The Erosion of the Right to Confrontation under the Cloak of Fairness at the ICTY' (2010) 8 *Journal of International Criminal Justice* 511;.

[29] E.g. R. May and M. Wierda, *International Criminal Evidence* (Transnational Publishers, 2002); K.A.A. Khan, C. Buisman, and C. Gosnell (eds), *Principles of Evidence in International Criminal Justice* (OUP, 2010); M. Klamberg, *Evidence in International Criminal Trials: Confronting Legal Gaps and the Reconstruction of Disputed Events* (Martinus Nijhoff, 2013).

[30] T. Anderson, D. Schum, and W. Twining, *Analysis of Evidence* (2nd edn, CUP, 2009), xvii; W. Twining, 'Taking Facts Seriously' in W. Twining, *Rethinking Evidence: Exploratory Essays* (CUP, 2009), 14. Exclusionary rules have also been at the forefront of teaching evidence in law school curricula too, with teaching rarely paying attention to the techniques of fact-finding that underpin evidence and proof: P. Roberts, 'The Priority of Procedure and the Neglect of Evidence and Proof: Facing Facts in International Criminal Law' (2015) 13 *Journal of International Criminal Law* 479, 481. See further, J.D. Jackson, 'Analysing the New Evidence Scholarship: Towards a New Conception of the Law of Evidence' (1996) 16 *Oxford Journal of Legal Studies* 309; J. Jackson and P. Roberts, 'Beyond Common Law Evidence: Reimagining, and Reinvigorating, Evidence Law as Forensic Science' in D.K. Brown, J.I. Turner, and B. Weisser (eds), *The Oxford Handbook of Criminal Process* (OUP, 2019), 787, 809; R.O. Lempert, 'The New Evidence Scholarship: Analyzing the Process of Proof' (1986) 66 *Boston University Law Review* 439; W. Twining, 'The New Evidence Scholarship' (1991–2) 13 *Cardozo Law Review* 295; P. Roberts, 'Groundwork for a Jurisprudence of Criminal Procedure' in R.A. Duff and S.P. Green (eds), *Philosophical Foundations of Criminal Law* (OUP, 2011), 379; S. Haack, *Evidence Matters: Science, Proof, and Truth in the Law* (CUP, 2014); L. Laudan, *Truth, Error, and Criminal Law: An Essay in Legal Epistemology* (CUP, 2006); P. Dawid, W. Twining, and M. Vasilaki (eds), *Evidence, Inference and Enquiry* (OUP, 2011).

[31] M. Klamberg, 'Epistemological Controversies and Evaluation of Evidence in International Criminal Trials' in K.J. Heller et al. (eds), *The Oxford Handbook of International Criminal Law* (OUP, 2020), 450. See also N. Combs, *Fact-Finding without Facts: The Uncertain Evidentiary Foundations of International Criminal Convictions* (CUP, 2010) and the special issue edited by K. McGregor Richmond, 'Transforming Evidence and Proof in International Criminal Trials' (2022) 22 *International Criminal Law Review* 827.

[32] It does not discuss disclosure, which is a procedural matter typically considered separately from the law of evidence: see also P. Roberts and A. Zuckerman, *Roberts and Zuckerman's Criminal Evidence* (3rd edn, OUP, 2022), 41; for a detailed treatment of this topic, see S. Rigney, *Fairness and Rights in International Criminal Procedure* (Edinburgh University Press, 2022), Chapter 4. Moreover, although

about whether international criminal evidence aligns most closely with the adversarial or inquisitorial legal traditions, the development of a coherent framework for proving international crimes should be driven by two guiding principles: rectitude of decision and the highest standards of fairness.[33]

It is hoped that this book will not only be of interest to academic lawyers with an interest in international criminal law and those working in international criminal justice institutions, but that its insights will also prove useful to investigators, judges, and lawyers based in domestic jurisdictions, as well as advocates for justice worldwide and system designers considering the creation of new international criminal tribunals. Outside of international criminal law and the law of evidence, this book may provide useful insights to scholars of other branches of law, particularly human rights and criminal law, and other disciplines such as international relations, epistemology, and legal philosophy.

The remainder of this chapter examines, the nature of international criminal evidence, highlighting four key features that guide the tribunals' treatment of evidence, in section B; section C discusses some of the unique challenges of proving international crimes, while section D presents an overview of the remaining chapters of this book.

B. The nature of international criminal evidence

Several works on international criminal evidence have noted the increasingly inquisitorial character of relevant procedures over time.[34] In general, however,

this book focuses on proving international crimes through adjudication, it cannot be denied that a lot of fact handling in international criminal law occurs outside of adjudication: the parties gather and evaluate evidence in decisions on what material to present in supporting their arguments and what to exclude in processes that are rarely made known to the wider public. In the case of the prosecution, decisions on situation and case selection and prioritisation take the prospect of eventual conviction in light of the evidence into account long before an arrest warrant is issued or a trial commenced. See further, M. Bergsmo and C. Stahn (eds), *Quality Control in Preliminary Examination: Volumes 1 and 2* (TOAEP, 2018); A. Whiting, 'Dynamic Investigative Practice at the International Criminal Court' (2014) 76 *Law and Contemporary Problems* 163, 185, and, setting out the OTP's guidelines for source evaluation, X. Agirre Aranburu, 'The Contribution of Analysis to the Quality Control in Criminal Investigation' in X. Agirre et al. (eds), *Quality Control in Criminal Investigation* (TOAEP, 2020), 117.

[33] See Chapter 2.

[34] E.g. B. Van Schaak, 'Witness Proofing and International Criminal Law' (*Int Law Grrls*, 26 November 2008) (noting that, '[i]n a series of procedural rulings, the International Criminal Court is asserting its inquisitorial character'); Klamberg, n 29, 503; V. Nerlich, 'Daring Diversity: Why There Is Nothing Wrong with "Fragmentation" in International Criminal Procedure' (2013) 26 *Leiden Journal of International Law* 777, 778; R. Karemaker et al., 'Witness Proofing in International Criminal Tribunals: A Critical Analysis of Widening Procedural Divergence' (2008) 21 *Leiden Journal of International Law* 683; M. Langer, 'The Rise of Managerial Judging in International Criminal Law' (2005) 53 *American Journal of Comparative Law* 835. Here, I understand the 'inquisitorial' and 'adversarial' categories as 'ideal types', although it is possible to interpret the terms in historical, theoretical, or traditional senses: A. Heinze, 'Bend it Like Bentham: The Ambivalent "Civil Law" vs. "Common

the broad classification of practices into 'inquisitorial' or 'adversarial' is less than helpful, given the absence of any pure example of either system in any one country or legal system.[35] It is nevertheless necessary at times to draw parallels with how domestic legal systems deal with the same issues. How, then, to categorise international practice, if not along the traditional adversarial/inquisitorial divide? Damaška proposed examining key factors, including the extent of lay participation in decision-making, whether proceedings are party-driven or judge-led, and whether investigations are led by a non-partisan investigator, in classifying legal systems as either 'hierarchical' or 'coordinate'.[36]

On these measures, international criminal law does not fit neatly as either an example of a 'hierarchical' or a 'co-ordinate' model. The absence of a jury in international criminal trials in favour of professional judges as fact-finders is a notably 'hierarchical' feature and could be said to account for the absence of strict admissibility rules. On the other hand, despite increased managerialism[37] and the fact that some benches are more proactive and interventionist than others,[38] it is fair to say that international criminal proceedings are party-driven. Furthermore, despite Article 54(1)(a) of the ICC Statute, which incorporates a prosecutorial duty to investigate inculpatory and exculpatory evidence equally, international criminal investigations are largely partisan in practice.[39]

Law" Dichotomy within International Criminal Adjudication' in M. Bergsmo et al. (eds), *Power in International Criminal Justice* (TOAEP, 2020), 155, 172–81.

[35] J.F. Nijboer, 'Common Law Tradition in Evidence Scholarship Observed from a Continental Perspective' (1993) 41 *American Journal of Comparative Law* 299, 305; M.R. Damaška, 'Evidentiary Barriers to Conviction and Two Models of Criminal Procedure: A Comparative Study' (1973) 121 *University of Pennsylvania Law Review* 506, 559; J. Jackson, 'Taking Comparative Evidence Seriously' in P. Roberts and M. Redmayne (eds), *Innovations in Evidence and Proof: Integrating Theory, Research and Teaching* (Hart, 2007), 291, 304–12; M.R. Damaška, *The Faces of Justice and State Authority* (Yale University Press, 1986); M.R. Damaška, 'Models of Criminal Procedure' (2001) 51 *Zbornik* 477, 481–5; M. Langer, 'From Legal Transplants to Legal Translations: The Globalization of Plea Bargaining and the Americanization Thesis in Criminal Procedure' (2004) 45 *Harvard International Law Journal* 1 proposed a 'new theoretical framework to reconceptualize the adversarial and inquisitorial systems'.

[36] M. Damaška, 'Structures of Authority and Comparative Criminal Procedure' (1975) 84 *Yale Law Journal* 480; Damaška, n 25; see further, H.H. Koh, 'Mirjan Damaška: A Bridge between Two Legal Cultures' in J. Jackson, M. Langer, and P. Tillers (eds), *Crime, Procedure and Evidence in a Comparative and International Context: Essays in Honour of Professor Mirjan Damaška* (Hart, 2008), 29.

[37] Langer, n 33.

[38] On the divergent practices regarding judicial interventions from the bench, see R. Byrne, 'The New Public International Lawyer and the Hidden Art of Trial Practice' (2010) 25 *Connecticut Journal of International Law* 243.

[39] C. Buisman, 'The Prosecutor's Obligation to Investigate Incriminating and Exonerating Circumstances Equally: Illusion or Reality' (2014) 27 *Leiden Journal of International Law* 205, 215; M.A. Fairlie, 'Defense Issues at the International Criminal Court' (2019) 47 *Georgia Journal of International and Comparative Law* 619, 620–2; M.A. Fairlie, 'The Unlikely Prospect of Non-Adversarial Trials at the International Criminal Court' (2018) 16 *Journal of International Criminal Justice* 295. An exception is the ECCC; there, two Co-Investigating Judges (one Cambodian and one international) bear joint responsibility over investigations: Article 23*new*, The Law on the Establishment of the Extraordinary Chambers as amended, 27 October 2004 (hereafter, 'ECCC Law'). On investigative methodology, see M. Bergsmo and W.H. Wiley, 'Human Rights Professionals and the Criminal Investigation and Prosecution of Core International Crimes' in S. Skåre, I. Burkey and H.

Thus, international criminal tribunals' practices on issues of evidence and proof do not lend themselves easily to analogy with any one domestic system or family of systems.[40] Instead, international criminal evidence should be viewed as a uniquely pluralistic (and at times experimental) melting pot of rules and procedures curated from domestic practice,[41] with some elements that are unique to international criminal law alone.[42] As Jackson has noted, evidence scholars need to depart from the classification of systems along common law/civil law divides, and to examine the extent to which human rights law provides the opportunity to move beyond this dichotomy 'towards a vision of proof rooted in rights of participation that is genuinely *sui generis*'.[43] Such a reimagining is certainly feasible

Mørk (eds), *Manual on Human Rights Monitoring: An Introduction for Human Rights Field Officers* (Norwegian Centre for Human Rights, 2008), Chapter 10; X. Agirre, 'Methodology for the Criminal Investigation of International Crimes' in A. Smeulers, *Collective Violence and International Criminal Justice: An Interdisciplinary Approach* (Intersentia, 2010), 353.

[40] A. Zahar and G. Sluiter, *International Criminal Law: A Critical Introduction* (OUP, 2007), 394; *Prosecutor v Erdemović*, Judgment, IT-96-22-A, 7 October 1997, Separate and Dissenting Opinion of Judge Cassese, para. 4.

[41] Jackson and Brunger, n 26; D.M. Amann, 'Harmonic Convergence? Constitutional Criminal Procedure in an International Context' (2000) 75 *Indiana Law Journal* 809; Jackson and Roberts, n 30, 815. On the blending of procedural models in international criminal law, see K. Ambos, 'International Criminal Procedure: "Adversarial", "Inquisitorial", or "Mixed"?' (2003) 3 *International Criminal Law Review* 1; C. Schuon, *International Criminal Procedure: A Clash of Legal Cultures* (TMC Asser Press, 2010); A.M.M. Orie, 'Accusatorial v. Inquisitorial Approach in International Criminal Proceedings' in A. Cassese, P. Gaeta, and J.R.W.D. Jones (eds), *The Rome Statute of the International Criminal Court: A Commentary, Volume 2* (OUP, 2002), 1439; M. Delmas-Marty, 'Reflections on the "Hybridisation" of Criminal Procedure' in J. Jackson, M. Langer, and P Tillers (eds), *Crime, Procedure and Evidence in a Comparative and International Context: Essays in Honour of Professor Mirjan Damaška* (Hart, 2008), 251; F. Pocar, 'Common and Civil Law Traditions in the ICTY Criminal Procedure: Does Oil Blend with Water?' in J. Walker and O.G. Chase (eds), *Common Law, Civil Law and the Future of Categories* (LexisNexis, 2010), 437; O.-G. Kwon, 'The Challenge of an International Criminal Trial as Seen from the Bench' (2007) 5 *Journal of International Criminal Justice* 360; A. Whiting, 'The ICTY as a Laboratory of International Criminal Procedure' in B. Swart et al. (eds), *The Legacy of the International Criminal Tribunal for the Former Yugoslavia* (OUP, 2011), 83, 91. On hybridisation in international criminal evidence specifically, see J.D. Jackson, 'Finding the Best Epistemic Fit for International Criminal Tribunals: Beyond the Adversarial-Inquisitorial Dichotomy' (2009) 7 *Journal of International Criminal Justice* 17;M. Caianiello, 'Law of Evidence at the International Criminal Court: Blending Accusatorial and Inquisitorial Models' (2010) 36 *North Carolina Journal of International Law and Commerical Regulation* 287; M. Caianiello, 'First Decisions on the Admission of Evidence at ICC Trials—A Blending of Accusatorial and Inquisitorial Models?' (2011) 9 *Journal of International Criminal Justice* 385; Klamberg, n 29; P. Roberts, 'Why International Criminal Evidence' in Roberts and Redmayne, n 35, 347.

[42] For example, the expansive treatment of the 'judicial notice' doctrine, normally reserved for facts of common knowledge, to incorporate facts proven in earlier trials is a unique facet of international criminal procedure. See, for example, *Prosecutor v Milošević*, Decision on Prosecutor's Interlocutory Appeal against the Trial Chamber's 10 April 2003 Decision on Prosecution Motion for Judicial Notice of Adjudicated Facts, IT-02-54-AR73.5, 28 October 2003, and the appended Separate Opinion of Judge Shahabuddeen and Dissenting Opinion of Judge Hunt; *Prosecutor v Karemera* et al., Decision on Prosecutor's Interlocutory Appeal of Decision on Judicial Notice, ICTR-98-44-AR73(C), 16 June 2006.

[43] Jackson, n 35, 294; J.D. Jackson, 'The Effect of Human Rights on Criminal Evidentiary Processes: Towards Convergence, Divergence, or Realignment?' (2005) 68 *Modern Law Review* 737; J.D. Jackson and S.J. Summers, *The Internationalisation of Criminal Evidence* (CUP, 2012), 285–324; see further D. Giannoulopoulos, *Improperly Obtained Evidence in Anglo-American and Continental Law* (Hart, 2019), 2.

from the perspective of institutional culture: numerous studies have noted that international criminal lawyers have often served in more than one international criminal tribunal and may take more inspiration from their previous international experience than from the procedure of their home countries.[44]

We will define specific concepts and discuss relevant rules and jurisprudence on international criminal evidence over the course of this book. For example, Chapter 3 explores the meanings of admissibility and relevance, and the factors that are considered in determining the relevance or admissibility of a piece of evidence. Chapter 4 examines the standard of proof at different procedural stages, while Chapters 5 and 6 unpack approaches to the evaluation of different forms of evidence and the record of evidence as a whole and Chapter 7 discusses appellate review standards.

For now, however, it is worth noting four defining features of international criminal evidence, namely: the flexibility and discretion afforded to Chambers; the free assessment of evidence; the centrality of fairness; and the search for the truth.[45] The latter two features are discussed in detail in Chapter 2, where rectitude of decision and the highest standards of fairness are framed as the two central principles that should drive the future development of international criminal evidence as a body of law and practice. Suffice to note for now that considerations of fairness and potential prejudice to the accused are central to decisions of admissibility and exclusion of evidence,[46] and that the Chamber retains

[44] Jackson and Brunger, n 26, 162; E. Baylis, 'Tribunal-Hopping with the Post-Conflict Justice Junkies' (2008) 10 *Oregon Review of International Law* 361; N. Eltringham, *Genocide Never Sleeps: Living Law at the International Criminal Tribunal for Rwanda* (CUP, 2019), 100–5; F. Mégret, 'International Criminal Justice as a Juridical Field' (2016) 13 *Champ pénal/Penal field*, para. 26 ('Although international criminal lawyers may emerge from and draw on the authority of fields of domestic criminal practice as validators of their expertise, they also seek to emancipate themselves from them in an effort to deprovincialize their credentials'). Cf. Byrne, n 38, 261.

[45] See similarly, *Prosecutor v Lubanga*, Decision on the admissibility of four documents, ICC-01/04-01/06-1399, 13 June 2008, para. 19 ('There are four key factors arising from the provisions contained within the statutory framework which provide the necessary starting-point for an investigation of the Trial Chamber's general approach to this issue [the admissibility of evidence other than direct oral evidence]').

[46] Evidence will, however, be excluded where the right to a fair trial outweighs its probative value, under Article 69(7), Rome Statute of the International Criminal Court (adopted 17 July 1998, entered into force 1 July 2002), 2187 UNTS 90 (hereafter, 'ICC Statute'). Similar provisions can be found in Rule 89(D), Rules of Procedure and Evidence of the International Criminal Tribunal for the former Yugoslavia (adopted 11 February 1994, last amended 8 July 2015), IT/32/Rev.50 (hereafter, 'ICTY RPE'); Rule 70(F), Rules of Procedure and Evidence of the International Criminal Tribunal for Rwanda (adopted 29 June 1995, last amended 13 May 2015), ITR/3/Rev.24 (hereafter, 'ICTR RPE') (referring to the Trial Chamber's power under the general admissibility rule of Rule 89(C) 'to exclude evidence if its probative value is substantially outweighed by the need to ensure a fair trial'); Rule 149(D), Rules of Procedure and Evidence of the Special Tribunal for Lebanon (adopted 20 March 2009, last amended 18 December 2020), STL-BD-2009-01-Rev.11 (hereafter 'STL RPE'); Rule 105(D), Rules of Procedure and Evidence of the International Residual Mechanism for Criminal Tribunals (adopted 8 June 2012, last amended 4 December 2020), MICT/1/Rev.7 (hereafter 'IRMCT RPE'); Rule 87(3), ECCC Internal Rules Rev. 9 (adopted 12 June 2007, last amended 16 January 2015) (hereafter 'ECCC IR'). See also n 72, on improperly obtained evidence.

significant control over the presentation of evidence to ensure the determination of the truth.[47] The centrality of the search for the truth also impacts upon the Prosecutor, who is 'not only ... a Party to adversarial proceedings but is an organ of the Tribunal and an organ of international criminal justice whose object is not simply to secure a conviction but to ... assist the Chamber to discover truth in a judicial setting'.[48]

i. Flexibility

International criminal law has a long history of unmooring itself from technical rules of evidence,[49] which are perceived as particularities of domestic legal systems that international criminal trials can operate without. This was reflected in the words of Judge Cassese at the establishment of the ICTY:

> [T]his Tribunal does not need to shackle itself to restrictive rules which have developed out of the ancient trial by jury system. There will be no jury sitting at the Tribunal, needing to be shielded from irrelevancies or given guidance as to the weight of the evidence they have heard.[50]

[47] Regulation 43, ICC Regulations of the Court (adopted 26 May 2004, last amended 12 November 2018) (hereafter 'ICC Regulations') ('Subject to the Statute and the Rules, the Presiding Judge, in consultation with the other members of the Chamber, shall determine the mode and order of questioning witnesses and presenting evidence so as to: (a) Make the questioning of witnesses and the presentation of evidence fair and effective for the determination of the truth; (b) Avoid delays and ensure the effective use of time').

[48] *Prosecutor v Kupreškić*, Decision on Communications between the Parties and Their Witnesses, IT-95-16-T, 21 September 1998, 2. See further Chapter 2.

[49] Article 19, Charter of the International Military Tribunal, London, 8 August 1945 (hereafter, 'IMT Charter') ('The Tribunal shall not be bound by technical rules of evidence. It shall adopt and apply to the greatest possible extent expeditious and non-technical procedure and shall admit any evidence which it deems to have probative value'); Article 13(a), Charter of the International Military Tribunal for the Far East (hereafter, 'IMTFE Charter'); Rule 89(C), ICTY RPE; Rule 89(C), ICTR RPE; Rule 105(C), IRMCT RPE; Rule 89(C), Rules of Procedure and Evidence of the Special Court for Sierra Leone (adopted 16 January 2002, last amended 31 May 2012) (hereafter, 'SCSL RPE'); Rule 149(C), STL RPE; Articles 64(9), 69(3) and 69(4), ICC Statute; Rules 63(2) and 63(5), Rules of Procedure and Evidence, International Criminal Court, *Official Records of the Assembly of States Parties to the Rome Statute of the International Criminal Court, First session, New York, 3–10 September 2002* (ICC-ASP/1/3 and Corr.1) (hereafter, 'ICC RPE'); Rule 23, Rules of Procedure and Evidence before the Kosovo Specialist Chambers including Rules of Procedure for the Specialist Chamber of the Constitutional Court (adopted 17 March 2017, last amended 2 June 2020) (hereafter, 'KSC RPE'), and Article 37, Law on Specialist Chambers and Specialist Prosecutor's Office, 05/L-053, 3 August 2015 (hereafter, 'KSC Law'), stating that the admissibility of evidence collected prior to the establishment of the KSC shall be decided 'pursuant to international standards on the collection of evidence' and Article 22 of the Constitution of Kosovo (on the applicability of international human rights law treaties).

[50] A. Cassese, *Annual Report of the International Tribunal for the Prosecution of Persons Responsible for Serious Violations of International Humanitarian Law Committed in the Territory of the Former Yugoslavia since 1991*, A/49/342, S/1994/1007, 29 August 1994, para. 72.

Yet, as will be discussed further in Chapter 3, evidence rules can be seen as more than 'a child of the jury'.[51] Judges can be as vulnerable to cognitive biases and logical fallacies as lay jury members, given that susceptibility to systematic errors in reasoning are a product of our humanity.[52] Rules of evidence play a broader role in preserving judicial economy and the fairness and integrity of proceedings.[53]

Judges are afforded significant leeway to determine key evidential issues, such as the modalities for the admission of evidence, the time limits to be imposed on the parties for the presentation of their cases, witness preparation, the admission of prior recorded testimony,[54] and the questioning of witnesses. Before the ICC, the Trial Chamber must consult the parties 'and adopt such procedures as are necessary to facilitate the fair and expeditious conduct of the proceedings'.[55] The presiding judge may give directions for the conduct of proceedings to ensure they are carried out in a fair and impartial manner.[56] On the one hand, judicial discretion has been described as 'the oil in the procedural machine' which prevents the parts of the criminal justice system from grinding against one another, or seizing up altogether.[57] On the other, the flexibility afforded to judges in shaping the conduct of trials has led to significant 'intra-institutional pluralism',[58] whereby different chambers of the same court take distinct approaches to issues of procedure

[51] In the words of J.B. Thayer, *A Preliminary Treatise on Evidence at the Common Law* (Little, Brown, and Co., 1898), 266.

[52] R. Nisbett and E. Borgida, 'Attribution and the Psychology of Prediction' (1975) 32 *Journal of Personality and Social Psychology* 932; D. Kahneman, P. Slovic, and A. Tversky (eds), *Judgment and Uncertainty: Heuristics and Biases* (CUP, 1982); D. Kahneman and A. Tversky, 'Subjective Probability' (1972) 3 *Cognitive Psychology* 430. Cf. L.J. Cohen, 'Can Human Irrationality Be Experimentally Demonstrated?' (1981) 4 *The Behavioral and Brain Sciences* 317. There is a debate about the appropriateness of a system where the judge(s) who have the power to decide on the admissibility of evidence and exclude that evidence because of its prejudicial effect later determine the guilt or innocence of the accused, given that there is a risk that the excluded evidence may have already contaminated the judge's mind. As was stated in a case before the Grand Chamber of the European Court of Human Rights, *Dvorski v Croatia*, App. No. 25703/11, 20 October 2015 (Concurring Opinion of Judge Zupančič, para. 8), it difficult to squeeze the genie back into the bottle once it has been released. See also M. Damaška, 'Free Proof and Its Detractors' (1995) 43 *American Journal of Comparative Law* 343, 348–52.

[53] By preventing the Chamber from having to spend time evaluating what Murphy and Baddour term 'evidential debris', which they define as evidence which 'even if in fact authentic, cannot be accorded any real probative value': P. Murphy and L. Baddour, 'Evidence and Selection of Judges in International Criminal Tribunals: The Need for a Harmonized Approach' in van Sliedregt and Vasiliev, n 25, 368, 369.

[54] Rule 68(2) ICC RPE.

[55] Article 64(3)(a), ICC Statute.

[56] The presiding judge of the Pre-Trial Chamber has an identical power under Rule 122(1), ICC RPE. See e.g. *Prosecutor v Yekatom and Ngaïssona*, Initial Directions on the Conduct of the Proceedings, ICC-01/14-01/18-631, 26 August 2020; *Prosecutor v Al Hassan*, Decision on the Conduct of Proceedings, ICC-01/12-01/18-789, 6 May 2020, with one public annex; *Prosecutor v Ongwen*, Initial Directions on the Conduct of Proceedings, ICC-02/04-01/15-497, 13 July 2016; *Prosecutor v Ntaganda*, Decision on the Conduct of Proceedings, ICC-01/04-02/06-619, 2 June 2015; *Prosecutor v Katanga and Ngudjolo*, Directions for the Conduct of the Proceedings and Testimony in accordance with Rule 140, ICC-01/04-01/07-1665-Corr, 1 December 2009.

[57] Roberts and Zuckerman, n 32, 45.

[58] van Sliedregt and Vasiliev, n 25, 27–8; Whiting, n 41, 91 (noting 'enormous variation in the application of the Rules from one Trial Chamber to another').

and evidence. This can lead to unpredictability for the parties and can have an impact on their ability to prepare for trial.[59]

Flexibility also presents in the constructive ambiguity of the relevant legal frameworks.[60] For example, Article 69 of the ICC Statute notes that the parties '*may* submit evidence relevant to the case', and 'the Court *may* rule on the relevance or admissibility of any evidence'.[61] Even where the wording of a provision seems to afford less discretion to the Chamber, such as in Article 69(2), which states that '[t]he testimony of a witness at trial *shall* be given in person',[62] this is tempered by 'except to the extent provided by the measures set forth in article 68 or in the Rules of Procedure and Evidence'. Under the original Rule 68 of the ICC RPE, prior recorded testimony could only be introduced in the place of oral testimony where the opposing party had the opportunity to cross-examine the witness at the time the testimony was recorded, or where the witness was present and available for examination.[63] Rule 68 was amended in 2013 to closely mirror Rules 92 *bis*, 92 *ter*, 92 *quater*, and 92 *quinquies* of the ICTY RPE.[64] Rule 68(1) states that a Trial Chamber may allow the introduction of prior recorded testimony in accordance with the conditions set out in the rest of the Rule, provided that it would not be prejudicial to or inconsistent with the rights of the accused.[65] Rule 68(2)(b) relates to prior recorded testimony not pertaining to the acts and conduct of an accused, while Rules 68(2)(c) and (d) pertains to the prior recorded testimony of a person

[59] Whiting, n 41.

[60] Review of the International Criminal Court and the Rome Statute System, Final report of the Group of Independent Experts, ICC-ASP/19/16, 30 September 2020, para. 839, defining constructive ambiguity as 'a legislative drafting technique designed to produce a text that all who are debating or arguing over the point can live with'.

[61] Articles 69(3) and 69(4), ICC Statute (emphasis added). See also Article 64(9), ICC Statute (The Trial Chamber 'shall have, *inter alia*, the power ... to (a) Rule on the admissibility or relevance of evidence').

[62] Emphasis added.

[63] ICC-ASP/1/3 (2002), Rule 68. See further, M. Fairlie, 'The Abiding Problem of Witness Statements in International Criminal Trials' (2017) 50 *NYU Journal of International Law and Politics* 75.

[64] These amendments are discussed at length in Murphy, n 28; Kay, n 28; O'Sullivan and Montgomery, n 28; M. Fairlie, 'The Marriage of Common and Continental Law at the ICTY and Its Progeny, Due Process Deficit' (2004) 4 *International Criminal Law Review* 243; P.M. Wald, 'To Establish Incredible Events by Credible Evidence: The Use of Affidavit Testimony in Yugoslavia War Crimes Tribunal Proceedings' (2001) 42 *Harvard International Law Journal* 535. Comparing the two sets of Rules in detail, see Fairlie, n 63.

[65] See *Prosecutor v Abd-Al-Rahman*, Public redacted version of the First Decision on the Prosecution's Request to Introduce Prior Recorded Testimonies under Rule 68(3), ICC-02/05-01/20-559-Red, 20 January 2022, para. 11 ('A Chamber's determination to allow prior recorded testimony is discretionary and requires a case-by-case assessment'), citing *Prosecutor v Yekatom and Ngaïssona*, Decision on the Prosecution Requests for Formal Submission of Prior Recorded Testimonies under Rule 68(3) of the Rules concerning Witnesses P-1962, P-0925, P-2193, P-2926, P-2927, P-1577, and P-0287, ICC-01/14-01/18-907-Red, 10 March 2021, para. 9; *Prosecutor v Al Hassan*, Decision on Prosecution's Requests to Introduce Prior Recorded Testimonies under Rule 68(3) of the Rules, ICC-01/12-01/18-987-Red, 5 August 2020, para. 7; *Prosecutor v Gbagbo and Blé Goudé*, Judgment on the appeals of Mr Laurent Gbagbo and Mr Charles Blé Goudé against the decision of Trial Chamber I of 9 June 2016 entitled 'Decision on the Prosecutor's Application to Introduce Prior Recorded Testimony under Rules 68(2)(b) and 68(3), ICC-02/11-01/15-744 OA8, 1 November 2016, paras 69–72.

who is unavailable to testify orally (either because they are dead or owing to 'obstacles that cannot be overcome with reasonable diligence'), or who has been subjected to witness interference. Prior recorded testimony under Rules 68(2)(c) and (d) can go to proving acts or conduct of an accused, although the Chamber may consider this a factor against its introduction.[66]

Prior recorded testimony under Rule 68(3), which is today a central feature of ICC proceedings,[67] allows the introduction of prior recorded testimony if the witness is present before the Chamber and does not object to its introduction, provided that both parties, and the Chamber, have the opportunity to examine the witness.[68] Because the witness appears before the Court (albeit for a limited examination by the calling party) and the parties have an opportunity to examine them, Rule 68(3) evidence is seen as complementing, rather than replacing, the expectation of oral evidence, while also maintaining the efficiency of proceedings.[69]

ii. Free assessment of evidence

> [T]he drafters of the Statute framework have clearly and deliberately avoided proscribing certain categories or types of evidence, a step which would have limited—at the outset—the ability of the Chamber to assess evidence 'freely'. Instead, the Chamber is authorised by statute to request any evidence that is necessary to determine the truth, subject always to such decisions on relevance and admissibility as are necessary, bearing in mind the dictates of fairness.[70]

Closely related to the flexibility principle discussed in the previous section is the authority of the Court to assess evidence 'freely'. This principle of free evaluation of the evidence permeates both the admission and evaluation of evidence. In practice, it means that judges are not bound by restrictions as to the type of evidence they

[66] *Prosecutor v Al Hassan*, Judgment on the appeal of the Prosecution against Trial Chamber X's 'Decision on second Prosecution request for the introduction of P-0113's evidence pursuant to Rule 68(2)(b) of the Rules', ICC-01/12-01/18-2222, 13 May 2022, paras 74–87 (recognising that recourse to Rule 68 requires a cautious assessment to ensure that the rights of the accused are not imperilled).

[67] See e.g. *Prosecutor v Ntaganda*, Supplemental Decision on Matters Related to the Conduct of Proceedings, ICC-01/04-02/06-1342, 27 May 2016, para. 15 (encouraging the Prosecution to consider increased use of Rule 68 where appropriate); *Prosecutor v Said*, Decision on the Prosecution's Request under Rule 68(3) to Introduce the Prior Recorded Testimony of P-2931, P-0481, P-0349, P-2328, P-0834, P-2573, P-2232, P-0884, P-2251, and P-0291, ICC-01/14-01/21-571-Red, 21 December 2022.

[68] Rule 68(3), ICC RPE.

[69] *Abd Al Rahman* Rule 68(3) decision, n 65, para. 12. Cf. *Prosecutor v Gbabgo and Blé Goudé*, Decision on the Prosecution's application to conditionally admit the prior recorded statements and related documents of Witnesses P-0108, P-0433, P-0436, P-0402, P-0438, P-0459 and P-0109 under rule 68(3) and for testimony by means of video-link technology for witnesses P-0436, P-0402, P-0438, P-0459 and P-0109 under rule 67(1), ICC-02/11-01/15-870, 7 April 2017, para. 15 (assessing the potential time savings as low).

[70] *Lubanga* Four Documents Decision, n 45, para. 24.

can admit or consider relevant.[71] This is subject to certain exceptions, such as the exclusion of improperly obtained evidence where its admission would damage the integrity of proceedings or where the violation casts substantial doubt on the reliability of the evidence.[72] Unlike the Rules of other tribunals, which provided that a Chamber 'may exclude a piece of evidence if its probative value is substantially outweighed by the need to ensure a fair trial',[73] Article 69(4) of the ICC Statute takes a different formulation. It provides that the degree of probative value of the evidence, and any prejudice that such evidence may cause to a fair trial or the fair evaluation of the testimony of a witness, should be taken 'into account' by the Court in ruling on relevance or admissibility,[74] thereby moving away from the earlier 'substantially outweighed' standard and granting more flexibility to the Court.[75]

The free evaluation of evidence also means that there are no formal restrictions on the weight to be given to a particular type of evidence or formal requirements for corroboration, as discussed further in Chapter 5.[76] As noted by the Appeals Chamber in *Lubanga*:

> Depending on the circumstances, a single piece of evidence, such as a video image of a person, may suffice to establish a specific fact. However, as recognised by the Trial Chamber, this does not mean that *any* piece of evidence provides a sufficient evidentiary basis for a factual finding.[77]

Some authors have questioned the tribunals' 'free proof' approach, arguing that it can lead to inefficiencies and unfairness in practice because it permits the introduction of weaker forms of evidence (such as non-governmental organisations (NGO) reports relying on anonymous hearsay, where the original source of the

[71] Article 69(4), ICC Statute; Rule 63(2), ICC RPE. Similarly, *Prosecutor v Blaškić*, Judgment, IT-95-14-T, 3 March 2000, paras 34–5 (outlining the Chamber's 'extensive admissibility of evidence' approach, and the purported benefits thereto).

[72] Article 69(7), ICC Statute, discussed at length below, Chapter 3, section D. Similar provisions can be found in Rule 95, ICTY RPE; Rule 95, ICTR RPE; Rule 95, SCSL RPE; Rule 162, STL RPE; Rule 117, IRMCT RPE; Rules 138(2) and (3), KSC RPE. There is no specific rule on the exclusion of improperly obtained evidence in the ECCC IR, but relevant provisions of the Cambodian constitution and code of criminal procedure, read in conjunction with Article 15 of the Convention against Torture, were cited in: *NUON Chea and KHIEU Samphân ('Case 002/01')*, Decision on Evidence Obtained through Torture, 002/19-09-2007/ECCC/TC, 5 February 2016.

[73] Rule 89(D), ICTY RPE; Rule 89(D), ICTR RPE; Rule 149(D), STL RPE; Rule 105(D), IRMCT RPE; Rule 87(3), ECCC IR; Rule 138(1), KSC RPE.

[74] Article 69(4), ICC Statute. Note the use of the term '*inter alia*' in this provision, suggesting that other relevant factors aside from probative value, prejudice, and impact on the evaluation of witness testimony could also be considered.

[75] D. Piragoff and P. Clarke, 'Article 69' in O. Triffterer and K. Ambos (eds), *Rome Statute of the International Criminal Court: Article-by-Article Commentary* (4th edn, Beck/Hart, 2021), 2035 at 2041.

[76] Chapter 3 also discusses concepts such as credibility, reliability, and authenticity, as elucidated in the case law.

[77] *Prosecutor v Lubanga*, Public redacted Judgment on the appeal of Mr Thomas Lubanga Dyilo against his conviction, ICC-01/04-01/06-3121-Red, 1 December 2014, para. 218.

information cannot be located), which judges must wade through in evaluating the evidentiary record as a whole.[78]

C. The unique challenges of proving international crimes

It is a truism that international criminal tribunals conduct their fact-finding role in a uniquely challenging landscape. In each trial, a dazzlingly diverse 'mosaic of evidence',[79] incorporating tens (if not hundreds) of witnesses' live testimonies, thousands of pages of evidence and transcripts, maps, videos, recordings, sketches, photographs, and judicially noticed facts from other trials, is presented.[80] From that evidence, judges are expected to consider the most convincing explanation of what happened years, if not decades, earlier,[81] and whether the individual(s) standing trial before them bear criminal responsibility for those atrocities. The logical processing of this information requires extraordinary cognitive capacity.[82]

Added to the volume of evidence is the challenge of the reliability or otherwise of that evidence. Concerns have been raised about witness interference since the inception of the contemporary international criminal tribunals.[83] Furthermore, the party-driven nature of investigations and a lack of strong enforcement powers can mean that witnesses are unwilling to come forward to testify, and that parties struggle to gain access to the best evidence.[84] In recent years, the

[78] Murphy and Baddour, n 53; Fairlie, n 63.

[79] *Prosecutor v Krstić*, Judgment, IT-98-33-T, 2 August 2001, para. 4.

[80] See further, Y. McDermott, 'Inferential Reasoning and Proof in International Criminal Trials' (2015) 13 *Journal of International Criminal Justice* 507, 508 (giving some examples of the voluminous evidentiary records of international criminal trials).

[81] On the issues of time and distance from the events and trials, see N. Combs, 'Evidence' in W.A. Schabas and N. Bernaz (eds), *The Routledge Handbook of International Criminal Law* (Routledge, 2011), 323; on the limitations of human memory, see A. Roberts, 'The Frailties of Human Memory and the Accused's Right to Accurate Procedures' (2019) 11 *Criminal Law Review* 912; D. Davis and E. Loftus, 'Inconsistencies between Law and the Limits of Human Cognition: The Case of Eyewitness Identification' in L. Nadel and W. Sinnott-Armstrong (eds), *Memory and Law* (OUP, 2012), 47.

[82] On the limits of human cognition, see G.A. Miller, 'The Magical Number Seven, Plus or Minus Two: Some Limits on Our Capacity for Processing Information' (1956) 63 *Psychological Review* 81; A.D. Baddeley and G.J. Hitch, 'Working Memory', in G.H. Bower (ed.), *The Psychology of Learning and Motivation, vol. 8* (Academic Press, 1974), 47.

[83] R. Cryer, 'Witness Tampering and International Criminal Tribunals' (2014) 27 *Leiden Journal of International Law* 191; A.-M. de Brouwer, 'The Problem of Witness Interference before International Criminal Tribunals' (2015) 15 *International Criminal Law Review* 700. There have been a number of convictions for witness interference, including: *Prosecutor v Nshogoza*, Judgment, ICTR-07-91-T, 7 July 2009; *Prosecutor v Bemba et al.*, Judgment pursuant to Article 74 of the Statute, ICC-01/05-01/13-1989, 19 October 2016; *Prosecutor v Haraqija and Morina*, Judgment, IT-04-84-R77.4, 17 December 2008; *Specialist Prosecutor v Gucati and Haradinaj*, Public Redacted Version of the Trial Judgment, KSC-BC-2020-07, 18 May 2022.

[84] See K. de Meester, K. Pitcher, R. Rastan, and G. Sluiter, 'Investigation, Coercive Measures, Arrest, and Surrender' in G. Sluiter et al. (eds), *International Criminal Procedure: Principles and Rules* (OUP, 2013), 171.

ICC Prosecutor has been criticised for an over-reliance on secondary accounts, such as NGO reports,[85] poor evidence preservation practices,[86] delegating investigative responsibilities to and failing to exercise proper oversight over intermediaries,[87] and a failure to present evidence that links the crimes committed to the accused.[88]

Cultural differences also pose a difficulty in the assessment of evidence in international criminal trials. The assessment of witness reliability tends to be firmly grounded in cultural mores, and behaviour that may come across as evasiveness or uncertainty to one observer may in fact be attributable to the witness's manner of speaking, showing respect, or nervousness.[89] Generalisations can play a significant role in the fact-finder's evaluation of the evidence,[90] yet, as I have argued elsewhere, it would be difficult for most international judges to say with certainty how one might be expected to act in the face of machete-wielding genocidaires.[91] The culture clash can also arise between judges themselves, who hail from a wide range of jurisdictions and professional backgrounds,[92] and these prior experiences may have an impact on how they assess the evidence presented.[93]

[85] *Prosecutor v Gbagbo*, Decision adjourning the hearing on the confirmation of charges pursuant to article 61(7)(c)(i) of the Rome Statute, ICC-02/11-01/11-432, 3 June 2013, paras 28–36; *Prosecutor v Bemba*, Judgment on the appeal of Mr Jean-Pierre Bemba Gombo against Trial Chamber III's 'Judgment pursuant to Article 74 of the Statute', ICC-01/05-01/08-3636-Red, Separate Opinion of Judge Van den Wyngaert and Judge Morrison, ICC-01/05-01/08-3636-Anx2, 8 June 2018, para. 64.

[86] *Gbagbo* Reasons, n 5, Opinion of Judge Tarfusser, n 7, paras 91–2; *Gbagbo* Reasons, n 5, Reasons of Judge Henderson, n 7, paras 34–5.

[87] *Prosecutor v Lubanga*, Judgment pursuant to Article 74 of the Statute, ICC-01/04-01/06-2842, 14 March 2012, para. 482.

[88] *Gbagbo* Reasons, n 5, Reasons of Judge Henderson, paras 85–91.

[89] Combs, n 31, 63–105. Some psychological research suggests that accents have a bearing on native speakers' assessment of the credibility of non-native speakers: S. Lev-Ari and B. Keysar, 'Why Don't We Believe Non-Native Speakers? The Influence of Accent on Credibility' (2010) 46 *Journal of Experimental Social Psychology* 1093. Cf. G. Chlevickaitė, B. Holá and C. Bijleveld, 'Suspicious Minds? Empirical Analysis of Insider Witness Assessments at the ICTY, ICTR and ICC' (2023) 20 *European Journal of Criminology* 185, 191 and 197 (finding that witnesses' demeanour on the stand has a strong bearing on judges' evaluation of their testimony).

[90] Anderson, Schum, and Twining, n 30, 262–88.

[91] Y. McDermott, 'Strengthening the Evaluation of Evidence in International Criminal Trials' (2017) 17 *International Criminal Law Review* 682, 698–9, referring to *Prosecutor v Gatete*, Judgment and Sentence, ICTR-2000-61-T, 31 March 2011, para. 232 (where the Chamber noted that it had concerns on the reliability of a witness, because it was 'not convinced that she would have moved to only metres away from the Accused at the roadblock when *Interahamwe*, who according to her testimony had killed persons with "bladed weapons", were present').

[92] Pursuant to Article 36(3)(b) and Article 36(5), ICC Statute, at least nine judges of the Court are chosen on the basis of their proven competence in criminal law and procedure and at least five are elected on the basis of their competence in a relevant area of international law, such as human rights law or international humanitarian law. Article 36(8)(a) requires the States Parties to take into account equitable geographical representation and the representation of the world's principal legal systems in selecting judges.

[93] See e.g. *Bemba* Appeal Judgment, Separate Opinion of Judge Van den Wyngaert and Judge Morrison, n 7, para. 4 ('While we do not presume to speak for our colleagues, it is probably fair to say that we attach more importance to the strict application of the burden and standard of proof. We also seem to put more emphasis on compliance with due process norms that are essential to protecting the rights of the accused in an adversarial trial setting').

D. Structure of this book

Chapter 2 elucidates the two underpinning principles of international criminal evidence that I argue should guide the development of international criminal evidence as a coherent body of law: rectitude of decision and the highest standards of fairness. Starting first with an analysis of the meaning of the idea of a 'principle' of international criminal evidence, it then examines each of these two overarching principles (which incorporate other sub-principles, such as upholding the integrity of proceedings) in turn. Conclusions are drawn on how these principles have a bearing on numerous key aspects of international criminal evidence, including rules on admissibility and relevance, exclusionary rules, standards of proof, the evaluation of evidence, and appellate standards of review.

A relatively recent development before the ICC has been the deferral of decisions on admissibility and relevance until the end of trials. Chapter 3 analyses the relative benefits and disadvantages of this turn towards the 'submission approach' in place of admissibility, whereby the evidence is considered to have been submitted to the Chamber, with a decision on its relevance and probative value deferred to a later stage. This chapter also examines the key admissibility considerations of relevance, probative value and prejudice to the accused and how they have been interpreted in practice. Chapter 3 concludes with an analysis of the jurisprudence on the exclusion of improperly obtained evidence and argues that international criminal tribunals could take a more rights-protective role in this regard.

No book on proving international crimes would be complete without a thorough evaluation of the burden and standard of proof. In relation to the former, Chapter 4 discusses the fact that the burden of proof lies with the prosecution, and what that means in practice, as well as the exceptions to this principle. This chapter also analyses the standards of proof that apply throughout proceedings, from the relatively low threshold at the earliest stages to proof beyond reasonable doubt for conviction, with a particular focus on the relevant standards applicable before the International Criminal Court. Several leading authors have suggested that the 'beyond reasonable doubt' standard is too taxing in light of the various evidentiary challenges posed in international criminal trials;[94] this chapter argues that such proposals are ill-advised and would contravene the central tenets of international criminal evidence.

Chapter 5 examines the different forms of evidence used in proving international crimes and how they have been evaluated. It sets out the general framework for the

[94] L. May and S. Fyfe, *International Criminal Tribunals: A Normative Defense* (CUP, 2017), 160; Combs, n 31, 343–64. Similarly, D. Robinson, 'The Other Poisoned Chalice: Unprecedented Evidentiary Standards in the Gbagbo Case? (Part 1)' (*EJIL:Talk!*, 5 November 2019), appears to suggest that the judges' 'Cartesian approach' goes too far in its rigorous evaluation of (incriminatory) evidence ('the zeal for impeccable standards swings too far, and produces a method that is so rigid, formalistic, and hypersceptical that it loses sight of substance and feasibility').

evaluation of evidence, which is characterised by several key principles and practices. It then evaluates the factors that have been considered when assessing, first, testimonial evidence of witnesses, and second, other forms of evidence. In fitting with a common theme of this book, it shows some divergence in practice, leaving the parties at times uncertain about the sort of supporting information they should provide to demonstrate the probative value of a piece of evidence.

A live debate in practice and scholarship is about the manner in which evidence should be weighed and evaluated in reaching findings of fact—broadly categorised as 'atomistic' or 'holistic' approaches. Chapter 6 argues that the two approaches have emerged as something of a false dichotomy in scholarship and practice, with no 'true' example of a holistic or atomistic approach. Instead, it is posited that at the heart of this debate is a divergence in opinion on the extent to which other evidence on the record can 'remedy' some of the flaws in a piece of evidence on the record and the level of detail that the Chamber needs to provide in showing how the evidence led to a particular finding of fact or an inference supporting a finding of fact. As such, Chapter 6 explores options for the structuring of trial judgments, and argues that a combined framework derived from argumentation theory could be applied to combine the necessary micro- and macro- levels of assessment in a new approach to structuring judgments.

Chapter 7 assesses appellate review standards, with a particular focus on the standard of review for alleged errors of fact. It highlights an evolution in the ICC's practice over time on the relevant standard of review for factual errors to one of 'tempered deference' to the Trial Chamber in more recent practice. It also examines other issues relating to proof on appeal, including the introduction of new evidence on appeal and at retrial, and the circumstances under which a final judgment can be reviewed.

Chapter 8 concludes the book by discussing the future of proving international crimes, examining whether international criminal evidence can emerge as a coherent body of law. It summarises the key findings of the work and implications for future research and argues that recent efforts by ICC judges to settle contentious issues and reach compromises suggest a concerted effort to address some of the ambiguities that plagued practice in the ICC's first two decades. This chapter also discusses how technology might shape the future of proving international crimes.

2
Principles of International Criminal Evidence

A. Introduction

As noted in Chapter 1, the law and procedure of international criminal evidence has emerged as a *sui generis* model, incorporating a blend of practices from domestic legal traditions, with certain aspects that are unique. As shall be shown in the following chapters, the flexibility inherent in the legal frameworks of all international criminal tribunals means that international criminal evidence cannot be viewed as a fixed and immutable construct, but rather as one that constantly evolves and changes. The procedural uncertainty and inconsistency in practice that results from this flexibility is a central theme of this book. On the other hand, while recognising the consequences of flexibility, one cannot argue that international criminal evidence should remain permanently settled, just as the law of evidence in any jurisdiction should be amenable to amendment and evolution.

This leads, then, to the question of what principles should buttress the development and crystallisation of international criminal evidence as a body of law. This chapter argues that further development of the law and practice of proving international crimes should be underpinned by two key principles: rectitude of decision and the highest standards of fairness. Before the chapter explores each of these core principles, section B examines the meaning of a 'principle' in this context and explores how principles might come to bear on the development of international criminal evidence. Section C then defines rectitude of decision, and section D examines the meaning of the highest standards of fairness.

B. Identifying principles of international criminal evidence

A common theme in this book, and in writing on international criminal evidence more generally, is the lack of certainty and consistency that abounds in relation to the practice of international criminal courts.[1] Judges, writing extrajudicially, often

[1] M. Karnavas, 'The Kosovo Specialist Chambers' Rules of Procedure and Evidence: More of the Same Hybridity with Added Prosecutorial Transparency' (2020) 20 *International Criminal Law Review* 77, at 122–3 ('Should not a mature criminal procedure ... ensure predictability, uniformity, and

Proving International Crimes. Yvonne McDermott, Oxford University Press. © Yvonne McDermott 2024.
DOI: 10.1093/oso/9780198842972.003.0002

make the point that they have willingly abandoned some cherished aspects of their 'native' criminal procedure to meet the particular needs of conducting complex international criminal trials and to compromise with colleagues.[2] Yet, as shall be seen in Chapter 3's discussion of the early jurisprudence on the submission and admission models for evidence, the legal background of the presiding judge can bear an influence on the procedures adopted in practice. Regardless of the impact or otherwise of the judge's legal training or background, we can see fundamentally divergent approaches to a range of evidentiary and procedural matters, such as, perhaps most strikingly, witness preparation.[3]

Before the International Criminal Tribunal for the former Yugoslavia (ICTY) and International Criminal Tribunal for Rwanda (ICTR), as noted in Chapter 1, judge-made procedural law was amended frequently, often to address particular issues that had arisen in the course of trials, such as the unavailability of witnesses or defendants' unwillingness or inability to appear in court.[4] At the International Criminal Court (ICC), while presiding judges have the authority to determine the conduct of proceedings,[5] judges' role as procedural lawmakers is much more limited. Unlike many tribunals where the Rules of Procedure and Evidence (RPEs) were drafted and amended by a plenary of judges, the ICC's RPEs, and amendments

certainty in its application ... irrespective of the judges' predilections informed from and shaped by their domestic procedures and legal traditions?').

[2] B. Schmitt, 'Legal Diversity at the International Criminal Court: Reflections of a Judge' (2021) 19 *Journal of International Criminal Justice* 485, at 509; A.M.M. Orie, 'Accusatorial v. Inquisitorial Approach in International Criminal Proceedings' in A. Cassese, P. Gaeta, and J.R.W.D. Jones (eds), *The Rome Statute of the International Criminal Court: A Commentary, Volume 2* (OUP, 2002), 1439; O.-G. Kwon, 'The Challenge of an International Criminal Trial as Seen from the Bench' (2007) 5 *Journal of International Criminal Justice* 360; H. Morrison, 'Judging in International Criminal Cases: Challenges, Aspirations and Duties' in M. Böse et al. (eds), *Justice Without Borders: Essays in Honour of Wolfgang Schomburg* (Brill, 2018), 299; P. Wald, 'Judging War Crimes' (2000) 1 *Chicago Journal of International Law* 189, 196. Cf. *Prosecutor v Jelisić*, Judgment, IT-95-10-A, 5 July 2001, para. 34 ('Judges of the Tribunal come from different legal cultures, as do counsel appearing before it. The Trial Chamber in this case consisted wholly of non-common law judges; account must be taken of that fact in interpreting the language in which their judgement was cast').

[3] Schmitt, n 2, 503–5, noting that 'the practice leaves a judge with a civil law background perplexed'; J.D. Jackson and Y.M. Brunger, 'Witness Preparation in the ICC: An Opportunity for Principled Pragmatism' (2015) 13 *Journal of International Criminal Justice* 601. This remains a live issue, as demonstrated by the diverging positions set out in the Institute for International Legal and Advocacy Training (IILAT) Debate, 'Witness Preparation: Is failing to prepare, preparing to fail?', The Hague, 3 October 2022. The Independent Expert Review was agnostic on best practices, finding that '[t]he decision on this issue is one for the discretion of the Chamber or Presiding Judge in managing the proceedings and not a matter that requires regulation. On the other hand, it could be a matter for regulation if that is the wish of an absolute majority of the Judges': Independent Expert Review of the International Criminal Court and the Rome Statute System. Final Report, 30 September 2020, para. 551.

[4] See e.g. M. Fairlie, 'Rulemaking from the Bench: A Place for Minimalism at the ICTY' (2004) 39 *Texas International Law Journal* 257; Y. McDermott, 'The Admissibility and Weight of Written Witness Testimony in International Criminal Law: A Socio-Legal Analysis' (2013) 26 *Leiden Journal of International Law* 971; L. Moranchek, 'Protecting National Security Evidence while Prosecuting War Crimes: Problems and Lessons for International Justice from the ICTY' (2006) 31 *Yale Journal of International Law* 478, 480–1.

[5] Article 64(8)(b), ICC Statute.

thereto, are adopted by a two-thirds majority of State Parties.[6] Nevertheless, judges have found ways to overcome the constraints imposed on their procedural law-making powers by the ICC's statutory framework, and the sluggishness of the Assembly of States Parties-centred process.[7] These include through formal means such as the adoption and amendment of judge-made Regulations of the Court[8] and conduct of proceedings decisions by each individual Trial Chamber, but also through less formal means such as the adoption and amendment of a 'Chambers Practice Manual'[9] and reaching understandings at judicial retreats that are publicly announced via press releases.[10] The latter category of recommendations and guidelines are, of course, non-binding, and may not be consistently applied in practice.[11]

Given that international criminal evidence as a body of law is ever evolving, this raises the question: what are the optimal epistemic conditions for proving international crimes? Combs, approaching this question from the other direction, has argued that there are three factors that are most likely to lead to inaccurate fact-finding: the distance between the location of the alleged crimes and the fact-finding body; the scope of the crime; and the body prosecuting the atrocity.[12] She

[6] Article 51(2), ICC Statute. Under an emergency procedure included in Article 51(4) of the Statute, a two-thirds majority of judges may adopt temporary rules, which remain in force until the next meeting of the Assembly of States Parties (ASP). At that session, the ASP can vote to adopt the provisional rule into the permanent RPEs, or to amend or reject it.

[7] The Study Group on Governance was established in 2010 to facilitate 'a structured dialogue' between the Court and States Parties: ASP, Establishment of a Study Group on Governance, ICC-ASP/9/Res.2, 10 December 2010. See further: Study Group on Governance, *Lessons Learnt: First Report of the Court to the Assembly of States Parties*, ICC-ASP/11/31/Add. 1, 23 October 2012; ASP, *Strengthening the International Criminal Court and the Assembly of States Parties*, ICC-ASP/11/Res.8, 21 November 2012, and, for a detailed overview, P. Ambach, 'A Look towards the Future: The ICC and "Lessons Learnt"' in C. Stahn (ed.), *The Law and Practice of the International Criminal Court* (OUP, 2015), 1277, at 1285–7.

[8] Article 52(1), ICC Statute.

[9] Discussed at length in Y. McDermott, 'The International Criminal Court's Chambers Practice Manual: Towards a Return to Judicial Law Making in International Criminal Procedure?' (2017) 15 *Journal of International Criminal Justice* 873. The seventh edition of the Chambers Practice Manual was adopted following a judicial retreat in 2023, and is available online at https://www.icc-cpi.int/about/judicial-divisions/chambers-practice-manual (last accessed 3 December 2023).

[10] See e.g. 'ICC Judges Agree on Reforms in Response to Independent Expert Review at Annual Retreat', Press Release, ICC-CPI-20211121-PR1627, 22 November 2021, announcing that the judges had adopted a model for the decision on Directions for the Conduct of Proceedings, incorporating the submission model (as discussed in Chapter 3) for evidence and other key procedures, such as the order of evidence and matters relating to witness testimony and protection of witnesses. This model decision is included as a confidential annex to the Chambers Practice Manual, ibid.

[11] McDermott, n 9. There has been some judicial debate about the extent to which the Chambers Practice Manual should be followed: see e.g. *Prosecutor v Gbagbo and Blé Goudé*, Judgment on the appeal of Mr Laurent Gbagbo against the decision of Trial Chamber I entitled 'Decision giving notice pursuant to Regulation 55(2) of the Regulations of the Court', ICC-02/11-01/15-369, 18 December 2015, para. 54; *Prosecutor v Al Mahdi*, Decision on the confirmation of charges against Ahmad Al Faqi Al Mahdi, ICC-01/12-01/15-84, 24 March 2016, Separate Opinion of Judge Kovács, ICC-01/12-01/15-84-Anx, 9 May 2016, para. 13, and *Prosecutor v Ongwen*, Decision on the Defence request for leave to appeal the decision on the confirmation of charges, ICC-02/04-01/15-428, 29 April 2016, Partially dissenting opinion of Judge Perrin de Brichambaut, ICC-02/04-01/15-428-Anx, 10 May 2016, para. 13.

[12] N.A. Combs, 'Deconstructing the Epistemic Challenges to Mass Atrocity Prosecutions' (2018) 75 *Washington & Lee Law Review* 223.

concludes that the ideal fora for trying and proving international crimes may be domestic courts, rather than prosecution being undertaken by international criminal tribunals.[13] This points to a broader systemic issue with the design of international criminal trials as models of 'distant justice',[14] tasked with uncovering the truth of what happened in situations of mass atrocity that often took place many miles from the seat of the court and years before the start of the trial.

The structural difficulties that impede international criminal tribunals' fact-finding abilities are important to consider in light of the widespread assumption that trials by *international* criminal tribunals are the primary means to establish criminal accountability for international crimes. At the time of writing, there were calls to establish a new international criminal tribunal for Ukraine with jurisdiction to prosecute the crime of aggression.[15] Further, a working group in 2021 developed a definition for a new international crime of ecocide and was lobbying States Parties to the ICC to adopt a Statute amendment to incorporate it.[16] At the heart of each of these initiatives is the premise that the best way to achieve 'justice' is through international criminal tribunals as we know them today, but the recent revival of universal jurisdiction prosecutions and the domestic prosecution of international crimes across the world[17] suggest that a large part of international criminal law's future may well lie in the domestic realm.[18]

Regardless of the shift towards increasing domestic prosecution of international crimes, international criminal trials per se, and the International Criminal Court in particular, will continue to play a central role in the search for accountability for atrocity crimes worldwide. Given the complexity of proceedings and the scope of international criminal trials, some have argued for a dramatic reimagining of the current format and structure of international criminal trials. For example, Darryl Mundis, a former Senior Legal Officer at the ICTY, proposed an approach that

[13] Ibid. See, in a similar vein, J.D. Jackson, 'Finding the Best Epistemic Fit for International Criminal Tribunals: Beyond the Adversarial-Inquisitorial Dichotomy' (2009) 7 *Journal of International Criminal Justice* 17, arguing that international criminal evidence is ill-suited to meeting its aims of providing fair and reliable verdicts.

[14] A term taken from P. Clark, *Distant Justice: The Impact of the International Criminal Court on African Politics* (CUP, 2018).

[15] Council of Europe, 'Secretary General Joins the Summit of Leaders for Creation of Special Tribunal on the Crime of Aggression against Ukraine', Strasbourg, 9 May 2023, online at https://www.coe.int/en/web/portal/-/secretary-general-joins-the-summit-of-leaders-for-creation-of-special-tribunal-on-the-crime-of-aggression-against-ukraine (last accessed 13 May 2023).

[16] Independent Expert Panel for the Legal Definition of Ecocide, *Commentary and Core Text*, June 2021, online at https://www.stopecocide.earth/legal-definition (last accessed 13 May 2023).

[17] See e.g. K. Aksamitowska, *Justice at Home, Justice Abroad: The Accountability Efforts Relating to the Conflicts in Eastern Ukraine, Northern Iraq, and Syria* (PhD thesis, Swansea University, 2023); C. Gabriele et al., 'The Role of Mobile Technology in Documenting International Crimes: The *Affaire Castro et Kizito* in the Democratic Republic of Congo' (2021) 19 *Journal of International Criminal Justice* 107; M. Langer and M. Eason, 'The Quiet Expansion of Universal Jurisdiction' (2019) 30 *European Journal of International Law* 779.

[18] Or the regional realm: see e.g. African Union, Protocol on Amendments to the Protocol on the Statute of the African Court of Justice and Human Rights, 27 June 2014 (Malabo Protocol) in relation to the jurisdiction of the African Court on Human and Peoples' Rights over international crimes.

would bifurcate the 'crime base' and 'linkage' elements of cases, with a public commission taking evidence and making findings on the broader crime base—that is, what crimes occurred, where, and when—but being precluded from determining questions of individual criminal responsibility.[19] Trials themselves would focus on the individual accused and their alleged link to the crimes for which they allegedly bear responsibility.[20]

While intuitively attractive, this proposal faces some practical obstacles. First, and most fundamentally, Mundis foresees that the accused would not be able to challenge the findings of the commission unless they can show that an error of law was committed.[21] This could have very serious consequences both for the individual accused and for the broader legitimacy of the international criminal justice project, if a finding of fact that no reasonable Trial Chamber could have reached were permitted to stand.[22] Second, the initial tribunal may find it very difficult, if not impossible, to refrain from straying into the arena of international criminal responsibility under such a model. Many recent analyses of the work of human rights commissions of inquiry have revealed how their functions and approaches have evolved to consider and apply international criminal law concepts.[23] Indeed, because all crimes have an *actus reus* and a *mens rea* element, it would in fact be impossible to determine that a crime has been committed without analysing the mental element.[24] It could be argued that the commission would only examine the intent or knowledge of the principal perpetrators, with the later trial focusing on the link between these perpetrators and 'higher-level' accused, but international criminal tribunals can and do prosecute those who have directly committed the

[19] D.A. Mundis, Book Review of G. Boas, *The Milošević Trial: Lessons for the Conduct of Complex International Criminal Proceedings* (2008) 102 *American Journal of International Law* 691, at 694–5. See also P.M. Wald, *Tyrants on Trial: Keeping Order in the Courtroom* (Open Society Justice Initiative, 2009), 26. Others (e.g. M.C. Bassiouni and W.A. Schabas, *The Legislative History of the International Criminal Court* (2nd edn, Brill Nijhoff, 2016), 203) have suggested that it would have been preferable to have an investigative judge tasked with gathering all the evidence, under judicial supervision. A similar argument on delegation will be made in Simon De Smet's book, *Rethinking Fact-Finding by International Courts*, forthcoming with Cambridge University Press. De Smet's argument is more nuanced in that it proposes that such delegation is acceptable only if judges retain the ability to critically review the findings in detail, which requires a formalised method of analysis articulating the findings.

[20] Mundis, n 19, 695.

[21] Ibid.

[22] In Chapter 7 we discuss 'proof on appeal' with a particular focus on the standard of review for alleged errors of fact.

[23] C. Schwöbel-Patel, 'Commissions of Inquiry: Courting International Criminal Courts and Tribunals', and T. Mariniello, 'The Impact of International Commissions of Inquiry on the Proceedings before the International Criminal Court' in C. Henderson (ed.), *Commissions of Inquiry: Problems and Prospects* (Hart, 2017), 145, 171; L. van den Herik and C. Harwood, 'Commissions of Inquiry and the Charm of International Criminal Law: Between Transactional and Authoritative Approaches', and 'C. Stahn and D. Jacobs, 'The Interaction between Human Rights Fact-Finding and International Criminal Proceedings: Toward a (New) Typology' in P. Alston and S. Knuckey (eds), *The Transformation of Human Rights Fact-Finding* (OUP, 2016), 233, 255.

[24] D. Jacobs and C. Harwood, 'International Criminal Law Outside the Courtroom: The Impact of Focusing on International Crimes for the Quality of Fact-Finding by International Commissions of Inquiry' in M. Bergsmo (ed.), *Quality Control in Fact-Finding* (TOAEP, 2013), 325, at 355.

alleged crimes. It would therefore be difficult, if not impossible, to split the responsibility for adjudicating over 'crime base' factual allegations and 'linkage' factual allegations pertaining to the specific accused. Third, the prospect of amending the 'unique compromise'[25] reached by the drafters of the ICC Statute to boldly reformulate the structure of decision-making so radically seems highly unlikely, as does the prospect of a new international criminal tribunal adopting a judicial structure that is virtually unheard of in international and domestic law.[26]

Therefore, for the purposes of this chapter, we can take as our starting point the reality that international criminal tribunals exist in their current format and continue to form an important part of the landscape in proving international crimes. They are mandated to try individuals within the confines of a broadly adversarial adjudicative process, with parties carrying out their own investigations and a single Trial Chamber assessing all of the evidence that has been presented at the end of trial. Within those confines, what principles are central to the development and application of international criminal evidence as a body of law?

The notion of a 'principle' is itself contested. Judgments and secondary sources do, on occasion, refer to 'principles' without explaining what constitutes a principle or how such principles might be derived.[27] For example, the Special Tribunal for Lebanon's Trial Judgment in *Ayyash et al.* outlined numerous 'principles on the application of the standard of proof'. These included the presumption of innocence, the standard of proof beyond reasonable doubt, and the *in dubio pro reo* principle,[28] but the methodology used to identify those principles was not clear. Other judgments have set out general approaches to the evaluation of particular forms of evidence, but have not framed these as 'rules' or 'principles'.[29] Werle and Jeßberger, in their book *Principles of International Criminal Law*, comprehensively set out the history and key concepts of international criminal law, as well as a detailed overview of each of the crimes.[30] Part II of this book, titled 'General Principles', covers the structure of crimes under international criminal law (*actus*

[25] C. Kreß, 'The Procedural Law of the International Criminal Court in Outline: Anatomy of a Unique Compromise' (2003) 1 *Journal of International Criminal Justice* 603.

[26] The closest parallel is probably the International Military Tribunal (IMT) at Nuremberg's appointment of Commissioners to hear evidence in relation to the organisations, which heard evidence from 101 witnesses and received thousands of affidavits: A.M.S. Neave, Final Report on the Evidence of Witnesses for the Defense of Organizations Alleged to be Criminal, Heard Before a Commission Appointed by the Tribunal Pursuant to Paragraph 4 of the Order of the 13th of March, 1946, Nuremberg Trial Proceedings Volume 42, August 1946.

[27] E.g. K.A.A. Khan, C. Buisman, and C. Gosnell (eds), *Principles of Evidence in International Criminal Justice* (OUP, 2010).

[28] *Prosecutor v Ayyash et al.*, Judgment, STL-11-01/T/TC, 18 August 2020 ('*Ayyash et al.* Judgment'), para. 201.

[29] E.g. *Prosecutor v Ongwen*, Trial Judgment, ICC-02/04-01/15-1762, 4 February 2021, paras 251–60; 613 *et seq*; 847–50; *Prosecutor v Lubanga*, Judgment pursuant to Article 74 of the Statute, ICC-01/04-01/06-2842, 14 March 2012, paras 92–123; *Prosecutor v Katanga*, Judgment pursuant to Article 74 of the Statute, ICC-01/04-01/07-3436, 7 March 2014, paras 68–110; *Prosecutor v Ntaganda*, Judgment, ICC-01/04-02/06-2359, 8 July 2019, paras 44–76.

[30] G. Werle and F. Jeßberger, *Principles of International Criminal Law* (3rd edn, OUP, 2014).

reus and *mens rea*), modes of liability, defences, and immunity, among other substantive issues.[31]

Other scholarship tends to perceive 'principles' as more of an abstract concept than an extrapolation of what already happens. For Hart, principles, as opposed to rules, are 'broad, general, or unspecific, in the sense that often what would be regarded as a number of distinct rules can be exhibited as the exemplifications or instantiations of a single principle'.[32] To this end, principles can go some way to justifying or explaining the content or rationale of particular rules.[33] Vasiliev has likened the notion of principles of international criminal procedure to constitutional principles in domestic law: they are 'highly abstract, non-conclusive, but absolute provisions' that are 'not subject to fragmentation'.[34] For example, while 'the principle of orality' is often mentioned in proceedings, it can hardly be viewed as a general principle of international criminal evidence, given that it can be weighed against other factors and has been framed as less of 'an absolute restriction' and more as 'a preference for the oral introduction of evidence'.[35] The editors of *International Criminal Procedure: Principles and Rules*, and members of the working groups that contributed to that comprehensive volume, adopted the following condensed version of Vasiliev's definition: 'Principles are general, highly abstract, and inconclusive legal prescriptions which are (or must be) shared by all individual tribunals due to their fundamental and mandatory nature (i.e. not subject to fragmentation in the macro-dimension of international criminal justice).'[36]

Determining what principles might underpin and inform the development of international criminal evidence as a body of law necessitates an examination of the purpose of international criminal trials in general, and their rules of evidence in particular.[37] A broad spectrum of goals—ranging from deterrence to creating a historical record—have been ascribed to international criminal tribunals.[38] However, at its heart, the purpose of the trial is to determine whether the defendant bears criminal responsibility for the crimes with which they have been charged, and to

[31] Ibid., 165–288.

[32] H.L.A. Hart, *The Concept of Law* (3rd edn, OUP, 2012), 260.

[33] Ibid. (noting that principles are regarded 'not only as providing an explanation or rationale of the rules, which exemplify them, but as at least contributing to their justification').

[34] S. Vasiliev, 'General Rules and Principles of International Criminal Procedure: Definition, Legal Nature and Identification' in G. Sluiter and S. Vasiliev (eds), *International Criminal Procedure: Towards a Coherent Body of Law* (Cameron May, 2009), 19, 88–9.

[35] *Prosecutor v Halilović*, Decision on Interlocutory Appeal Concerning Admission of Record of Interview of the Accused from the Bar Table, IT-01-48-AR73.2, 19 August 2005, para. 17. See further Vasiliev, ibid., 56.

[36] G. Sluiter et al., 'Introduction' in G. Sluiter et al. (eds), *International Criminal Procedure: Principles and Rules* (OUP, 2013), 21.

[37] For a thorough overview, see C. Wheeler, *Fairness and the Goals of International Criminal Trials* (Routledge, 2023).

[38] M.R. Damaška, 'What is the Point of International Criminal Justice?' (2008) 83 *Chicago-Kent Law Review* 329.

do so in a fair and ethical manner.[39] Jackson and Brunger have noted that civil and common law systems are guided by 'two rather different goals'—'the need to find the truth and the need for dispute resolution', respectively—and that it is unclear which of those goals international criminal tribunals should prioritise.[40] However, the notion of 'dispute resolution' in the context of a criminal trial—which necessarily involves duly considering the arguments presented and any evidence provided in support of, or against, those arguments in the course of the trial—is not necessarily opposed to the search for the truth.[41]

While some have argued that rules of evidence are designed to apportion risk between the parties,[42] a more convincing view of their purpose is to enable the court to *find the truth in an ethical way.*[43] Roberts and Zuckerman identified 'five foundational principles of criminal evidence': accurate fact-finding; preventing wrongful convictions; the protection of liberty; humane treatment; and maintaining high standards of propriety in the criminal process.[44] The first two principles (accuracy and preventing wrongful convictions) are inextricably linked, as are the latter three, which all fall under the need to protect the rights of the accused and the integrity of proceedings.

From that purposive view, we can extract two overarching principles underpinning proof in international criminal trials: rectitude of decision and the highest standards of fairness. Each of these will be examined in turn below. These principles are reflected in the legal frameworks of the international criminal tribunals, which seek to fill lacunae in their rules through the application of 'rules of evidence *which will best favour a fair determination of the matter before [the court]* and are consonant with the spirit of the Statute and the general principles of law'.[45]

There are other principles that have been suggested as providing an ideal epistemic framework; for example, Jackson suggested equality of arms and the right to adversarial procedure as the two factors to which international criminal evidence

[39] A. Duff et al., 'Introduction: Judgment and Calling to Account' in A. Duff et al. (eds), *The Trial on Trial: Volume Two* (Hart, 2006), 1; H.L. Ho, *A Philosophy of Evidence Law: Justice in the Search for Truth* (OUP, 2008), discussed at text to n 86.

[40] J.D. Jackson and Y.M. Brunger, 'Fragmentation and Harmonization in the Development of Evidentiary Practices in International Criminal Tribunals' in E. van Sliedregt and S. Vasiliev, *Pluralism in International Criminal Law* (OUP, 2014), 159, 162.

[41] Compare The Rt Hon Lord Bonomy LLD, 'Is Our Adversarial System Fit for Purpose?', Lecture delivered at the Inner Temple, London, 12 June 2023 (arguing that the adversarial system 'may result in an outcome determined by argument rather than evidence given that it is not an investigation into or search for truth but a contest of proof').

[42] A. Stein, *Foundations of Evidence Law* (OUP, 2005).

[43] Ho, n 39, 50.

[44] P. Roberts and A. Zuckerman, *Roberts and Zuckerman's Criminal Evidence* (3rd edn, OUP, 2022), 19–24.

[45] Rule 89(B), ICTY RPE; Rule, 89(B), ICTR RPE; Rule 89(B), SCSL RPE (emphasis added). Rule 149(B) STL RPE is worded slightly differently ('a Chamber shall apply rules of evidence which best favour a fair determination of the matter before it and are consonant with the highest standards of international criminal procedure').

should be aligned.[46] These factors can be subsumed into the broader principles of rectitude of decision and fairness: an adversarial procedure enables both sides to be heard in a manner that leads to the proper determination of the truth, while equality of arms is a key component of the right to a fair trial. Similarly, the integrity of proceedings could be seen as a standalone principle of international criminal evidence, but, as argued below, this falls under the wider principle of the highest standards of fairness.[47]

C. Rectitude of decision

The term 'rectitude of decision' was used by Jeremy Bentham to describe the idea of achieving justice through the accurate determination of true relevant past facts and their correct application to the substantive law.[48] Bentham saw rectitude of decision as the purpose of adjectival (or procedural) law.[49] To this end, in a position that is now widely acknowledged to have gone 'too far',[50] Bentham argued in favour of abolishing *all* rules of evidence, under what became known as 'the non-exclusion principle':

> Be the dispute what it may—see everything that is to be seen: hear everybody who is likely to know anything about the matter: hear everybody, but most attentively of all, and first of all, those who are likely to know most about it—the parties.[51]

We will return to the utility of exclusionary rules and rules on the admission of evidence in the next chapter.[52] For now, returning to the notion of 'rectitude of decision', the sound application of law to true facts may seem like an uncontroversial proposition. Yet, post-structuralist theories contest the notion of 'truth' as something to be found, rather than constructed.[53] This school of thought contends

[46] J.D. Jackson, 'Finding the Best Epistemic Fit for International Criminal Tribunals: Beyond the Adversarial-Inquisitorial Dichotomy' (2009) 7 *Journal of International Criminal Justice* 17.

[47] See also Chapter 3 on the exclusion of evidence.

[48] J. Bentham, *Rationale of Judicial Evidence: Specially Applied to English Practice, Volume I* (Hunt and Clarke, 1827), 1–4. See further, W. Twining, *Rethinking Evidence: Exploratory Essays* (CUP, 2009), 79–80; W. Twining, 'Moving Beyond Law: Interdisciplinarity and the Study of Evidence' in P. Dawid, W. Twining, and M. Vasilaki (eds), *Evidence, Inference and Enquiry* (OUP, 2011), 73.

[49] 'To give execution and effect throughout to the main, or substantive, branch of the body of the law is, or ought to be, the main positive end or object of the other branch, viz. the adjective, or that which regulates the system of procedure': J. Bentham, *Rationale of Judicial Evidence: Specially Applied to English Practice, Volume VI* (Hunt and Clarke, 1827), 210.

[50] Twining, n 48, 76.

[51] J. Bentham, *Rationale of Judicial Evidence: Specially Applied to English Practice, Volume X* (Hunt and Clarke, 1827), 599.

[52] Chapter 3, section D.

[53] M. Parlevliet, 'Considering Truth: Dealing with a Legacy of Gross Human Rights Violations' (1998) 16 *Netherlands Quarterly of Human Rights* 141 and J. Frank, *Courts on Trial, Myth and Reality in*

that there is no objective truth, only perspectives and interpretations.[54] This can be compared with the pragmatist theory of truth, as pioneered by Charles Sanders Peirce, who reminded readers that truth means that something is 'so', regardless of whether one thinks otherwise, 'for if thinking otherwise is going to make it otherwise, there is no use in reasoning or in studying logic'.[55] Enlightenment thinkers such as Hume saw truth as knowledge which corresponds to objective reality and 'best discovered through reason, understood as the exercise of formal logic (scientific rationality)'.[56] More recently, philosophers like Susan Haack have convincingly argued that while some claims may be only be partially true, or may only be true in a particular context, place, or time, it is incorrect to extrapolate from that to conclude that there is no such thing as 'truth'.[57]

In practice, several judges have expressly disavowed any role in determining broader historical truths in the conflict at issue.[58] B.V.A. Röling, the Dutch Judge

American Justice (Princeton University Press, 1973), 23–4 (both arguing that 'truth' and 'facts' are not 'found' but rather constructed, based on a subjective evaluation of the evidence presented); T. Franck and H. Fairley, 'Procedural Due Process in Human Rights Fact-Finding by International Agencies' (1980) 74 *American Journal of International Law* 308, 309 ('Lawyers know that there are few "pure" facts').

[54] W. Kaufmann, *The Portable Nietzsche* (Viking Press, 1954), 458. On the 'myth of objectivity', see T. Nagel, *The View from Nowhere* (OUP, 1986), 11 and R. Rorty, *Objectivity, Relativism, and Truth: Philosophical Papers, Volume 1* (CUP, 1991), 7.

[55] C.S. Peirce, 'The Objectivity of Truth' in C. Hartshorne and P. Weiss (eds), *The Collected Papers of Charles Sanders Peirce, Volume II: Elements of Logic* (Harvard University Press, 1932), 135.

[56] D. Nicolson, 'Gender, Epistemology, and Ethics: Feminist Perspectives on Evidence Theory' in M. Childs and L. Ellison (eds), *Feminist Perspectives on Evidence* (Taylor & Francis, 2000), 13, 14. See e.g. D. Hume, *Enquiries Concerning the Human Understanding and Concerning the Principles of Morals* (2nd edn, OUP, 1902), 69–179.

[57] S. Haack, *Evidence Matters: Science, Proof, and Truth in the Law* (CUP, 2014), 297; M. Mekki, 'Preuve et Vérité en France' in Association Henri Capitant (ed.), *La Preuve: Journées internationales 2013 d'Amsterdam, Pays-Bas et Liège, Belgique, Vol. LXIII* (Bruylant, 2015), 813, 817 (arguing that the judge both discovers and constructs a truth, the judicial truth, which is the product of probative reasoning).

[58] See e.g. the comments of an ICTR Presiding Judge: 'We are running a trial now. We are not a truth commission': *Prosecutor v Karemera et al.*, Transcript, ICTR-98-44-T, 2 November 2006, 30, and the remark that the 'Chamber's purpose is not to serve the academic study of history' in *Prosecutor v Karadžić*, Decision on the Accused's Holbrooke Agreement Motion, IT-95-5/18-PT, 8 July 2009, para. 46. Much has been written on the (unintended) role of international criminal tribunals in the historiography of the conflicts on which they adjudge: e.g. B. Sander, 'History on Trial: Historical Narrative Pluralism Within and Beyond International Criminal Courts' (2018) 67 *International & Comparative Law Quarterly* 547; R.A. Wilson, *Writing History in International Criminal Trials* (CUP, 2011); F. Gaynor, 'Uneasy Partners: Evidence, Truth and History in International Trials' (2012) 10 *Journal of International Criminal Justice* 1257; N. Eltringham, '"We are not a Truth Commission": Fragmented Narratives and the Historical Record at the International Criminal Tribunal for Rwanda' (2009) 11 *Journal of Genocide Research* 55; N. Eltringham, *Genocide Never Sleeps: Living Law at the International Criminal Tribunal for Rwanda* (CUP, 2019); B. Sander, *Doing Justice to History: Confronting the Past in International Criminal Courts* (OUP, 2021); M. Aksenova, 'The Role of International Criminal Tribunals in Shaping the Historical Accounts of Genocide' in U. Belavusau and A. Gliszczyńska-Grabias (eds), *Law and Memory: Towards Legal Governance of History* (CUP, 2017), 48. As Schuppli argued in the context of the ICTY's archival holdings, 'what emerges … is ultimately the extent to which the Tribunal itself becomes a processing machine that works over the materials that enter its legal infrastructure, and in the process also actively transforms them': S. Schuppli, 'Entering

at the IMTFE, distinguished between what he called a 'trial truth', constrained by the scope of the trial's inquiry and the arguments and evidence put forward by the parties, and the 'real truth'.[59] Before the Special Tribunal for Lebanon (STL), the Trial Chamber noted that it was neither a truth and reconciliation commission nor a commission of inquiry.[60] As such, it decided it was 'not therefore equipped to establish an "objective truth"—behind what is pleaded in an indictment and is proved by the evidence before it—if in fact an "objective truth" exists'.[61] The latter part of this quote seems an unusual standpoint for a Tribunal established 'to prosecute persons responsible for the attack of 14 February 2005 resulting in the death of former Lebanese Prime Minister Rafiq Hariri'[62] to take. If, in fact, *no* objective truth exists as to who was responsible for that attack, then the Tribunal's only completed trial seems hardly the most productive use of the 15 years of legal proceedings and $1 billion it cost. The quote may be explained in part by its context, in a section about participating victims' rights and the extent to which they could avail of the right to a reasoned opinion—a right that the Trial Chamber found inured primarily to the accused.[63] In this way, it might be explained as limiting the concept of truth to the purpose of the trial, although the side note that objective truth may not exist seems somewhat superfluous.

Nevertheless, judges should be wary about veering into postmodern theory that 'there is no such thing as truth',[64] as the STL appeared to do in the above-cited passage. As eloquently stated by Norman Geras:

> If there is no truth, there is no injustice. Stated less simplistically, if truth is wholly relativized or internalized to particular discourses or language games or social practices, there is no injustice. The victims and protesters of any *putative* injustice are deprived of their last and often best weapon, that of telling what really happened. They can only tell their story, which is something else. Morally and politically, therefore, anything goes.[65]

Evidence: Cross-Examining the Court Records of the ICTY' in *Forensis: The Architecture of Public Truth* (Sternberg Press/Forensic Architecture, 2014), 279, 282.

[59] B.V.A. Röling, *The Tokyo Trial and Beyond: Reflections of a Peacemonger* (Polity Press, 1993) (edited and with an introduction by A. Cassese), 50–4. See also Gaynor, n 58, 1260.

[60] *Ayyash et al.* Judgment, n 28, para. 938.

[61] Ibid. The word 'behind' may be a typographical error here—the judges may have meant 'beyond'.

[62] Agreement between the United Nations and the Lebanese Republic on the establishment of a Special Tribunal for Lebanon, Annex to UN Security Council Resolution 1757 (2007), 30 May 2007, Article 1(1).

[63] *Ayyash et al.* Judgment, n 28, para. 940. This point of who is entitled to fair trial rights is discussed further in section D of this chapter.

[64] Cf. C. Buisman, *Ascertainment of the Truth in International Criminal Justice* (PhD thesis, Brunel University London, 2012).

[65] N. Geras, 'Language, Truth and Justice' (1995) 1 *New Left Review*, online at https://newleftreview.org/issues/i209/articles/norman-geras-language-truth-and-justice.pdf (last accessed 16 May 2023). I am indebted to my colleague Gideon Calder for this point. Cf. H. White, 'Response to Arthur Marwick' (1995) 30 *Journal of Contemporary History* 233, 244 (arguing that postmodernists are not

On the other hand, other Chambers have emphasised their role in searching for the truth.[66] More recently, several judges have highlighted the dangers of 'fake news' and the 'post-truth' era, and the importance of grounding their judgments solidly in the evidence as a result.[67] The right to the truth for victims of human rights violations has been mentioned as a key determinant.[68]

In evidence scholarship, the leading 'rationalist tradition' has as a key underlying hypothesis that the purpose of evidence in the law is to discover the truth.[69] Zuckerman has argued that the law of criminal evidence is a 'continual search for a balance between competing demands, the first of which is the desire to discover the truth',[70] while Schwikkard perceived 'accuracy' as a core value that the law of evidence seeks to protect.[71] Twining dubbed the leading scholars in this tradition—Gilbert, Bentham, Stephen, and Thayer—as 'optimistic rationalists', because they all believed that their proposed changes to evidence laws would enhance the rationality of adjudication.[72] More recently, scholars have argued that

'opposed to the truth', but rather merely recognise that reality is as much constructed as it is discovered). This distinction is discussed in further depth in Sander, *Doing Justice to History*, n 58, 37–40.

66 *Prosecutor v Akayesu*, Judgment, ICTR-96-4-T, 2 September 1998, para. 131; *Prosecutor v Deronjic*, Sentencing Judgment, IT-02-61-S, 30 March 2004, para. 133. For example, Judge Antonetti noted: 'I am a bit like Diogenes, who was walking in Athens with a lantern in daylight and he was asked what he was doing, and he answered, I'm looking for a human, a human being. I myself am looking for the truth. I'm the judicial counterpart of this famous person, and I'm looking for the truth.' *Prosecutor v Prlić*, Transcript, IT-04-74, 10 February 2009, p. 36692, lines 2–5.

67 *Prosecutor v Bemba*, Judgment on the appeal of Mr Jean-Pierre Bemba Gombo against Trial Chamber III's 'Judgment pursuant to Article 74 of the Statute', ICC-01/05-01/08-3636-Red, 8 June 2018 ('*Bemba* Appeal Judgment'), Separate Opinion of Judge Van den Wyngaert and Judge Morrison, para. 5; *Prosecutor v. Gbagbo and Blé Goudé*, Reasons for oral decision of 15 January 2019 on the Requête de la Défense de Laurent Gbagbo afin qu'un jugement d'acquittement portant sur toutes les charges soit prononcé en faveur de Laurent Gbagbo et que sa mise en liberté immédiate soit ordonnée, and on the Blé Goudé Defence no case to answer motion, ICC-02/11-01/15-1263, 16 July 2019, Reasons of Judge Henderson, ICC-02/11-01/15-1263-AnxB-Red, 16 July 2019, para. 4.

68 *Prosecutor v Katanga and Ngudjolo*, Decision on the Set of Procedural Rights Attached to Procedural Status of Victim at the Pre-Trial Stage of the Case, ICC-01/04-01/07-474, 13 May 2008, para. 32.

69 D. Accatino, 'Legal Evidence Theory: Are We All "Rationalists" Now?' (2020) 40 *Revus* 85. See further, T. Anderson, D. Schum, and W. Twining, *Analysis of Evidence* (2nd edn, CUP, 2009), 79–82. There is a rich tradition of scholarship in the rationalist tradition in the Spanish language, by authors such as J. Ferrer Beltrán (*Prueba y Verdad en el Derecho* (2nd edn, Marcial Pons, 2005); *La Valoración Racional de la Prueba* (Marcial Pons, 2007), and *Motivación y Racionalidad de la Prueba* (Grijley, 2016)). See also M. Gascón Abellán, *Los Hechos en el Derecho: Bases Argumentales de la Prueba* (2nd edn, Marcial Pons, 2004); D. González Lagier, 'Tres Modos de Razonar Sobre Hechos (y Algunos Problemas Sobre la Prueba Judicial Planteados a Partir de Ellos)' in C. Vázquez (ed.), *Hechos y Razonamiento Probatorio* (Ceji, 2018), 17; and C. Vázquez, *De la Prueba Científica a la Prueba Pericial* (Marcial Pons, 2015). See further, Twining, n 48, 35–98; D. Nicolson, *Evidence and Proof in Scotland: Context and Critique* (Edinburgh University Press, 2019), 29.

70 A.A.S. Zuckerman, *The Principles of Criminal Evidence* (OUP, 1989).

71 P.J. Schwikkard, 'Convergence, Appropriate Fit and Values in Criminal Process' in P. Roberts and M. Redmayne (eds), *Innovations in Evidence and Proof: Integrating Theory, Research and Teaching* (Hart, 2007), 331, 332.

72 Anderson, Schum, and Twining, n 69, 81; Twining, n 48, 70–82. For an overview of each proponent's recommendations (Gilbert's 'best evidence rule'; Bentham's free proof approach; Stephen's test of relevancy, and Thayer's conception of evidence rules as a group of exceptions to the principle of free proof), see Anderson, Schum, and Twining, n 69, 290.

rules of evidence can create the conditions for finding the truth in an ethical and epistemically sound way.[73]

The search for truth, which is after all an obligation on the ICC,[74] can be squared with some judges' apparent reluctance to engage in writing history per se,[75] by moving away from broad theoretical questions about the nature of truth and whether one objective truth exists. The judge's role is to determine the truth of whether the evidence that has been presented is sufficient to meet the standard of proof, not any broader questions of 'what really happened'.[76] Importantly, as Simon de Smet has emphasised, the judicial role is not just establishing the truth, it is finding the truth *with an appropriate level of certainty* to comply with the requisite standard of proof.[77] The Trial Chamber must identify potential sources of doubt.[78] If there is evidence to lend some support to the proposition of guilt but it is not enough to prove guilt beyond reasonable doubt, then it must acquit the defendant.[79] Thus, the judge's role is truth-seeking, rather than truth-neutral, but they must determine the truth only on the narrow question of whether the culpability of the accused for the crimes charged has been proven beyond reasonable doubt.[80] As a consequence of this, there are particular facts that must be

[73] Ho, n 39; cf. Stein, n 42, arguing that the purpose of the law of evidence is to 'apportion the risk of error in conditions of uncertainty'.

[74] Article 69(3), ICC Statute. The search for the truth is also a prosecutorial duty, per Article 54(1)(a), ICC Statute. *Prosecutor v Ngudjolo*, Judgment on the Prosecutor's appeal against the decision of Trial Chamber II entitled 'Judgment pursuant to article 74 of the Statute', ICC-01/04-02/12-271-Corr, 7 April 2015 ('*Ngudjolo* Appeal Judgment'), para. 256.

[75] *Prosecutor v Lubanga*, Public redacted Judgment on the appeal of Mr Thomas Lubanga Dyilo against his conviction, ICC-01/04-01/06-3121-Red, 1 December 2014 ('*Lubanga* Appeal Judgment'), Dissenting opinion of Judge Anita Ušacka, ICC-01/04-01/06-3121-Anx2, 1 December 2014, para. 42 (arguing that the ICC cannot sacrifice fairness and the need for sufficient evidence at the altar of preserving an historical record).

[76] Though this may be an inevitable side-product of their endeavours: see Wilson, n 58; Sander, n 58, 29; Gaynor, n 58; M. Osiel, *Mass Atrocity, Collective Memory, and the Law* (Transaction Publishers, 1997), 241; P.M. Wald, 'Foreword: War Tales and War Trials' (2008) 106 *Michigan Law Review* 901, 911.

[77] S. de Smet, 'Enhancing the Quality of Reasoning about the Link Between Evidence and Factual Propositions', Indian Law Institute, New Delhi, 22 February 2019, online at www.cilrap.org/cilrap-film/190222-smet/ (last accessed 16 May 2023).

[78] Ibid.

[79] The general principle of *in dubio pro reo* means that in cases of doubt, the benefit of the doubt must go to the accused: see e.g. *Gbagbo and Blé Goudé*, Reasons of Judge Henderson, n 67, para. 2. We return to this point in Chapter 4.

[80] On the idea of 'procedural truth', see P. Murphy (ed.), *Evidence, Proof, and Facts: A Book of Sources* (OUP, 2003), 6; G.L. Certoma, 'The Accusatory System v the Inquisitorial System: Procedural Truth v Fact?' (1982) 56 *Australian Law Journal* 288; T. Weigend, 'Is the Criminal Process About Truth? A German Perspective' (2003) 26 *Harvard Journal of Law & Public Policy* 157, 160; 170–3. On 'legal truth', see R.S. Summers, 'Formal Legal Truth and Substantive Truth in Judicial Fact-Finding: Their Justified Divergence in some Particular Cases' (1999) 18 *Law & Philosophy* 497; J.M. Fernandez, 'An Exploration of the Meaning of Truth in Philosophy and Law' (2009) 11 *University of Notre Dame Australia Law Review* 53 at 79–80. R.S. Frase, 'The Search for the Whole Truth about American and European Criminal Justice' (2000) 3 *Buffalo Criminal Law Review* 785. Ho Hock Lai has argued against these distinctions, finding them unhelpful. He notes: 'That factfinding is conducted for a higher purpose—to enforce the law or determine legal rights and liabilities—is consistent with the claim that the adjudication of factual disputes, which is the definitive business of the trial, is aimed at ascertaining

proven,[81] which may contribute to a broader historical narrative or provide a starting point for discussion about the past,[82] but that narrative is filtered through 'certain legal or juridical categories that shape its form and substance'.[83]

When considering the development of new practices or procedures in relation to evidence and proof, judges should ask: does this help in my search for the truth? Of course, two equally qualified judges may disagree on whether a measure helps or hinders that truth-finding role. For example, as shall be discussed in Chapter 3 in relation to the submission model for evidence, proponents of this approach believe that it impedes the truth to unnecessarily filter the evidentiary record through admissibility determinations. On the other hand, its opponents may argue that flooding the record with material that may be limited in relevance, reliability, or probative value may make it unnecessarily difficult for judges to determine the truth. Similarly, some judges may believe that witness preparation hinders the search for the truth, by removing the spontaneity of testifying in court, while others may believe that familiarising a witness is crucial to enabling them to tell their story to their fullest ability.[84] In such circumstances, some discussion between judges may be required to find a compromise or consensus.[85]

There are also some circumstances in which the search for the truth may come into conflict with other important considerations. For example, a piece of evidence obtained through torture might be relevant in proving a fact at issue, but to admit it would seriously undermine the fairness and integrity of proceedings. In circumstances where the integrity of proceedings would be seriously damaged, it is clear that such evidence must be excluded.[86] This leads us to our second foundational principle of international criminal evidence: the highest standards of fairness.

the truth': H.L. Ho, 'Evidence and Truth' in C. Dahlman, A. Stein, and G. Tuzet, *Philosophical Foundations of Evidence Law* (OUP, 2021), 11, 14.

[81] And the Chamber may invite the Prosecutor to reduce the scope of the indictment: Rule 73 *bis*(D), ICTY RPE.

[82] Sander has argued that it is better to see international criminal judgments as 'discursive beginnings for victims, local communities and future generations to engage with and debate the past beyond the courtroom' rather than expect them to provide 'narrative closure': Sander, n 58, 334.

[83] L. Douglas, 'The Didactic Trial: Filtering History and Memory into the Courtroom' (2006) 14 *European Review* 513, 514; see further Sander, n 58, 54. See further J.D. Jackson, 'Modern Trends in Evidence Scholarship: Is All Rosy in the Garden?' (2001–3) 21 *Quinnipiac Law Review* 893, 904, who sees the purpose of the law as providing 'closure to the issues under examination' from the perspective of establishing the truth; L. Prosperi and A.Z. Borda, 'A Partial View of History: ICTY Judgments as "Judicial Truths"' in C. Stahn et al. (eds), *Legacies of the International Criminal Tribunal for the Former Yugoslavia: A Multidisciplinary Approach* (OUP, 2020), 174.

[84] Jackson and Brunger, n 3.

[85] This appears to be the case in relation to the submission model before the ICC, as discussed in Chapter 3, and in amendments to the Rules of Procedure and Evidence in other tribunals: D.A. Mundis, 'From "Common Law" Towards "Civil Law": The Evolution of the ICTY Rules of Procedure and Evidence' (2001) 14 *Leiden Journal of International Law* 367; G. Boas, 'A Code of Evidence and Procedure for International Criminal Law? The Rules of the ICTY' in G. Boas and W.A. Schabas (eds), *International Criminal Law Developments in the Case Law of the ICTY* (Nijhoff, 2003), 1.

[86] See further Chapter 3, section D.

D. The highest standards of fairness

International criminal evidence must do more than ensure rectitude of decision.[87] As eloquently stated by Ho Hock Lai: 'The court must not only find truth in order to reach a just outcome, it must also do justice in the course of ascertaining the truth.'[88] It is for this reason that legal systems exclude certain forms of evidence that could potentially lead to a greater elucidation of the truth, including evidence obtained in violation of human rights or a recognised privilege, to ensure the continued fairness and integrity of the legal system.[89] This is also the case in international criminal law, where the creation of an accurate historical record is but one of the competing goals that trials seek to achieve.[90] Other goals, such as encouraging respect for the rule of law and deterring future human rights violations, would be defeated if international criminal trials decided to permit the admission of evidence that would undermine the integrity of proceedings.[91] To do justice in the process of fact-finding means to do so in a manner that respects the highest standards of fairness.

As I have argued at length elsewhere, the idea of 'the highest standards of fairness' is a construct of the international criminal tribunals themselves, who note their commitment to conducting trials to this standard in their own publicity and judgments.[92] In *Fairness in International Criminal Trials*, I argued that the right to a fair trial forms a 'unique construct of fairness', distinct from broader theories of fairness in its concrete and prescriptive nature.[93] The right to a fair trial is made up of a number of minimum procedural guarantees, such as the right to equality of arms, the right to trial without undue delay, the right to trial by an independent and impartial tribunal, and the right to silence.[94] The 'highest standards of fairness', in turn, can be defined as a full respect for all those procedural guarantees making up the right to a fair trial, combined with key principles of fairness including consistency, equality before the law, publicity, impartiality, non-retroactivity, and legal certainty.[95]

[87] Ho, n 39, 133. See also Ho, n 39, 79 (on the right to a 'just verdict, where justice must be understood to impose ethical demands on the manner in which the court conducts the trial, and importantly, on how it deliberates on the verdict').

[88] Ibid., 49.

[89] Schauer has argued that exclusionary rules that may occasionally produce bad outcomes in individual cases are likely to produce better decisions in the long term: F. Schauer, 'In Defense of a Rule-Based Evidence Law—and Epistemology Too' (2008) 5 *Episteme* 295.

[90] Damaška, n 38; Wheeler, n 37.

[91] Y. McDermott, *Fairness in International Criminal Trials* (OUP, 2016), 125–48.

[92] Ibid., 21–40; Y. McDermott, 'Rights in Reverse: A Critical Analysis of Fair Trial Rights under International Criminal Law' in W.A. Schabas et al. (eds), *The Ashgate Research Companion to International Criminal Law: Critical Perspectives* (Ashgate, 2013) 165. Cf. M. Damaška, 'Reflections on Fairness in International Criminal Justice' (2012) 10 *Journal of International Criminal Justice* 611; J. Nicholson, '"Too High", "Too Low", or "Just Fair Enough"? Finding Legitimacy Through the Accused's Right to a Fair Trial' (2019) 17 *Journal of International Criminal Justice* 351.

[93] McDermott, n 92, 21–40.

[94] Ibid., 41–104.

[95] Ibid., 21–40; see further, S. Rigney, *Fairness and Rights in International Criminal Procedure* (Edinburgh University Press, 2022).

One issue that has emerged in practice is whether fairness in the context of international criminal proceedings means fairness to the accused alone, or to other actors such as the prosecution or victims.[96] As the ICC Appeals Chamber noted in *Ngudjolo*, this is a vexed question.[97] The KSC Appeals Chamber interpreted the right to equality of arms as requiring 'that *neither of the parties* is put at a disadvantage when presenting their case'.[98] However, its authority for this proposition was the European Court of Human Rights judgment in *Dombo Beheer v The Netherlands*, a judgment relating to civil proceedings,[99] and therefore the reference to 'each party' in that case referred to two adversaries on an equal footing, where the claimant bears the evidential burden. By contrast, in criminal prosecutions, there is a structural imbalance that disadvantages the accused, who comes against the power of the state.[100] The right to equality of arms seeks to remedy that disadvantage by ensuring the accused has a fair ability to present their case. The institutional strength of the prosecution is also a feature in international criminal trials, where the prosecution is a permanent actor with dedicated staff and resources,[101] and often (though not always) benefits from state co-operation and the support of the international community in the collection of evidence.[102] Further, the prosecution's job is, by design, more difficult than the defence, in light of the burden of proof,[103] and the notion of ensuring the prosecution benefits from equality with the accused seems to overlook this important fact. While all parties to the trial should be afforded an adequate opportunity to present their case,[104] the right to a fair trial is an individual right owed to the person who stands on trial and not any broader procedural actors. Some may argue that limiting fairness to the accused alone ignores the rights of victims, the prosecution, and even the

[96] Discussed at length in McDermott, n 92, 105–24.

[97] *Ngudjolo* Appeal Judgment, n 74, paras 255–6. Compare *Ngudjolo* Appeal Judgment, n 74, Joint Dissenting Opinion of Judge Trendafilova and Judge Tarfusser, ICC-01/04-02/12-271-AnxA, 27 February 2015, para. 12 ('It is our strong conviction that the judicial duty to ensure fairness of the trial, as enjoined by virtue of article 64(2) of the Statute, encompasses the obligation of the Trial Chamber to safeguard the rights of the accused and *equally* the procedural rights of the Prosecutor, acting in the public interest').

[98] *Specialist Prosecutor v Gucati and Haradinaj*, Appeal Judgment, KSC-CA-2022-01, 2 February 2023 ('*Gucati and Haradinaj* Appeal Judgment'), para. 50.

[99] *Dombo Beheer B.V. v the Netherlands*, App. No. 14448/88, 27 October 1993, para. 33.

[100] Mekki, n 57, 840.

[101] McDermott, n 91, 116. See also W.A. Schabas and Y. McDermott, 'Article 66' in O. Triffterer and K. Ambos (eds), *Rome Statute of the International Criminal Court: Article-by-Article Commentary* (4th edn, Beck/Hart, 2021), 1947; McDermott, n 92, 165.

[102] McDermott, n 91, 116.

[103] *Prosecutor v Orić*, Interlocutory Decision on Length of Defence Case, IT-03-68-AR73.2, 20 July 2005, para. 7 ('The Prosecution has the burden of telling an entire story, of putting together a coherent narrative and proving every necessary element of the crimes charged beyond a reasonable doubt. Defence strategy, by contrast, often focuses on poking specifically targeted holes in the Prosecution's case, an endeavour which may require less time and fewer witnesses').

[104] *Ngudjolo* Appeal Judgment, n 74, para. 256; *Prosecutor v Lubanga*, Decision on the Defence request for leave to appeal regarding the transmission of applications for victim participation, ICC-01/04-01/06-672, 6 November 2006, 7.

international community.[105] But, as has been argued at length elsewhere, any extension of fair trial rights to other parties risks diluting the rights of the accused in the interests of 'balance'.[106]

The detailed understanding of the right to a fair trial that has been developed through international criminal tribunals and international human rights bodies, particularly the case law of the European Court of Human Rights, where Article 6 is amongst the most litigated rights,[107] 'implicitly enshrines a framework for the development of evidence rules'.[108] As Jackson and Summers have argued, the field of criminal evidence, which was traditionally the preserve of domestic legal traditions, has been internationalised through human rights principles that can provide a 'cross-jurisdictional notion of procedural fairness'.[109]

For example, in accordance with the right to be informed of the charges, the highest standards of fairness require that the factual allegations against the accused are clear, specific, and grounded in the evidence, as discussed in Chapter 4 on the 'substantial grounds to believe' standard of proof for the confirmation of charges. In recent years, however, the presentation and evaluation of the evidence at this stage of proceedings has been lowered, in a drive towards greater efficiency in proceedings.[110] Yet, the number of cases where some or all of the charges have been dropped at or before the confirmation hearing shows the value of this stage and the need for scrutiny of the evidence against the applicable (lower) standard of proof. Relatedly, as analysed in detail in Chapters 5 and 6, the right to a reasoned judgment means that the Trial Chamber must clearly indicate how it reached its decision, and on the basis of which evidence.[111] This is also indispensable for the full realisation of the right to appeal. As shall be argued in Chapter 7, Trial Chambers need not set out why they relied upon or did not rely upon each piece of evidence,[112] but conviction decisions must make clear how the Chamber reached its conclusions based on the evidence presented before it, in order to allow for meaningful appellate review.[113]

[105] For a detailed discussion of such arguments, see McDermott, n 92, 105–24.

[106] McDermott, n 91, 38–9.

[107] Council of Europe, *Annual Report 2022 of the European Court of Human Rights* (Council of Europe, 2023), 142. For an analysis of the Article 6 case law, see R. Goss, *Criminal Fair Trial Rights: Article 6 of the European Convention on Human Rights* (Hart, 2014); S. Trechsel and S. Summers, *Human Rights in Criminal Proceedings* (OUP, 2006).

[108] R. Stoykova, 'The Right to a Fair Trial as a Conceptual Framework for Digital Evidence Rules in Criminal Investigations' (2023) 49 *Computer Law & Security Review*, article 105801.

[109] J.D. Jackson and S.J. Summers, *The Internationalisation of Criminal Evidence* (CUP, 2012), 80.

[110] For a detailed discussion, see McDermott, n 9. The Independent Expert Review report, n 3, paras 483–9 noted what it saw as continuing inefficiencies in the confirmation process and urged Pre-Trial Chambers to consistently adhere to the guidance set out in the Chambers Practice Manual.

[111] *Prosecutor v Karera*, Judgment, ICTR-01-74-A, 2 February 2009 ('*Karera* Appeal Judgment'), para. 20; *Prosecutor v Kvočka et al.*, Judgment, IT-98-30/1-A, 28 February 2005, para. 23.

[112] *Karera* Appeal Judgment, n 112, para. 20; *Prosecutor v Furundžija*, Judgment, IT-95-17/1-A, 21 July 2000 ('*Furundžija* Appeal Judgment'), para. 69.

[113] *Lubanga* Appeal Judgment, n 75, Dissenting opinion of Judge Anita Ušacka, para. 26. See further Chapter 7.

The highest standards of fairness require the rigorous evaluation of the evidence, which clearly links established facts to the evidence presented to support that proposition.[114] This aligns with the presumption of innocence and *in dubio pro reo* principles, as discussed in Chapter 4, and with the protection against the reversal of the burden of proof.[115] As Judge Ušacka noted in *Lubanga*, 'the accused must always be given the benefit of any doubt as to the proof of guilt'.[116] Where evidence is unclear or where two reasonable readings of the evidence are possible, the interpretation that favours the accused must be taken.[117]

In situations where questions are raised about the reliability of a particular form of evidence, the Trial Chamber must be mindful of the risk of miscarriage of justice that might result from the reliance on that evidence.[118] For example, in relation to identification evidence, the ICTY Appeals Chamber noted the need to carefully articulate the factors that were taken into account when evaluating that evidence.[119] As shall be discussed in Chapter 5, the tribunals have incorporated the human rights principle that a conviction should not be based 'solely or to a decisive extent' on untested witness accounts.[120]

The highest standards of fairness are also closely interlinked with the need to ensure the integrity of the proceedings, given the function that procedural fairness plays in the perceived legitimacy of international institutions.[121] If international criminal evidence is to mature as a body of law, international criminal tribunals need to tackle issues that may call the fairness and integrity of their proceedings into question head on. Thus, as analysed in Chapter 3, the high threshold for the exclusion of evidence in some cases, and the ICC's unwillingness to consider the exclusion of evidence that technically does not fall under Article 69(7)'s exclusionary rule but nevertheless casts a pall over the perceived fairness and integrity of proceedings in others, may fix short-term issues but cause a longer-term dent in the reputation of the Court.

114 J.H. Wigmore, *The Science of Judicial Proof: As Given by Logic, Psychology, and General Experience, and Illustrated in Judicial Trials* (3rd edn, Little, Brown & Co., 1937), 5 called these two notions the '*factum probandum*' (the proposition to be established) and the '*factum probans*' (material evidencing that proposition).

115 See M. Coleman, *The Presumption of Innocence in International Human Rights and Criminal Law* (Routledge, 2021), 78–105.

116 *Lubanga* Appeal Judgment, n 75, Dissenting opinion of Judge Anita Ušacka, para. 79.

117 Discussed further in Chapter 4.

118 *Furundžija* Appeal Judgment, n 112, para. 34.

119 Ibid., para. 39.

120 *Prosecutor v Gotovina*, Judgment, IT-06-90-T, 15 April 2011, para. 43; *Prosecutor v Ntaganda*, Public redacted version of Judgment on the appeals of Mr Bosco Ntaganda and the Prosecutor against the decision of Trial Chamber VI of 8 July 2019 entitled 'Judgment', ICC-01/04-02/06-2666-Red, 30 March 2021, paras 629–30; *Prosecutor v Prlić et al.*, Judgment, IT-04-74-A, 29 November 2017, para. 137. See further Chapter 5.

121 T. Franck, *Fairness in International Law and Institutions* (OUP, 1995), 90–1. On the legitimacy of international criminal tribunals and its link with the law of evidence, see Jackson and Summers, n 109, 145–6.

E. Conclusion

Noting that international criminal evidence has emerged as an ad hoc and often inconsistent and unpredictable set of practices, this chapter proposed two key principles that ought to drive its crystallisation into a consistent body of law. Having discussed the nature of a 'principle' in this context, the chapter argued that the development of international criminal evidence should be underpinned by two principles: rectitude of decision and the highest standards of fairness. An approach driven by these two factors would lead to a greater consistency and coherence in practice, and more reasoned procedural law-making as international criminal evidence emerges as a standalone body of law.

Rectitude of decision requires judges to incorporate practices that lead to the accurate discovery of the past facts. Post-structuralist theories, which deny that one objective truth exists, were analysed and it was argued that judges *do* search for the truth, even if discomfort is sometimes expressed at the idea of 'writing history' through international criminal trials. It was argued that judges in international criminal trials are tasked with discovering the truth, albeit a narrow truth that is filtered through the lens of the crimes charged, and as such, rectitude of decision is a core principle that should shape international criminal evidence as a body of law.

The highest standards of fairness demand full respect for the rights of the accused (whom, it was argued, is the only beneficiary of the right to a fair trial), in a manner consistent with key principles of fairness such as legal certainty, equality before the law, non-retroactivity, and impartiality. It is clear to see how several important facets of the right to a fair trial, including the presumption of innocence, the right to challenge the evidence against one, the right to be informed of the charges, and the right to an appeal can influence the development of international criminal evidence.

3

The Admission and Exclusion of Evidence

A. Introduction

Questions surrounding the admission of evidence have been the subject of significant debate since the birth of international criminal law. This is unsurprising, given that there are few areas of practice that diverge so dramatically between different legal systems as that of the admissibility of evidence and the exclusion thereof.[1] How domestic legal systems deal with these issues does not always fit neatly along the civil law/common law divide,[2] and human rights law has not provided a common standard in relation to the admission and exclusion of evidence.[3]

While this book is principally about the processes of proof, and it supports the recent turn in international criminal evidence scholarship away from a predominant focus on admissibility rules to one that takes a more holistic view of the weight given to evidence as well as its admissibility,[4] the admission and exclusion of evidence is worthy of deeper consideration in this chapter, for three key reasons. The first is that, as is a common theme throughout this book, this is an area that remains beset with uncertainty, inconsistency, and significant fragmentation in practice. The second is that practice in this sphere speaks volumes about the values and principles underpinning proof in international criminal trials, and how judges perceive the Court's role in encouraging best practices in the collection, preservation, and presentation of evidence to ensure rectitude of decision and the highest standards of fairness. The third is that, while overlooking the analysis of evidence in favour of an extensive focus on admissibility rules may be akin to 'treating

[1] F. Guariglia, '"Admission" v. "Submission" of Evidence at the International Criminal Court: Lost in Translation?' (2018) 16 Journal of International Criminal Justice 315; B. Schmitt, 'Legal Diversity at the International Criminal Court: Reflections of a Judge' (2021) 19 *Journal of International Criminal Justice* 485. On the exclusion of evidence, there is a difference between common law 'exclusion' and civil law 'nullity'—in the latter, the focus is on the act of obtaining the evidence, while the former looks at the evidence itself. In practice, however, the effect is the same: exclusion from the consideration of the fact-finder, who cannot base their judgment on it (D. Giannoulopoulos, *Improperly Obtained Evidence in Anglo-American and Continental Law* (Hart, 2019), 5–6).

[2] M. Klamberg, 'General Requirements for the Admission of Evidence' in G. Sluiter et al., *International Criminal Procedure: Principles and Rules* (OUP, 2013), 1015–16.

[3] The European Court of Human Rights, for example, considers the overall fairness of proceedings in the context of the facts of the case, rather than setting down common standards for admissibility and exclusion: see e.g. *Schenk v Switzerland*, App. No. 10862/84, 12 July 1988; *Al-Khawaja and Tahery v United Kingdom*, App. Nos 26766/05 and 22228/06, 15 December 2011; see further R. Goss, *Criminal Fair Trial Rights* (Hart, 2014), 60.

[4] See Chapter 1, text to nn 30 *et seq.*

Proving International Crimes. Yvonne McDermott, Oxford University Press. © Yvonne McDermott 2024.
DOI: 10.1093/oso/9780198842972.003.0003

England as a suburb of London',[5] the evaluation of evidence cannot be viewed in a vacuum from the decisions around how that evidence was admitted, and an examination of the checks and balances that are in place to exclude weak or problematic evidence from the record.

Section B of this chapter outlines the processes for the admission of evidence before international criminal tribunals. It analyses the International Criminal Court's recent turn towards an approach that favours the widespread 'submission' of evidence, deferring decisions on the admissibility of evidence until the close of trial—an approach that has now been followed by the Kosovo Specialist Chambers.[6] Section C analyses the key admissibility considerations of relevance, probative value, and prejudice to the accused, while section D assesses the jurisprudence on the exclusion of improperly obtained evidence.

B. Admissibility processes

At the London Conference, negotiations around how the parties would seek to admit their evidence, and challenge that of the opposing party, led to some heated exchanges. Justice Jackson expressed a concern that the wording of draft Article 24(d) of the Charter ('The Tribunal shall ask the prosecution and the defence what evidence (if any) they wish to submit to the Tribunal and the Tribunal shall rule on the admissibility of any such evidence'[7]) would cause considerable delays.[8] He feared that this provision might be read as requiring the prosecution to make a complete statement of all the evidence it wished to submit after delivering its opening statement, and have the Tribunal rule on its admissibility, with the Tribunal then doing the same on all of the proposed evidence for the defence.[9] A proposal to change the word 'shall' to 'may' was strongly opposed by Professor Trainin, who felt the proposal 'would change the whole procedure too much'.[10] Trainin's colleague from the Soviet delegation, General Nikitchenko, expressed an understanding that before the trial the prosecution would have filed the majority of its evidence with the Tribunal in support of the indictment, and that this

[5] W. Twining, *Theories of Evidence: Bentham and Wigmore* (Weidenfeld & Nicolson, 1985), 164.

[6] *Specialist Prosecutor v Shala*, Decision on the submission and admissibility of non-oral evidence, KSC-BC-2020-04/F00461, 17 March 2023; *Specialist Prosecutor v Mustafa*, Decision on the submission and the admissibility of evidence, KSC-BC-2020-05/F00169, 25 August 2021.

[7] Draft of Agreement and Charter, Reported by Drafting Subcommittee, 11 July 1945, Article 24(d). The Memorandum on Changes in Subcommittee Draft Desired by American Delegation, 31 July 1945 noted: 'Article 24 makes no provision as to when the prosecution shall offer its evidence, or the defendant its evidence, or the prosecution shall offer rebuttal evidence. This omission may be taken to mean that no evidence is to be offered on the trial and appropriate additions should be made.'

[8] Report of Robert H. Jackson, United States Representative to the International Conference on Military Trials: London, 1945, Minutes of Conference Session of 2 August 1945, 411.

[9] Minutes of Conference Session of 2 August 1945, 411.

[10] Ibid., 412.

paragraph would only apply to new evidence not lodged with the indictment, which the Tribunal could pass judgment on its relevance in determining whether it should be admitted.[11] Jackson, in reply, voiced a fear 'that we are getting the delays of both systems into this trial'.[12]

This exchange is interesting, because it reflects a difference between legal systems on the extent to which the evidence underpinning each of the charges should be presented with the indictment. We see a similar debate ongoing to this day before the International Criminal Court around the necessary 'trial-readiness' of cases by the confirmation of charges hearing, as discussed further in Chapter 4. At Nuremberg, ultimately, the provision was retained in Article 24(d) of the final IMT Charter,[13] while Article 20 noted: 'The Tribunal may require to be informed of the nature of any evidence before it is offered so that it may rule on the relevance thereof.' The indictment did not refer explicitly to the evidence underpinning each charge, although Rule 2 of the Rules of Procedure provided that each defendant would be provided with a translated copy of the Indictment as well as 'any other documents lodged with the indictment'.[14] Throughout proceedings, reference was made to bundles of documentary evidence, the majority of which was captured by the Allied armies in German government buildings, army headquarters, and elsewhere.[15] As such, the authenticity of these documents was broadly unchallenged by the defendants,[16] and the judgment noted that 'copies of all the documents put in evidence by the Prosecution' were supplied to the defence.[17]

Before the ICTR, ICTY, IRMCT, SCSL, and STL, the admissibility of evidence was, as noted in Chapter 1,[18] governed by a general provision that the tribunal was not bound by national rules of evidence, but instead would apply rules of evidence that would 'best favour a fair determination of the matter before it', in a manner consistent with the spirit of its Statute and general principles of law.[19] This echoed the IMT and IMTFE Charters, which provided that the Tribunals were not bound by technical rules of evidence, but instead were to adopt expeditious and non-technical procedure and admit any evidence deemed to have probative value.[20] Similarly, the ICTY's Rules 89(C) and (D), and its equivalent provisions

[11] Ibid., 413.

[12] Ibid., 413–14.

[13] The equivalent provision in the IMTFE Charter (Article 15(d)) adopted a slightly different formulation: 'The prosecution and defense may offer evidence and the admissibility of the same shall be determined by the Tribunal.'

[14] Rule 2(a) Rules of Procedure, adopted 29 October 1945.

[15] Judgment of the International Military Tribunal, 30 September 1946, in *Nuremberg Trial Proceedings Volume 22*, 412.

[16] Ibid.

[17] Ibid.

[18] See Chapter 1, section B.

[19] Rule 89(B), ICTY RPE; Rule 89(B), ICTR RPE; Rule 89(B), SCSL RPE; Rule 105(B), IRMCT RPE; Rule 149(B), STL RPE.

[20] Article 13(a), IMTFE Charter; Article 19, IMT Charter.

in other tribunals' Rules of Procedure and Evidence,[21] stated that a Chamber could admit any relevant evidence deemed to have probative value, and could exclude any evidence where its probative value was 'substantially outweighed by the need to ensure a fair trial'. The meaning of relevance, probative value, and prejudice to the accused as factors to be considered in determining admissibility are discussed in detail in section C below.

The Rules of Procedure and Evidence of many international criminal tribunals also contained specific provisions on written statements in lieu of oral testimony.[22] These were developed over the lifetimes of the tribunals and evolved significantly over time, usually in response to judicial developments and a desire to promote efficiency in proceedings by gradually undermining the initial preference for orality.[23] For example, Rule 92 *bis*, under which written statements could be introduced in lieu of oral testimony where they did not go to the acts and conduct of the accused, was introduced in 2000. Shortly afterwards, the prosecution in *Milošević* was permitted to introduce witness statements under the more general Rule 89(F), thereby enabling it to produce evidence-in-chief in the form of written statements, with the witnesses present in court to attest to the veracity of their statements.[24] Rule 92 *ter* was subsequently adopted, allowing evidence to be admitted in this way, thereby avoiding recourse to the *lex generalis* of Rule 89(F). Specific procedural rules relating to the admissibility of expert witness evidence,[25] the inadmissibility of evidence relating to the prior sexual conduct of the victim in cases of sexual assault,[26] and a provision enabling the Chamber to order the production of additional evidence[27] were also developed over the lifetimes of the ad hoc Tribunals.

[21] Rules 89(C) and (D), ICTR RPE; Rule 89(C), SCSL RPE; Rule 149(C) and (D), STL RPE; Rules 105(C) and (D), IRMCT RPE; Rule 137, KSC RPE; under Rule 87(1), ECCC IR, unless otherwise provided for in the Rules, *all* evidence is admissible, but the Chamber may reject, pursuant to Rule 87(3), evidence that it finds to be repetitious or irrelevant. The Chamber takes into account whether evidence is irrelevant or repetitious, impossible to obtain within a reasonable time, unsuitable to prove the facts it purports to prove, not allowed under the law, or intended to prolong proceedings.

[22] Rules 92 *bis*, 92 *ter*, 92 *quater* and 92 *quinquies*, ICTY RPE; Rule 92 *bis*, ICTR RPE; Rules 110–13, IRMCT RPE; Rules 92 *bis*, 92 *ter* and 92 *quater*, SCSL RPE; Rules 155–58, STL RPE; Rules 153–55, KSC RPE.

[23] O.G. Kwon, 'The Challenge of an International Criminal Trial as Seen from the Bench' (2007) 5 *Journal of International Criminal Justice* 360; I. Bonomy, 'The Reality of Conducting a War Crimes Trial' (2007) 5 *Journal of International Criminal Justice* 348.

[24] *Prosecutor v Milošević*, Decision on Interlocutory Appeal on the Admissibility of Evidence-in-Chief in the Form of Written Statements, IT-02-54-AR73.4, 30 September 2003 (overturning *Prosecutor v Milošević*, Decision on Prosecution Motion for the Admission of Evidence-in-Chief of Its Witnesses in Writing, IT-02-54-T, 16 April 2003); see further, Kwon, n 23, 365. Rule 89(F) was adopted in 2000 to change the old preference in Rule 90(A) that witnesses be heard directly by the Chambers. Rule 89(F) provided: 'A Chamber may receive the evidence of a witness orally or, where the interests of justice allow, in written form.'

[25] Rule 94 *bis*, ICTY RPE; Rule 94 *bis*, ICTR RPE; Rule 116, IRMCT RPE; Rule 94 *bis*, SCSL RPE; Rule 161, STL RPE; Rule 149, KSC RPE.

[26] Rule 96, ICTY RPE; Rule 96, ICTR RPE; Rule 118, IRMCT RPE; Rule 96, SCSL RPE; Rule 148, KSC RPE.

[27] Rule 98, ICTY RPE; Rule 98, ICTR RPE; Rule 120, IRMCT RPE; Rule 165, STL RPE; Rule 87(4), ECCC IR.

At trial,[28] evidence was generally admitted to the record either through a witness, who could attest to its relevance, probative value, and reliability,[29] or 'from the bar table', where documentary evidence is not produced through a witness. The latter practice has been described as a 'a long-standing practice in international criminal law proceedings that promotes judicial economy, particularly in relation to the unopposed admission into evidence of documents'.[30] Even though the ICC's legal framework does not include a specific provision allowing for evidence to be produced from the bar table, in practice this has been permitted, although differently constituted ICC chambers have taken diverging approaches.[31] On the one hand, the *Gbagbo and Blé Goudé* Trial Chamber positively encouraged the use of bar table motions in the interests of efficiency,[32] as did the Trial Chamber in *Bemba et al.*[33] and *Yekatom and Ngaïssona*.[34] On the other hand, Trial Chamber VI in *Ntaganda* refused to admit documents through the bar table where the prosecution had 'failed to provide sufficiently specific reasons why they ha[d] not been entered through a witness'.[35] The Chamber considered that documentary evidence should normally be tendered through a witness, and the absence of a witness to authenticate the document may negatively impact upon its assessment of the admissibility of the document.[36] Similarly, the *Ruto and Sang* Trial Chamber

[28] At pre-trial, the Rules required the parties to provide lists of the witnesses they intended to call and the exhibits they intended to offer: see Rule 65 *ter* (E) and (G), ICTY RPE. In addition, the prosecution had to include a summary of the evidence underpinning each count in the indictment in its pre-trial brief: Rule 65 *ter* (E)(i), ICTY RPE.

[29] See e.g. *Prosecutor v Prlić* et al., Decision on Admission of Evidence, IT-04-74-T, 13 July 2006, Annex, para. 1. *Prosecutor v Boškoski & Tarčulovski*, Decision on Prosecution's Motion for Admission of Exhibits from the Bar Table with Confidential Annexes A to E, IT-04-82-T, 14 May 2007, para. 10.

[30] *Prosecutor v Ayyash et al.*, Judgment, STL-11-01/T/TC, 18 August 2020, para. 354.

[31] *Prosecutor v Bemba*, Public Redacted Version of the First Decision on the Prosecution and Defence Requests for the Admission of Evidence, dated 15 December 2011, ICC-01/05-01/08-2012-Red, 9 February 2012 ('*Bemba* admissibility decision'), para. 55 stated that, '[w]hile the use of a "bar table" motion is one permissible way to seek the admission of documentary evidence, it is not the only one'.

[32] *Prosecutor v Gbagbo & Blé Goudé*, Amended Directions, ICC-02/11-01/15-498-AnxA, 4 May 2016, para. 43; *Prosecutor v Gbagbo and Blé Goudé*, Decision concerning the Prosecutor's submission of documentary evidence on 13 June, 14 July, 7 September, and 19 September 2016, ICC-02/11-01/15-773, 9 December 2016, para. 34 ('the introduction of evidence other than through witnesses must not be regarded as extraordinary, but as common practice that this Chamber has urged the parties to use in order to expedite proceedings, insofar as this is not prejudicial to the rights of the accused') ('*Gbagbo* submission decision').

[33] *Prosecutor v Bemba et al.*, Decision on Prosecution Requests for Admission of Documentary Evidence, ICC-01/05-01/13-1285, 24 September 2015 ('*Bemba et al.* Documentary Evidence decision'); *Prosecutor v Bemba et al.*, Decision on 'Prosecution's Fifth Request for the Admission of Evidence from the Bar Table', ICC-01/05-01/13-1524, 14 December 2015, para. 3.

[34] *Prosecutor v Yekatom and Ngaïssona*, Initial Directions on the Conduct of the Proceedings, ICC-01/14-01/18-631, 26 August 2020, para. 63 ('Oral submission of evidence used during the hearing should be done exceptionally').

[35] *Prosecutor v Ntaganda*, Decision on Prosecution's Request for Admission of Documentary Evidence, ICC-04/01-02/06-1838, 28 March 2017, para. 13.

[36] Ibid. See also *Prosecutor v Katanga and Ngudjolo*, Decision on the Prosecutor's Bar Table Motions, ICC-01/04-01/07-2635, 17 December 2010 ('*Katanga and Ngudjolo* Bar Table Decision'), para. 12.

considered 'admission of evidence through a witness to be a preferable approach, where possible'.[37]

In a similar development of practice over time, recent cases before the ICC have availed of a 'submission approach', whereby admissibility determinations are deferred until the end of the trial.[38] This approach was described in the *Bemba et al.* case as follows:

> The Chamber determines that, as a general rule, these proceedings will be conducted more efficiently if the Chamber defers its assessment of the admissibility of evidence until deliberating its judgment pursuant to Article 74(2) of the Statute. The Chamber will consider the relevance, probative value and potential prejudice of each item of evidence submitted at that time, though it may not necessarily discuss these aspects for every item submitted in the final judgment.[39]

In practice, submission means that the parties can submit evidence for the purposes of proving or disproving a fact at issue, upon their own initiative or in response to a request by the Trial Chamber, in accordance with a pre-established procedure.[40] In *Bemba et al.* such submissions were made via email, through a bar table motion, or orally during the hearing.[41] The opposing party can make objections at the time of submission based on the standard evidentiary criteria (relevance, probative value, and/or potential prejudice),[42] but an assessment of those objections will be deferred until the deliberation phase.[43] The only exception to this is where a preliminary examination of the evidence is required to determine whether the Chamber would be procedurally barred from considering the standard admissibility criteria, for example if an Article 69(7) challenge has been raised,[44] or if a party alleges that the procedural prerequisites of Rule 68 have not

[37] *Prosecutor v Ruto and Sang*, Decision on the Joint Defence Application for Admission of Documentary Evidence Related to the Testimony of Witness 536, ICC-01/09-01/11-1436, 15 July 2014, para. 11.

[38] This practice has received surprisingly little scholarly attention, although important contributions have been made by Guariglia, n 1; L. Freeman and R. Vazquez Llorente, 'Finding the Signal in the Noise: International Criminal Evidence and Procedure in the Digital Age' (2021) 19 *Journal of International Criminal Justice* 163.

[39] *Bemba et al.* Documentary Evidence decision, n 33, para. 9.

[40] *Prosecutor v Bemba*, Judgment on the appeals of Mr Jean-Pierre Bemba Gombo and the Prosecutor against the decision of Trial Chamber III entitled 'Decision on the admission into evidence of materials contained in the prosecution's list of evidence', ICC-01/05-01/08-1386, 3 May 2011, para. 43 ('*Bemba* admissibility appeal'). See further C. Schuon, 'The Appeals Decision in the ICC's *Jean-Pierre Bemba Gombo* Case on the Trial Chamber's 'Decision on the Admission into Evidence of Materials Contained in the Prosecution's List of Evidence' (2012) 25 *Leiden Journal of International Law* 511.

[41] *Prosecutor v Bemba et al.*, Judgment pursuant to Article 74 of the Statute, ICC-01/05-01/13-1989, 19 October 2016, para. 190 ('*Bemba et al.* Trial Judgment'). The Appeals Chamber in *Bemba* held that the Trial Chamber erred where it had admitted items included in the Prosecutor's list of evidence that had not been formally submitted to the Chamber: *Bemba* admissibility appeal, n 40, para. 46.

[42] Discussed further in section C.

[43] *Bemba et al.* Documentary Evidence decision, n 33, para. 9; *Bemba et al.* Trial Judgment, n 41, paras 190–2.

[44] Discussed further in section D.

been met,[45] or if the evidence is of prior sexual conduct of a victim or witness, which is inadmissible under Rule 71.[46]

The Appeals Chamber has confirmed that the word 'may' in Article 69(4) of the Statute means that the Trial Chamber has the discretion to rule on admissibility at the time the evidence is submitted to the Chamber, or to defer its consideration of the admissibility criteria until the end of proceedings.[47] In that same decision, however, the Appeals Chamber found that the Trial Chamber had erred by making a blanket '*prima facie* finding of admissibility' without conducting an item-by-item assessment of the evidence.[48] In essence, then, it is open to each Trial Chamber to determine its own approach to admissibility: the Chamber can either rule on the relevance and/or admissibility of an item of evidence at the time of its submission, as a pre-condition to recognising it as 'submitted' pursuant to Article 74(2), or it can recognise the submission of the evidence, deferring the considerations of relevance and admissibility until the deliberation phase.[49]

In practice, this means that two Chambers of the same Court, running trials concurrently under the same roof, can do so with almost unrecognisable approaches to the admission of evidence. This flexibility was built into the ICC Statute, which provides that, at trial, 'the presiding judge may give directions for the conduct of proceedings', and that the parties may submit evidence in accordance with those directions.[50] This is supplemented by Rule 140 of the Rules of Procedure and Evidence, which gives discretion to the presiding judge to opt not to give directions for the conduct of proceedings at all, leaving it to the parties to decide between themselves on how evidence will be submitted to the Chamber.[51]

The upshot of this flexibility, when it comes to admissibility, is that Chambers' approaches generally tended to cleave along the lines of whether the presiding judge was trained or experienced in the Romano-Germanic or the Common Law legal tradition.[52] For example, the Trial Chamber in *Bemba*, presided over by Judge

[45] *Gbagbo* submission decision, n 32, para. 33; *Bemba* et al. Trial Judgment, n 41, para. 191.

[46] *Bemba* admissibility appeal, n 40, para. 52.

[47] *Bemba* admissibility appeal, n 40, para. 37.

[48] *Bemba* admissibility appeal, n 40, para. 57; Judge Ozaki, in her dissent to Trial Chamber III's decision, had similarly considered the concept of *prima facie* admissibility to have no basis in the ICC's legal framework: *Prosecutor v Bemba*, Decision on the admission into evidence of materials contained in the prosecution's list of evidence, ICC-01/05-01/08-1022, 19 November 2010 ('*Bemba prima facie* admission decision'), Dissenting Opinion of Judge Ozaki on the Decision on the Admission into Evidence of Materials Contained in the Prosecution's List of Evidence, ICC-01/05-01/08-1028, 23 November 2010, para. 4.

[49] *Prosecutor v Bemba et al.*, Judgment on the appeals of Mr Jean-Pierre Bemba Gombo, Mr Aimé Kilolo Musamba, Mr Jean-Jacques Mangenda Kabongo, Mr Fidèle Babala Wandu and Mr Narcisse Arido against the decision of Trial Chamber VII entitled 'Judgment pursuant to Article 74 of the Statute', ICC-01/05-01/13-2275, 8 March 2018, para. 598 ('*Bemba et al.* Appeal Judgment').

[50] Article 64(8)(b), ICC Statute; see further, V. Nerlich, 'Daring Diversity: Why There Is Nothing Wrong with "Fragmentation" in International Criminal Procedure' (2013) 26 *Leiden Journal of International Law* 777, 780.

[51] If no agreement can be reached, the Presiding Judge shall issue directions: Rule 140(1), ICC RPE.

[52] S. De Smet, 'All Roads Lead to Rome: Lifting the Veil on the ICC's Procedural Pluriformity' in P. Šturma (ed.), *The Rome Statute of the ICC at Its Twentieth Anniversary* (Brill, 2019), 191–206, 195.

Steiner (Brazil), introduced a concept of *prima facie* admissibility[53] and, when that was later overturned by the Appeals Chamber,[54] embraced the submission approach, deferring admissibility considerations until the deliberation phase (and, in the view of the Majority of the Appeals Chamber, failing to do so with sufficient thoroughness[55]). The same approach was adopted in *Bemba et al.*,[56] *Ongwen*,[57] and *Al Hassan*,[58] with Judges Schmitt (Germany) and Mindua (Democratic Republic of the Congo) as Presiding Judges respectively. By contrast, in *Ruto and Sang*, presided over by Judge Eboe-Osuji (Nigeria), the Trial Chamber opted to make an individual assessment of the admissibility of each piece of evidence, conducting an item-by-item analysis.[59] Most strikingly, the *Gbagbo and Blé Goudé* Trial Chamber under Presiding Judge Henderson (Trinidad and Tobago) set out directions on the conduct of proceedings in September 2015, emphasising the principle of orality and indicating that it would rule on admissibility on an item-by-item basis.[60] Just months later, following the appointment of Judge Tarfusser (Italy) as Presiding Judge, the procedures changed dramatically (and against the wishes of the prosecution, defence, and victims) to one that wholeheartedly embraced the submission approach.[61] As Simon de Smet has pointed out, it is difficult to imagine that the drafters, in including a measure of flexibility in the Court's legal framework, would have foreseen a system where the same Trial Chamber in the same case adopts markedly different approaches to the admission of evidence.[62]

This distinction based on the legal system of the Presiding Judge does not always hold true, however. While some vociferous dissenting judges to the submission approach have tended to be judges trained in the adversarial legal tradition,[63]

[53] *Bemba prima facie* admission decision, n 48.

[54] *Bemba* admissibility appeal, n 40.

[55] *Prosecutor v Bemba*, Judgment on the appeal of Mr Jean-Pierre Bemba Gombo against Trial Chamber III's 'Judgment pursuant to Article 74 of the Statute', ICC-01/05-01/08-3636, 8 June 2018 ('*Bemba* Appeal Judgment'); *Bemba* Appeal Judgment, Separate Opinion of Judge Van den Wyngaert and Judge Morrison; *Bemba* Appeal Judgment, Concurring Separate Opinion of Judge Eboe-Osuji. Cf. *Bemba* Appeal Judgment, Dissenting Opinion of Judges Monageng and Hofmański.

[56] *Bemba et al.* Documentary Evidence decision, n 33.

[57] *Prosecutor v Ongwen*, Decision on Prosecution request to submit interception related evidence, ICC-02/04-01/15-615, 1 December 2016, para. 7.

[58] *Prosecutor v Al Hassan*, Decision on the conduct of proceedings, ICC-01/12-01/18-789, 6 May 2020, Annex A: Directions on the conduct of proceedings, para. 29.

[59] *Prosecutor v Ruto and Sang*, Decision on the Prosecution's Request for Admission of Documentary Evidence, ICC-01/09-01/11-1353, 10 June 2014 ('*Ruto and Sang* Documentary Evidence Decision'), para. 19.

[60] *Prosecutor v Gbagbo and Blé Goudé*, Directions on the conduct of proceedings, ICC-02/11-01/15-205, 3 September 2015, paras 54; 60.

[61] *Prosecutor v Gbagbo and Blé Goudé*, Decision on the submission and admission of evidence, ICC-02/11-01/15-405, 29 January 2016 ('*Gbagbo* Decision on the submission and admission of evidence'). The former Presiding Judge issued a strongly worded dissent: *Gbagbo* Decision on the submission and admission of evidence, Dissenting Opinion of Judge Henderson, ICC-02/11-01/15-405-Anx, 1 February 2016.

[62] De Smet, n 52, 206.

[63] *Prosecutor v Gbagbo & Blé Goudé*, Decision concerning the Prosecutor's submission of documentary evidence, ICC-02/11-01/15-1172, 1 June 2018, Dissenting Opinion of Judge Henderson, ICC-02/

this is not always the case. Judge Ozaki (Japan) was a strong advocate for the principle of orality both in relation to admissibility considerations generally[64] and specifically expressing the view that the admission of prior recorded testimony should only be permitted in exceptional circumstances.[65] Interestingly, Judge Morrison (United Kingdom) did not dissent against the practice as a member of the Appeals Chamber in *Bemba et al.*, but later joined Judge Van den Wyngaert (Belgium) in a joint separate opinion in the main *Bemba* case to opine that the approach may be appropriate for cases charging offences against the administration of justice, but was not so for the prosecution of the ICC's core crimes.[66] They suggested that, for prosecutions under Article 5 of the Statute, 'Not only is it necessary to rule on the admissibility of all evidence submitted by the parties, the Trial Chamber must also apply the admissibility criteria of article 69(4) of the Statute sufficiently rigorously to avoid crowding the case record with evidence of inferior quality'.[67]

It is important to note that, at a retreat held in 2021, the judges of the ICC adopted a model decision on 'Directions for the Conduct of Proceedings', which is appended to the Chambers Practice Manual in a confidential annex.[68] It is clear from directions on the conduct of proceedings decisions issued since that date that the judges agreed to adopt a submission approach, deferring the ultimate assessment of the standard evidentiary criteria to the deliberation phase.[69] The predictability that arises from this judicial agreement cannot be gainsaid; indeed, the stated objective of this model decision is to 'facilitate the efficiency and consistency of proceedings'.[70] However, the Chambers Practice Manual is, of course, not binding on Chambers, and it could be amended further by decision of the judges at any time in the future. The Appeals Chamber has taken quite a detached view of this matter to date, emphasising that it is for each Trial Chamber to decide on the conduct of proceedings, within the confines of the Court's legal framework.[71] It is apposite, then, to examine the relative strengths and weaknesses of the practice,

11-01/15-1172-Anx, 1 June 2018; *Bemba* Appeal Judgment, n 55, Concurring Separate Opinion of Judge Eboe-Osuji, ICC-01/05-01/08-3636-Anx3, 14 June 2018, paras. 95–104.

64 *Bemba prima facie* admission decision, n 48, Dissenting Opinion of Judge Ozaki on the Decision on the Admission into Evidence of Materials Contained in the Prosecution's List of Evidence, para. 5.

65 *Prosecutor v Gbagbo & Blé Goudé*, Judgment on the appeals of Mr Laurent Gbagbo and Mr Charles Blé Goudé against the decision of Trial Chamber I of 9 June 2016 entitled 'Decision on the Prosecutor's application to introduce prior recorded testimony under Rules 68(2)(b) and 68(3)', ICC-02/11-01/15-744, 1 November 2016, Partially Dissenting Opinion of Judge Ozaki, 16 December 2016, para. 8.

66 *Bemba* Appeal Judgment, n 55, Separate opinion of Judge Van den Wyngaert and Judge Morrison, para. 18.

67 Ibid.

68 ICC, Chambers Practice Manual, 7th edn, adopted following the judicial retreat of 2023, para. 84.

69 *Prosecutor v Abd-Al-Rahman*, Directions on the conduct of proceedings, ICC-02/05-01/20-478, 4 October 2021 ('*Al Rahman* Directions'), para. 23.

70 Chambers Practice Manual, n 68, para. 84.

71 *Bemba* admissibility appeal, n 40, paras 36–7.

since future Trial Chambers will have the option to continue with or abandon the submission approach.

Six key arguments are generally raised in favour of the submission approach over an item-by-item evaluation of admissibility and relevance as each item is introduced. The first is that the Chamber is better placed to assess the standard evidentiary criteria of relevance, probative value, and prejudice to the accused at the end of the trial, in light of the full record of evidence that has been presented.[72] This argument contends that sometimes, the relevance of a piece of evidence only becomes apparent later on, when viewed in conjunction with another item of evidence, or the totality of the evidentiary record.[73] In the words of Trial Chamber I in *Gbagbo and Blé Goudé*:

> A determination on the admissibility or the relevance of a given item of evidence upon its submission would unduly restrict the Chamber's power to assess that particular piece of evidence in light of all the others [*sic*] pieces which are yet to be submitted, and to amend its assessment if and as required; as such, it would result in unnecessarily restraining the Chamber's right and duty 'to assess freely all evidence submitted in order to determine its relevance or admissibility in accordance with article 69' as provided in Rule 63(2) of the Rules.[74]

It may be the case, in certain circumstances, that the relevance of a piece of evidence only becomes clear when viewed in conjunction with another piece of evidence, or the evidentiary record as a whole.[75] However, this seems unlikely to be a common occurrence—the tendering party should be able to explain to the Chamber why the item of evidence is relevant to its case and admissible at the time of its submission. If they are unable to do so, that should raise questions as to the probative value of this item of evidence. The assumption that a Trial Chamber will be better able to see the relevance or admissibility of an item of evidence than the party tendering it and will be able to draw links between disparate items of evidence that the parties themselves may have missed assumes an omniscience on the part of judges. Moreover, this approach seems to conflate the distinct notions of probative value (an admissibility consideration) and weight (which is relevant to the Court's final assessment of the evidence as a whole). It may be the case that a piece of evidence appears to bear some probative value at the time of its admission, but that other items of evidence call its reliability into question, and thus it is given limited weight in the Chamber's final determination. It is well established that the assessment of a piece of evidence for the purposes of admissibility is distinct

[72] *Bemba et al.* Appeal Judgment, n 49, para. 554.
[73] Ibid.
[74] *Gbagbo* Decision on the submission and admission of evidence, n 61, para. 13.
[75] *Bemba et al.* Documentary Evidence decision, n 33, para. 10.

from the ultimate weight the Chamber may afford to that piece of evidence.[76] The submission approach, however, appears to commingle the considerations of admissibility and weight.[77] Lastly, in the paragraph quoted above, the reference to 'amending its assessment [of admissibility] if and as required' is problematic, as it suggests that an initial such assessment has been made without informing the parties. This gives the impression that the submission approach is simply a system of blanket *prima facie* admissibility, which the Appeals Chamber explicitly overruled in *Bemba*,[78] under another guise. The Appeals Chamber was clear that when the Chamber makes its determination on the standard admissibility criteria, whether that is at the time of submission or deferred until the deliberation phase, it 'must be clear from the reasons of the decision that the Chamber carried out the required item-by-item analysis, and how it was carried out'.[79]

The second argument put forward in favour of submission is that international criminal judges are professional fact-finders and, unlike juries, do not need to be shielded from marginally relevant or prejudicial material.[80] This is a point that has been made for decades in eschewing 'technical rules of evidence' in international criminal trials.[81] However, this is a rather narrow view of the purpose of evidentiary rules; while screening the jury from considering inappropriate materials is one function of such rules in jury trials, there are other important reasons to exclude irrelevant or inappropriate evidence from the record. Such exclusion protects the integrity of proceedings: if it seems to external observers that international criminal judgments are founded on weak evidence,[82] that will have an impact on the legitimacy of their proceedings. Admissibility rules also protect judicial economy and the efficiency of proceedings by preventing the record from being flooded with irrelevant material or evidence to which very limited weight

[76] *Prosecutor v Al Hassan*, Public redacted version of 'Decision on requests related to the submission into evidence of Mr Al Hassan's statements', ICC-01/12-01/18-1475, 17 May 2021, para. 29; *Gbagbo* Decision on the submission and admission of evidence, n 61, Dissenting Opinion of Judge Henderson, para. 16.

[77] *Gbagbo* Decision on the submission and admission of evidence, n 61, Dissenting Opinion of Judge Henderson, para. 16.

[78] *Bemba* admissibility appeal, n 40.

[79] Ibid., para. 59.

[80] Guariglia, n 1, 326.

[81] E.g. A. Cassese, *Annual Report of the International Tribunal for the Prosecution of Persons Responsible for Serious Violations of International Humanitarian Law Committed in the Territory of the Former Yugoslavia since 1991*, UN Doc. A/49/342, S/1994/1007, 29 August 1994, para. 72 ('This Tribunal does not need to shackle itself to restrictive rules that have developed out of the ancient trial-by-jury system. There will be no jury sitting at the Tribunal, needing to be shielded from irrelevancies or given guidance as to the weight of the evidence they have heard. The judges will be solely responsible for weighing the probative value of the evidence before them. Consequently, all relevant evidence may be admitted to the Tribunal unless its probative value is substantially outweighed by the need to ensure a fair trial (rule 89) or where the evidence was obtained by a serious violation of human rights (rule 95)'); *Prosecutor v Tadić*, Decision on Defence Motion on Hearsay, IT-94-1-T, 5 August 1996, para. 17.

[82] N. Combs, 'Grave Crimes and Weak Evidence: A Fact-finding Evolution in International Criminal Law' (2017) 58 *Harvard International Law Journal* 47; N. Combs, *Fact-Finding without Facts: The Uncertain Evidentiary Foundations of International Criminal Convictions* (CUP, 2010).

could reasonably be accorded. The need to avoid flooding the record is particularly important when one considers that ICC judges are not always trained professional judges; pursuant to Article 36 of the Statute, judges can come from a criminal law or an international law background, and those from the criminal law list have not necessarily served as judges.[83]

Relatedly, the third argument we frequently see in favour of submission relates to the efficiency of proceedings. The argument posits that the Trial Chamber saves time by deferring assessment of each item's relevance and probative value until all the evidence is before it. In *Gbagbo and Blé Goudé*, for example, the Chamber noted that intermediate rulings on evidence may prove disruptive if they lead to interlocutory appeals, causing inefficiencies and delays in the trial process.[84] This assumes that interlocutory litigation is generally undesirable. Yet, there is a value to litigation on admissibility, as can be seen from numerous cases where issues with evidence were remedied as a direct result of litigation. For example, before the ICTY, intercept evidence was deemed of insufficient reliability to be introduced via the bar table, but decisions emphasised that such evidence could be tendered through a witness.[85] This shows that admissibility determinations bear an important corrective function; under a submission approach, the same evidence would only be deemed inadmissible after proceedings have ended, and the tendering party would not have the opportunity to provide further information supporting its relevance and/or probative value. It may be argued that, as the tendering party needs to provide information relevant to admissibility determinations at the time of submission,[86] these issues will not need to be remedied if the tendering party simply submits their best evidence from the outset.[87] However,

[83] On the selection of judges, see M. Bohlander, 'The International Criminal Judiciary: Problems of Judicial Selection, Independence and Ethics' in M. Bohlander (ed.), *International Criminal Justice: A Critical Analysis of Institutions and Procedures* (Cameron May, 2007), 325–90. See further, M. Caianiello, 'Law of Evidence at the International Criminal Court: Blending Accusatorial and Inquisitorial Models' (2011) 36 *North Carolina Journal of International Law & Commercial Regulation* 287, 304; P.M. Wald, 'ICTY Judicial Proceedings: An Appraisal from Within' (2004) 2 *Journal of International Criminal Justice* 466, 473; P. Murphy and L. Baddour, 'Evidence and Selection of Judges in International Criminal Tribunals: The Need for a Harmonized Approach' in E. van Sliedregt and S. Vasiliev, *Pluralism in International Criminal Law* (OUP, 2014), 368.

[84] *Gbagbo* Decision on the submission and admission of evidence, n 61, para. 14.

[85] See e.g. *Prosecutor v Karadžić*, Decision on Prosecution's First Bar Table Motion, IT-95-5/18-T, 13 April 2010, para. 13; *Prosecutor v Karadžić*, Decision on Prosecution's First Bar Table Motion for the Admission of Intercepts, IT-95-5/18-T, 14 May 2012, para. 16. See further, *Gbagbo* Decision on the submission and admission of evidence, n 61, Dissenting Opinion of Judge Henderson, para. 15.

[86] Pursuant to Rule 64(1) of the ICC RPE, issues as to admissibility of evidence, including on any of the standard evidentiary criteria, must be raised at the time when the evidence is submitted to the Chamber or immediately after such an issue becomes known.

[87] *Gbagbo* Decision on the submission and admission of evidence, n 61, para. 18 ('In the view of the Majority, the need to ensure the impartiality of the proceedings does not allow the Chamber to assist the parties with their preparations for the case or, even less, to permit them to "remedy" any flaws which might affect their case, including their possible failure to satisfy their respective burden of proof. The Majority does expect that all the parties and participants will "conduct their investigations and prepare their respective cases in light of all evidence submitted" and that they will address the Chamber "in such a manner so as to cover all eventualities"; indeed, this appears to the Majority an essential

with the advent of new forms of evidence, such as online open source evidence,[88] it is difficult to know what information the Chamber may require to demonstrate its authenticity or reliability, in the absence of item-by-item admissibility rulings.[89] Conversely, if parties provide superfluous material to support the case for admissibility of their evidence, this may risk, in the words of Judge Henderson, 'the Chamber and parties wasting valuable time and resources on duplicative evidence'[90] or the parties expending time and resources preparing submissions relating to evidence that is ultimately deemed inadmissible by the Chamber.[91] Thus, submission may lead to greater inefficiencies in practice. Relatedly, the argument is sometimes advanced that the submission model still grants discretion to the Trial Chamber to make individual admissibility decisions for particularly important pieces of evidence,[92] and indeed it must do so where the exclusion of evidence (as outlined in section D below) is at issue. What this means in practice is that the party seeking to argue against the admission of particular evidence will make detailed submissions on the matter, to which the proponent will have to respond and upon which the Chamber will have to render a decision, thereby reducing some of the purported efficiency savings of the submission model.

The fourth argument in favour of submission over item-by-item admissibility determinations is that it is required by the ICC Statute.[93] This seems curious, given the relatively recent emergence of the practice, and the fact that the first decade or so of proceedings before the ICC operated, like the non-permanent international criminal tribunals that preceded it, with an approach that made admissibility decisions as evidence was tendered. Nevertheless, there is some support for this argument in Article 69(3) of the Statute, which states that 'the parties may *submit* evidence' and 'the Court has the authority to request the *submission* of all evidence that it considers necessary for the determination of the truth'.[94] Rule 63(2) of the Rules of Procedure and Evidence refers to the free assessment of 'all evidence *submitted* in order to determine its relevance or admissibility in accordance with

component of the parties' professionalism'). As Colleen Rohan points out, 'this observation is surprising, given the Chamber's equal concern that it fulfils its obligation to search for the truth': C. Rohan, 'The Hybrid System of International Criminal Law: A Work in Progress or Just a Noble Experiment?' in M. Aksenova et al., *Breaking the Cycle of Mass Atrocities* (Hart, 2019), 95, at 110.

[88] See further, Human Rights Center, University of California, Berkeley and Office of the United Nations High Commissioner for Human Rights, *Berkeley Protocol on Digital Open Source Investigations* (OHCHR, 2020); Special Issue, 'New Technologies and the Investigation of International Crimes' (2021) 19 *Journal of International Criminal Justice* 1–233; S. Dubberley et al. (eds), *Digital Witness* (OUP, 2019).

[89] Compare *Katanga and Ngudjolo* Bar Table Decision, n 36, which sets out detailed guidance for the criteria indicating the authenticity and reliability of different types of evidence.

[90] *Gbagbo* Decision on the submission and admission of evidence, n 61, Dissenting Opinion of Judge Henderson, para. 14.

[91] Ibid., para. 11.

[92] See e.g. *Al Rahman* Directions, n 69, paras 26–28.

[93] *Bemba et al.* Documentary Evidence decision, n 33, para. 5.

[94] Article 69(3) (emphasis added).

article 69'.[95] Evidence 'submitted' is also referred to in Article 74(2) on the requirements for the decision. In addition, the wording of the 'admissibility' provisions of the Statute (Articles 64(9)(a) and 69(4)) are worded in such terms as to suggest that rulings on the admissibility or relevance of evidence are discretionary. They state that the Trial Chamber has the power to make such rulings, and Article 69(4) states the Court 'may' rule on relevance or admissibility. On the other hand, the requirement in Rule 64 that parties raise any issues on the admissibility of evidence at the time of submission demands, in the words of Judge Eboe-Osuji, 'as a matter of *necessary* implication ... trial judges to play their own incidental part, by ruling upon the evidential concerns raised by the parties'.[96] Furthermore, the drafting history of Article 69 suggests that the key emphasis was on the Court's ability to play an active role in trial proceedings, and the submission approach was not explicitly discussed in the negotiations.[97] As noted above, flexibility was at the heart of the drafters' approach to the Statute's evidence provisions in order to achieve a compromise between seemingly incompatible legal systems.[98] We can tell from the drafting history that the drafters rejected two extremes: one that proposed that all evidence should be admissible in principle, and another that 'obligated the Court to assess all evidence for the purpose of admissibility'.[99] Constructive ambiguity was key to reaching a compromise, under which the Court is permitted, but not obliged, to assess the admissibility of evidence.[100] This shows that submission is one possible interpretation of the Statute, but it seems a stretch to suggest that it is the approach most true to the intention of the drafters.

The fifth and sixth arguments in favour of submission pertain to the principles of certainty and fairness. In the words of the Trial Chamber in *Gbagbo and Blé Goudé*:

> [D]eferring the Chamber's determination to the time of the judgment as a general rule will also ensure that all the evidence submitted will be subjected to a uniform treatment; whether the Chamber decides or not to anticipate its ruling at an earlier stage will not depend on the fact that an issue has or has not be raised by one of the parties at a given moment, but rather on the Chamber's exercise of its discretion in light of its statutory obligations. The Chamber believes that this will contribute to the overall certainty and fairness of the proceedings as a whole.[101]

[95] Emphasis added.

[96] *Bemba* Appeal Judgment, n 55, Concurring Separate Opinion of Judge Eboe-Osuji.

[97] D. Piragoff and P. Clarke, 'Article 69' in O. Triffterer and K. Ambos (eds), *Rome Statute of the International Criminal Court: Article-by-Article Commentary* (4th edn, Beck/Hart, 2021), 2035, 2039.

[98] See Chapter 1, section B.· See also *Prosecutor v Lubanga*, Decision on the defence request to reconsider the 'Order on numbering of evidence' of 12 May 2010, ICC-01/04-01/06-2705, 30 March 2011, Separate Opinion of Judge Blattmann.

[99] Piragoff and Clarke, n 97, 2041.

[100] Ibid.

[101] *Gbagbo* Decision on the submission and admission of evidence, n 61, para. 15.

Yet, it is difficult to see how certainty can be a result of the parties effectively submitting their evidence in a vacuum, unclear as to whether which pieces of that evidence will ultimately be deemed admissible. Without clarity on admissibility, the parties remain uncertain on the extent to which they can rely on a piece of submitted evidence in their submissions. Submission may also lead to false hope that particular pieces of evidence will be admitted when the Chamber has no intention of finding them admissible. For example, as noted above, in *Gbagbo and Blé Goudé*, a submission approach was taken by the Trial Chamber under Presiding Judge Tarfusser. The Prosecutor may have been surprised to read the following in his Opinion accompanying the main decision ('Reasons') acquitting the defendants:

> For almost four years, I have also been sifting through mountains of documents purportedly supporting [the prosecution] case, none of which could confirm it in the slightest, whether taken individually or as a whole; many, as highlighted in the Reasons, 'of doubtful authenticity' and/or 'containing significant anonymous hearsay'. As also stated in the Reasons, 'there are pervasive problems affecting a considerable number of documents that make their authenticity questionable', making it 'probably fair to say that a majority of documentary exhibits that were submitted by the Prosecutor in this case would not pass even the most rudimentary admissibility test in many domestic systems'.[102]

The point is that submission leaves the parties in the dark as to how the Chamber is going to interpret their evidence, unaware of such 'pervasive problems' until it is too late.

Aside from granting certainty to the parties, there is a broader value in clarity on these matters when considering the ICC's self-declared role in observing the 'highest standards of fairness and due process'.[103] As such, other entities, such as the International Nuremberg Principles Academy in drafting its 'Principles on Digital Evidence', look to the Court when establishing best practices. Yet, in the absence of specific rulings on admissibility of particular forms of evidence, these principles can be difficult to discern. A common approach taken by Trial Chambers is to emphasise that submission does not require a discussion of the admissibility of each piece of submitted evidence in the judgment.[104] For example, in *Bemba et al.*, the parties provided competing arguments as to whether material found from an individual's Facebook account was necessarily reliable and attributable to that

[102] *Prosecutor v Gbagbo and Blé Goudé*, Reasons for Oral Decision of 15 January 2019 on the Requête de la Défense de Laurent Gbagbo afin qu'un jugement d'acquittement portant sur toutes les charges soit prononcé en faveur de Laurent Gbagbo et que sa mise en liberté immédiate soit ordonnée, ICC-02/11-01/15-1263, 16 July 2019, Opinion of Judge Tarfusser, para. 4 (references omitted).

[103] Discussed at length in Y. McDermott, *Fairness in International Criminal Trials* (OUP, 2016).

[104] *Bemba et al.* Trial Judgment, n 41, para. 193.

person, given that anyone could, in principle, set up an account under someone else's name.[105] The Chamber did not explicitly address the admissibility of these photographs found on Facebook in its judgment, which means that parties in future cases seeking to admit such evidence have no guidance as to what is needed to show authenticity and reliability. This is relevant for UN investigative mechanisms, such as the International, Impartial and Independent Mechanism (IIIM) for Syria and the Independent Investigative Mechanism for Myanmar (IIMM), which are mandated to preserve relevant evidence for future prosecutions. Without guidance as to what might be needed to demonstrate authenticity, reliability, and/or chain of custody of evidence extracted from social media, these mechanisms simply have to come up with their own interpretation of best practices on preservation and hope for the best.

On the overall fairness of proceedings, Judge Henderson in *Gbagbo and Blé Goudé* noted that the submission approach can adversely impact the defendant, who, having seen the prosecution case, may stay silent or elect to give evidence in their own defence.[106] It also 'hardly assists the Prosecution in determining whether it has discharged its evidential burden at the close of its case, let alone at the conclusion of the evidentiary stage of proceedings'.[107] Without clarity as to what prosecution evidence will ultimately be admitted to the record, the defence's ability to shape and prepare its case can be undermined.[108] In deciding where to expend time in preparing submissions and its closing statement, there is a risk that the defence will expend excessive resources on disproving evidence that is ultimately deemed inadmissible, while spending less time on other evidence that it believes will be inadmissible, only to find that the Chamber has admitted it and relied upon it in its judgment.[109] This risk can be seen in the *Bemba et al.* Appeal judgment, where the defence argued that they felt 'ambushed' by certain evidence the relevance of which was only explained in the prosecution's closing statement,[110] and the *Bemba* Appeal Judgment, where the defendant argued that he did not know what evidence was used to convict him and why.[111] Before the ICTY and ICTR, uncertainty as to what the Trial Chamber would ultimately rely on (in those cases, unpleaded facts) was held to materially impact on the defence's ability to prepare

[105] *Prosecutor v Bemba et al.*, Public Redacted Version of Defence Response to Prosecution's Third Request for the Admission of Evidence from the Bar Table, ICC-01/05-01/13-1245, 9 October 2015; see further, L. Freeman, 'Digital Evidence and War Crimes Prosecutions' (2018) 41 *Fordham International Law Journal* 283, 327.

[106] *Gbagbo* Decision on the submission and admission of evidence, n 61, Dissenting Opinion of Judge Henderson, para. 9.

[107] Ibid., para. 8.

[108] Ibid. It is interesting to note that this case was a rare example of an acquittal following a 'no case to answer' motion after the close of the prosecution case.

[109] *Gbagbo* Decision on the submission and admission of evidence, n 61, Dissenting Opinion of Judge Henderson, paras 10–11.

[110] *Bemba et al.* Appeal Judgment, n 49, paras 558–66.

[111] *Bemba* Appeal Judgment, n 55, Concurring Separate Opinion of Judge Eboe-Osuji, para. 293.

its case.[112] To date, however, the ICC has generally found no prejudice in the submission approach.[113]

The foregoing analysis shows that the six arguments frequently adduced in favour of the submission approach may not stand up to scrutiny. The efficiency of the approach remains unproven, and it can lead to considerable uncertainty and potential unfairness for the parties throughout the trial, which may have a detrimental impact to how their cases are prepared and pleaded. In the current context in human rights investigations—where significant efforts are placed on the preservation of evidence, especially new forms of digital evidence such as videos and photographs from social media—for future prosecutions some guidance from the ICC on proving the authenticity and reliability of this type of material would be highly beneficial, but this cannot be guaranteed without individual admissibility determinations.

C. Admissibility considerations: Relevance, probative value, and prejudice

Having examined the processes by which evidence is admitted to the record, this section briefly analyses the three key admissibility considerations: the evidence's relevance, probative value, and any likely prejudice that might be caused by its admission.[114] The ICC Statute distinguishes between admissibility and relevance as distinct constructs to be considered by the Court.[115] In *Lubanga,* a three-stage admissibility test was developed, with *prima facie* relevance of the piece of evidence as the first consideration.[116] In the second stage of the test, its probative value will be determined, and, in the third stage, that probative value will be weighed against its prejudicial effect.[117] The submission approach, as outlined in section B, means

[112] *Prosecutor v Nyiramasuhuko et al.*, Judgment, ICTR-98-42-A, 14 December 2015, para. 1280, citing *Prosecutor v Ntakirutimana and Ntakirutimana*, Judgment, ICTR-96-10-A and ICTR-96-17-A, 13 December 2004, para. 28, referring to *Prosecutor v Kupreškić et al.*, Judgment, IT-95-16-A, 23 October 2001, paras 110, 119.

[113] *Bemba et al.* Appeal Judgment, n 49, paras 602–28. The *Bemba* admissibility appeal, n 40 rejected *prima facie* admissibility as being unduly prejudicial but implicitly accepted that Chambers might opt to take a submission approach.

[114] Article 69(4), ICC Statute; Rule 63(2), ICC RPE; Rules 89(C) and (D), ICTY RPE; Rules 89(C) and (D), ICTR RPE; Rule 89(C), SCSL RPE; Rule 149(C) and (D), STL RPE; Rules 105(C) and (D), IRMCT RPE; Rule 137, KSC RPE; cf. Rule 87, ECCC IR (under which, unless otherwise provided for in the Rules, *all* evidence is admissible). Note that relevance is the only criterion in Rule 89(C), SCSL RPE.

[115] Article 64(9) states that 'the Court may rule on the relevance *or* admissibility of any evidence, taking into account, inter alia, the probative value of the evidence and any prejudice that such evidence may cause to a fair trial or to a fair evaluation of the testimony of a witness, in accordance with the Rules of Procedure and Evidence' (emphasis added) See also Article 69, ICC Statute; Rules 63 and 64, ICC RPE.

[116] *Prosecutor v Lubanga*, Decision on the Admissibility of Four Documents, ICC-01/04-01/06-1399, 16 June 2008, paras 26–32 ('*Lubanga* Four Documents Decision').

[117] *Katanga and Ngudjolo* Bar Table Decision, n 36, para. 14.

that these standard admissibility criteria would be considered at the judgment stage instead of having a separate procedural step where the Trial Chamber considers these criteria and issues a ruling on the admissibility and relevance of a piece of evidence.[118]

'Relevance' has been defined as the quality that makes the existence of a fact at issue more or less likely.[119] This may be clear from the piece of evidence itself, but if not, the tendering party bears the responsibility to explain, first, how a specific factual proposition is relevant to a material fact of the case, and second, how the item of evidence makes that factual proposition more or less probable.[120] Relevant evidence may pertain to the context of the alleged crimes, the conduct of the accused, and/or the actions of the alleged principal perpetrator(s).[121]

Assuming *prima facie* relevance has been proven, the Chamber will consider whether the piece of evidence has sufficient probative value. Evidence has probative value if it tends to prove or disprove an issue of fact at issue in the case.[122] The Trial Chamber in *Lubanga* noted that there were 'innumerable factors which may be relevant' to an evaluation of probative value.[123] A decision on probative value 'will turn on the issues in the case, the context in which the material is to be introduced into the overall scheme of the evidence and a detailed examination of the circumstances of the disputed evidence'.[124]

There are two key aspects to assessing the probative value of a piece of evidence: the item's reliability and its significance.[125] Reliability may be indicated by a large range of factors, including: the item's source or author, including their role in

[118] Ibid., paras 25–6; *Prosecutor v Ongwen*, Trial Judgment, ICC-02/04-01/15-1762, 4 February 2021, para. 235.

[119] *Prosecutor v Katanga & Ngudjolo*, Decision on the Bar Table Motion of the Defence of Germain Katanga, ICC-01/04-01/07-3184, 21 October 2011 ('*Katanga* Defence Bar Table Motion Decision'), para. 16; *Bemba* et al. Trial Judgment, n 41, para. 195; *Katanga and Ngudjolo* Bar Table Decision, n 36, para. 16 ('If the evidence tendered makes the existence of a fact at issue more or less probable, it is relevant.'); *Lubanga* Four Documents Decision, n 115, para. 27.

[120] *Katanga* Defence Bar Table Motion Decision, n 119, para. 16. See also *Prosecutor v Bemba*, Decision Pursuant to Article 61(7)(a) and (b) of the Rome Statute on the Charges of the Prosecutor Against Jean-Pierre Bemba Gombo, ICC-01/05-01/08-424, 15 June 2009, para. 41; *Prosecutor v Ruto et al.*, Decision on the Confirmation of Charges Pursuant to Article 61(7)(a) and (b) of the Rome Statute, ICC-01/09-01/11-373, 23 January 2012, para. 66; *Prosecutor v Muthaura et al.*, Decision on the Confirmation of Charges Pursuant to Article 61(7)(a) and (b) of the Rome Statute, ICC-01/09-02/11-382, 23 January 2012, para. 79 (confirming the need for a nexus between the evidence and a fact to be proven to show *prima facie* relevance).

[121] C. Gosnell, 'Admissibility of Evidence' in K.A.A. Khan et al. (eds), *Principles of Evidence in International Criminal Justice* (OUP, 2010), 375, 436–7; *Katanga and Ngudjolo* Bar Table Decision, n 36, para. 24.

[122] *Prosecutor v Blagojević and Jokić*, Decision on the Admission into Evidence of Intercept-Related Materials, IT-02-60-T, 18 December 2003, para. 17.

[123] *Lubanga* Four Documents Decision, n 115, para. 28.

[124] Ibid., para. 29.

[125] Ibid.; *Katanga* Defence Bar Table Motion Decision, n 118, para. 15. For a helpful diagram, see N. Mehandru and A. Koenig, 'Open Source Evidence and the International Criminal Court' (2019) 4 *Harvard Human Rights Journal*, online at https://harvardhrj.com/2019/04/open-source-evidence-and-the-international-criminal-court/ (last accessed 20 May 2023).

events and whether they may have a particular bias or motive; the circumstances under which the document was created; whether it is an original or a copy, and whether it is sealed, stamped, or certified in any way; its legibility; its chain of custody, to the extent that it is known; whether the information therein is consistent with other evidence on the record, and the Chamber's ability to conduct an independent evaluation of the evidence.[126] The absence of information on any of these factors will not lead a Chamber to automatically consider a document to be devoid of reliability.[127]

In some circumstances, Chambers may attach a rebuttable presumption of authenticity to a class of documents; for example, the ECCC found that documents produced by the Documentation Centre of Cambodia (DC-Cam) were presumed relevant and reliable unless proven otherwise,[128] while Rule 94(B) of the ICTY, ICTR, and SCSL RPE created a rebuttable presumption that documents admitted in a previous trial were authentic.[129] Unlike the ICTY, which deemed that challenges to the authenticity of a piece of evidence goes to weight, rather than admissibility,[130] the ICC has previously held that '[u]nder no circumstances can the Chamber admit unauthenticated documentary evidence since, by definition, such

[126] *Prosecutor v Bemba*, Judgment pursuant to Article 74 of the Statute, ICC-01/05-01/08-3343, 21 March 2016 ('*Bemba* Judgment'), para. 23 (noting that the Chamber that it would examine an item's contents, in addition to its 'provenance, source or author, as well as their role in the relevant events, the chain of custody from the time of the item's creation until its submission to the Chamber, and any other relevant information' in assessing its reliability); see further, *Lubanga* Four Documents Decision, n 115, paras 28–30; *Katanga and Ngudjolo* Bar Table Decision, n 36, para. 13; *Bemba* admissibility decision, n 31, para. 15; *Prosecutor v Karemera*, Decision on the Prosecution Motion for Admission into Evidence of Certain Exhibits from Other Trials, ICTR-98-44-T, 30 October 2007, para. 6; *KHIEU Samphân* ('*Case 002/02*'), Judgment, 002/19-09-2007/ECCC/TC (E465), 16 November 2018, para. 61; *Prosecutor v Musema*, Judgment, ICTR-96-13-T, 27 January 2000, paras 66–7.

[127] See e.g. *Prosecutor v Lubanga*, Decision on the Confirmation of the Charges, ICC-01/04-01/06-803, 29 January 2007, para. 96 ('nothing in the Statute or the Rules expressly states that the absence of information about the chain of custody ... affects the admissibility or probative value of Prosecution evidence') but cf. *Prosecutor v Brđanin and Talić*, Order on the Standards Governing the Admission of Evidence, IT-99-36-T, 15 February 2002, para. 18, emphasising the importance of chain of custody.

[128] *NUON Chea et al. ('Case 002/01')*, Decision on Objections to Documents Proposed to be Put Before the Chamber on the Co-Prosecutors' Annexes A1-A5 and to Documents Cited in Paragraphs of the Closing Order Relevant to the First Two Trial Segments of Case 002/01, 002/19-09-2007/ECCC/TC (E185), 9 April 2012, para. 28. See further Y. McDermott, 'The ECCC's Approach to Evidence and Proof' (2020) 18 *Journal of International Criminal Justice* 747.

[129] *Prosecutor v Stanišić and Župljanin*, Decision Granting in Part the Prosecution's Bar Table Motion and Granting the Prosecution's Supplemental Bar Table Motion, IT-08-91-T, 1 February 2011, para. 14 (noting that the moving party still had to demonstrate relevance to make the case for admission of such evidence).

[130] *Prosecutor v Orić*, Order Concerning Guidelines on Evidence and the Conduct of the Parties during Trial Proceedings, IT-03-68-T, 21 October 2004, guideline (v); *Prosecutor v Brdanin and Talić*, Order on the Standards Governing the Admission of Evidence, IT-99-36-T, 15 February 2002, para. 19. A. Appazov, *Expert Evidence and International Criminal Justice* (Springer, 2016), 54, argues that the ICC's (perhaps former) demand of *prima facie* reliability to be demonstrated before evidence can be admitted is therefore different to the position of the ad hoc tribunals. Before the ICC (if this position is followed in later jurisprudence, which it may not be) 'the subsequent attribution of weight to the evidence is therefore informed by a prior demonstration of its intrinsic validity'.

evidence has no probative value'.[131] However, later Trial Chambers applying the 'submission' model for evidence as discussed in section B may take a different approach. In *Abd-Al-Rahman*, the Chamber noted that objections to the admissibility of material with reference to such decisions were 'not applicable *vis-à-vis* the present ruling, on the basis that in these cases the Chambers adopted a different approach to the reception of materials into evidence, i.e. that of "admission" rather than "submission"'.[132] The Chamber noted that, as is now standard practice, the standard admissibility criteria (and all objections) would be considered at the judgment stage.[133] Ultimately, regardless of whether the 'submission' or 'admission' approach is followed, if a piece of evidence is apparently lacking in reliability, the Chamber has the discretion to either exclude it as inadmissible, or to admit it and consider its lack of reliability when determining its weight.[134] Generally speaking, given that they are not bound by national rules of evidence and Chambers have significant discretion in considering all types of evidence,[135] international criminal tribunals can be expected in most cases to admit the evidence and consider reliability 'as a component of the evidence when determining its weight'.[136]

Significance pertains to the extent to which a piece of evidence can 'advance the Chamber's inquiries', either by speaking to the existence or otherwise of a material fact, or in shedding light on the reliability of other evidence to some significant degree.[137] A consideration of significance asks: 'How strong is this evidence in favouring or disfavouring the fact it seeks to prove?' A piece of evidence may appear broadly relevant, but if the Chamber finds that its likely impact on the determination of the issues is limited, then it may be of limited probative value and may not be admitted on that basis.[138]

The probative value of a piece of evidence must then be weighed against its potentially prejudicial effect.[139] A Chamber must ensure that fairness to the accused and the fair evaluation of witness testimony are not prejudiced by the admission of evidence.[140] These two facets map directly to the two principles of international criminal evidence outlined in Chapter 2—the highest standards of fairness and rectitude of decision. In *Lubanga*, the Trial Chamber noted:

[131] *Katanga and Ngudjolo* Bar Table Decision, n 36, para. 22; see also *Katanga* Defence Bar Table Motion Decision, n 118, para. 17; *Ruto and Sang* Documentary Evidence Decision, n 59, para. 44.

[132] *Prosecutor v Abd-Al-Rahman*, Decision on the Prosecution's Bar Table Motion, ICC-02/05-01/20-885, 27 February 2023, para. 25.

[133] Ibid., paras 25–6.

[134] *Lubanga* Four Documents Decision, n 115, para. 28.

[135] Ibid., para. 24.

[136] *Prosecutor v Katanga and Ngudjolo*, Decision on the Confirmation of Charges, ICC-01/04-01/07-717, 30 September 2008, paras 77–8.

[137] *Katanga and Ngudjolo* Bar Table Decision, n 36, para. 34.

[138] Ibid., para. 35.

[139] Article 69(4), ICC Statute. See further, *Katanga and Ngudjolo* Bar Table Decision, n36, para. 14; *Ruto and Sang* Documentary Evidence Decision, n 59, para. 16.

[140] Article 69(4), ICC Statute.

> Whilst it is trite to observe that all evidence that tends to incriminate the accused is also 'prejudicial' to him, the Chamber must be careful to ensure that it is not unfair to admit the disputed material, for instance because evidence of slight or minimal probative value has the capacity to prejudice the Chamber's fair assessment of the issues in the case.[141]

For example, in *Katanga*, evidence that would take up a disproportionate amount of time to be presented to or evaluated by the Chamber, relative to its probative value, was given as an example of evidence that would be inadmissible on this basis.[142]

In assessing the admissibility of a piece of evidence, the Chamber may have to weigh up whether to exclude it because of concerns as to its relevance, probative value, or potential prejudice or to admit it despite those concerns, which may instead be a decisive factor in the ultimate weight given to the evidence.[143] As outlined in section C above, the concept of 'probative value' can be distinguished from that of 'weight'. The former requires an examination of the individual characteristics of a piece of evidence in deciding upon its admissibility;[144] by contrast, 'weight' relates to the extent to which a Chamber is willing to attach importance to an item of evidence in the context of the broader evidentiary record.[145] We will return to the evaluation of specific forms of evidence in Chapter 5, and the weighing of the record of evidence as a whole in Chapter 6.

D. Exclusion of evidence

In addition to the general guiding principles of relevance, probative value, and prejudice, most of the international criminal tribunals have incorporated a rule on the exclusion of evidence obtained in violation of human rights, or where the means through which it was obtained casts substantial doubt on its reliability or risks damaging the integrity of proceedings.[146] Further exclusionary rules apply to

[141] *Lubanga* Four Documents Decision, n 115, para. 29; *Ruto and Sang* Documentary Evidence Decision, n 59, para. 16.

[142] *Katanga and Ngudjolo* Bar Table Decision, n 36, para. 41.

[143] *Lubanga* Four Documents Decision, n 115, para. 30.

[144] *Katanga and Ngudjolo* Bar Table Decision, n 36, para. 13.

[145] Ibid. ('Probative value is determined on the basis of a number of considerations pertaining to the inherent characteristics of the evidence. Evidentiary weight, however, is the relative importance that is attached to an item of evidence in deciding whether a certain issue has been proven or not. It depends on the intrinsic quality and characteristics of the item of evidence, but also on the amount and quality of other available evidence on the same issue.')

[146] There was no equivalent rule before the IMT or IMTFE: see Piragoff and Clarke, n 97, 2044. However, exclusionary rules of this nature can be found in Rule 95, ICTY RPE; Rule 95, ICTR RPE; Rule 117, IRMCT RPE; Rule 95, SCSL RPE; Rule 138(2), KSC RPE; Article 69(7), ICC Statute; Rule 162, STL RPE.

specific types of evidence, such as evidence pertaining the prior sexual conduct of a victim.[147] Regardless of whether the Chamber is following the admission or the submission approach, decisions on the application of exclusionary rules must be made at trial. This section focuses specifically on the exclusionary rule for improperly obtained evidence.

The exclusion of wrongfully obtained evidence is usually justified on one of three grounds. First, under the so-called deterrence rationale, exclusion can be seen as a mechanism to impose particular standards of behaviour, by providing a procedural sanction.[148] Second, the 'fair trial rationale' justifies exclusion to uphold the fairness of proceedings.[149] Third, the 'integrity rationale' posits that even if no harm can be shown to the accused from admission of the evidence, admitting wrongfully obtained evidence damages the credibility of the legal system and the authority of the system seeking to 'blame' the alleged wrongdoer.[150]

International criminal tribunals have, generally speaking, declined to take a rights-protective approach to wrongfully obtained evidence.[151] Some Chambers have emphasised that the deterrence rationale is inapplicable to international criminal proceedings, where they do not have control over domestic law enforcement authorities and therefore cannot effectively punish their wrongful conduct through exclusion.[152] Others have emphasised the fact that illegally obtained evidence, such as intercepts, can help the Court in its search for the truth, and this has to be weighed against the potential damage to the integrity of proceedings.[153] Two key recent decisions are worthy of further discussion: the admission of large-scale

[147] Rule 96, ICTY RPE; Rule 96, ICTR RPE; Rule 118, IRMCT RPE; Rule 96, SCSL RPE; Rule 148, KSC RPE; Rules 70 and 71, ICC RPE.

[148] P. Chau, 'Excluding Integrity? Revisiting Non-Consequentialist Justifications for Excluding Improperly Obtained Evidence in Criminal Trials' in J. Hunter et al. (eds), *The Integrity of the Criminal Process* (Hart, 2016), 267, 268; S. Zappala, *Human Rights in International Criminal Proceedings* (OUP, 2003), 152.

[149] Although H.L. Ho, 'The Fair Trial Rationale for Excluding Wrongfully Obtained Evidence', in S. Gless (ed.), *Do Exclusionary Rules Ensure a Fair Trial?* (Springer, 2019), 283–305, argues that the fair trial rationale would benefit from deeper reflection on how wrongfully obtained evidence undermines fairness.

[150] A. Ashworth, 'Exploring the Integrity Principle in Evidence and Procedure', in P. Mirfield and R.J. Smith (eds), *Essays for Colin Tapper* (OUP, 2005) 112; A. Ashworth, 'Excluding Evidence as Protecting Rights' [1977] *Criminal Law Review* 723. In the international criminal law context, see K. Vanderpuye, 'The International Criminal Court and Discretionary Evidential Exclusion' (2005–6) 14 *Tulane Journal of International & Comparative Law* 127, at 169.

[151] See, e.g., *Prosecutor v Lubanga*, Decision on the admission of material from the 'bar table', ICC-01/04-01/06-1981, 24 June 2009 ('*Lubanga* Bar Table Decision'), paras 45–8; *Bemba et al.* Appeal Judgment, n 49, paras 288–9; cf. *Bemba et al.* Appeal Judgment, n 49, Separate Opinion of Judge Henderson, paras 22 and 29.

[152] *Lubanga* Bar Table Decision, n 150, paras 45–6; *Prosecutor v Brđanin*, Decision on the Defence 'Objection to Intercept Evidence', IT-99-36-T, 3 October 2003, para. 63.

[153] *Brđanin* Decision on the Defence Objection to Intercept Evidence, n 151, para. 61; *Prosecutir v Delalić* et al., Decision on the Tendering of Prosecution Exhibits 104–8, IT-96-21-T, 9 February 1998, para. 20 ('The Trial Chamber is of the opinion that it would constitute a dangerous obstacle to the administration of justice if evidence which is relevant and of probative value could not be admitted merely because of a minor breach of procedural rules which the Trial Chamber is not bound to apply').

call data records by the Special Tribunal for Lebanon, and the admission of allegedly torture-tainted evidence in the *Al Hassan* case before the ICC.

The STL's *Ayyash et al.* case relied heavily on cell tower data, which can show the approximate location of the person who made the call at the time the call was made.[154] The Prosecutor had been given access to an enormous dataset of phone records, outlining every text message and phone call made by every person in Lebanon between 2003 and 2010, and it sought to admit call sequence tables from phones allegedly connected to the defendants that it had created using this data. The defence objected on the grounds that the collection of this information was a disproportionate breach of the right to privacy. The Appeals Chamber, in upholding the admission of this evidence, found that that the absence of judicial control over the Prosecutor's request for, and collection of, call data records from Lebanese telecommunications firms did not lead to a human rights violation that would justify their exclusion.[155] This decision followed from numerous other decisions that declined to exclude evidence where the right to privacy had apparently not been fully respected,[156] but what is notable about the STL's decision is the sheer scale of data collected and transferred to the Office of the Prosecutor. In an era of 'big data', questions of consent and proportionality ought to inform the operation of exclusionary rules of evidence.

The *Al Hassan* case before the ICC raised the difficult issue of so-called torture-tainted evidence. The accused was detained in Mali by national authorities, who allegedly subjected him to torture and inhumane and degrading treatment, a *jus cogens* norm. Over 19 days while he was in that detention, he was interviewed by the ICC's Office of the Prosecutor (OTP), whom he purportedly told that he had been denied access to food for three days and that his conditions were 'like Guantanamo'.[157] The OTP sought to have the interviews conducted at this time admitted into evidence; they argued that the interviews were voluntary, while the defence argued for their exclusion because they were tainted by torture.[158] In May 2021, the Trial Chamber held that the interviews were admissible. In so doing, the Chamber limited its analysis to the question of whether the interviews themselves were obtained via torture, and not the broader conditions around the accused's detention and how those conditions might have impacted on his statements.[159]

154 *Prosecutor v Ayyash et al.*, Judgment, STL-11-01/T/TC, 18 August 2020.

155 *Prosecutor v Ayyash et al.*, Decision on Appeal by Counsel for Mr Oneissi Against the Trial Chamber's Decision on the Legality of the Transfer of Call Data Records, STL-11-01/T/AC/AR126.9, 28 July 2015, para. 10.

156 *Bemba et al.* Appeal Judgment, n 49, para. 285; *Lubanga* Bar Table Decision, n 150, paras 17–50 (also outlining the approach of the Pre-Trial Chamber and relevant jurisprudence of other international courts).

157 *Prosecutor v Al Hassan*, Public redacted version of 'Corrigendum to "Defence Request to terminate the proceedings"', ICC-01/12-01/18-885-Corr-Red3, 29 July 2020, para. 48.

158 *Prosecutor v Al Hassan*, Public redacted version of 'Decision on requests related to the submission into evidence of Mr Al Hassan's statements', ICC-01/12-01/18-1475, 17 May 2021, paras 1–7.

159 Ibid., paras 71–2.

Luban has argued that this decision may lead to some unfortunate unintended consequences, in view of the parallels between it and the Guantanamo Military Commission's case law, where the accused was re-interrogated in apparently non-coercive circumstances (by so-called clean teams) after years of detention and inhumane and degrading treatment at the hands of the CIA, and the later evidence was deemed admissible.[160] The decision in *Al Hassan* highlights the problematic bipartite nature of Article 69(7), which necessarily limits the scope of the exclusionary rule. Article 69(7) requires, first, an assessment of whether the evidence in question was 'obtained *by means of*'[161] a violation of the Statute or internationally recognised human rights, before the Chamber can assess whether that violation casts substantial doubt on the reliability of the evidence or whether its admission would be antithetical to and would damage the integrity of proceedings.[162] Having found that the first limb of the test was not satisfied (as the evidence itself was not gathered by means of a violation of internationally recognised human rights), the Chamber could not move to the second limb.[163] One potential argument in favour of the exclusion of this evidence, which does not seem to have been raised by the defence,[164] could have been to distinguish between the term 'by means of' in the ICC Statute, and the language of the ICTY and other tribunals' Rules, which refer to the 'methods' of obtaining the contested evidence.[165]

[160] D. Luban, 'Torture Evidence and the Guantanamo Military Commissions' (*Just Security*, 26 May 2021), online at https://www.justsecurity.org/76640/torture-evidence-and-the-guantanamo-military-commissions/ (last accessed 21 December 2023).

[161] Article 69(7) (emphasis added). For a critique of the 'discretionary standard', and arguing that a 'genuinely nondiscretionary framework in the application of an exclusionary provision under the Rome Statute [should] be adopted', see Vanderpuye, n 149, 130.

[162] See also, *Prosecutor v Abd-Al-Rahman*, Decision on the admissibility of video (DAR-OTP-0216-0119) and records of telephone calls (DAR-OTP-0216-0127, DAR-OTP-0216-0128), ICC-02/05-01/20-876, 17 February 2023 ('*Abd-Al-Rahman* Admissibility Decision'), para. 18.

[163] Interestingly, an earlier draft of the Statute referred to evidence 'obtained directly or indirectly' by means of a serious violation of the Statute, internationally protected human rights, or other rules of international law: Preparatory Committee on the Establishment of an International Criminal Court, 1–12 December 1997, Decisions Taken by the Preparatory Committee at its Session held from 1 to 12 December 1997, 25 and 64. See further A. Alamuddin, 'Collection of Evidence' in K.A.A. Khan et al. (eds), *Principles of Evidence in International Criminal Justice* (OUP, 2010), 231, 239.

[164] *Prosecutor v Al Hassan*, Public redacted version of 'Article 69(7) Application', ICC-01/12-01/18-1346, 8 March 2021, paras 17–30, arguing instead that there was no attenuation between the original acts of torture and cruel treatment and the accused's statements to the prosecution, which the defence argued should be considered as involuntary. The defence also referred to a statement of the UN Special Rapporteur which stated (with reference to the Inter-American Court of Human Rights case of *Cabrera García and Montiel Flores v México*, Inter-American Court of Human Rights, Series C, No. 220, judgment of 26 November 2010): 'The exclusionary rule extends not only to confessions and other statements obtained under torture, but also to all other pieces of evidence subsequently obtained through legal means, but which originated in an act of torture': *Prosecutor v Al Hassan*, Public redacted version of 'Article 69(7) Application', ICC-01/12-01/18-1346, 8 March 2021, para. 17, referring to UN Human Rights Council, 25th session, Report of the Special Rapporteur on torture and other cruel, inhuman or degrading treatment or punishment, Juan E. Méndez, UN Doc. A/HRC/25/60, 10 April 2014, para. 29.

[165] Rule 95, ICTY RPE; Rule 95, ICTR RPE; Rule 117, IRMCT RPE; Rule 162, STL RPE. Rule 138, KSC RPE uses the term 'means', while Rule 95 SCSL RPE simply states that no evidence shall be admitted if its admission would bring the administration of justice into serious disrepute.

In the law of armed conflict, 'means and methods of warfare' are distinct concepts, with 'means' referring to the weapons employed, and 'methods' pertaining to broader strategical or tactical choices.[166] To draw an analogy, it could be argued that the Trial Chamber focused on the *methods* (that is, how the OTP carried out its interviews), whereas the *means* through which the evidence was obtained involved a broader strategy of co-ordination with the Malian authorities who held the accused in detention.

In general, both this decision and the STL call records decision demonstrate that the bar for excluding evidence on the basis of a violation of international human rights is quite high, which might give pause for reflection in view of the principles of rectitude of decision and the highest standards of fairness. On the other hand, a recent decision in *Abd-Al-Rahman* shows that the structure and wording of Article 69(7) does not make it impossible to exclude wrongfully obtained evidence.[167] In that decision, records of telephone calls between the Office of the Prosecutor and the accused were found to be inadmissible because they were obtained in breach of Article 55(2) of the Statute (under which the accused should have been informed of his rights in advance of being questioned) and that their admission would be antithetical to the integrity of proceedings.[168]

E. Conclusion

This chapter sought to set out the processes, principles, and practices underpinning the admission and exclusion of evidence in international criminal trials. One overarching conclusion that can be drawn is that practice is inconsistent, not just between different tribunals, or even different Chambers of the same tribunal, but sometimes even in the same Chamber of the same tribunal under a different presiding judge. This was particularly true as regards the practice of 'submission' before the International Criminal Court, where the conduct of proceedings around the admission of evidence varies quite dramatically between different Trial Chambers depending on the composition of the bench. Some might see this as an inevitable divergence in a system designed to represent a 'unique compromise' between the Romano-Germanic and Common Law legal traditions.[169] It does appear that the disputes that could not be resolved at the Rome conference were simply

[166] See M. Longobardo and D. Fleck, 'Means of Combat' and S. Oeter, 'Methods of Combat' in D. Fleck (ed.), *The Handbook of International Humanitarian Law* (4th edn, OUP, 2021), 129; 170.

[167] *Abd-Al-Rahman* Admissibility Decision, n 161. Judge Henderson also found a violation of Article 69(7) in *Bemba et al.* Appeal Judgment, n 49, Separate Opinion of Judge Henderson, ICC-01/05-01/13-2275-Anx, 8 March 2018, paras 1–37.

[168] *Abd-Al-Rahman* Admissibility Decision, n 161, para. 60.

[169] C. Kress, 'The Procedural Law of the International Criminal Court in Outline: Anatomy of a Unique Compromise' (2003) 1 *Journal of International Criminal Justice* 603.

left to be resolved through a flexible model that leaves a great deal of discretion to the judges, perhaps at the expense of predictability and consistency.[170]

At the time of writing, ICC judges had, through the non-binding Chambers Practice Manual, agreed on a model decision for the conduct of proceedings which apparently embraces the submission model. However, this chapter argued for a re-thinking of that practice, on the basis that submission can lead to uncertainty as to which evidence the Chamber will rely upon, inefficiencies in the submission of duplicative or unnecessary supporting evidence, and a lack of guidance on the proper preservation and presentation of certain types of evidence, particularly 'new evidence' such as user-generated evidence, where the Court could play an important standard-setting function.[171]

This chapter also provided, in section C, an overview of how the admissibility criteria of relevance, probative value, and preventing undue prejudice have been interpreted in practice. Again, practice demonstrates that judges have broad discretion in how they interpret these criteria, and the supporting information that might demonstrate the relevance and probative value of evidence (or lack thereof). Regardless of whether the 'admission' or 'submission' approach is followed, Trial Chambers have taken an inclusive approach to the admissibility of evidence, with any weaknesses in the evidence more likely to speak to its ultimate weight than to its probative value for the purposes of admissibility. Similarly, when it comes to the exclusion of evidence obtained through methods that might cast doubt on the integrity of proceedings, section D demonstrated that Chambers have leaned towards the admission of evidence, even in cases where serious violations of human rights have been alleged. The rest of this book now turns to an examination of what happens to evidence once it is admitted to the record—through an evaluation of the burden and standard of proof in Chapter 4; an assessment of the evaluation of evidence, both individually and collectively, in Chapters 5 and 6 respectively; and an analysis of the appellate standard of review in Chapter 7.

[170] P. Behrens, 'Assessment of International Criminal Evidence: The Case of the Unpredictable Genocidaire' (2011) 71 *ZaöRV* 661.

[171] See also Freeman and Vazquez Llorente, n 38.

4
The Burden of Proof and Standards of Proof

A. Introduction

That the burden of proof lies with the Prosecutor, who must prove the guilt of the accused beyond reasonable doubt if they are to be convicted, is well known and ought to be uncontroversial. In practice, however, the meaning and implications of both the burden and standard of proof have been the subject of significant jurisprudence before international criminal tribunals. This chapter provides a thorough examination of the burden and standards of proof, as well as some of the controversies that have arisen in practice.

Section B assesses the meaning of the burden of proof and the interpretation of the presumption of innocence in international criminal trials. It also analyses the 'no case to answer' or 'decision on a motion for a judgment of acquittal' procedure as a function of the presumption of innocence, and how Trial Chambers have interpreted the requisite standard of proof for such motions. Section C then discusses the varying standards of proof applicable at different stages in proceedings, with a particular focus on the law and practice of the International Criminal Court, given the centrality of the Court in contemporary international criminal prosecutions. As such, some of the standards of proof discussed in section C—such as 'substantial grounds to believe' for the confirmation of the charges—do not apply to other international criminal tribunals, given that their pre-trial structures are different to those of the ICC.[1] However, the standard of proof for a conviction—beyond reasonable doubt—is universal in international criminal proceedings.[2] Section D analyses an argument that has recently gained traction in the scholarly literature, which is that the 'beyond reasonable doubt' standard of proof for conviction is too taxing and should be lowered. It argues against such a move, in light of the central tenets of rectitude of decision and the highest standards of fairness, as outlined in Chapter 2.

[1] D. Jacobs, 'Standard of Proof and Burden of Proof' in G. Sluiter et al. (eds), *International Criminal Procedure: Principles and Rules* (OUP, 2013) 1128, 1129; M. Coleman, *The Presumption of Innocence in International Human Rights and Criminal Law* (Routledge, 2021), 83.

[2] A curious quirk of the ECCC is that its internal rules refer to 'beyond reasonable doubt' in the English version, and *'l'intime conviction de sa culpabilité'* in the French: Rule 87(1), ECCC IR. See further, section C.iii.

Proving International Crimes. Yvonne McDermott, Oxford University Press. © Yvonne McDermott 2024.
DOI: 10.1093/oso/9780198842972.003.0004

B. The burden of proof

The presumption of innocence is famously the 'golden thread' of criminal proceedings.[3] A corollary of the presumption is that it is for the prosecution to prove the guilt of the accused beyond reasonable doubt[4] and, relatedly, that the defendant should not have any onus placed upon them to prove their innocence. The principle of *in dubio pro reo*—that any doubt should be interpreted in favour of the accused—is also a facet of the presumption of innocence,[5] and has been recognised as such in international criminal law.[6]

Roberts and Zuckerman have argued that the presumption of innocence goes beyond merely being a rule of evidence and should instead be seen as a 'complex legal and political doctrine'.[7] This is because the 'proof structure' of criminal trials (that is, the prosecutorial burden of proof combined with the beyond reasonable doubt standard of proof) is often justified in terms of error distribution. Blackstone's famous aphorism that it is better for ten guilty people to be acquitted than for one innocent to be wrongly convicted is well known.[8] It is for this reason that the burden on the prosecution is necessarily higher than that placed on the accused, who is under no obligation to present a defence.[9] This explains why notions of extending fair trial rights to parties other than the accused, as discussed in Chapter 2, are misplaced.

[3] *Woolmington v DPP* [1935] UKHL 1.

[4] The STL rightly took issue with wording from other tribunals that suggested that the court must determine the 'guilt or innocence' of the accused beyond reasonable doubt, emphasising that it is only guilt that must be proven to this standard: *Prosecutor v Ayyash et al.*, Judgment, STL-11-01/T/TC, 18 August 2020 ('*Ayyash et al.* Trial Judgment'), para. 202.

[5] G.P. Fletcher, 'Two Kinds of Legal Rules: A Comparative Study of Burden-of-Persuasion Practices in Criminal Cases' (1968) 77 *Yale Law Journal* 880; L. Kaplow, 'Burden of Proof' (2012) 121 *Yale Law Journal* 738.

[6] E.g. *Prosecutor v Galić*, Judgment and Opinion, IT-98-29-T, 5 December 2003, Separate and Partially Dissenting Opinion of Judge Nieto-Navia, para. 17 (describing the principle as a 'foundational precept of criminal law'); *Prosecutor v Renzaho*, Judgment, ICTR-97-31-A, 1 April 2011, para. 474; *Prosecutor v Limaj et al.*, Judgment, IT-03-66-A, 27 September 2007, para. 21.

[7] P. Roberts and A. Zuckerman, *Criminal Evidence* (2nd edn, OUP, 2010), 231.

[8] W. Blackstone, *Commentaries on the Laws of England: Vol. 4* (JB Lippincott Company, 1769), ch. 27, 352 ('for the law holds, that it is better that ten guilty persons escape, than that one innocent suffer'). Evidence scholars are similarly familiar with the '25 prisoners' dilemma: 25 prisoners are exercising in a prison yard when 24 of them spontaneously attack a guard. There is no way of telling which one of the 25 prisoners did not participate in the attack. Even though the probability of guilt would be high (96%), very few would justify randomly selecting one of the 25 prisoners and convicting them.

[9] *Prosecutor v Lubanga*, Judgment on the Appeals of the Prosecutor and the Defence against Trial Chamber I's Decision on Victims' Participation of 18 January 2008 ('*Lubanga* Victim Participation Appeal Decision'), ICC-01/04-01/06-1432, 11 July 2008, Partly Dissenting Opinion of Judge Pikis, para. 14 ('The adversary of the accused is the Prosecutor and none other. The defendant cannot have more than one accuser. It is not for the accused to prove his innocence. He is presumed to be innocent. The ultimate question is whether the Prosecution proved its case beyond reasonable doubt'). See also, *Murray v United Kingdom*, App. No. 18731/91, Judgment, Grand Chamber, 8 February 1996, para. 51 ('Conversely if the case presented by the prosecution had so little evidential value that it called for no answer, a failure to provide one could not justify an inference of guilt').

Lippke links the presumption of innocence to a 'moral assurance' approach, stating that 'we make trials rigorous tests of the government's accusations in order to assure ourselves that, when we convict and punish people for crimes, we do so justifiably'.[10] This 'moral assurance' hypothesis links the presumption of innocence to the principle of rectitude of decision, as outlined in Chapter 2, and the broader legitimacy of international criminal tribunals. As Nancy Combs has noted, even if there were doubts as to the broader sociological aims of international criminal law, such as the place of trials in broader deterrence or reconciliation efforts, trials were, at a minimum, 'considered useful mechanisms for determining who did what to whom during a mass atrocity'.[11] Her book *Fact-finding without Facts* argued that this assumption was not always well founded, based on scrutiny of transcripts and judgments that showed unexplained inconsistencies in witnesses' accounts.[12] If international criminal judgments cannot rigorously demonstrate the evidence and inference that led to particular conclusions, as discussed in Chapter 6, this could jeopardise their legitimacy and claim to authority to try and punish alleged perpetrators of international crimes.

i. Key issues in the interpretation of the burden of proof and the presumption of innocence

The ICC Statute goes further than the statutes of other international criminal tribunals[13] in containing a separate statutory provision on the presumption of innocence in Article 66. This article has three sub-provisions on: the presumption of innocence; the prosecutorial burden of proof; and the standard of proof beyond reasonable doubt for conviction. In addition, Article 67 on the rights of the accused contains two highly relevant minimum guarantees: the right to remain silent and the right not to have imposed on them 'any reversal of the burden of proof or any onus of rebuttal'.[14] In *Bemba*, as discussed in Chapter 3, a decision determined that evidence could be deemed '*prima facie* admissible'.[15] The upshot of this decision

[10] R. Lippke, *Taming the Presumption of Innocence* (OUP, 2016), 105.

[11] N. Combs, *Fact-Finding without Facts: The Uncertain Evidentiary Foundations of International Criminal Convictions* (CUP, 2010), 4.

[12] Ibid.

[13] The IMT, IMTFE, ICTY, ICTR, SCSL, ECCC, STL, and IRMCT did not have specific statutory provisions stating that the burden of proof rested with the prosecution, but this was held by the ICTY to be implicit in the presumption of innocence: *Prosecutor v Delić*, Judgment, IT-04-83-T, 15 September 2008, para. 23; *Prosecutor v Limaj et al.*, Judgment, IT-03-66-T, 30 November 2005, para. 10.

[14] Articles 67(1)(g) and (i), ICC Statute. The presumption also forms the basis of other rights, such as the right to interim release pending trial save in exceptional circumstances: W.A. Schabas and Y. McDermott, 'Article 66' in O. Triffterer and K. Ambos (eds), *Rome Statute of the International Criminal Court: Article-by-Article Commentary* (4th edn, Beck/Hart, 2021), 1947, 1948.

[15] *Prosecutor v Bemba*, Decision on the admission into evidence of materials contained in the prosecution's list of evidence, ICC-01/05-01/08-1022, 19 November 2010 ('*Bemba prima facie* admission decision'); cf. *Bemba prima facie* admission decision, Dissenting Opinion of Judge Ozaki, ICC-01/05-01/08-1028, 23 November 2010. See further, Chapter 3, text to nn 46–53.

was that all of the prosecution witness statements could be admitted, save where the defence had disproved their admissibility.[16] While overturning this decision, the Appeals Chamber disagreed that *prima facie* admissibility reversed the burden of proof.[17]

Four other aspects of international criminal practice can also raise tensions with the rule that the burden of proof lies with the prosecution, and that no reverse onus can be placed on the accused. The first is directions such as those given in *Lubanga*, to the effect that the parties should highlight relevant evidence in their closing submissions to support their arguments and, if they fail to do so, the Chamber cannot be expected to find that evidence in the record itself.[18] This direction is perhaps understandable, given the volume of evidence submitted over the course of trials. The Trial Chamber explained that it cannot be expected 'to read each and every one of the documents ... respectively submitted, guessing at what might be the unexplained relevance of the particular piece of paper'.[19] But, as Roberts has cogently argued, this direction 'is particularly troubling in the context of the rights of the accused, in that it explicitly states that if [one of] the parties, including the defence, does not refer to evidence in its written closing statement, the Chamber could very well not take that piece of evidence into consideration'.[20] This is a good example of the tension that can arise in a mixed procedural system, where the admission of evidence is relatively unfettered and the judges have a duty to search for the truth, yet the collection and submission of that evidence is left to the parties locked in an adversarial contest.[21]

The second potential area of tension with the 'no reverse onus' protection is the taking of judicial notice of adjudicated facts from earlier proceedings, a common practice before many international criminal tribunals.[22] In *Krajišnik*, the ICTY

[16] *Prosecutor v Bemba*, Judgment on the appeals of Mr Jean-Pierre Bemba Gombo and the Prosecutor against the decision of Trial Chamber III entitled 'Decision on the admission into evidence of materials contained in the prosecution's list of evidence', ICC-01/05-01/08-1386, 3 May 2011.

[17] Ibid, para. 72. However, it did find merit in the suggestion that *prima facie* admissibility placed an 'additional burden of disproving the admissibility of items' (ibid, para. 73).

[18] *Prosecutor v Lubanga*, Transcript, ICC-01/04-01/06-T-342-ENG, 1 April 2011, 64.

[19] Ibid.; see also, *Prosecutor v Lubanga*, Order on the Timetable for Closing Submissions, ICC-01/04-01/06-2722, 12 April 2011, paras 5–6; *Prosecutor v Lubanga*, Judgment pursuant to Article 74 of the Statute, ICC-01/04-01/06-2842, 14 March 2012, paras 95–7.

[20] R.C.E. Roberts, 'The *Lubanga* Trial Chamber's Assessment of Evidence in Light of the Accused's Right to the Presumption of Innocence' (2012) 10 *Journal of International Criminal Justice* 923, 932.

[21] In Romano-Germanic systems, a judicial authority would bear responsibility for gathering evidence and compiling a dossier: see e.g. French Code of Criminal Procedure, Article 14; Italian Code of Criminal Procedure, Title III ('Means for Obtaining Evidence'); German Code of Criminal Procedure, s. 162.

[22] Rule 94, ICTY RPE; Rule 94, ICTR RPE; Rule 94, SCSL RPE; Rule 155, IRMCT RPE; Rule 160, STL RPE; Rule 157, KSC RPE. Article 69(6), ICC Statute allows the Court to take judicial notice of 'facts of common knowledge', while the ECCC's legal framework does not allow for judicial notice to be taken of either adjudicated facts or facts of common knowledge: *IENG Sary ('Case 002')*, Decision on Ieng Sary's Motions Regarding Judicial Notice of Adjudicated Facts from Case 001 and Facts of Common Knowledge being Applied in Case 002, 002/19-09-2007-ECCC/TC (E69/1), 4 April 2011. See further, Y. McDermott, *Fairness in International Criminal Trials* (OUP, 2016), 44–6; K.G. Shannon, 'Passing the Poisoned Chalice: Judicial Notice of Genocide by the ICTR' (2006) 19 *Revue Québécoise*

Trial Chamber found that judicial notice creates a 'well-founded presumption for the accuracy of this fact, which therefore does not have to be proven again at trial—*unless* the other party brings out new evidence and successfully challenges and disproves the fact at trial'.[23] The Appeals Chamber in *Milošević* approved this presumption of accuracy, meaning that the moving party does not need to prove the fact at issue, but the opposing party may introduce evidence to rebut it.[24] It has been argued that this practice effectively introduces a rebuttable presumption in favour of the prosecution.[25] The ICC Statute, by contrast, allows the Chamber to take judicial notice of facts of common knowledge, but not adjudicated facts from other cases.[26]

The third area of potential tension is Article 28 of the ICC Statute's definition of superior responsibility, which renders a superior liable for the acts and conduct of their subordinates where they have failed to prevent or punish the criminal acts committed. As has been noted:

de Droit International 95; J.G. Stewart, 'Judicial Notice in International Criminal Law: A Reconciliation of Potential, Peril and Precedent' (2003) 3 *International Criminal Law Review* 245; F. Gaynor, 'Judicial Notice and Agreed Facts' in G. Sluiter et al. (eds), *International Criminal Procedure: Principles and Rules* (OUP, 2013), 1107, 1127; N.H.B. Jørgensen, 'Judicial Notice' in K.A.A. Khan et al. (eds), *Principles of Evidence in International Criminal Justice* (OUP, 2010), 695.

[23] *Prosecutor v Krajišnik*, Decision on Prosecution Motions for Judicial Notice of Adjudicated Facts and for Admission of Written Statements of Witnesses pursuant to Rule 92*bis*, IT-00-39&40, 28 February 2003, para. 16 (emphasis in original). See further, *Prosecutor v Karemera et al.*, Decision on Prosecutor's Interlocutory Appeal of Decision on Judicial Notice, ICTR-98-44-AR73(C), 16 June 2006, para. 48; *Prosecutor v Milošević*, Decision on the Prosecution's Interlocutory Appeal Against the Trial Chamber's 10 April 2003 Decision on Prosecution Motion for Judicial Notice of Adjudicated Facts, IT-02-54-AR73.5, 28 October 2003 and *Milošević* Decision on the Prosecution's Interlocutory Appeal Against the Trial Chamber's 10 April 2003 Decision on Prosecution Motion for Judicial Notice of Adjudicated Facts, Separate Opinion of Judge Shahabuddeen. Cf. *Prosecutor v Fofana*, Decision on Appeal Against 'Decision on Prosecution's Motion for Judicial Notice and Admission of Evidence', SCSL-04-14-AR73, 16 May 2005, para. 32, and *Fofana* Decision on Appeal Against 'Decision on Prosecution's Motion for Judicial Notice and Admission of Evidence', Separate Opinion of Judge Robertson, para. 9.

[24] *Milošević* Decision on the Prosecution's Interlocutory Appeal Against the Trial Chamber's 10 April 2003 Decision on Prosecution Motion for Judicial Notice of Adjudicated Facts, n 23, 4, overturning *Prosecutor v Milošević*, Decision on Prosecution Motion for Judicial Notice of Adjudicated Facts, IT-02-54-T, 10 April 2003. Judge O-gon Kwon, who was on the bench of the Trial Chamber that rejected the 'well-founded presumption of accuracy' approach in the original decision, discusses this in O.G. Kwon, 'The Challenge of an International Criminal Trial as Seen from the Bench' (2007) 5 *Journal of International Criminal Justice* 360, 371.

[25] *Milošević* Decision on the Prosecution's Interlocutory Appeal Against the Trial Chamber's 10 April 2003 Decision on Prosecution Motion for Judicial Notice of Adjudicated Facts, n 23, Dissenting Opinion of Judge Hunt, paras 11; 14.

[26] Article 69(6), ICC Statute. The Chamber considered itself unable to do so in *Prosecutor v Ngudjolo*, Judgment pursuant to Article 74 of the Statute, ICC-01/04-02/12-3, 18 December 2012 ('*Ngudjolo* Trial Judgment'), para. 37; *Prosecutor v Katanga*, Judgment pursuant to Article 74 of the Statute, ICC-01/04-01/07-3436, 7 March 2014, para. 71. In *Prosecutor v Katanga and Ngudjolo*, Decision on the request by the Defence for Germain Katanga seeking to admit excerpts from the judgment rendered in *Lubanga*, ICC-01/04-01/07-3279, 26 April 2012, paras 12–13, the Chamber noted that there was no legal basis for the taking of judicial notice of facts tried in other cases, but took the view that there was no impediment, in principle, to the admission of judgments as documentary evidence pursuant to the *lex generalis* of Article 69.

> The practical effect of Article 28, once proof of commission of crimes by subordinates has been made, is to force the accused to testify in order to rebut the presumption of negligence, and to establish that the superior took 'all necessary and reasonable measures within his or her power to prevent or repress their commission or to submit the matter to the competent authorities for investigation and prosecution' (Art. 28(1)(b)). Consequently, there is an effective reversal of the onus of proof.[27]

The fourth, and perhaps most controversial, issue on the protection against a reverse onus is the burden of proof where an affirmative defence is raised. Where an accused raises a defence of alibi, it does not seem unreasonable to suggest that they should provide some evidence to substantiate their claim to have been in another place at the relevant time.[28] The burden of proof remains with the prosecution—the question for the Trial Chamber will be whether the alleged alibi gives rise to a reasonable doubt as to the accused's culpability.[29] If it does, the court must acquit. As Michelle Coleman has convincingly argued, if the judges do not find the claim of alibi gives rise to a reasonable doubt, because it is insufficiently evidenced or for any other reason, this does not constitute a breach of the presumption of innocence.[30] The burden remains on the prosecution to prove each element of the crime beyond reasonable doubt and if it fails to do so, the court must acquit, even if the defendant's claim to an alibi or other affirmative defence is unsuccessful.[31]

The distinction between the burden of persuasion and the burden of production (or 'evidential burden'[32]) also arises where an accused pleads a lack of mental capacity. In *Delalić et al.*, the ICTY Trial Chamber held that there was a presumption of sanity, which the defence could bring evidence to rebut, and the standard of proof for such rebuttal was the balance of probabilities.[33] There is a question about whether requiring a defendant to prove insanity, even to a balance of probabilities standard, would accord with the ICC Statute's explicit prohibition on 'any reversal of the burden of proof or any onus of rebuttal'.[34]

[27] Schabas and McDermott, n 14, 1955.

[28] *Prosecutor v Renzaho*, Judgment, ICTR-97-31-A, 1 April 2011, para. 303; *Prosecutor v Setako*, Judgment, ICTR-04-81-A, 28 September 2011, para. 224.

[29] *Prosecutor v Delalić* et al., Judgment, IT-96-21-T, 16 November 1998 ('*Delalić et al.* Trial Judgment'), paras 1157–72; See further, *Prosecutor v Ntawukulilyayo*, Judgment, ICTR-05-82-A, 14 December 2011, paras 101–4; Coleman, n 1, 87.

[30] Coleman n 1.

[31] Ibid. ('Thus, the fact-finder can reject the alibi but still find that the prosecutor has not proven it was the defendant who was responsible.')

[32] R. May and M. Wierda, *International Criminal Evidence* (Transnational Publishers, 2002), 122–3; *R v Fontaine* [2004] 1 SCR 702 (Supreme Court of Canada, 22 April 2004), para. 11 (noting that the evidential burden is not a burden of proof).

[33] *Delalić et al.* Trial Judgment, n 29, paras 1157–60, 1172; see further M. Klamberg, *Evidence in International Criminal Trials: Confronting Legal Gaps and the Reconstruction of Disputed Events* (Martinus Nijhoff, 2013), 125.

[34] W.A. Schabas, *The International Criminal Court: A Commentary on the Rome Statute* (OUP, 2017), 1049.

In *Ongwen*, the ICC Trial Chamber dismissed the defences raised under Articles 31(1)(a) and (d) of the Statute, finding that there was insufficient evidence to support a claim of historical mental disease or defect[35] and of duress.[36] The defence appeal brief argued that the Trial Chamber had erred in failing to articulate the standard of proof for affirmative defences that would be applied prior to the defence case.[37] The defence further submitted that, in relation to affirmative defences, the accused bore no evidentiary burden, and that the Trial Chamber erred in failing to apply the burden of proof to the prosecution in respect of the defendant's affirmative defences.[38] The Appeals Chamber called for *amicus curiae* briefs on, *inter alia*, 'the burden of proof when asserting a ground for excluding criminal responsibility and the standard of proof applicable to the assessment of mental disease or defect or duress'.[39] The role of *amici* is generally to inform the Court about matters outside its competence,[40] so the request for briefs on this question of the applicable law was itself curious, as determining the relevant burden and standard of proof would seem to fit squarely within the judges' ability. This seems part of a broader willingness on the Court's part to engage with perspectives from academic research through the *amicus curiae* mechanism, as seen in other cases.[41] On the one hand, it could be argued that this approach offers more focused results than the Chamber (and its legal officers) conducting independent research into academic literature on the topic and is therefore more efficient. On the other hand, a Chamber asking for input on some apparently straightforward questions of legal interpretation could lead to allegations of inconsistency and criticisms of outsourcing the role of the judge and parties in determining fundamental legal questions such as the appropriate burden and standard of proof. It might be argued that the judges did not strictly require *amicus* input on these questions, but merely saw it as desirable to canvas a broad range of views, but this raises questions of efficiency and judicial economy, given that several days of

[35] *Prosecutor v Ongwen*, Trial Judgment, ICC-02/04-01/15-1762, 4 February 2021 ('*Ongwen* Trial Judgment'), para. 2580.

[36] Ibid., para. 2669.

[37] *Prosecutor v Ongwen*, Public Redacted Version of 'Corrected Version of "Defence Closing Brief"', filed on 24 February 2020, ICC-02/04-01/15-1722-Corr-Red, 13 March 2020, paras 91–6.

[38] *Prosecutor v Ongwen*, Public Redacted Version of 'Defence Appeal Brief Against the Convictions in the Judgment of 4 February 2021', filed on 21 July 2021 as ICC-02/04-01/15-1866-Conf, ICC-02/04-01/15-1866-Red, 19 October 2021, para. 4.

[39] *Prosecutor v Ongwen*, Order inviting expressions of interest as *amici curiae* in judicial proceedings (pursuant to Rule 103 of the Rules of Procedure and Evidence), ICC-02/04-01/15-1884, 25 October 2021, para. 19 (iii).

[40] S. Williams, H. Woolaver, and E. Palmer, *The Amicus Curiae in International Criminal Justice* (Hart, 2020), 75–111. Rule 103, ICC RPE allows the Court to admit *amici curiae* at any stage of proceedings, 'if it considers it desirable for the proper determination of the case'.

[41] E.g. *Prosecutor v Gbagbo*, Amicus Curiae Observations of Professors Robinson, deGuzman, Jalloh and Cryer, ICC-02/11-01/11-534, 9 October 2013; *Prosecutor v Al Bashir*, Amicus Curiae Observations of Professors Robinson, Cryer, deGuzman, Lafontaine, Oosterveld, and Stahn, ICC-02/05-01/09-362, 18 June 2018.

oral submissions accompanied the lengthy written *amicus* submissions that were produced.[42]

In its judgment, the Appeals Chamber confirmed that

> in all circumstances, including when a ground for excluding criminal responsibility is raised, the onus is on the Prosecutor to prove the guilt of the accused (article 66(2) of the Statute) and in order to convict the accused, the Court must be convinced of the guilt of the accused beyond reasonable doubt (article 66(3) of the Statute).[43]

The Appeals Chamber also underscored that the Prosecutor does not have to disprove a ground excluding the accused's responsibility, as such.[44] Rather, the burden remains with the Prosecutor to establish the guilt of the accused beyond reasonable doubt, even when a defence has been raised, and to this end, he or she may seek to address and rebut the evidence adduced by the accused.[45] This follows from earlier jurisprudence that the prosecution cannot be expected to rebut claims that are 'frivolous or merely hypothetical',[46] or 'a bare assertion or mere conjecture'.[47] Here again, we can distinguish between the burden of persuasion and the burden of production or evidential burden, which falls to a party seeking to raise a particular issue to adduce evidence to 'give an air of realism to the issue aimed at by the evidence in question'.[48]

Lastly, it is worthy of note that in several decisions, Chambers or individual judges have made the point that just because an accused has been acquitted, it does not necessarily mean that they are innocent, just that the standard of proof has not been met. For example, in *Ngudjolo*, the Trial Chamber noted that 'finding an accused person not guilty does not necessarily mean that the Chamber considers

[42] *Prosecutor v Ongwen*, Revised directions on the conduct of the hearing, ICC-02/04-01/15-1979, 8 February 2022 (outlining the time allocated for *amici* submissions, responses and questions over three court days, from 14 to 16 February 2022). See also Independent Expert Review of the International Criminal Court and the Rome Statute System ('IER'), Final Report, 30 September 2020, paras 533–45; R202, criticising inefficiencies and inconsistency in practice.

[43] *Prosecutor v Ongwen*, Judgment on the appeal of Mr Ongwen against the decision of Trial Chamber IX of 4 February 2021 entitled 'Trial Judgment', ICC-02/04-01/15-2022-Red, 15 December 2022 ('*Ongwen* Appeal Judgment'), para. 337.

[44] Ibid., para. 338.

[45] Ibid.

[46] *Prosecutor v Abd-Al-Rahman*, Decision on the Confirmation of Charges Against Ali Muhammad Ali Abd-Al-Rahman ('Ali Kushayb'), ICC-02/05-01/20-433, 9 July 2021, para. 78.

[47] *Prosecutor v Ruto and Sang*, Decision No. 5 on the Conduct of Trial Proceedings (Principles and Procedure on 'No Case to Answer' Motions), ICC-01/09-01/11-1334, 3 June 2014 ('*Ruto and Sang* Decision No. 5'), Separate Further Opinion of Judge Eboe-Osuji, ICC-01/09-01/11-1334-Anx-Corr, 5 June 2014, para. 80.

[48] Ibid. See also *Ongwen* Appeal Judgment, n 43, para. 340; *Prosecutor v Al-Senussi*, Judgment on the appeal of Mr Abdullah Al-Senussi against the decision of Pre-Trial Chamber I of 11 October 2013 entitled 'Decision on the admissibility of the case against Abdullah Al-Senussi', ICC-01/11-01/11-565, 24 July 2014, para. 167 (considering that the Pre-Trial Chamber 'was reasonable in in placing an "evidential" burden on the Defence sufficiently to substantiate the factual allegations it was making.')

him or her to be innocent. Such a finding merely demonstrates that the evidence presented in support of the accused's guilt has not satisfied the Chamber "beyond reasonable doubt".'[49] Such statements are highly problematic from the perspective of the presumption of innocence, under which the Trial Chamber should presume the innocence of the accused unless their guilt has been proven beyond reasonable doubt, and should be avoided in future practice.

ii. Motions for a judgment of acquittal/'No case to answer'

Another important facet of the presumption of innocence and the prosecutorial burden of proof is the existence of so-called no case to answer motions, now commonly referred to as a 'motion for a judgment of acquittal'.[50] This type of motion allows the defence, after the close of the prosecution case, to invite the Trial Chamber to acquit on some or all of the charges, on the basis that the evidence presented by the prosecution would be insufficient to sustain a conviction, even before any exonerating evidence is produced by the defence. No case to answer motions were not included in the Statutes or Rules of the ICTY or ICTR, but defence motions to dismiss the charges upon the close of the prosecution case were nevertheless entertained in the early days of the ICTY,[51] and Rule 98 *bis* formalising the practice was adopted in time.[52] Charges were rarely dismissed in full at this stage in proceedings, though on occasion a judgment of acquittal was entered for particular charges.[53] Of particular note was the dropping of some genocide charges in the *Karadžić* trial, a decision that was later overturned by the Appeals Chamber.[54] The ICC Statute and Rules are also silent on no case to

[49] *Ngudjolo* Trial Judgment, n 26, para. 36.

[50] See e.g. *Prosecutor v Abd-Al-Rahman*, Transcript, ICC-02/05-01/20-T-116-Red-ENG, 19 April 2023 ('*Abd-Al-Rahman* Decision on Motion for Judgment of Acquittal'), 4.

[51] *Prosecutor v Tadić*, Decision on Defence Motion to Dismiss Charges, IT-94-1-T, 13 September 1996; *Prosecutor v Delalić* et al., Order on the Motions to Dismiss the Indictment at the Close of the Prosecutor's Case, IT-96-21-T, 18 March 1998.

[52] Rule 98 *bis* was first adopted in ICTY RPE Rev. 13, 10 July 1998. In an amendment in ICTY RPE Rev.33, 8 December 2004, the wording of the standard was changed from 'the evidence is insufficient to sustain a conviction' to 'if there is no evidence capable of supporting a conviction'. See also Rule 98 *bis*, ICTR RPE; Rule 98, SCSL RPE; Rule 167, STL RPE; Rule 130, KSC RPE; Rule 121, IRMCT RPE.

[53] E.g. *Prosecutor v Krajišnik*, Transcript, IT-00-39-T, 19 August 2005. There was a partial acquittal in *Prosecutor v Hadžihasanović and Kubura*, Decision on Requests for Acquittal Pursuant to Rule 98 *bis* of the Rules of Procedure and Evidence, IT-01-47-T, 27 September 2004 and *Prosecutor v Strugar*, Decision on Defence Motion Requesting Judgment of Acquittal Pursuant to Rule 98 *bis*, IT-01-42-T, 21 June 2004; *Prosecutor v Ndindiliyimana et al.*, Decision on Defence Motions Pursuant to Rule 98 *bis*, ICTR-00-56-T, 20 March 2007.

[54] *Prosecutor v Karadžić*, Transcript, IT-95-5/18-T, 28 June 2012; *Prosecutor v Karadžić*, Judgment, IT-95-5/18-AR98*bis*.1, 11 July 2013 ('*Karadžić*, 98 *bis* Appeal'). See further, Y. McDermott, '*Prosecutor v Karadžić* (ICTY)' (2013) 52 *International Legal Materials* 1117. The Trial Chamber ultimately acquitted the accused on these charges and the Appeals Chamber did not overturn the acquittal. The implications of the no case to answer decision are discussed in A. Niv, 'Revisiting the "No Case to Answer" Procedure—The First Step in the Right Direction' (*Opinio Juris*, 28 May 2021).

answer motions, but they were first permitted in the *Ruto and Sang* case as being consistent with the Court's statutory framework, particularly the presumption of innocence and the right to a fair and speedy trial,[55] and the charges were vacated at this stage of proceedings.[56]

The standard of proof applicable to no case to answer motions before the ICC, and particularly the degree of evidentiary evaluation that must be undertaken at this stage, remains subject to some ambiguity.[57] At the ad hoc tribunals, the standard was interpreted as whether the evidence presented to date, if taken at its highest, would be sufficient to sustain a conviction.[58] This accorded with the revised formulation of Rule 98 *bis* adopted in 2004, which stated: 'At the close of the Prosecutor's case, the Trial Chamber shall, by oral decision and after hearing the oral submissions of the parties, enter a judgment of acquittal on any count if there is no evidence capable of supporting a conviction.'

Before the ICC, in *Ruto and Sang*, it was noted that the Chamber should not consider questions of the credibility or reliability of the evidence, 'save where the evidence in question is incapable of belief by any reasonable Trial Chamber'.[59] In *Gbagbo and Blé Goudé*, however, the situation was somewhat different insofar as the Chamber had followed the 'submission' model discussed at length in Chapter 3—that is, the relevance and probative value of the evidence was not assessed at the time of its introduction.[60] Judge Henderson argued that this meant that some scrutiny of the evidence was required, given that its relevance and probative value could not be taken as a given.[61] The Prosecutor's appeal in *Gbagbo and Blé Goudé* took issue with the degree of rigour the Trial Chamber had subjected the evidence to at the no case to answer stage.[62] The Appeals Chamber found that there had been no error, noting:

[55] *Ruto and Sang* Decision No. 5, n 47, para. 12.

[56] *Prosecutor v Ruto and Sang*, Decision on Defence Applications for Judgments of Acquittal, ICC-01/09-01/11-2027, 5 April 2016 ('*Ruto and Sang* Decision on Motions for Acquittal'); cf. *Ruto and Sang* Decision on Motions for Acquittal, Dissenting Opinion of Judge Herrera Carbuccia, ICC-01/09-01/11-2027-AnxI, 5 April 2016.

[57] P. Bradfield, 'No Case to Answer? Show Me the (Standard of) Proof!' (*Opinio Juris*, 20 January 2019).

[58] *Karadžić*, 98 *bis* Appeal, n 54, paras 21 and 37.

[59] *Ruto and Sang* Decision No. 5, n 47, para. 32; *Ruto and Sang* Decision on Motions for Acquittal, n 56, Reasons of Judge Fremr, paras 17–19 and 116.

[60] *Prosecutor v Gbagbo and Blé Goudé*, Reasons for oral decision of 15 January 2019 on the Requête de la Défense de Laurent Gbagbo afin qu'un jugement d'acquittement portant sur toutes les charges soit prononcé en faveur de Laurent Gbagbo et que sa mise en liberté immédiate soit ordonnée, and on the Blé Goudé Defence no case to answer motion, ICC-02/11-01/15-1263, 16 July 2019 ('*Gbagbo* Reasons'), Reasons of Judge Henderson, ICC-02/11-01/15-1263-AnxB-Red, 16 July 2019, para. 20, citing *Prosecutor v Gbagbo and Blé Goudé*, Decision on the submission and admission of evidence, ICC-02/11-01/15-405, 29 January 2016.

[61] Reasons of Judge Henderson, ibid., paras 20–30.

[62] *Prosecutor v Gbagbo and Blé Goudé*, Further public redacted version of 'Prosecution Document in Support of Appeal', ICC-02/11-01/15-1277-Conf-Red2, 15 October 2019, paras 123–4.

> In the assessment of the evidence for purposes of a no case to answer motion, the Trial Chamber is not precluded from sensibly weighing credibility and reliability of the evidence thus far presented, in order to satisfy the applicable standard of proof... Judges have the prerogative of assessment of credibility and reliability of the evidence at any point in the proceedings when such an assessment falls to be made.[63]

The precise standard of proof applied by the Trial Chamber in *Gbagbo and Blé Goudé* was difficult to discern, not least owing to the format of the judgment, which comprised a short majority decision, lengthy 'Reasons' by one of the majority judges (Judge Henderson), and a separate opinion by the other judge in the majority (Judge Tarfusser), as well as a dissenting opinion by the third judge on the bench (Judge Herrera Carbuccia). To add to the confusion, Judge Tarfusser expressed his view that no case to answer proceedings had no place before the ICC, while simultaneously issuing a no case to answer decision.[64] Judge Henderson, conversely, found the legal basis for no case to answer proceedings in Article 66(2) of the Statute, on the presumption of innocence and the burden of proof.[65] The Appeals Chamber disagreed, finding that Article 66(2) 'does not regulate the contents of a decision further to an acquittal nor the procedure for the issuance of that decision ... The only provision in the Statute that sets out the requirements for a decision of acquittal is Article 74(5).'[66] This can be distinguished from an earlier Appeals Chamber ruling in *Ntaganda*, which derived the ability to consider no case to answer motions from the Chamber's power to rule on relevant matters under Article 64(6)(f) of the Statute, and said that the discretion to allow no case to answer proceedings must be decided on a case-by-case basis bearing in mind the fairness and efficiency of proceedings.[67] Thus, the precise statutory basis for no

[63] *Prosecutor v Gbagbo and Blé Goudé*, Judgment in the appeal of the Prosecutor against Trial Chamber I's decision on the no case to answer motions, ICC-02/11-01/15-1400-Red, 31 March 2021 ('*Gbagbo and Blé Goudé* Appeal Judgment'), paras 312–14. The Appeals Chamber did add, however, that it 'encourages trial chambers to exercise great care and circumspection in their pronouncements regarding findings on credibility and reliability of the evidence, in order to avoid undue awkwardness in the event that the trial may have to continue before the same composition of the trial chamber': *Gbagbo and Blé Goudé* Appeal Judgment, para. 316.

[64] *Gbagbo* Reasons, n 60, Opinion of Judge Tarfusser, ICC-02/11-01/15-1263-AnxA, 16 July 2019, para. 65. Judge Tarfusser reiterated this view in a later interview: G. Chiarini, 'Can We Return to the Law, Please? Rethinking the Judicial Interpretation of Procedural Rules in the ICC—A Conversation with Judge Tarfusser after the *Gbagbo-Blé Goude* Appeal Judgment' (*Opinio Juris*, 13 April 2021). However, Judge Tarfusser did add in the same interview: 'What would be the necessity in terms of efficiency, of effectiveness of the trial, in terms of the right of the accused to a fair and expeditious trial, to continue it by hearing exculpatory evidence, if the Prosecutor has failed to submit sufficient inculpatory evidence as to the criminal responsibility of the defendants for the crimes charged? Well, the answer is none. Hence, the only solution, for judges faced with evidence which might be, well, massive in numbers but "exceptionally weak" in quality, is to acquit the defendants, by applying Article 74.'

[65] *Gbagbo* Reasons, n 60, Reasons of Judge Henderson, paras 14–15.

[66] *Gbagbo and Blé Goudé* Appeal Judgment, n 63, para. 121.

[67] *Prosecutor v Ntaganda*, Judgment on the appeal of Mr Bosco Ntaganda against the "Decision on Defence request for leave to file a 'no case to answer' motion", ICC-01/04-02/06-2026, 5 September

case to answer proceedings remains unclear. An amendment of the Regulations of the Court could remedy this issue.[68]

Given the lack of legislative footing for such motions, it is perhaps unsurprising that differences of opinion on the requisite standard of proof have emerged in practice. In *Gbagbo and Blé Goudé*, the prosecution alleged that the Trial Chamber erred in failing to 'articulate a clear and consistent standard of proof or approach to assess the sufficiency of evidence' in the no case to answer proceedings.[69] One of the Trial Chamber judges, Judge Tarfusser, would later refute a suggestion that it is the role of a Trial Chamber to articulate standards of proof in this way—in his view, only the Court's Statute can define standards of proof.[70] In the Trial Chamber's decision, apparently distinct approaches were taken, although the majority's conclusion was clear—the prosecution case was so weak that they must acquit.[71] Judge Henderson followed the standard set out in *Ruto and Sang*—that is, whether the prosecution has provided sufficient evidence such that a reasonable chamber could enter a conviction on a charge or charges.[72] Judge Tarfusser's approach, on the other hand, was somewhat unclear, insofar as he referred to the 'beyond reasonable doubt' standard in his written separate opinion,[73] but in the oral decision he stated:

> the dissenting judge is mistaken in stating that the majority has acquitted Mr Gbagbo and Mr Blé Goudé by applying the beyond a reasonable doubt standard. The majority limited itself to assessing the evidence submitted and whether the Prosecutor has met the onus of proof to the extent necessary for warranting the Defence to respond.[74]

The Appeals Chamber later set the following statement of the applicable standard of proof:

2017, paras 44–5. This was also the statutory basis set out in *Prosecutor v Ongwen*, Decision on Defence Request for Leave to File a No Case to Answer Motion, ICC-02/04-01/15-1309, 18 July 2018, paras 4–5.

[68] ICC judges, at the time of writing, appeared to be considering this possibility: International Criminal Court, 'ICC Judges Complete Assessment of IER Recommendations Concerning the Judiciary at their Annual Retreat', Press Release, 5 June 2023 ('The judges discussed the Court's practice to date and agreed on the value of regulating the procedure applicable to potential motions for a judgment of acquittal. The judges will continue their discussion to develop proposals for amendments to the Court's legal texts').

[69] *Prosecutor v Gbagbo and Blé Goudé*, Prosecutor's Appeal Brief, n 62, para. 122.

[70] Chiarini, n 64.

[71] *Gbagbo* Reasons, Reasons of Judge Henderson, n 60, para. 2041; *Gbagbo* Reasons, n 60, Opinion of Judge Tarfusser, n 64, para. 124.

[72] *Gbagbo* Reasons, Reasons of Judge Henderson, n 60, para. 14.

[73] *Gbagbo* Reasons, n 60, Opinion of Judge Tarfusser, n 64, para. 65.

[74] *Prosecutor v Gbagbo and Blé Goudé*, Transcript, ICC-02/11-01/15-T-234-ENG, 16 January 2019, 4.

> In the event of a motion for a finding of no case to answer, the test that guides the trial chamber's decision may be expressed as follows: upon the conclusion of the evidence presented by the prosecution (and on behalf of the victims, as appropriate), the trial chamber shall acquit the defendant or, as the case may be, dismiss one or more of the charges, where the evidence thus far presented is insufficient in law to sustain a conviction on one or more of the charges.[75]

In other words, the standard of proof beyond reasonable doubt is employed at this stage in assessing whether the evidence presented to date would be capable of sustaining a conviction.[76] The Appeals Chamber confirmed that

> it is only when the evidence has satisfied the standard of proof beyond reasonable doubt that it can be said to have been 'sufficient to sustain a conviction', or 'capable of supporting a conviction'; or evidence upon which 'a jury properly directed [...] could convict' or evidence upon which 'a jury properly directed could [...] properly convict.' Nothing less would do.[77]

The reference to proof beyond reasonable doubt is confusing and appears inappropriate, given that this is the standard of proof employed for the ultimate judgment under Article 74. For one thing, it renders it practically impossible for the Chamber to dismiss a motion for judgment of acquittal and later acquit the accused, unless the defence has produced evidence. By contrast, where the standard is whether the prosecution evidence taken at its highest passes a *prima facie* assessment, this hypothetical is feasible.[78] The Appeals Chamber noted that applying the beyond reasonable doubt standard at this stage of proceedings could raise concerns of prejudgment of the case to the detriment of the defence.[79] However, it observed that dismissing a no case to answer motion does not preclude an acquittal, because the Chamber might still find at the end of trial that the prosecution had not in fact proven guilt beyond reasonable doubt.[80]

Moreover, the Appeals Chamber judgment reflected earlier case law by emphasising that the test is whether the prosecution evidence forms a sufficient basis on which the Court *could* convict, not whether the Chamber *would* convict on this evidence.[81] The standard of proof set out in *Ruto and Sang* therefore appears more appropriate than an assessment of whether the evidence presented

[75] *Gbagbo and Blé Goudé* Appeal Judgment, n 63, para. 301.

[76] Ibid., paras 304–5, citing *Prosecutor v Jelisić*, Judgment, IT-95-10-A, 5 July 2001 ('*Jelisić* Appeal Judgment'), para. 35 ('it is only if the evidence is not capable of satisfying the reasonable doubt test that it can be described as "insufficient to sustain a conviction" within the meaning of Rule 98 *bis*(B)').

[77] *Gbagbo and Blé Goudé* Appeal Judgment, n 63, para. 309.

[78] *Ruto and Sang* Decision No. 5, Separate Further Opinion of Judge Eboe-Osuji, n 47, para. 85.

[79] *Jelisić* Appeal Judgment, n 76, para. 37.

[80] Ibid.

[81] *Gbagbo and Blé Goudé* Appeal Judgment, n 63, para. 309.

meets the standard of proof beyond reasonable doubt. The *Ruto and Sang* standard requires a *prima facie* assessment of whether the evidence, taken at its highest, is such that a reasonable chamber *could* enter a conviction on a charge or charges.[82] Nevertheless, the Appeals Chamber's judgment in *Gbagbo and Blé Goudé* appears likely to be followed in later decisions on motions for judgment of acquittal.[83]

C. Standards of proof

Standards of proof 'tell the court how much uncertainty may remain in its final factual conclusion'.[84] As the United States Supreme Court noted in *Re Winship*, 'a standard of proof represents an attempt to instruct the factfinder concerning the degree of confidence our society thinks he should have in the correctness of factual conclusions for a particular type of adjudication'.[85] Different standards of proof may be 'quantitatively imprecise'[86] but they illustrate to the fact-finder the degree of confidence they must have for their factual conclusions to meet the requisite standard. These statements on degrees of confidence could be seen as rather subjective in character, linking the standard of proof to the fact-finder's strength of belief. But satisfying the standard of proof at any stage must be objectively rational—that is to say, there must be a link between the fact-finder's belief and the facts that are established by evidence.[87] As shall be seen in Chapters 5 and 6, 'free

[82] *Ruto and Sang* Decision No. 5, n 47, paras 23–4 and 31–2; *Ruto and Sang* Decision No. 5, n 47, Separate Further Opinion of Judge Eboe-Osuji, paras 2 and 11; *Gbagbo* Reasons, Reasons of Judge Henderson, n 60, paras 4–6; para. 30; *Ruto and Sang* Decision on Motions for Acquittal, Dissenting Opinion of Judge Herrera Carbuccia, n 56, para. 3. Cf. D. Hunt, 'The Meaning of a *Prima Facie* Case' in R. May et al. (eds), *Essays on ICTY Procedure and Evidence—In Honour of Gabrielle Kirk McDonald* (Kluwer, 2001), 137, 139 and *Jelisić* Appeal Judgment, n 76, para. 35 (considering that establishing whether a *prima facie* case capable of supporting a conviction has been made necessarily invokes the beyond reasonable doubt standard).

[83] For example, this standard was followed in *Abd-Al-Rahman* Decision on Motion for Judgment of Acquittal, n 50, 7–9.

[84] S. De Smet, 'The International Criminal Standard of Proof at the ICC—Beyond Reasonable Doubt or Beyond Reason?' in C. Stahn (ed.), *The Law and Practice of the International Criminal Court* (OUP, 2015), 861. See also *Prosecutor v Bemba*, Decision Pursuant to Article 61(7)(a) and (b) of the Rome Statute on the Charges of the Prosecutor Against Jean-Pierre Bemba Gombo, ICC-01/05-01/08-424, 15 June 2009 ('*Bemba* Confirmation Decision'), para. 27 ('The nature of these evidentiary limits depends on each different stage of the procedure and is also consistent with the foreseeable impact of the decision in question on the fundamental rights of the accused person'); L. Laudan, *Truth, Error, and Criminal Law: An Essay in Legal Epistemology* (CUP, 2006), 52–64.

[85] *In re Winship* (1970) 397 U.S. 358, 370.

[86] Ibid.

[87] J. Ferrer Beltrán, 'Legal Proof and Fact Finders' Beliefs' (2006) 12 *Legal Theory* 293–314; S. De Smet, 'Controlling the Quality of Reasoning About the Link Between Evidence and Factual Findings' in X. Agirre et al. (eds), *Quality Control in Criminal Investigation* (TOAEP, 2020), 611; O. Triffterer and A. Kiss, 'Article 74' in O. Triffterer and K. Ambos (eds), *Rome Statute of the International Criminal Court: Article-by-Article Commentary* (4th edn, Beck/Hart, 2021) 2188, 2204 ('The judgment is not an act of subjective intuition but reasoning showing the evidentiary confirmation of the guilt of the accused; the decision must test rationally the viability of the arguments and discard competing hypotheses, based on practical reason and experience').

evaluation' is the preferred framework for assessing the evidence, but judges' discretion in this regard is tempered by the duty to provide a reasoned opinion.

This section discusses the three main standards of proof set out in the ICC Statute in relation to the culpability of an accused individual:[88] 'reasonable grounds to believe' for the issuance of an arrest warrant or summons to appear;[89] 'substantial grounds to believe' for the confirmation of charges;[90] and 'beyond reasonable doubt' for final judgment.[91] Each of these thresholds, according to Pre-Trial Chamber II in *Bemba*, 'depends on the different stages of the proceedings and is also consistent with the foreseeable impact of the relevant decisions on the fundamental human rights of the person charged'.[92] This chapter does not analyse other standards of proof that do not relate directly to the culpability of the accused, such as the 'reasonable basis to proceed' standard for the initiation of an investigation,[93] or the relevant standards of proof for sentencing[94] and reparations decisions.[95] Nor does it discuss the standard of appeal for findings of fact, which is analysed in depth in Chapter 7. Throughout this section, we will see that uncertainty abounds as to the quantity and quality of evidence required to meet each standard of proof. There is also a lack of consistency when it comes to the level of evaluation of the evidence that is required at each stage and the quantity and quality of evidence that can satisfy each threshold standard. This is a theme to which we will return in Chapter 6 on the evaluation of evidence.

i. Reasonable grounds to believe

Before the IMT and IMTFE, there was no judicial control over the indictment, which was approved by a committee comprising all the Chief Prosecutors.[96] Under the

[88] This chapter therefore excludes the 'reasonable basis to proceed' standard for the initiation of an investigation by the ICC Prosecutor. This distinction was drawn by the ICC Pre-Trial Chamber in *Situation in the Republic of Kenya*, Decision Pursuant to Article 15 of the Rome Statute on the Authorization of an Investigation into the Situation in the Republic of Kenya, ICC-01/09-19-Corr, 31 March 2010, para. 29.

[89] Article 58(1)(a), ICC Statute.

[90] Articles 61(5), 61(6), and 61(7), ICC Statute.

[91] Article 66(3), ICC Statute.

[92] *Bemba* Confirmation Decision, n 84, para. 27.

[93] Articles 15(3) and (4) and Article 53(1), ICC Statute. For an excellent overview, see M.E. Cross, 'The Standard of Proof in Preliminary Examinations' in M. Bergsmo and C. Stahn (eds), *Quality Control in Preliminary Examination: Vol. 2* (TOAEP, 2018), 213. The standard of 'reasonable basis to proceed' has been interpreted as entailing 'a sensible or reasonable justification for a belief that a crime falling within the jurisdiction of the Court has been or is being committed': *Situation in Kenya*, Decision Pursuant to Article 15, n 88, para. 35.

[94] The standard of proof for aggravating factors is beyond reasonable doubt: *Prosecutor v Lubanga*, Decision on Sentence Pursuant to Article 76 of the Statute, ICC-01/04-01/06-2901, 10 July 2012, para. 33.

[95] The requisite standard of proof is 'a balance of probabilities': *Prosecutor v Lubanga*, Order for Reparations, ICC-01/04-01/06-3129-AnxA, 3 March 2015, para. 65.

[96] Article 14, IMT Charter. See further Jacobs, n 1, 1130.

statutory frameworks of many non-permanent international criminal tribunals, if the Prosecutor believed there was 'sufficient evidence to provide reasonable grounds for believing' that a suspect had committed a crime falling within the jurisdiction of the tribunal,[97] he or she prepared an indictment for confirmation by a single judge.[98] Aside from the SCSL, which confirmed an indictment if the crimes charged fell within the jurisdiction of the Court,[99] and the KSC, which referred to a 'well-grounded suspicion' standard,[100] most tribunals required that a *prima facie* case be established by the Prosecutor.[101] The establishment of a *prima facie* case and issuance of an indictment before the ICTY has been described as a 'very brief and rudimentary legal process',[102] although the single judge could request more evidence or, in some tribunals, adjourn the review, asking the Prosecutor to amend the indictment.[103]

In the case law, a *prima facie* case was defined as 'a credible case which, if accepted and uncontradicted, would be a sufficient basis on which to convict the accused'.[104] This seems to unnecessarily conflate the standard with that for no case to answer proceedings—which, as discussed in the previous section, arises at a much later stage in proceedings—with that for establishing a *prima facie* case, which should be a lower standard.[105] An earlier pronouncement by Judge Sidhwa in *Rajić* seems a more appropriate understanding of the standard of proof for establishing reasonable grounds for believing:

[97] Rule 47(B), ICTY RPE; Rule 47(B), ICTR RPE; Rule 48(B), IRMCT RPE. Rule 68(B), STL RPE sets out a standard of 'sufficient evidence that a suspect has committed a crime', while Rule 86(1) KSC RPE refers to a 'well-grounded suspicion' that a suspect committed or participated in the commission of a crime within the jurisdiction of the Specialist Chambers. Rule 47(B), SCSL RPE required the Prosecutor to be satisfied that the suspect had committed a crime within the jurisdiction of the Special Court.

[98] Article 18(4), ICTY Statute; Article 17(4), ICTR Statute; Article 17(4), STL Statute; Rule 47, SCSL RPE; Article 16(4), IRMCT Statute; Article 38(4), KSC Law. The situation before the ECCC was slightly different, given its inquisitorial nature: ECCC Co-Prosecutors, where they had 'reason to believe' that crimes within the jurisdiction of the ECCC had been committed, would transmit this decision to the Co-Investigating Judges, who would carry out their own investigation and issue a Closing Order (which was the ECCC's equivalent of an indictment) if there was 'sufficient evidence against the charged person': Rules 53 and 67(3)(c) ECCC IR.

[99] Rule 47(E), SCSL RPE. See further, *Prosecutor v Norman et al.*, Decision on amendment of the consolidated indictment, SCSL-04-14-AR73, 16 May 2005, para. 49.

[100] Article 39(2), KSC Law.

[101] Article 19(1), ICTY Statute; Article 18(1), ICTR Statute; Article 18(1), STL Statute; Article 17(1), IRMCT Statute.

[102] A.T. Cayley, 'Constraints and Quality Control in Preliminary Examination: Critical Lessons Learned from the ICTY, the ICC, the ECCC and the United Kingdom' in M. Bergsmo and C. Stahn, *Quality Control in Preliminary Examination: Volume 1* (TOAEP, 2018), 35, 39.

[103] Rule 47(F), ICTY RPE; Rule 47(F), ICTR RPE; Rule 48(F), IRMCT RPE; Rule 68(I), STL RPE; Rule 86(4), KSC RPE.

[104] *Prosecutor v Milošević*, Decision on Review of Indictment, IT-01-51-I, 22 November 2001, para. 14.

[105] In a similar vein, in relation to the confirmation of charges at the ICC (unquestionably a higher standard of proof than that at issue here), the Pre-Trial Chamber in *Abu Garda* noted that the Chamber 'shall not evaluate whether the evidence is sufficient to sustain a future conviction. Such a high standard is not compatible with the standard under Article 61(7) of the Statute': *Prosecutor v Abu Garda*, Decision on the Confirmation of Charges, ICC-02/05-02/09-243, 8 February 2010, para. 40.

> [R]easonable grounds, therefore, point to such facts and circumstances as would justify a reasonable or ordinarily prudent man to believe that a suspect has committed a crime ... The evidence ... need not be overly convincing or conclusive; it should be adequate or satisfactory to warrant the belief that the suspect has committed the crime.[106]

Before the ICC, the Pre-Trial Chamber will issue an arrest warrant against an individual upon the request of the Prosecutor only where it is satisfied, based on the evidence and information provided by the Prosecutor, that there are 'reasonable grounds to believe that the person has committed a crime within the jurisdiction of the Court'.[107] While the ad hoc tribunals closely linked the confirmation of the indictment to the issuance of an arrest warrant,[108] the ICC separates these two processes, with the issuance of an arrest warrant or summons to appear needing to satisfy a lower standard of proof than the confirmation of charges, as discussed in the next section.

Ambos argues that the ICTY and ICTR's '*prima facie* case' standard for confirmation of an indictment is higher than the ICC's 'reasonable grounds' standard for issuing an arrest warrant.[109] This is not self-evident from the relevant legal frameworks, which refer to 'reasonable basis for believing'[110] and 'reasonable grounds to believe'[111] respectively, but it does seem to be justified by the judicial interpretation of these standards. As discussed above, the 'reasonable basis for believing' standard before the ad hoc tribunals was interpreted as requiring that the prosecution puts forward a credible case that would, if accepted, form a sufficient basis for conviction.[112] The ICC, conversely, has linked 'reasonable grounds to believe' to the 'reasonable suspicion' standard taken from human rights law.[113]

106 *Prosecutor v Rajić*, Review of the Indictment, IT-95-12-I, 29 August 1995, 8.
107 Article 58(1)(a), ICC Statute.
108 Article 19(2), ICTY Statute.
109 K. Ambos, *Treatise on International Criminal Law Vol. III: International Criminal Procedure* (OUP, 2016), 401. Cf. T. Mariniello, 'Questioning the Standard of Proof: The Purpose of the ICC Confirmation of Charges Procedure' (2015) 13 *Journal of International Criminal Justice* 579, at 585–6, noting similarities between the two standards.
110 See n 97.
111 Article 58(1)(a), ICC Statute.
112 *Milošević*, Decision on Review of Indictment, n 103; *Prosecutor v Kordić et al.*, Decision on the Review of the Indictment, IT-95-14-I, 10 November 1995, 2–3.
113 E.g. *Prosecutor v Gbagbo*, Public redacted version of 'Decision on the Prosecutor's Application Pursuant to Article 58 for a warrant of arrest against Laurent Koudou Gbagbo', ICC-02/11-01/11-9-Red, 20 December 2011, para. 27, stating that the Chamber considered the reasonable suspicion standard under Article 5(1)(c) of the ECHR and was also guided by Inter-American Court of Human Rights jurisprudence on Article 7 (the right to liberty); *Prosecutor v Ntaganda*, Decision on the Prosecutor's Application under Article 58, ICC-01/04-02/06-36-Red, 13 July 2012, para. 16; *Prosecutor v Al Bashir*, Judgment on the appeal of the Prosecutor against the 'Decision on the Prosecution's Application for a Warrant of Arrest against Omar Hassan Ahmad Al Bashir', ICC-02/05-01/09-73, 3 February 2010 ('*Bashir* Arrest Warrant Appeal Decision'), para. 31; *Prosecutor v Harun and Abd-Al-Rahman*, Decision on the Prosecution Application under Article 58(7) of the Statute, ICC-02/05-01/07-1-Corr, 27 April

It has been argued that the conflation of 'reasonable grounds to believe' with 'reasonable suspicion' effectively lowers the standard of proof, because 'suspicion' is more vague and less concrete than 'belief'.[114] However, 'reasonable suspicion' is made more tangible by the relevant case law of the European Court of Human Rights (ECtHR), which 'requires the existence of some facts or information which would satisfy an objective observer that the person concerned may have committed the offence'.[115] Ryngaert notes that, perhaps as a result of this academic criticism, more recent decisions do not explicitly mention the 'reasonable suspicion' standard, but nor do they clarify how the evidence has been evaluated.[116] Nevertheless, recent case law clearly demonstrates a scrutiny of the evidence presented, albeit without defining the standard of proof. For example, in *Mokom*, the Chamber refused to conclude that there were reasonable grounds to believe that the suspect bore criminal responsibility for crimes committed in the location of Guen, because the prosecution had not presented evidence linking the principal perpetrators with Mokom or other alleged leaders of the Anti-Balaka movement.[117]

In *Al Bashir*, the Appeals Chamber considered that the Pre-Trial Chamber erred when it declined to issue an arrest warrant for the crime of genocide on the grounds that the existence of genocidal intent was 'one of several reasonable conclusions available on the materials provided by the Prosecution'.[118] The Appeals Chamber (and Judge Ušacka in her dissent to the original decision[119]) found that requiring a fact to be the 'only reasonable conclusion' would conflate the standard of proof with that of proof beyond reasonable doubt for final conviction.[120] This conclusion seems logical on its face, but as Ramsden and Chung have argued, it is problematic to equate 'reasonable grounds to believe' with just one of the reasonable conclusions that can be inferred from the indirect evidence presented, in light of the provision's aim to shield the Court from considering unfounded

2007, para. 28; *Prosecutor v Bemba*, Decision on the Prosecutor's Application for a Warrant of Arrest against Jean-Pierre Bemba Gombo, ICC-01/05-01/08-14-tENG, 12 June 2008, para. 24.

[114] M. Ramsden and C. Chung, '"Reasonable Grounds to Believe": An Unreasonably Unclear Evidentiary Threshold in the ICC Statute' (2015) 13 *Journal of International Criminal Justice* 555, 563–5.

[115] *O'Hara v United Kingdom* (2002) 34 EHRR 32, para. 34; *Fox, Campbell and Hartley v United Kingdom*, Judgment of 30 August 1990, vol. 182, Series A, page 16, para. 32; *Labita v Italy* (2008) 46 EHRR 50, para. 155.

[116] C. Ryngaert, 'Article 58' in O. Triffterer and K. Ambos (eds), *Rome Statute of the International Criminal Court: Article-by-Article Commentary* (4th edn, Beck/Hart, 2021), 1708, 1718.

[117] *Prosecutor v Mokom*, Public Redacted Version of 'Warrant of Arrest for Maxime Jeoffroy Eli Mokom Gawaka', ICC-01/14-01/22-2-Red2, 22 March 2022, para. 15.

[118] *Bashir* Arrest Warrant Appeal Decision, n 113, paras 32–3.

[119] *Prosecutor v Al Bashir*, Decision on the Prosecution's Application for a Warrant of Arrest against Omar Hassan Ahmad Al Bashir, ICC-02/05-01/09-3, 4 March 2009, Separate and Partly Dissenting Opinion of Judge Ušacka, paras 28–34.

[120] *Bashir* Arrest Warrant Appeal Decision, n 113, para. 31.

allegations.[121] We have some clarity on what the 'reasonable grounds to believe' standard does *not* require (including certainty[122] and that a finding be the only reasonable conclusion[123]), but the case law to date has been less concrete in setting out what it *does* require.[124]

ii. Substantial grounds to believe

To confirm a charge, Article 61(7) of the ICC Statute requires the Pre-Trial Chamber to determine 'whether there is sufficient evidence to establish substantial grounds to believe that the person committed each of the crimes charged'. The Chamber can then confirm the charges, decline to confirm those charges for which there is insufficient evidence, or adjourn the hearing to request the Prosecutor to either provide more evidence or amend the charges. This confirmation of charges procedure plays an important role in ensuring that 'only those persons against whom sufficiently compelling charges beyond mere theory or suspicion have been brought',[125] thereby protecting accused persons 'against wrongful and wholly unfounded charges'.[126] In defining the scope of the charges,[127] the confirmation of the charges process is intended to encourage more efficient administration of justice[128] and protect the rights of the accused.[129] However, concerns have been raised about

[121] Ramsden and Chung, n 114, 560.

[122] *Bashir* Arrest Warrant Appeal Decision, n 113, para. 31.

[123] *Bashir* Arrest Warrant Appeal Decision, n 113, para. 33.

[124] E.g. *Prosecutor v Gicheru and Bett*, Decision on the 'Prosecution's Application under Article 58(1) of the Rome Statute', ICC-01/09-01/15-1-Red, 10 September 2015; *Prosecutor v Al Werfalli*, Warrant of Arrest, ICC-01/11-01/17-2, 15 August 2017; *Prosecutor v Bemba et al.*, Warrant of arrest for Jean-Pierre Bemba Gombo, Aimé Kilolo Musamba, Jean-Jacques Mangenda Kabongo, Fidèle Babala Wandu and Narcisse Arido, ICC-01/05-01/13-1-Red2-tENG, 20 November 2013 (not elaborating on the meaning of the 'reasonable grounds to believe' standard of proof). Cf. *Prosecutor v Lubanga*, Judgment on the appeal of Mr. Thomas Lubanga Dyilo against the decision of Pre-Trial Chamber I entitled 'Décision sur la demande de mise en liberté provisoire de Thomas Lubanga Dyilo', ICC-01/04-01/06-824, 13 February 2007, Separate Opinion of Judge Pikis, para. 5 (providing a detailed overview of his understanding of the relevant standard) and *Prosecutor v Katanga*, Judgment in the Appeal by Mathieu Ngudjolo Chui of 27 March 2008 against the Decision of Pre- Trial Chamber I on the Application of the Appellant for Interim Release, ICC-01/04-01/07-572 (OA 4), 9 June 2008, para. 18 ('Belief denotes... acceptance of fact... The facts placed before the Chamber must be cogent to the extent of creating a reasonable belief that the person committed the crimes.)

[125] *Prosecutor v Lubanga*, Decision on the Confirmation of Charges, ICC-01/04-01/06-803, 29 January 2007, para. 37. See also *Prosecutor v Katanga and Ngudjolo*, Decision on Evidentiary Scope of the Confirmation Hearing, Preventive Relocation and Disclosure under Article 67(2) of the Statute and Rule 77 of the Rules, ICC-01/04-01/07-428, 25 April 2008, para. 6; *Bemba* Confirmation Decision, n 84, para. 28.

[126] *Lubanga* Confirmation of Charges Decision, n 125, para. 37.

[127] *Prosecutor v Bemba*, Judgment pursuant to Article 74 of the Statute, ICC-01/05-01/08-3343, 21 March 2016, para. 32.

[128] Jacobs, n 1, 1147.

[129] *Katanga and Ngudjolo*, Decision on the Confirmation of Charges, ICC-01/04-01/07-717, 30 September 2008, para. 63; *Lubanga* Confirmation of Charges Decision, n 125, para. 37.

its unwieldiness in practice and the fact that the standard of proof remains unclear and inconsistent.[130]

The standard of proof of 'substantial grounds to believe' is clearly higher than the 'reasonable grounds' standard discussed in the previous section, and lower than the 'beyond reasonable doubt' standard for conviction discussed in the next section. In attempting to define the meaning of 'substantial grounds to believe', the *Bemba* Pre-Trial Chamber consulted the *Oxford English Dictionary*, finding that 'substantial' can be understood as 'significant', 'solid', 'material', 'well built', and 'real' as opposed to 'imagined'.[131] It confirmed that the prosecution must offer 'concrete and tangible proof demonstrating a clear line of reasoning underpinning its specific allegations'.[132] A number of cases have referred to ECtHR case law on the 'strong grounds for believing' standard that applies when assessing whether an applicant might be exposed to a violation of Articles 2 or 3 of the Convention if deported.[133] Some decisions have effectively incorporated that standard into the interpretation of 'substantial grounds to believe'.[134] This is rather curious, given that the ECHR standard of proof has emerged from a different legal regime in a distinct context to the international criminal trial.[135]

There is some inconsistency in practice on the quantum of evidence that should be presented for a confirmation decision. Article 61(3) requires the accused to be provided with a copy of the document containing the charges and an account of the evidence that the Prosecutor seeks to rely upon at the hearing, while Article 61(5) states that, at the confirmation hearing, 'the Prosecutor shall support each charge with sufficient evidence to establish substantial grounds to believe that the person committed the crime charged. The Prosecutor may rely on documentary or summary evidence and need not call the witnesses expected to testify at the trial.'[136]

The first issue is the meaning of 'each charge' in Article 61(5). In *Gbagbo*, the initial confirmation hearing was postponed to enable the prosecution to bring more evidence.[137] The majority held that the Prosecutor must prove 'a sufficient number of incidents' to establish the context element of an 'attack against

[130] IER Report, n 42, paras 483–9.

[131] *Bemba* Confirmation Decision, n 84, para. 29.

[132] Ibid., para. 29, quoting *Lubanga* Confirmation of Charges Decision, n 125, para. 39.

[133] *Mamatkulov and Askarov v Turkey*, Judgment of 4 February 2005, Applications Nos. 46827/99 and 46951/99, para. 7; *Chahal v United Kingdom*, Judgement of 15 November 1996, Application No. 22141/93, para. 97.

[134] *Lubanga* Confirmation of Charges Decision, n 125, para. 38; cited with approval in *Katanga and Ngudjolo* Confirmation of Charges Decision, n 129, para. 65; *Abu Garda* Confirmation of Charges Decision, n 105, para. 36.

[135] Jacobs, n 1, 1137.

[136] Article 61(5), ICC Statute.

[137] *Prosecutor v Gbagbo*, Decision adjourning the hearing on the confirmation of charges pursuant to Article 61(7)(c)(i) of the Rome Statute, ICC-02/11-01/11-432, 3 June 2013 ('*Gbagbo* Adjournment Decision'), paras 44–7.

any civilian population' to the substantial grounds to believe standard.[138] The Chamber stressed that, to demonstrate substantial grounds to believe that such an attack occurred, the prosecution should include, *inter alia*, details about the perpetrators' identity 'or at least information as to the group they belonged to', as well as the identity of the victims 'or at least their political or other allegiance'.[139]

The second issue is what constitutes 'sufficient evidence to establish substantial grounds to believe'. In practice, much of the evidence presented by the prosecution at this stage of proceedings tends to be documentary in nature, including NGO reports and the reports of international organisations, witness statements, and press articles.[140] However, in *Gbagbo*, the Pre-Trial Chamber criticised the prosecution's reliance on evidence of this nature, noting that it was 'not prepared to accept allegations proven solely through anonymous hearsay in documentary evidence'.[141] In her dissenting opinion to this decision, Judge Fernández de Gurmendi criticised what she saw as her colleagues' 'piecemeal' approach to the evidence, which she saw as inappropriate when assessing 'systemic forms of criminality'.[142] The 'atomistic vs. holistic' approach is a debate to which we will return in Chapter 6. For now, it suffices to note that evidence must be provided to support each charge, and that the lower standard of proof is not an excuse for not providing sufficiently solid evidence.[143] However, the evidence presented should comprise a 'limited and careful selection of the best evidence'.[144] Relevant direct evidence with an unbroken chain of custody is clearly going to bear a higher weight than indirect evidence with an unclear link to the charges or weaker forms of evidence, such as

[138] Ibid., para. 23. Similarly, see, *Prosecutor v Mbarushimana*, Decision on the Confirmation of Charges, ICC-01/04-01/10-465, 16 December 2011, paras 244–67 (finding that the Prosecutor had not presented sufficient evidence to satisfy the Chamber to the requisite threshold of substantial grounds to believe that there was a policy to attack the civilian population).

[139] *Gbagbo* Adjournment Decision, n 137, para. 22.

[140] W.A. Schabas, E. Chaitidou, and M. El Zeidy, 'Article 61' in O. Triffterer and K. Ambos (eds), *Rome Statute of the International Criminal Court: Article-by-Article Commentary* (4th edn, Beck/Hart, 2021), 1759, 1804.

[141] *Gbagbo* Adjournment Decision, n 137, para. 37.

[142] Ibid., Dissenting opinion of Judge Fernandez de Gurmendi, ICC-02/11-01/11-432-Anx-Corr, 3 June 2013, para. 48.

[143] *Prosecutor v Ruto, Kosgey & Sang*, Decision on the Confirmation of Charges Pursuant to Article 61(7)(a) and (b) of the Rome Statute, ICC-01/09-01/11-373, 23 January 2012, Dissenting Opinion of Judge Kaul, paras 53–7; *Gbagbo* Adjournment Decision, n 137, para. 35.

[144] *Katanga and Ngudjolo*, Decision on Evidentiary Scope of the Confirmation Hearing, n 125, para. 81. See also *Prosecutor v Abd-Al-Rahman*, Decision on the Prosecutor's Request for Postponement of the Confirmation Hearing and related deadlines, ICC-02/05-01/20-196, 2 November 2020, para. 42 and *Prosecutor v Said*, Second order on disclosure and postponement of the confirmation hearing, ICC-01/14- 01/21-112, 30 June 2021, para. 20 (requesting that the document containing the charges be accompanied by a separate pre-confirmation brief 'where each statement of fact should have a corresponding footnote referring specifically, with hyperlinks, to *the most probative supporting evidence*, duly explaining which evidence is believed to support each charge and the reason why that would be the case' (emphasis added).

anonymous hearsay.[145] The defence, too, can submit evidence, but is not obliged to do so.[146] Ultimately, the presiding judge has discretion as to the conduct of confirmation proceedings and whether the parties can call witnesses, and if so, how many.[147] However, this discretion is tempered somewhat by detailed guidance now set out in the Chambers Practice Manual,[148] the impact of which we shall consider in more detail below.

To what extent should evidence presented be evaluated at the confirmation stage of proceedings? In several cases, the prosecution has urged against any 'in depth examination of the evidence', arguing that questions such as reliability and credibility of the evidence should be left to the Trial Chamber.[149] That is incorrect. The confirmation standard is not a *prima facie* one whereby only a cursory evaluation of the evidence is carried out,[150] and neither the Statute nor the Rules draw a distinction as to the means in which a Trial Chamber and a Pre-Trial Chamber should evaluate evidence.[151] Rather, the evidence should be fully evaluated in accordance with the free assessment of the evidence, but applying the requisite lower standard of proof.[152]

What would such an evaluation look like, in light of the 'substantial grounds' standard of proof? As Judge Van den Wyngaert has made clear, 'charges should only be confirmed if the evidence has a realistic chance of supporting a conviction beyond reasonable doubt ... there must be at least enough of an evidentiary

[145] *Gbagbo* Adjournment Decision, n 137, paras 27–8. *Prosecutor v Yekatom and Ngaïssona*, Decision on the Confirmation of Charges against Alfred Yekatom and Patrice Edouard Ngaïssona, ICC-01/14-01/18-403-Corr-Red, 14 May 2020, para. 59 and *Prosecutor v Abu Garda*, Decision on the Confirmation of Charges, ICC-02/05-02/09-243, 8 February 2010, Separate Opinion of Judge Tarfusser, para. 4 (referring to situations where a link cannot be established between the events and the suspect, owing to the evidence being 'flimsy, inconsistent, or otherwise inadequate').

[146] Rule 121(6), ICC RPE; *Lubanga* Victim Participation Appeal Decision, Partly Dissenting Opinion of Judge Pikis, n 9, para. 43.

[147] Rule 122, ICC RPE. For example, the defence teams were instructed to call a maximum of two live witnesses per suspect in *Prosecutor v Katanga and Ngudjolo*, Decision on the Admissibility for the Confirmation Hearing of the Transcripts of Interview of Deceased Witness 12, ICC-01/04-01/07-412, 18 April 2008, 4 and *Ruto, Kosgey & Sang* Confirmation Decision, n 143, para. 14 ('in light of the limited scope and purpose of the confirmation of charges hearing').

[148] International Criminal Court, Chambers Practice Manual, 7th edition, adopted following the judicial retreat of 2023, 13–16.

[149] See *Ruto, Kosgey & Sang* Confirmation Decision, n 143, Dissenting Opinion of Judge Kaul, para. 55; *Prosecutor v Abu Garda*, Decision on the 'Prosecution's Application for Leave to Appeal the "Decision on the Confirmation of Charges"', ICC-02/05-02/09-267, 23 April 2010, paras 4–12.

[150] *Lubanga* Confirmation of Charges Decision, n 125, para. 39 (noting the Chamber's role in carrying out 'an exacting scrutiny of all the evidence'). See further, M. Miraglia, 'Admissibility of Evidence, Standard of Proof, and Nature of the Decision in the ICC Confirmation of Charges in *Lubanga*' (2008) 6 *Journal of International Criminal Justice* 489, 498. Cf. D.D. Ntanda Nsereko, 'Prosecutorial Discretion before National Courts and International Tribunals' (2005) 3 *Journal of International Criminal Justice* 124, 140 (stating that the 'substantial grounds to believe' standard is 'the equivalent of the prima facie standard used by the ad hoc Tribunals')

[151] *Abu Garda*, Decision on the Prosecution's Application for Leave to Appeal the Confirmation Decision, n 149, para. 6 ('The Statute vests all Chambers, regardless of the stage of proceedings, with discretion to freely assess the evidence presented by the parties').

[152] *Prosecutor v Al Mahdi*, Decision on the confirmation of charges against Ahmad Al Faqi Al Mahdi, ICC-01/12-01/15-84, 24 March 2016, Separate Opinion of Judge Kovács, ICC-01/12-01/15-84-Anx, 9 May 2016, paras 11–13.

basis to sustain a possible conviction, on the assumption that these questions are resolved in favour of the Prosecutor at trial'.[153] Conversely, the Pre-Trial Chamber in *Abu Garda* expressly said that the Chamber should 'not evaluate whether the evidence is sufficient to sustain a future conviction'.[154] These two statements seem incompatible on first glance, but they can be squared. Judge Van den Wyngaert's reference to the potential of sustaining a *possible* conviction, if the prosecution evidence is found to be sufficient over the course of the trial and if reasonable doubt does not otherwise emerge, is compatible with the bare statement set out in *Abu Garda* that the Pre-Trial Chamber should not assess the sufficiency of the evidence to secure a conviction at that moment in time.

The many cases in which some or all charges have been dismissed at the confirmation stage[155] speak volumes as to Article 61's important function in weeding out weaker cases in advance of trial. However, there have been criticisms over the Court's lifetime of the inefficiency of the confirmation stage and its time-consuming nature.[156] In light of the intention that the confirmation procedure should not become a mini-trial or a 'trial within a trial',[157] some have argued that certain decisions, such as the adjournment decision in *Gbagbo*,[158] set too high a standard in requiring 'largely completed investigation'.[159] On the other hand, it must be recalled that the confirmation stage of proceedings is different to the issuance of an indictment before the ad hoc tribunals, insofar as the accused has been identified and transferred to the seat of the Court,[160] and he or she has the right to

[153] *Prosecutor v Gbagbo*, Decision on the confirmation of charges against Laurent Gbagbo, ICC-02/11-01/11-656-Red, 12 June 2014, Dissenting Opinion of Judge Van den Wyngaert, ICC-02/11-01/11-656-Anx, 12 June 2014, para. 4.

[154] *Abu Garda*, Decision on the Confirmation of Charges, n 105, para. 40.

[155] E.g. *Abu Garda*, Decision on the Confirmation of Charges, n 105; *Mbarushimana*, Decision on the Confirmation of Charges, n 138; *Ruto, Kosgey & Sang* Confirmation Decision, n 143 (declining to confirm the charges against Kosgey); *Prosecutor v Muthaura et al.*, Decision on the Confirmation of Charges Pursuant to Article 61(7)(a) and (b) of the Rome Statute, ICC-01/09-02/11-382, 23 January 2012 (declining to confirm the charges against Ali); *Yekatom and Ngaïssona* Confirmation Decision, n 144 (declining to confirm some of the charges); *Prosecutor v Said*, Decision on the confirmation of charges against Mahamat Said Abdel Kani, ICC-01/14-01/21-218, 9 December 2021, paras 125–53 (declining to confirm the charges relating to the CEDAD compound, because the evidence presented was insufficient to establish a link between the events and the suspect).

[156] Schabas, n 34, 734–5 (describing the process as 'a rather significant, costly, and time-consuming process, resulting in decisions numbering in the hundreds of pages'); Ambos, n 108, 356; H. Friman, 'Charges' in G. Sluiter et al. (eds), *International Criminal Procedure: Principles and Rules* (OUP, 2013), 381, 471.

[157] *Katanga and Ngudjolo*, Confirmation of Charges Decision, n 129, paras 62–4; *Abu Garda*, Decision on the Confirmation of Charges, n 105, para. 38; *Mbarushimana*, Decision on the Confirmation of Charges, n 138, para. 41.

[158] *Gbagbo* Adjournment Decision, n 137, para. 25.

[159] T. Mariniello and N. Pons, 'The Confirmation of Charges at the International Criminal Court: A Tale of Two Models' in T. Mariniello (ed.), *The International Criminal Court in Search of its Purpose and Identity* (Routledge, 2015), 217.

[160] By contrast, the arrest warrant followed the issuance of an indictment before the ICTY/ICTR and it was widely accepted that the prosecution still had investigations to carry out into this individual accused once the indictment was issued. However, if the accused was captured and transferred to the

be fully informed of the charges and supporting evidence against them.[161] To confirm the charges on the basis of one body of evidence and then allow the prosecution to gather different evidence to be presented at trial would effectively ambush the defence at trial. What is more, we might ask whether, with the benefit of hindsight and in light of Laurent Gbagbo's ultimate acquittal, as discussed at length in section B above, the Pre-Trial Chamber's adjournment decision was arguably not as wrongheaded as commentators at the time thought it to be.

In recent years, we have witnessed a move towards more slimmed-down confirmation of charges decisions and a less thorough evaluation of the evidence at this stage. The judges' move towards this more streamlined approach is apparently influenced by (or reflected in) the Court's Chambers Practice Manual, a document written by the judges themselves which is not anticipated by the legal framework of the Court and is therefore not binding on any Chamber.[162] On some occasions, the Manual has been treated as holding a normative force that ought not to attach to a non-binding document.[163] For example, the Independent Expert Review (IER) chided '[t]he failure of the Pre-Trial Division to consistently follow the guidance of the Chambers Practice Manual in relation to the way the confirmation decision should be set out'.[164] The IER welcomed the decision confirming the charges in *Ongwen* as 'an example of the clarity that would result were the Division as a whole to adhere to the agreed recommendation contained in the Chambers Practice Manual'.[165] Let us examine that model of clarity in depth. The 'findings' part of the *Ongwen* confirmation decision totals fewer than 50 pages, with only 37 footnotes,[166] thus making it unclear what the evidentiary basis for those findings (on 70 counts of crimes against humanity and war crimes) actually was.[167] The list of charges confirmed is almost the same length as the complete statement of the Chamber's factual and legal findings. By way of comparison, the confirmation decision issued in the case of Charles Blé Goudé in December 2014, confirming just four counts of crimes against humanity, has an 'analysis of the

Tribunal, then proceedings had to start promptly, which meant that the prosecution was sometimes taken by surprise, as Andrew Cayley describes vividly in his account of the *Blaškić* case: Cayley, n 102.

[161] Article 67(1)(a), ICC Statute.

[162] Discussed at length in Y. McDermott, 'The International Criminal Court's Chambers Practice Manual: Towards a Return to Judicial Law Making in International Criminal Procedure?' (2017) 15 *Journal of International Criminal Justice* 873.

[163] Ibid.; cf. K.L. Ring, 'The Evolution of the Procedure for Reviewing Victim Applications at the International Criminal Court' (2023) 21 *Journal of International Criminal Justice* 29, 52 (arguing that the approach set out in the Manual for review of victim participation applications was effectively ignored for years until the Manual was amended to reflect what Chambers were actually doing.

[164] IER Report, n 42, para. 489, citing the *Yekatom and Ngaïssona* and *Al Hassan* confirmation decisions as examples.

[165] Ibid.

[166] *Prosecutor v Ongwen*, Decision on the confirmation of charges against Dominic Ongwen, ICC-02/04-01/15-422-Red, 23 March 2016, paras 46–159.

[167] Discussed further in McDermott, n 162, 894–5.

evidence' that spans 72 pages with no fewer than 421 footnotes referencing the evidence.[168]

This example shows that the newer model of confirmation decision—as expressly encouraged by the Independent Expert Review—has led to a less in-depth evaluation of the evidence presented. As Judge Perrin de Brichambaut pointed out in a dissenting opinion, plenty of evidence was set out in detail by the prosecution, but it was simply not referenced in the confirmation decision, making it difficult for the parties to determine the evidentiary basis for each finding.[169] The Manual similarly 'streamlines' the proceedings for confirmation hearings, with provisions against live witnesses and in-depth analysis charts,[170] which earlier Pre-Trial Chambers found helpful in determining whether the requisite standard of proof had been met.[171] It would be unfortunate if the purported efficiencies of this less rigorous approach led to weaker cases proceeding to trial, causing greater inefficiencies and cost, not just to the budget of the Court but also to the liberty of the accused, in the long run.

iii. Beyond reasonable doubt

Almost universally, international criminal tribunals have adopted proof beyond reasonable doubt as the requisite standard for entering a conviction.[172] The IMT and IMTFE did not expressly include a standard of proof in their founding documents, but the idea that the guilt of the accused must be proven beyond reasonable doubt was expressed on several occasions.[173] The ECCC included beyond

[168] Ibid., 895, citing *Prosecutor v Blé Goudé*, Decision on the Confirmation of Charges against Charles Blé Goudé, ICC-02/11-02/11-186, 11 December 2014, paras 17–182.

[169] *Prosecutor v Ongwen*, Decision on the Defence Request for Leave to Appeal the Decision on the Confirmation of Charges, ICC-02/04-01/15-428, 29 April 2016, Partially dissenting opinion of Judge Perrin de Brichambaut, ICC-02/04-01/15-428-Anx, 10 May 2016, paras 9–10.

[170] Chambers Practice Manual, n 148, paras 42–4. Cf. however, the decisions in *Abd-Al-Rahman* and *Said*, n 144, asking for a brief that links each statement of fact with the underpinning evidence supporting that statement.

[171] *Prosecutor v Bemba*, Decision Adjourning the Hearing pursuant to Article 61(7)(c)(ii) of the Rome Statute, ICC-01/05-01/08-388, 3 March 2009, para. 11.

[172] Article 66(3), ICC Statute; Rule 87(A), ICTY RPE; Rule 87(A), ICTR RPE; Rule 87(A), SCSL RPE; Rule 104(A), IRMCT RPE; Rule 140(1), KSC RPE; Article 16(3)(c), STL Statute.

[173] Nuremberg Trial Proceedings, Vol. 22, Two Hundred and Eighteenth Day, 1 October 1946, 555; 572–3 (acquitting Schacht and van Papen because their guilt had not been established beyond reasonable doubt); IMTFE, Opening Statement of President Webb ('The onus will be on the prosecution to establish guilt beyond a reasonable doubt'): see B.V.A. Röling and C.F. Rüter (eds), *The Tokyo Judgment: The International Military Tribunal for the Far East (IMTFE) 29 April 1946–12 November 1948, Vol II* (Amsterdam University Press, 1977), 22–3; *United States v Flick et al.*, US Military Tribunal at Nuremberg, Judgment, 22 December 1947, 3 ('Some safeguards written in the constitution and statutes of the United States as to persons charged with crime, among others such as the presumption of innocence, the rule that conviction is dependent upon proof of the crime charged beyond reasonable doubt, and the right of the accused to be advised and defended by counsel, are recognized as binding on the Tribunal, as they were recognized by the International Military Tribunal').

reasonable doubt in the English and Khmer-language versions of its Internal Rules, but the French version referred to the judge's '*intime conviction*'.[174]

This discrepancy before the ECCC led to an interesting discussion as to whether there is a substantive difference between the notions of reasonable doubt and '*l'intime conviction*'.[175] The literature generally distinguishes between the objective nature of the former and the subjective, or inward-looking, nature of the latter.[176] For proof beyond reasonable doubt (which is rarely defined in the legal systems in which it is employed[177]), the fact-finder's doubt must be reasonable. Reasonableness in this context is generally understood in the negative: it does not require 'proof beyond a shadow of a doubt'[178] nor the entertaining of 'fanciful possibilities'.[179] In *Rutaganda*, the ICTR Appeals Chamber defined the standard as follows:

> The reasonable doubt standard in criminal law cannot consist in imaginary or frivolous doubt based on empathy or prejudice. It must be based on logic and common sense, and have a rational link to the evidence, lack of evidence, or inconsistencies in the evidence.[180]

The French Code of Criminal Procedure, by contrast, shows the subjectivity of *l'intime conviction*, asking judges to 'question themselves in silence and reflection and to seek in the sincerity of their conscience what impression has been made on their reason by the evidence brought against the accused and the arguments of his defence' and ultimately consider 'are you inwardly convinced?'[181] In other Continental systems, we see a somewhat different approach; Spain's *Ley de*

[174] Rule 87(1), ECCC IR.

[175] *KAING Guek Eav* alias *Duch ('Case 001')*, Judgment, 001/18-07-2007/ECCC/TC (E188), 26 July 2010, paras 44–5; *NUON Chea et al. ('Case 002')*, Judgment, 002/19-09-2007/ECCC/TC (E313), 7 August 2014, para. 22.

[176] M. Klamberg, 'Epistemological Controversies and Evaluation of Evidence in International Criminal Trials' in K.J. Heller et al. (eds), *The Oxford Handbook of International Criminal Law* (OUP, 2020), 450.

[177] In England and Wales, juries are instructed that they must be 'sure': Crown Court Compendium, Part 1; *Miah* [2018] EWCA Crim 563; *R* v *Yap Chuan Ching* (1976) 63 Cr App Rep 7, para. 11. The doctrine is not without criticism: see F. Picinali, 'The Threshold Lies in the Method: Instructing Jurors about Reasoning Beyond Reasonable Doubt' (2015) 19 *International Journal of Evidence and Proof* 139; A. Keane and P. McKeown, 'Time to Abandon "Beyond Reasonable Doubt" and "Sure": The Case for a New Direction on the Criminal Standard and How It Should Be Used' (2019) 6 *Criminal Law Review* 505 (arguing that neither 'beyond reasonable doubt' nor 'sure' is fit for purpose, and should instead be replaced by 'no realistic doubt'); H.L. Ho, *A Philosophy of Evidence Law: Justice in the Search for Truth* (OUP, 2008), 455 ('It is a mystery why a doctrine held in such high esteem should yet be so elusive').

[178] Denning LJ in *Miller v Minister of Pensions* (1947) 2 ALL ER 272.

[179] Ibid.

[180] *Prosecutor v Rutaganda*, Judgment, ICTR-96-3-A, 26 May 2003, para. 488. Cited with approval in, *inter alia*, *Prosecutor v Ngudjolo*, Judgment on the Prosecutor's appeal against the decision of Trial Chamber II entitled 'Judgment pursuant to article 74 of the Statute', ICC-01/04-02/-12-271-Corr, 7 April 2015, para. 109.

[181] French Code of Criminal Procedure, n 21, Article 353.

Enjuiciamiento Civil refers to the '*reglas de la sana critíca*'[182] (the rules of sound critique), which are generally taken to incorporate 'common sense rules of reason and the average experience of the world' in evaluating the evidence.[183] In Italy, the concept of *prudente apprezzamento*[184] similarly urges prudence in weighing the evidence.[185] In these systems, Cumiz and dei Vecchi have argued:

> the ground for a rational evaluation of proof is not defined by reference to formal standards, but by requiring the court to articulate sound arguments based upon available and reliable background knowledge (the *Erfahrungssaetze* of the German literature or the *massime di esperienza* of the Italian legal theory) and to the standards of inference provided by the common culture.[186]

Thus, we can conclude that both formulations on the standard of proof for conviction require a rational foundation in the evidence,[187] and any difference between them may be a 'matter of semantics'.[188] This is especially so given the ICC Appeals Chamber's recent endorsement of the *reglas de la sana critíca* from the Spanish legal tradition in the context of the Court's beyond reasonable doubt standard, as discussed further in Chapter 7. The ECCC, ultimately, adopted what it called 'a common approach' based on 'the sufficiency of the evidence', whereby, 'upon a reasoned assessment of evidence', any doubt as to guilt was interpreted in favour of the accused.[189]

Proof beyond reasonable doubt requires that if any reasonable explanation of the evidence (or lack thereof) other than guilt exists, then the accused must be acquitted.[190] Thus, the Trial Chamber's role is not to consider which of the theories of the case (prosecution or defence) is the more convincing, but to analyse whether the prosecution theory of guilt is the only reasonable explanation of the evidence. The standard of proof does not require that *every* hypothesis or possibility of innocence be excluded, but if a rational conclusion can be drawn that is not one of guilt,

182 *Ley de Enjuiciamiento Civil*, Ley 1/2000, 7 January 2000, Articles 316, 348, and 376.

183 J. Cumiz and D. dei Vecchi, 'Estándares de prueba y ponderación de derechos en la Corte Penal Internacional' (2019) *InDret* 2.2019, online at https://indret.com/estandares-de-prueba-y-ponderacion-de-derechos-en-la-corte-penal-internacional/ (last accessed 24 June 2023), text to note 38 (translation author's own).

184 Italian Code of Criminal Procedure, n 21, Article 116.

185 M. Taruffo, 'Rethinking the Standards of Proof' (2003) 51 *American Journal of Comparative Law* 659.

186 Cumiz and dei Vecchi, n 183, text to note 39 (translation author's own).

187 Klamberg, n 176, 455 ('Under a more modern view, this purely subjective *conviction intime* no longer suffices; findings of fact must now also be supported by a high degree of objective (or intersubjective) probability').

188 M.G. Karnavas, 'Making Sense of the Standard & Burden of Proof in Hybrid Courts: Reflections on the Common Law & Civil Law Approaches to Proof—Part IV', 5 July 2016, online at https://michaelgkarnavas.net/blog/2016/07/05/standard-burden-of-proof-hybrid-courts-part-iv/ (last accessed 24 June 2023).

189 *Duch* Judgment, n 175, para. 45; *Nuon Chea* Judgment, n 175, para. 22.

190 *Lubanga* Trial Judgment, n 19, para. 111; *Ngudjolo* Trial Judgment, n 26, para. 71.

the court must acquit.[191] This raises a question about the compatibility of the provisions for majority judgments with the standard of proof; if one judge on a three-judge bench has doubts, the argument goes, surely that should be sufficient to raise reasonable doubt?[192] Ultimately, however, it is well established that collective certainty is not required; an individual judge can still dissent on the question of guilt while a valid conviction is entered by the majority.

A further issue is *what* must be proven beyond reasonable doubt. The Trial Chamber in *Bemba et al.* noted that the evidentiary standard 'must be applied to establish all the facts underpinning the elements of the particular offence and the mode of liability alleged against the accused'.[193] A distinction is drawn between so-called material facts, that is, those facts underpinning a specific element of a crime or mode of liability[194] and those facts that are indispensable for entering a conviction,[195] and 'subsidiary facts', which are pieces of background information or other

[191] *Prosecutor v Mrkšić* et al., Judgment, IT-95-13/1-A, 5 May 2009, para. 220 ('the proof must be such as to exclude not every hypothesis or possibility of innocence, but every fair or rational hypothesis which may be derived from the evidence, except that of guilt') (citations omitted). See also, *Prosecutor v Delalić et al.*, Judgment, IT-96-21-T, 16 November 1998, para. 601 (citing *Miller*, n 178: 'If the evidence is so strong against a man as to leave only a remote possibility in his favour, which can be dismissed with the sentence, "of course it is possible, but not in the least probable", the case is proved beyond a reasonable doubt, but nothing short of that will suffice'); *Prosecutor v Ngudjolo*, Judgment on the Prosecutor's appeal against the decision of Trial Chamber II entitled 'Judgment pursuant to article 74 of the Statute', ICC-01/04-02/12-271-Corr, 7 April 2015, Joint Dissenting Opinion of Judge Trendafilova and Judge Tarfusser, ICC-01/04-02/12-271-AnxA, 27 February 2015, para. 56 ('The "reasonable doubt" standard does not leave room for imaginary doubts or speculative observations on the guilt or innocence of the accused that cannot reasonably be derived from the evidence'); *Prosecutor v Karera*, Judgment, ICTR-01-74-A, 2 February 2009, para. 34.

[192] *Prosecutor v Galić*, Judgment and Opinion, IT-98-29-T, 5 December 2003, Separate and Partially Dissenting Opinion of Judge Nieto-Navia, para. 17 ('I had expected this plural Trial Chamber to accept my doubts as sufficient to establish that the Prosecution has failed to prove an allegation beyond a reasonable doubt'). See further R.C. Pruitt, 'Guilt by Majority in the International Criminal Tribunal for the Former Yugoslavia: Does This Meet the Standard of Proof "Beyond Reasonable Doubt"?' (1997) 10 *Leiden Journal of International Law* 557, 568–70; Schabas and McDermott, n 14, 1960; D. Jacobs, 'The ICC Katanga Judgment: A Commentary (Part 2): Regulation 55 and the Modes of Liability', *Spreading the Jam*, 11 March 2014, online at https://dovjacobs.com/2014/03/11/the-icc-katanga-judgment-a-commentary-part-2-regulation-55-and-the-modes-of-liability/ (last accessed 24 June 2023).

[193] *Ongwen* Trial Judgment, n 35, para. 231 (referring to the Prosecution's burden of proof beyond reasonable doubt 'with respect to the facts "indispensable for entering a conviction", namely, in this case, the absence of any ground excluding criminal responsibility and, thus, the guilt of the accused'); *Prosecutor v Bemba et al.*, Judgment pursuant to Article 74 of the Statute, ICC-01/05-01/13-1989, 19 October 2016, para. 186 ('the evidentiary standard of beyond reasonable doubt must be applied to establish all the facts underpinning the elements of the particular offence and the mode of liability alleged against the accused').

[194] *Prosecutor v Lubanga*, Public redacted Judgment on the appeal of Mr Thomas Lubanga Dyilo against his conviction, ICC-01/04-01/06-3121-Red, 1 December 2014, paras 121–3; see further *Prosecutor v Gotovina et al.*, Judgment, IT-06-90-T, 15 April 2011, para. 14 ('each and every element of the offences charged against an accused must be proven beyond a reasonable doubt').

[195] *Prosecutor v Halilović*, Judgment, IT-01-48-A, 16 October 2007, para. 129 ('a trier of fact is called upon to make findings beyond reasonable doubt based on all of the evidence on the trial record—direct or circumstantial—not only on facts which are essential to proving the elements of the crimes and the forms of responsibility. There might be other facts that need to be proven beyond reasonable doubt due to the way in which the case was pleaded in the indictment and presented during trial to the Defence and to the Trial Chamber. All facts underlying the elements of the crime or the form of responsibility alleged as well as all those, which are indispensable for entering a conviction, must be proven beyond reasonable doubt').

information from which a material fact can be inferred.[196] Material facts must be proven to the beyond reasonable doubt standard.[197] However, there may be circumstances where *some* material facts pleaded in the indictment/document containing the charges are proven to the beyond reasonable doubt standard and others are not. In those circumstances, the question is whether the material facts that *have* been proven to the requisite standard are sufficient to prove the constitutive elements of the crime and mode of liability charged.[198] The fact that some of the material facts have not been established beyond reasonable doubt may mean that some of the elements of the crime charged and mode of responsibility alleged are unproven, leading to a partial or full acquittal, depending on the circumstances. In recent years, there has been some debate among judges about a perceived erroneous approach whereby evidence is 'evaluated in a fragmentary manner or one which would lead to the application of the beyond reasonable doubt standard to all the facts in the case, and even to those not indispensable for entering a conviction'.[199] These questions pertaining to the evaluation of the evidence as a whole are discussed at length in Chapter 6.[200]

D. Lowering the beyond reasonable doubt standard?

In recent years, it has been suggested that perhaps the 'beyond reasonable doubt' standard is too high for international criminal tribunals, in light of the complexity of proving international crimes and the difficulties in carrying out effective investigations. Nevertheless, the idea of lowering the standard of proof has gained some academic traction.[201] The overarching argument seems to be founded on an assumption that incomplete and/or flawed evidence, incapable of meeting the standard of proof beyond reasonable doubt, is the best that international criminal tribunals can do, and that the goalposts need to shift to accept that.[202]

[196] E.g. *Prosecutor v Nourain and Jerbo*, Decision on the Confirmation of Charges, ICC-02/05-03/09-121-Corr-Red, 8 March 2011, para. 37.

[197] *Prosecutor v Ayyash et al.*, Judgment, STL-11-01/T/TC, 18 August 2020, para. 218 ('All facts underlying the elements of the crime or the form of responsibility alleged as well as all those, which are indispensable for entering a conviction, must be proven beyond reasonable doubt'); citing *Halilović* Appeals judgment, n 195, para. 129.

[198] *Prosecutor v Ntagerura et al.*, Judgment, ICTR-99-46-A, 7 July 2006, para. 174; *Ayyash et al.* Judgment, n 197, paras 201–22.

[199] *Prosecutor v Katanga*, Judgment pursuant to Article 74 of the Statute, ICC-01/04-01/07-3436, 7 March 2014, Concurring Opinion of Judges Diarra and Cotte, ICC-01/04-01/07-3436-AnxII-tENG, 13 March 2014, para. 4.

[200] Chapter 6, section C.

[201] L. May and S. Fyfe, *International Criminal Tribunals: A Normative Defense* (CUP, 2017), 160; Combs, n 11, 344.

[202] May and Fyfe, n 201 ('given the relatively poor access to solid evidence'); M. De Guzman, *Shocking the Conscience of Humanity: Gravity and the Legitimacy of International Criminal Law* (OUP, 2020), 145.

For example, Nancy Combs argued that a reconceptualization of the standard of proof may be needed, because reasonable doubt in international criminal cases is more likely attributable to flawed investigations than to a lack of sufficient evidence.[203] In other words, Combs assumed that evidence pointing to the guilt of the accused probably exists, it is just that prosecution investigators do not always manage to source it. This assumption seems incompatible with the presumption of innocence and the burden of proof which makes it very clear that it is for the prosecution to prove the guilt of the accused.[204]

Combs also argued that, compared to domestic cases, there is a greater likelihood that the defendant in an international criminal trial is responsible for *some* crime, even if it is not the specific crime or mode of liability charged, or that the defendant may bear some moral culpability as a high-ranking official at the time the crimes were committed by individuals who were politically or militarily aligned, even if the accused's liability cannot be proven.[205] As Simon de Smet has convincingly argued, there appears to be no empirical basis for these sweeping claims.[206] Aside from the obvious breaches of the right to a fair trial, especially the presumption of innocence, that would arise if we accepted Combs's argument that the accused is probably responsible for something and so should be convicted even if the requisite material facts are not proven beyond reasonable doubt, the argument is also highly problematic from the perspective of rectitude of decision. A judgment that convicts an accused where their culpability has not been proven to the requisite standard is nothing short of a miscarriage of justice.[207]

E. Conclusion

This chapter analysed the burden of proof applicable in international criminal trials and the standards of proof that are applied at each stage of proceedings. In relation to

[203] Combs, n 11, 343–64.

[204] See *Prosecutor v Lubanga*, Public redacted Judgment on the appeal of Mr Thomas Lubanga Dyilo against his conviction, ICC-01/04-01/06-3121-Red, 1 December 2014, Dissenting opinion of Judge Ušacka, ICC-01/04-01/06-3121-Anx2, 1 December 2014, para. 33 (describing the tendency to relax the standard of 'beyond reasonable doubt' in the international context as 'inconsistent with the explicit wording of the applicable legal framework').

[205] Combs also suggested that a lower standard may be applied by international criminal tribunals in practice while claiming to uphold the beyond reasonable doubt standard. This is discussed further in ibid., Dissenting opinion of Judge Ušacka ('In my view, if the exigencies of international criminal prosecutions require the application of a lower standard, the proper course of action would be to amend the applicable law, rather than paying lip service to the high threshold required to establish criminal responsibility, while *de facto* applying a lower standard.').

[206] De Smet, n 84, 884–7.

[207] X. Agirre Aranburu, 'Methodology for the Criminal Investigation of International Crimes' in A. Smeulers et al. (eds), *Collective Violence and International Criminal Justice: An Interdisciplinary Approach* (Intersentia, 2010), 353, 357 reflects that in the pre-modern era, lowering the standard of proof in the case of particularly atrocious crimes, justified by the maxim *in attrocissimis leviores coniecturae sufficiunt et licet iudice iura transgredi* ('in very atrocious crimes, light conjectures suffice, and it is licit for the judge to transgress the law'), was dismissed by Becarria as a 'cruel imbecility'.

the burden of proof, which rests with the prosecution, we discussed this provision's interplay with the presumption of innocence and analysed some recent controversies that have arisen in relation to the burden of proof. These included the question of the applicable burden of proof where the accused raises an affirmative defence, such as duress or diminished responsibility. It was argued that a distinction can be drawn between the burden of persuasion (which always remains with the prosecution) and the burden of production, under which a party is expected to substantiate claims with evidence to show that they are not merely hypothetical or frivolous.

The existence of 'no case to answer' or 'decision on a motion for a judgment of acquittal' proceedings was found to be an important consequence of the prosecutorial burden of proof. If, by the end of the prosecution case, there are charges that are not supported by the evidence, then the court must acquit on those charges. As we saw in section B above, given that this procedure was not incorporated in the statutory framework of the ICC, the precise standard of proof applicable was unclear from the inconsistent and sometimes contradictory jurisprudence on the question. The Appeals Chamber's ruling that the applicable standard of proof is 'beyond reasonable doubt' was argued to be misplaced, but this standard is likely to be followed in future cases.

The standard of proof for the issuance of a warrant of arrest, the confirmation of charges, and conviction were each analysed in depth in section C. In relation to the 'reasonable grounds to believe' standard for arrest warrants, we saw that the jurisprudence of the Court was detailed on what this standard does not require, but less clear on what it does. To satisfy the 'substantial grounds to believe' standard for the confirmation of the charges, it was seen that there has been a move towards shorter decisions in recent years with a less clear link between the evidence underpinning each charge and the charges confirmed. This streamlining was no doubt inspired by the frequent calls for efficiency in the Court's pre-trial procedures, and has been welcomed by some commentators, but a less thorough evaluation of the evidence (against the relevant standard of proof) is inconsistent with the ICC Statute and the purpose of confirmation processes. Moreover, this approach may not conform with the accused's right to be informed of the charges, where confirmed charges are listed at the end of the decision but the evidential reasoning that led to the confirmation of these charges is opaque.

The standard of proof for conviction—beyond reasonable doubt—was compared with the *intime conviction* standard applied in inquisitorial systems and ultimately it was argued that both standards require a rational link to be established between the evidence, the inferences that can be drawn from that evidence, and the ultimate probandum or thing that must be proven in the trial. This is a theme to which we will return in Chapter 6. Ultimately, proof beyond reasonable doubt requires that if two reasonable readings of the evidence are possible, and one of them suggests innocence, then the court must acquit. This chapter has argued that calls to lower the standard of proof in light of the unique challenges of international criminal investigations (as discussed in Chapter 1) are misplaced and founded on a serious assumption that weak evidence is the best that international courts can ever hope to collect—an assumption with no empirical foundation.

5
The Evaluation of Different Forms of Evidence

A. Introduction

The previous chapter analysed the prosecutorial burden of proof and its implications, as well as the different standards of proof that attach to distinct procedural stages. This chapter follows on from that discussion by examining how judges approach the weighing and assessment of different categories of evidence in determining whether the standard of proof beyond reasonable doubt has been met. As noted in Chapter 4, some have argued that judges should undertake a less thorough evaluation of the evidence at earlier stages of proceedings, such as the confirmation of charges stage, where the standard of proof is lower.[1] Relatedly, there is a debate over whether seemingly 'weaker' forms of evidence, such as media reports or the reports of non-governmental organisations, may suffice to prove an allegation to a lower standard of proof at an earlier stage in proceedings.[2] We discuss these forms of evidence, among others, in section D below.

This chapter examines, in section B, some general features of the framework for evidence evaluation in international criminal trials, including the principles of flexibility and free evaluation of the evidence, the need to exercise caution in certain circumstances, the duty to provide a reasoned opinion, and the principle of *in dubio pro reo*. Section C then discusses the evaluation of testimonial evidence, while section D outlines how other forms of evidence have been weighed. Chapter 6 builds upon this discussion by analysing Trial Chambers' approaches to weighing the totality of the evidence, in determining whether the guilt of the accused has been proven beyond reasonable doubt.

In keeping with a common theme of this work, this chapter demonstrates that there is a great deal of flexibility built into the legal frameworks of the international criminal tribunals, with wide judicial discretion over how much weight to afford to distinct pieces of evidence, which tends to be determined on a case-by-case basis. This discretion has led to some divergent approaches, with uncertainty at times about what information the tendering party needs to provide when submitting a piece of evidence to demonstrate its probative value.

[1] See Chapter 4, text to nn 129–53.
[2] See Chapter 4, section C.ii.

Proving International Crimes. Yvonne McDermott, Oxford University Press. © Yvonne McDermott 2024.
DOI: 10.1093/oso/9780198842972.003.0005

B. Features of the framework for evidence evaluation

i. General principles and practices

Chapter 1 analysed flexibility and the free evaluation of evidence as overarching features of international criminal evidence.[3] Flexibility pervades practices on weight as well as admissibility.[4] It means that, just as international criminal tribunals are unshackled from the strictures of domestic admissibility rules on the categories of acceptable evidence, national conventions on the weighing the evidence also have no place in international criminal trials.[5] While some domestic jurisdictions retain, for example, a rule of *unus testis, nullus testis* (one witness is no witness),[6] practice has consistently emphasised that there is no formal corroboration rule in international criminal law.[7] For example, in *Tadić*, the ICTY noted that the ad hoc tribunals had the power 'to accept as evidence the testimony of

[3] See Chapter 1, section B. See further, R. Dixon, 'Developing International Rules of Evidence for the Yugoslav and Rwanda Tribunals' (1997) 7 *Transnational Law and Contemporary Problems* 81; G. Boas, 'Creating Laws of Evidence for International Criminal Law: The ICTY and the Principle of Flexibility' (2001) 12 *Criminal Law Forum* 41; M. Klamberg, 'General Requirements for the Admission of Evidence' in G. Sluiter et al. (eds), *International Criminal Procedure: Principles and Rules* (OUP, 2013), 1016.

[4] G. McIntyre, 'ICTR—Assessment of Evidence', *Symposium on the Legacy of the International Criminal Tribunal for Rwanda*, 6–7 November 2014, Arusha, Tanzania, 1–3.

[5] *Prosecutor v Taylor*, Judgment, SCSL-03-01-A, 26 September 2013 ('*Taylor* Appeal Judgment'), para. 250; *Prosecutor v Gotovina*, Judgment, IT-06-90-T, 15 April 2011 ('*Gotovina* Trial Judgment'), para. 38.

[6] L. van Lent and I. Braam, 'The Dutch *Unus Testis, Nullus Testis* Rule' in J. Chalmers, F. Leverick, and A. Shaw (eds), *Post-Corroboration Safeguards Review Report of the Academic Expert Group* (Scottish Government, 2014), 250, discussing the relevant provisions from the Dutch Code of Criminal Procedure (1926) and recent case law on the rule. Note, however, that corroboration rules appear vanishingly rare: the editors of this report note that, 'While common lawyers sometimes speak loosely of civilian systems requiring corroboration, the group's enquiries have yielded no sign that this is true as a contemporary fact, apart from the Dutch recognition of the principle of *unus testis, nullus testis*' (Chalmers et al., 'Executive Summary', xx).

[7] Rule 63(4), ICC RPE ('Without prejudice to article 66, paragraph 3 [the guilt of the accused must be proven beyond reasonable doubt in order to convict], a Chamber shall not impose a legal requirement that corroboration is required in order to prove any crime within the jurisdiction of the Court, in particular, crimes of sexual violence'); *Prosecutor v Kayishema and Ruzindana*, Judgment, ICTR-96-10-A and ICTR-96-17-A, 13 December 2004, para. 132; *Prosecutor v Delalić* et al., Judgment, IT-96-21-A, 20 February 2001 ('*Čelebići* Appeal Judgment'), paras 492 and 506; *Specialist Prosecutor v Gucati and Haradinaj*, Appeal Judgment, KSC-CA-2022-01, 2 February 2023 ('*Gucati and Haradinaj* Appeal Judgment'), para. 36; *Prosecutor v D. Milošević*, Judgment, IT-98-29/1-A, 12 November 2009, para. 215; *Prosecutor v Aleksovski*, Judgment, IT-95-14/1-A, 24 March 2000, para. 62; *Prosecutor v Ntaganda*, Public redacted version of Judgment on the appeals of Mr Bosco Ntaganda and the Prosecutor against the decision of Trial Chamber VI of 8 July 2019 entitled 'Judgment', ICC-01/04-02/06-2666-Red, 30 March 2021 ('*Ntaganda* Appeal Judgment'), para. 782; *Prosecutor v Lubanga*, Public redacted Judgment on the appeal of Mr Thomas Lubanga Dyilo against his conviction, ICC-01/04-01/06-3121-Red, 1 December 2014 ('*Lubanga* Appeal Judgment'), para. 218; *Prosecutor v Haradinaj* et al., Judgment, IT-04-84-T, 3 April 2008, para. 14 ('*Haradinaj et al.* Trial Judgment'); *Prosecutor v Kupreškić* et al., Appeal Judgment, IT-95-16-A, 23 October 2001 ('*Kupreškić et al.* Appeal Judgment'), para. 33 (noting, however, Rule 90(B) ICTY RPE's rule that a judgment cannot be based on the uncorroborated testimony of a child witness testifying without a solemn declaration).

a single witness on a material fact without need for corroboration'.[8] In addition, many tribunals have specific rules outlining that corroboration is not required in cases of sexual assault.[9]

As is widely known, admissibility has no bearing on the weight to be attributed to a piece of evidence; any piece of evidence may be admitted but ultimately not be relied upon in any way in the final judgment.[10] Weight is defined as the 'qualitative assessment of the probative value that the Trial Chamber ascribes to a specific item of evidence in relation to facts in issue in the case'.[11] Because the evaluation of evidence occurs outwith the tribunals' legal frameworks, it is often said that fact-finding 'begins where the law ends'.[12]

While evidence is weighed holistically,[13] the probative value of a particular piece of evidence is determined by a multitude of factors, including whether the evidence is direct or indirect in nature, and whether it is corroborated by or consistent with other evidence on the record.[14] Credibility and reliability are two central facets in assessing evidence.[15] While closely related, these two crucial factors are distinct: 'credibility' pertains to the trustworthiness of the source,[16] while

[8] *Prosecutor v Tadić*, Judgment, IT-94-1-A, 15 July 1999, para. 65.

[9] Rule 96(i), ICTY RPE; Rule 96(i), ICTR RPE; Rule 139(3) KSC RPE; Rule 63(4) ICC RPE.

[10] *Prosecutor v Boškoski and Tarčulovski*, Judgment, IT-04-82-T, 10 July 2008, para. 10; *Prosecutor v Bemba*, Decision on the admission into evidence of items deferred in the Chamber's 'Decision on the Prosecution's Application for Admission of Materials into Evidence Pursuant to Article 64(9) of the Rome Statute', ICC-01/05-01/08-2721, 27 June 2013, para. 9; *Prosecutor v Bemba*, Public Redacted Version of 'Decision on the Prosecution's Application for Admission of Materials into Evidence Pursuant to Article 64(9) of the Rome Statute' of 6 September 2012, ICC-0l/05-01/08-2299-Red, 8 October 2012 ('*Bemba* Admissibility Decision'), para. 11; *Prosecutor v Ntaganda*, Decision on Prosecution's request for admission of documentary evidence, ICC-01/04-02/06-1838, 28 March 2017, para. 6; *Prosecutor v Ntaganda*, Decision on Prosecution's first request for admission of documentary evidence, ICC-01/04-02/06-1181, 19 February 2016, para. 7.

[11] *Prosecutor v Milutinović* et al, Judgment, IT-05-87-T, 26 February 2009, para. 36.

[12] G. Chlevickaitė, B. Holá, and C. Bijleveld, 'Suspicious Minds? Empirical Analysis of Insider Witness Assessments at the ICTY, ICTR and ICC' (2023) 20 *European Journal of Criminology* 185, 187, quoting M. Stone, 'Instant Lie Detection? Demeanour and Credibility in Criminal Trials' [1991] *Criminal Law Review* 821.

[13] See Chapter 6.

[14] *Prosecutor v Muthaura et al.*, Decision on the Defence Applications for Leave to Appeal the Single Judge's Order to Reduce the Number of *Viva Voce* Witnesses, ICC-01/09-02/11-275, 1 September 2011, para. 26.

[15] *Prosecutor v Ongwen*, Judgment on the appeal of Mr Ongwen against the decision of Trial Chamber IX of 4 February 2021 entitled 'Trial Judgment', ICC-02/04-01/15-2022-Red, 15 December 2022 ('*Ongwen* Appeal Judgment'), para. 17 (the Trial Chamber 'has the primary responsibility to determine the reliability and credibility of the evidence and then comprehensively assess the weight of the evidence'). See also, *Ntaganda* Appeal Judgment, n 7, para. 40.

[16] *Prosecutor v Bemba*, Judgment pursuant to Article 74 of the Statute, ICC-01/05-01/08-3343, 21 March 2016 ('*Bemba* Trial Judgment'), para. 229; *Lubanga* Appeal Judgment, n 7, Dissenting opinion of Judge Ušacka, ICC-01/04-01/06-3121-Anx2, 1 December 2014, footnote 32 ('The ICTY/ICTR's jurisprudence uses the words credibility and reliability as distinct concepts in relation to witness testimony. According to this jurisprudence, the assessment of credibility involves an assessment of whether a witness is truthful and should be believed, which does not necessarily depend on the actual veracity of the evidence presented. In contrast, an assessment of reliability involves an objective determination of whether the evidence presented proves the fact at issue'); *Prosecutor v Bikindi*, Judgment, ICTR-01-72-A, 18 March 2010, para. 114.

'reliability' refers to the quality of the information provided.[17] David Lagnado gives a good example of credible witnesses whose testimony transpired to be unreliable.[18] In 1912, a murder suspect in France had an alibi that he was drinking and playing cards with some friends at the time of the murder, and his friends confirmed that he was with them all night until they all went to bed at around 1 a.m. However, unbeknownst to the suspect's friends, he had set the clock forward by one hour, enabling him to slip out before midnight to meet his victim and commit the murder. The friends' accounts were credible, but transpired to be unreliable as they were founded on a false belief. Similarly, in *Lubanga*, Judge Ušacka noted:

> Although a witness may be honest (and therefore credible), the evidence he or she gives may nonetheless be unreliable due to the 'vagaries of human perception', or because it relates to facts that occurred a long time ago. For example, in our case, an honest and credible witness may be absolutely convinced that he saw children who he thought were twelve years old, but the children in question may actually have been fifteen.[19]

Although, as noted above, there is no formal corroboration rule in international criminal law, whether a piece of evidence is corroborated by other evidence on the record will be a factor in determining its probative value.[20] The ICTR Appeals Chamber reasoned:

> [E]ven if there are some doubts as to the reliability of the testimony of a certain witness, that testimony may be corroborated by other pieces of evidence leading the Trial Chamber to conclude that the witness is credible. Or, on the other hand, a seemingly convincing testimony may be called into question by other evidence which shows that evidence to lack credibility.[21]

[17] *Bemba* Trial Judgment, n 16, para. 230. See also, S. Ferro Ribeiro and D. van der Straten Ponthoz, *International Protocol on the Documentation and Investigation of Sexual Violence in Conflict* (2nd edn, UK Foreign and Commonwealth Office, 2017), 214–23.

[18] D. Lagnado, *Explaining the Evidence: How the Mind Investigates the World* (CUP, 2021), 132–3 (describing the case of Emile Gourbin).

[19] *Lubanga* Appeal Judgment, n 7, Dissenting opinion of Judge Ušacka, ICC-01/04-01/06-3121-Anx2, 1 December 2014, para. 25 (footnotes omitted).

[20] *Prosecutor v Ngudjolo*, Judgment on the Prosecutor's appeal against the decision of Trial Chamber II entitled 'Judgment pursuant to article 74 of the Statute', ICC-01/04-02/12-271-Corr, 7 April 2015 ('*Ngudjolo* Appeal Judgment'), Joint Dissenting Opinion of Judge Trendafilova and Judge Tarfusser, ICC-01/04-02/12-271-AnxA, 27 February 2015, para. 37 ('[T]he determination of whether an individual item of evidence is credible and reliable depends on the extent to which it is corroborated, if at all, by other pieces of evidence').

[21] *Prosecutor v Ntagerura et al.*, Judgment, ICTR-99-46-A, 7 July 2006 ('*Ntagerura et al.* Appeal Judgment'), para. 174.

Despite the absence of rules on the evaluation of evidence in their legal frameworks,[22] the international criminal tribunals have adopted practices on the evaluation of evidence that have been almost universally applied. For example, drawing heavily on the case law of the European Court of Human Rights,[23] they have adopted a practice that a conviction should not be based 'solely or to a decisive extent' on the depositions of a witness whom the accused had no opportunity to question.[24] It has been noted that even if untested evidence were corroborated, a conviction might still be found to have been based to a decisive extent on such evidence, depending on the content of, and importance attached to, both it and the corroborating evidence.[25]

Likewise, as regards circumstantial evidence (that is, evidence that does not speak directly to a fact but to circumstances from which a fact may be reasonably inferred), there appears to be a consistent practice that proof of a material fact must be the only reasonable inference available to the Chamber from that evidence.[26] For example, in a case before the STL, the Contempt Judge inferred that the accused must have received an email and an attached Order from the Tribunal.[27] The Appeals Chamber found that this was an error, because it could also have been inferred from the evidence that she did not receive the email. It stressed:

> This error violates the principle of *in dubio pro reo* and the requirement that all material facts have to be proven beyond reasonable doubt—if another reasonable

[22] An exception is the KSC RPE, which has Rule 139 on 'Assessment of Evidence for the Purposes of Judgment', outlining that: 1. inadmissible evidence shall not be considered by the Panel; 2. the evidence shall be assessed holistically in light of the entire body of evidence; 3. corroboration is not required; 4. the weight of witness testimony hinges on credibility and reliability; 5. circumstantial evidence should be assessed with caution; 6. the panel may accept parts of a piece of evidence and reject others, and 7. the manner in which evidence was collected and its likely impact on the fairness of proceedings will be taken into account.

[23] *Luca v Italy* (2003) 36 EHRR 807; *Al-Khawaja and Tahery v UK* (2009) 49 EHRR 1.

[24] *Prosecutor v Haraqija and Morina*, Judgment on Allegations of Contempt, IT-04-84-R77.4, 17 December 2008 ('*Haraqija and Morina* Trial Judgment'), para. 23; *Ntaganda* Appeal Judgment, n 7, paras 629–30; *Prosecutor v Prlić* et al., Judgment, IT-04-74-A, 29 November 2017, para. 137; *Prosecutor v Popović* et al., Judgment, IT-05-88-A, 30 January 2015 ('*Popović* Appeal Judgment'), para. 96; *KHIEU Samphân* ('*Case 002/02*'), Judgment, 002/19-09-2007-ECCC/TC (E465), 16 November 2018, para. 71; *Prosecutor v Ayyash* et al., Judgment, STL-11-01/T/TC, 18 August 2020 ('*Ayyash et al.* Trial Judgment'), para. 276. See further, Y. McDermott, 'Absent Witnesses and the Right to Confrontation: The Influence of the Jurisprudence of the European Court of Human Rights on International Criminal Law' in P. Lobba and T. Mariniello (eds), *Judicial Dialogue on Human Rights: The Practice of International Criminal Tribunals* (Brill, 2017), 225.

[25] *Haraqija and Morina* Trial Judgment, n 24, para. 24 ('[t]he mere existence of corroborating evidence, however, does not preclude a conviction from being based to a decisive extent on untested evidence. The issue is not one of quantity, but of quality; in other words, how much importance was attached to the corroborating evidence in convicting the accused').

[26] *Čelebići* Appeal Judgment, n 7, para. 458. Later cases noted that the only reasonable inference standard also applies to inferences drawn from direct evidence: *Popović* Appeal Judgment, n 24, para. 12.

[27] *In the Case Against Al Jadeed SAL/New TV SAL and Al Khayat*, Judgment, STL-14-05/T/CJ, 18 September 2015, paras 168–76.

> inference could have been drawn from the totality of the available circumstantial evidence, it necessarily follows that the fact in question was not proven beyond reasonable doubt.[28]

Another form of indirect evidence, hearsay, has been the subject of much commentary and controversy over the years. Chambers have expressed caution in relying on hearsay evidence, declaring 'that the weight or probative value to be afforded to that evidence will usually be less than that given to the testimony of a witness who has given it under a form of oath and who has been cross-examined, although even this will depend upon the infinitely variable circumstances which surround hearsay evidence'.[29] Some have set a more sweeping standard that a conviction will not be entered where the evidence supporting that conviction was based solely on hearsay.[30] The probative value of hearsay evidence (if any) will hinge on factors such as: whether the source of the information was known or anonymous,[31] and, if known, whether the opposing side had the opportunity to cross-examine him or her; whether that source gave the information voluntarily; whether it was 'first-hand' hearsay or more removed; and the level of detail that the witness was able to provide.[32] In their dissenting opinion to the *Ngudjolo* Appeal Judgment, Judges Tarfusser and Trendafilova acknowledged that hearsay generally has a lower probative value, but argued that the Trial Chamber erred in automatically excluding the accounts of several witnesses on the grounds that they were hearsay without considering whether that evidence was corroborated by other evidence on the record.[33]

[28] *In the Case Against Al Jadeed SAL/New TV SAL and Al Khayat*, Judgment on Appeal, STL-14-05/A/AP, 8 March 2016, para. 169.

[29] *Prosecutor v Aleksovski*, Decision on Prosecutor's Appeal on Admissibility of Evidence, IT-95-14/1-AR73, 16 February 1999 ('*Aleksovski* Admissibility Decision'), para. 15, citing *Prosecutor v Tadić*, Decision on the Defence Motion on Hearsay, IT-94-1-T, 5 August 1996, Separate Opinion of Judge Stephen, 2–3. See also, *Ngudjolo* Appeal Judgment, n 20, para. 226; *Prosecutor v Bemba* et al., Judgment pursuant to Article 74 of the Statute, ICC-01/05-01/13-1989, 19 October 2016 ('*Bemba et al.* Trial Judgment'), para. 620; *Prosecutor v Katanga*, Judgment pursuant to Article 74 of the Statute, ICC-01/04-01/07-3436, 7 March 2014 ('*Katanga* Trial Judgment'), para. 90; *Prosecutor v Ntaganda*, Judgment, ICC-01/04-02/06-2359, 8 July 2019 ('*Ntaganda* Trial Judgment'), paras 67–8; *Specialist Prosecutor v Gucati and Haradinaj*, Trial Judgment, KSC-BC-2020-07, 18 May 2022 ('*Gucati and Haradinaj* Trial Judgment'), paras 24–6 and 43; *Gotovina* Trial Judgment, n 5, paras 38, 43, and 49–59; *Taylor* Appeal Judgment, n 5, para. 176 and references therein. The post-Second World War *Ministries Trial* refused to convict one of the defendants (Berger) on one count where the key testimony rested on hearsay and the source of the hearsay was not called as a witness: *United States of America v von Weizsäcker et al. (Ministries)*, Judgment of 11 April 1949, in *Trials of War Criminals Before the Nuremberg Military Tribunals*, Vol. XIV, at 540.

[30] *Gotovina* Trial Judgment, n 5, para. 43.

[31] *Prosecutor v Gbagbo*, Decision adjourning the hearing on the confirmation of charges pursuant to article 61(7)(c)(i) of the Rome Statute, ICC-02/11-01/11-432, 3 June 2013 ('*Gbagbo* Adjournment Decision'), para. 28.

[32] *Aleksovski* Admissibility Decision, n 29, para. 15; *Ngudjolo* Appeal Judgment, *supra* n 20, para. 226; *Gotovina* Trial Judgment, n 5, para. 43.

[33] *Ngudjolo* Appeal Judgment, *supra* note 20, Joint Dissenting Opinion of Judge Trendafilova and Judge Tarfusser, para. 50.

The majority of the Appeals Chamber did not find the Trial Chamber's approach to hearsay unreasonable.[34]

The last overarching feature to note on the evaluation of evidence is the Trial Chamber's duty to provide a reasoned opinion.[35] The practical impact of this obligation is that the Trial Chamber is expected to give reasons as to how it reached the conclusions it did based on the evidence before it.[36] This is important when it comes to appeals, as the judgment 'must enable both the convicted person and the Appeals Chamber to understand *how* the Trial Chamber made its findings based on the evidence before it, to ensure that the accused can exercise his or her right to appeal and for the Appeals Chamber to conduct a meaningful review'.[37] Trial Chambers are not expected to refer to every submission or piece of evidence on the record,[38] nor to explain every step in their reasoning.[39] It is often presumed that the Chamber considered a piece of evidence or testimony even if it did not expressly refer to that evidence in its judgment.[40] However, there are circumstances where the Trial Chamber will be expected to expand on why a piece of evidence was relied upon or not. For example, in *Simba*, the ICTR Appeals Chamber noted

[34] *Ngudjolo* Appeal Judgment, n 20, para. 226.

[35] Article 74(5), ICC Statute; Article 22(2), ICTR Statute; Rule 98(C), ICTR RPE; Article 22(2), ICTY Statute; Rule 98*ter*(C), ICTY RPE; Article 22(2), SCSL Statute; Rule 88(C), SCSL RPE; Article 21(2), IRMCT Statute; Rule 122(C), IRMCT RPE; Article 23, STL Statute; Rule 168(2), STL RPE; Article 43, KSC Law; Rule 78(2), KSC RPE.

[36] *Prosecutor v Bemba* et al., Public Redacted Judgment on the appeals of Mr Jean-Pierre Bemba Gombo, Mr Aimé Kilolo Musamba, Mr Jean-Jacques Mangenda Kabongo, Mr Fidèle Babala Wandu and Mr Narcisse Arido against the decision of Trial Chamber VII entitled 'Judgment pursuant to Article 74 of the Statute', ICC-01/05-01/13-2275-Red, 8 March 2018 ('*Bemba et al.* Appeal Judgment'), para. 102; *Prosecutor v Bemba*, Judgment on the appeal of Mr Jean-Pierre Bemba Gombo against Trial Chamber III's 'Judgment pursuant to Article 74 of the Statute', ICC-01/05-01/08-3636-Red, 8 June 2018, para. 49. Cf. *Prosecutor v Simba*, Judgment, ICTR-01-76-A, 27 November 2007, para. 152 ('[A] Trial Chamber has the obligation to provide a reasoned opinion, but is not required to articulate the reasoning in detail ... There is no guiding principle on the question to determine the extent to which a Trial Chamber is obliged to set out its reasons for accepting or rejecting a particular testimony' (footnotes omitted)).

[37] *Lubanga* Appeal Judgment, n 7, Dissenting opinion of Judge Ušacka, ICC-01/04-01/06-3121-Anx2, 1 December 2014, para. 26 (emphasis in original). See also, *Prosecutor v Nchamihigo*, Judgment, ICTR-01-63-A, 18 March 2010, para. 165.

[38] *Prosecutor v Karera*, Judgment, ICTR-01-74-A, 2 February 2009 ('*Karera* Appeal Judgment'), para. 20; *Kupreškić* et al. Appeal Judgment, n 7, para. 39. *Prosecutor v Kamuhanda*, Judgment, ICTR-99-54A-A, 19 September 2005 ('*Kamuhanda* Appeal Judgement'), para. 32; *Prosecutor v Kajelijeli*, Judgment, ICTR-98-44A-A, 23 May 2005, para. 59; *Prosecutor v Semanza*, Judgment, ICTR-97-20-A, 20 May 2005, paras 130, 149; *Prosecutor v Niyitegeka*, Judgment, ICTR-96-14-A, 9 July 2004, para. 124; *Prosecutor v Rutaganda*, Judgment, ICTR-96-3-A, 26 May 2003, para. 536; *Prosecutor v Musema*, Judgment, ICTR-96-13-A, 16 November 2001 ('*Musema* Appeal Judgment'), paras 18, 277; *Čelebići* Appeal Judgment, n 7, para. 481.

[39] *Simba* Appeal Judgment, n 36, para. 143.

[40] *Prosecutor v Kvočka et al.*, Judgment, IT-98-30/1-A, 28 February 2005, para. 23 ('If the Trial Chamber did not refer to the evidence given by a witness, even if it is in contradiction to the Trial Chamber's finding, it is to be presumed that the Trial Chamber assessed and weighed the evidence, but found that the evidence did not prevent it from arriving at its actual findings'); *Musema* Appeal Judgment, n 38, paras 19; 152 ('there is no guiding principle on the question to determine the extent to which a Trial Chamber is obliged to set out its reasons for accepting or rejecting a particular testimony').

that, since the Trial Chamber had expressed its concerns over the credibility of one witness and decided that it would accept his testimony only where corroborated, it should have explained why it then relied on that witness's uncorroborated account, instead of that of another witness who testified to the contrary.[41] Similarly, discussing identification evidence, the ICTY Appeals Chamber ruled that the 'Trial Chamber must rigorously implement its duty to provide a "reasoned opinion". In particular, a reasoned opinion must carefully articulate the factors relied upon in support of the identification of the accused and adequately address any significant factors impacting negatively on the reliability of the identification evidence.'[42]

ii. Categorising forms of evidence

In the scholarly literature, evidence tends to be placed into one of three broad categories: oral (or testimonial) evidence, documentary evidence, and real evidence.[43] The category of oral evidence is self-explanatory, while documentary evidence can encompass not just 'documents' in a strict sense, but also photographs, video or audio recordings, and other items.[44] 'Real' evidence refers to tangible exhibits or other material objects that speak for themselves.[45] Some authors further distinguish between two forms of real evidence: physical and forensic.[46] Others categorise evidence as falling into one of four groups: testimonial, documentary, digital, or physical (including forensic) evidence.[47] A separate category

[41] *Simba* Appeal Judgment, n 36, para. 143.

[42] *Kupreškić et al.* Appeal Judgment, n 7, para. 39.

[43] H.L. Ho, 'The Legal Concept of Evidence' in E.N. Zalta (ed.), *The Stanford Encyclopaedia of Philosophy* (Stanford University, 2015), online at https://plato.stanford.edu/entries/evidence-legal/ (last accessed 23 May 2023). Wigmore identified just three basic forms of evidence: testimonial, circumstantial, and 'autoptic proference' (referring to any observable evidence given at trial): J.H. Wigmore, *The Principles of Judicial Proof: As Given by Logic, Psychology, and General Experience and Illustrated in Judicial Trials* (Little, Brown & Co., 1913), 7.

[44] See section D.

[45] *Prosecutor v Orić*, Order Concerning Guidelines on Evidence and the Conduct of Parties during Trial Proceedings, IT-03-68-T, 21 October 2004 ('*Orić* Guidelines'), para. 3 ('For the purposes of the trial, evidence will be taken to mean the information which will be put before the Trial Chamber in order to prove the facts at issue and may take the following forms: a) testimony, b) documents produced for the inspection of the Trial Chamber, c) real evidence, i.e. exhibits and other material objects, and d) admissions of fact.'). See further *Prosecutor v Katanga*, Decision on the Prosecutor's Bar Table Motions, ICC-01/04-01/07-2635, 17 December 2010 ('*Katanga* Bar Table Decision'), para. 24 (outlining that once the originality and integrity of audio-visual material is established, it may be regarded as 'real evidence').

[46] L. Freeman, 'Digital Evidence and War Crimes Prosecutions: The Impact of Digital Technologies on International Criminal Investigations and Trials' (2018) 41 *Fordham International Law Journal* 283, 295; D. Piragoff and P. Clarke, 'Article 69' in O. Triffterer and K. Ambos (eds), *Rome Statute of the International Criminal Court: Article-by-Article Commentary* (4th edn, Beck/Hart, 2021), 2035, 2055.

[47] See e.g. S. Ferro Ribeiro and D. van der Straten Ponthoz, *International Protocol on the Documentation and Investigation of Sexual Violence in Conflict: Best Practice on the Documentation of Sexual Violence as a Crime or Violation of International Law* (2nd edn, FCO, 2017), Chapter 10.

of evidence, 'demonstrative evidence', incorporating visual aids such as maps, models, diagrams, and 3D platforms introduced to enhance the presentation of the evidence and understanding of the context and landscape of the alleged crimes, could also be identified, and these models are increasingly used in international criminal trials.[48]

The legal frameworks of international criminal tribunals do not explicitly distinguish between the different forms of evidence.[49] This means that debates about whether, for example, video evidence is 'real' or 'documentary' in nature[50] are largely irrelevant, because the same principles of admission and evaluation apply to both categories.[51] Following recent ICC decisions, which distinguish between just two categories of evidence: 'witnesses' and 'documentary and other types of evidence',[52] sections C and D below provide an overview of how evidence falling under these broad categories have been evaluated in practice.

It should be noted at the outset, however, that there may be a difference between the approach outlined by a Trial Chamber and the practical application of those principles. For example, in *Lubanga*, Judge Ušacka opined that the Trial Chamber's stated 'cautious approach' in relation to making age assessments based

[48] For example, the Special Tribunal for Lebanon admitted three-dimensional models to give an overview of the crime scene prior to and after the explosion of 14 February 2005: *Prosecutor v Ayyash et al.*, Decision on Prosecution's Motion to Admit into Evidence Photographs, Videos, Maps, and 3-D Models, STL-11-01/PT/TC, 13 January 2014, paras 9–10. Interactive visual platforms created by SITU research were introduced in the ICC cases of *Al Hassan* and *Al Mahdi*, showing damage to Timbuktu: see *Prosecutor v Al Hassan*, Decision on Prosecution request under Regulation 35 and application under Rule 68(2)(b) of the Rules concerning the introduction into evidence of the prior recorded testimony of P-0204 and P-0630, ICC-01/12-01/18-1671, 30 August 2021. For further analysis, see S. Zarmsky, 'Why Seeing Should Not Always Be Believing: Considerations Regarding the Use of Digital Reconstruction Technology in International Law' (2021) 19 *Journal of International Criminal Justice* 213; K.M. Clarke and S. Kendall, 'The Beauty… Is That It Speaks for Itself: Geospatial Materials as Evidentiary Matters' (2019) 23 *Law Text Culture* 91; K. MacLean, 'Interactive Digital Platforms, Human Rights Fact Production, and the International Criminal Court' (2023) 15 *Journal of Human Rights Practice* 84.

[49] There is, however, some practice ordering that evidence which is 'testimonial in nature'—that is, a statement given by a person 'in the capacity of a witness in the context of or in anticipation of legal proceedings'—cannot be submitted through a bar table motion: see e.g. *Prosecutor v Yekatom and Ngaïssona*, Decision on the First Prosecution Submission Request from the Bar Table (Sexual and Gender Based Violence), ICC-01/14-01/18-1359, 12 April 2022, para. 16; cf. *Prosecutor v Abd-Al-Rahman*, Decision on the Prosecution's Bar Table Motion, ICC-02/05-01/20-885, 27 February 2023, paras 38–40 (finding that reports based on interviews are not themselves 'prior recorded testimony' and can be submitted from the bar table). See further, Chapter 3, section B.

[50] See the sources cited at n 45 for examples.

[51] The question of whether video evidence is 'real' evidence may be much more important in common law jurisdictions with a rule against hearsay. If it is considered hearsay, rather than real, evidence, then it would have to fall within one of the permitted exceptions. For example, in one case, a mechanically produced film of the echoes made by two ships which collided on the River Thames was objected to by the defence as inadmissible hearsay but was ultimately found to be 'in the nature of real evidence': *Sapporo Maru v Statue of Liberty* [1968] 1 WLR 739.

[52] E.g. *Prosecutor v Al Hassan*, Decision on the conduct of proceedings, ICC-01/12-01/18-789, 6 May 2020, Annex A: Directions on the conduct of proceedings, paras 35–80 and *Prosecutor v Ntaganda*, Decision on the conduct of proceedings, ICC-01/04-02/06-619, 2 June 2015, paras 20–57 (each with one section for 'witnesses' and one for documentary and other types of evidence).

on video excerpts was apparently not rigorously adhered to.[53] It is worth noting that it can be difficult to systematically ascertain from an external perspective whether the Chamber's stated approach to various types of evidence has been consistently applied. This is particularly so where a piece of evidence is referred to by its exhibit number but information on what that exhibit contains is not publicly available, or where a witness is referred to by a pseudonym without further information.[54] Nevertheless, sections C and D attempt to provide concrete examples of the approach to different types of evidence in practice, and the factors that may be important in the Chamber's evaluation of them.

C. The evaluation of oral evidence

Witness testimony is a central component to international criminal trials.[55] A range of factors that Trial Chambers use in determining the credibility of a witness and the reliability of their account can be identified from the case law. In their ground-breaking empirical research on witness assessments at the ICTY, ICTR, and ICC, Gabrielė Chlevickaitė, Barbora Holá, and Catrien Bijleveld consolidated the 'ad hoc, consistently evolving jurisprudence'[56] into a comprehensive framework of factors comprising three overarching factors: the witness's objectivity, their competence, and the quality of their testimony.[57] Similarly, Agirre noted 14 'source evaluation' criteria extrapolated from ICC trial judgments issued between 2012 and 2019, which include consistency; plausibility; demeanour and apparent sincerity; indications of collusion or witness interference; relationship to

[53] *Lubanga* Appeal Judgment, n 7, Dissenting opinion of Judge Ušacka, ICC-01/04-01/06-3121-Anx2, 1 December 2014, para. 67.

[54] *Prosecutor v Bemba*, Judgment on the appeal of Mr Jean-Pierre Bemba Gombo against Trial Chamber III's 'Judgment pursuant to Article 74 of the Statute', ICC-01/05-01/08-3636-Red, 8 June 2018 ('*Bemba* Appeal Judgment'), Separate Opinion of Judge Van den Wyngaert and Judge Morrison, ICC-01/05-01/08-3636-Anx2, 8 June 2018, para. 6 (criticising 'the opacity of the Conviction Decision in terms of outlining the evidentiary basis for many of the findings').

[55] For example, in *Ongwen*, 130 witnesses appeared before the Chamber (69 for the prosecution, 54 for the defence, and 7 for participating victims), and a further 56 witnesses had their testimony introduced in writing: *Prosecutor v Ongwen*, Trial Judgment, ICC-02/04-01/15-1762, 4 February 2021 ('*Ongwen* Trial Judgment'), paras 19–22. In *Karadžić*, 434 witnesses testified over the course of the trial (195 prosecution, 1 Chamber, and 238 defence), with a further 152 written witness testimonies (142 prosecution, 10 defence) introduced under Rules 92 *bis* and *quater*: *Prosecutor v Karadžić*, Public Redacted Version of Judgment Issued on 24 March 2016, IT-95-5/18-T, 24 March 2016 ('*Karadžić* Trial Judgment'), paras 6136–46. See further, G. Chlevickaitė, B. Holá, and C. Bijleveld, 'Thousands on the Stand: Exploring Trends and Patterns of International Witnesses' (2019) 32 *Leiden Journal of International Law* 819, mapping an average number of 125 *viva voce* witnesses for each ICTY trial between 1997 and 2017. The mean number of witnesses was 66 and 64 for the ICTR and ICC respectively in the same time frame.

[56] G. Chlevickaitė, B. Holá, and C. Bijleveld, 'Judicial Witness Assessments at the ICTY, ICTR and ICC: Is There "Standard Practice" in International Criminal Justice?' (2020) 18 *Journal of International Criminal Justice* 185.

[57] Ibid., 194.

the accused; bias and motivation; contradictions with earlier statements or other evidence on the record; and the impact of trauma and the passage of time.[58] He observed a difference between Trial Chambers on the number of criteria considered, and whether these are couched in hypothetical (e.g. 'potential reasons' for giving flawed evidence or 'possible bias') rather than impartial descriptive terms, with Trial Chamber II in *Ngudjolo* and *Katanga* considering a broader range of factors than other Trial Chambers.[59]

Objectivity 'pertain[s] to the individual circumstances of each witness, potentially revealing the perceived reasons to be untruthful.'[60] Of course, witnesses may have multiple complex and inter-related motivations for testifying in international criminal trials,[61] and some may not have voluntarily appeared before the tribunal, but may have been compelled to do so by a summons or subpoena, if the tribunal has the power to make such orders.[62] In considering witness objectivity, the tribunal may consider factors such as whether the witness holds an animus against the accused[63] and their potential bias in favour of or against the accused, for example owing to their membership of an ethnic or political group.[64] Most notably, insider or accomplice witnesses may be highly motivated to downplay their own involvement.[65] They may also have sought to gain, financially or through a promise of non-prosecution in exchange for their testimony, or they may bear continued loyalty towards, or fear of retaliation from, their former allies.[66] However, as

[58] X. Agirre Aranburu, 'The Contribution of Analysis to the Quality Control in Criminal Investigation' in X. Agirre, M. Bergsmo, S. De Smet and C. Stahn (eds), *Quality Control in Criminal Investigation* (TOAEP, 2020), 117, 229–31.

[59] Ibid., 231–2.

[60] Chlevickaitė et al., n 12, 191.

[61] Agirre Aranburu, n 57, 194–5 lists 13 possible motives.

[62] Rule 54, ICTY RPE; Rule 54, ICTR RPE; Rule 54, SCSL RPE; Rule 48(2), KSC RPE; Rule 77, STL RPE; Rule 55, IRMCT RPE; Rule 41, ECCC IR. The situation before the ICC is a little more complicated: Article 64(6)(b), ICC Statute states that the Trial Chamber may require the attendance and testimony of witnesses as necessary, but Article 93(1)(e) refers to the role of states in facilitating the '*voluntary* appearance' of witnesses (emphasis added). The Appeals Chamber has held that the Court does have the power to compel witnesses under Article 64(6)(b), which is complemented by the obligation on states under Article 93(1)(b) to assist in 'the taking of evidence': *Prosecutor v Ruto and Sang*, Judgment on the appeals of William Samoei Ruto and Mr Joshua Arap Sang against the decision of Trial Chamber V (A) of 17 April 2014 entitled 'Decision on Prosecutor's Application for Witness Summonses and resulting Request for State Party Cooperation', ICC-01/09-01/11-1598, 9 October 2014.

[63] E.g. *Prosecutor v Vasiljević*, Judgment, IT-98-32-T, 29 November 2002, para. 85, fn. 190.

[64] E.g. *Prosecutor v Boškoski and Tarčulovski*, Judgment, IT-04-82-T, 10 July 2008, para. 11 (noting the residents of Ljuboten had 'a tendency to speak as if with one voice', and noting 'the relevance of group values, honour and family loyalty to the cultural background of witnesses with ethnic Albanian roots').

[65] Chlevickaitė et al., n 12; G. Chlevickaitė and B. Holá, 'Empirical Study of Insider Witnesses' Assessments at the International Criminal Court' (2016) 16 *International Criminal Law Review* 673.

[66] Chlevickaitė and Holá, n 65; see also *Prosecutor v Nchamihigo*, Judgment and Sentence, ICTR-01-63-T, 12 November 2008, para. 17 ('It is accepted both as a matter of law and common sense that the testimony of accomplices may be tainted by motives or incentives to falsely implicate an accused to gain some benefit or advantage in regard to their own case or sentence'); *Prosecutor v Brima et al.*, Judgment, SCSL-04-16-T, 20 June 2007 ('*AFRC* Trial Judgment'), paras 124–30; 358–70; *Haradinaj et al.* Trial

noted by the SCSL Trial Chamber, 'A witness with a self-interest to serve may seek to inculpate others and exculpate himself, but it does not follow that such a witness is incapable of telling the truth'.[67] Chambers may decide to accept part of a witness's account but not others, to rely on that witness's account only where it is corroborated, or to dismiss the witness's testimony entirely.[68]

Competence refers to the witness's ability to recall, observe, and comment on matters at issue.[69] For example, it is frequently noted that there may be cases where trauma suffered by a witness means that they may have difficulty recalling events in a clear and linear manner.[70] If the Chamber believes that the trauma suffered by the witness renders his or her account unreliable, it is expected to provide concrete reasons as to why that is the case.[71] Cultural and educational factors may also bear an impact on the perceived competence of a witness. Expert testimony in the *Akayesu* case outlined that witnesses may speak indirectly in answering questions, and that the tradition of relaying information orally 'inevitably carries the hazard of distortion of the information each time it is passed on to a new listener'.[72] The Chamber noted:

> Similar cultural constraints were evident in their difficulty to be specific as to dates, times, distances and locations. The Chamber also noted the inexperience of witnesses with maps, film and graphic representations of localities, in the light of this understanding, the Chamber did not draw any adverse conclusions regarding the credibility of witnesses based only on their reticence and their sometimes circuitous responses to questions.[73]

Judgment, n 7, para. 13; *Bemba et al.* Appeal Judgment, n 36, paras 1523–36; R. Cryer, 'Witness Tampering and International Criminal Tribunals' (2014) 27 *Leiden Journal of International Law* 191; International Bar Association, *Witnesses before the International Criminal Court* (July 2013), 43–9.

[67] *AFRC* Trial Judgment, n 66, para. 125. See also *Prosecutor v Kordić and Čerkez*, Judgment, IT-95-14/2-T, 26 February 2001, para. 629.

[68] *Karera* Appeal Judgment, n 38, para. 88; *Prosecutor v Blagojević and Jokić*, Judgment, IT-02-60-A, 9 May 2007, para. 82; *Ntagerura et al.* Appeal Judgment, n 21, para. 214; *Bemba et al.* Appeal Judgment, n 36, paras 1081–5; Chlevickaitė and Holá, n 65, 696.

[69] Chlevickaitė et al., n 56, 191.

[70] *Prosecutor v Akayesu*, Judgment, ICTR-96-4-T, 2 September 1998 ('*Akayesu* Trial Judgment'), paras 142–3; *Prosecutor v Kayishema and Ruzindana*, Judgment, ICTR-95-1-T, 21 May 1999 ('*Kayishema and Ruzindana* Trial Judgment'), paras 73–5; *Prosecutor v Lubanga*, Judgment, ICC-01/04-01/06-2842, 14 March 2012 ('*Lubanga* Trial Judgment'), para. 103. See further E. Smith, 'Trauma in the Witness Stand: Effective Evaluation of Trauma-Impacted Testimony at the International Criminal Court' in A. Heinze and V.E. Dittrich, *The Past, Present and Future of the International Criminal Court* (TOAEP, 2021), 439.

[71] *Prosecutor v Kunarac et al.*, Judgment, IT- 96-23 & IT-96-23/1-A, 12 June 2002, para. 324.

[72] *Akayesu* Trial Judgment, n 70, paras 155–6. See also, *Kayishema and Ruzindana* Trial Judgment, n 70, para. 69, on the sources of unreliability in eyewitness testimony. The Chamber noted these factors but concluded that it could not simply disregard eyewitness testimony on the basis that it might not be an exact recollection (*Kayishema and Ruzindana* Trial Judgment, n 70, para. 70).

[73] *Akayesu* Trial Judgment, n 70, para. 156.

In *Ntaganda*, the Chamber noted that delayed reporting of rape allegations was extremely common and concluded that late reporting would not impact upon its assessment of a witness's credibility.[74] It particularly relied on the expert evidence of psychotherapist Maeve Lewis, whose 'experience is based on areas outside the DRC' but was nevertheless relevant in this regard.[75] A contrasting position on the perceived competence of an expert witness was taken in *Ongwen*, where the Trial Chamber declined to rely on the expert testimony of Adam Branch, who provided a 'detailed account on the economic and security situation in IDP camps', on the basis that 'his own personal experience relates primarily to the situation in Pabbo camp, which is not directly relevant to the charges of the present case'[76] and that there was other, more direct evidence that the Chamber could rely upon instead.[77] When considering the weight to give to expert accounts, Chambers will consider factors such as the expert's qualifications, role, and experience; the validity of the methods they employed; the credibility of their findings in light of these aspects and the other evidence on the record, and the perceived relevance and reliability of their account.[78] Ultimately, equally qualified prosecution and defence expert witnesses can provide the Chamber with conflicting accounts and the assessment of their evidence may hinge more on the perceived quality of their evidence than their competence to offer such accounts.[79]

Quality refers to the extent to which the witness's account is deemed credible and reliable, based on factors such as: the precision and level of detail in the testimony; corroboration with other evidence; consistency with the witness's earlier statements; and the clarity of the witness's account and its perceived plausibility.[80] Perceptions of plausibility can be difficult, given the fact that judges often come from very different backgrounds to the witnesses and will likely have never experienced similar situations.[81] For this reason, Chambers may need to rely on the views of experts in assessing the plausibility of a narrative.[82] In *Ongwen*, for example, the

[74] *Ntaganda* Trial Judgment, n 29, para. 88.
[75] Ibid., footnote 192.
[76] *Ongwen* Trial Judgment, n 55, para. 598.
[77] Ibid.
[78] *Haradinaj et al.* Trial Judgment, n 7, para. 16; *Prosecutor v Ntaganda*, Decision on Defence Preliminary Challenges to Prosecution's Expert Witnesses, ICC-01/04-02/16-1159, 9 February 2016 ('*Ntaganda* Decision on Defence Preliminary Challenges to Prosecution's Expert Witnesses'). paras 8–9; A. Appazov, *Expert Evidence and International Criminal Justice* (Springer, 2016), 32–50; 55–7.
[79] Appazov, n 78, 84–92; 178.
[80] Chlevickaitė et al., n 56, 195.
[81] Chlevickaitė et al., n 56, 202.
[82] An expert witness is 'a person who, by virtue of some specialized knowledge, skill or training can assist the Chamber in understanding or determining an issue of a technical nature that is in dispute': *Prosecutor v Ntaganda*, Decision on Defence Preliminary Challenges to Prosecution's Expert Witnesses, ICC-01/04-02/16-1159, 9 February 2016 ('*Ntaganda* Decision on Defence Preliminary Challenges to Prosecution's Expert Witnesses'), para. 7. Experts are offered 'wide latitude to offer opinions' and bear a duty to testify 'with the utmost neutrality and objectivity': *Ntaganda* Decision on Defence Preliminary Challenges to Prosecution's Expert Witnesses, para. 9. See further, *Prosecutor v Popović* et al., Decision on Joint Defence Interlocutory Appeal concerning the Status of Richard Butler

Trial Chamber found it would have been 'impossible in practice' for the accused to successfully hide the complex symptoms of his mental disorders from those around him throughout the entire period of the charges, based on the evidence of psychological experts.[83]

The research of Chlevickaitė *et al.* shines an important light on the lack of scientific validity underpinning some of the practices of witness assessment in international criminal trials. Most notably, tribunals have consistently expressed the view that the Trial Chamber can assess the credibility of witnesses from observing their testimony in person.[84] There is little doubt that hearing live testimony in court adds to the public nature of the trial and enables the parties to rigorously test the evidence in front of judges, which may act to make the proceedings more vivid than, say, solely reviewing transcripts of cross-examination, when they come to recall witnesses' testimony and evaluate the trial record as a whole. In-person testimony also enables the judges to seek clarification on aspects of the witness's account that may be unclear.[85] But some have justified the need to observe witnesses on an apparent assumption that one can detect whether a witness is lying based on their demeanour,[86] which does not seem to be supported by the psychological literature.[87] For example, one former judge recalled an incident where she and her legal officer reached opposing conclusions on the credibility of a witness.[88] The legal officer, having not been in court at the time of the witness's testimony,

as an Expert Witness, IT-05–88-AR73.2, 30 January 2008; M. Gillett, *Prosecuting Environmental Harm before the International Criminal Court* (CUP, 2022), 194–201; Appazov, n 78, 23–62.

[83] *Ongwen* Trial Judgment, n 55, paras 2555–7.

[84] *Karadžić* Trial Judgment, n 55, para. 17; *Katanga* Trial Judgment, n 29, para. 87; *Prosecutor v Nahimana et al.*, Judgment, ICTR-99-52-A, 28 November 2007, paras 194–5.

[85] *Prosecutor v Bemba*, Judgment on the appeals of Mr Jean-Pierre Bemba Gombo and the Prosecutor against the Decision of Trial Chamber III entitled 'Decision on the admission into evidence of materials contained in the prosecution's list of evidence', ICC-01/05-01/08-1386, 3 May 2011 ('*Bemba* Admissibility Appeal Decision'), para. 76. See further, M. Fairlie, 'The Abiding Problem of Witness Statements in International Criminal Trials' (2017) 50 *NYU Journal of International Law and Politics* 77, 128.

[86] See e.g. *Katanga* Trial Judgment, n 29, para. 87; *Prosecutor v Kunarac*, Judgment, IT-96-23-T & IT-96-23/1-T, 22 February 2001, para. 679 (noting that the witness 'always testified clearly and without hesitation'); *Ongwen* Trial Judgment, n 55, para. 343. Cf. *Bemba* Appeal Judgment, n 54, Concurring Separate Opinion of Judge Eboe-Osuji, ICC-01/05-01/08-3636-Anx3, 14 June 2018, paras 58–73 (noting cases from domestic jurisdictions that signal a move away from making findings of fact based on witness demeanour).

[87] V. Denault and L. Jupe, 'Justice at Risk! An Evaluation of a Pseudoscientific Analysis of a Witness' Nonverbal Behavior in the Courtroom' (2017) 29 *Journal of Forensic Psychiatry and Psychology* 221; A. Vrij and J. Turgeon, 'Evaluating Credibility of Witnesses—Are We Instructing Jurors on Invalid Factors?' (2018) 11 *Journal of Tort Law* 231; A. Vrij, M. Hartwig, and P.A. Granhag, 'Reading Lies: Nonverbal Communication and Deception' (2019) 70 *Annual Review of Psychology* 295; G. Bogaard, E.H. Meijer, A. Vrij, and H. Merckelbach, 'Strong, But Wrong: Lay People's and Police Officers' Beliefs about Verbal and Nonverbal Cues to Deception' (2016) 11 *Plos One*, available at https://doi.org/10.1371/journal.pone.0156615 (last accessed 23 May 2023). As Chlevickaitė et al., n 12, 188 note, even if there were indicators in behaviour to suggest lying, these are unlikely to be universal in cross-cultural settings.

[88] T.A. Doherty, 'Evidence in International Criminal Tribunals: Contrast between Domestic and International Trials' (2013) 26 *Leiden Journal of International Law* 937.

reviewed the transcript and perceived the evidence of one witness as not credible because she repeated the same answer.[89] The judge disagreed with this assessment, recalling that the witness was 'very sure of her facts, very credible'.[90] Drawing from this experience, the judge 'quer[ied] how anyone can assess the credibility of a witness without observing his/her demeanour and make conclusions that the evidence in the transcripts did not support findings'.[91] These observations were made in the context of a critique on Nancy Combs's book *Fact-Finding without Facts*, which reviewed thousands of pages of transcripts in concluding that witness testimony before international criminal trials 'is frequently problematic in numerous regards'.[92] These problems included contradictory accounts given by the same witnesses; vague and incomplete answers to questions on key facts, rendering them difficult to verify and challenge; and false testimony in many trials.[93] The problems identified by Combs are clearly very different to the legal officer's reported concern about a witness on the basis that her testimony was repetitive, which itself seems a rather unusual conclusion, given that consistency tends to be a factor leaning in favour of credibility, but it is difficult to assess this without further information.

That being said, and while acknowledging problematic assumptions that particular 'tells' can reveal whether a witness is lying, especially in cross-cultural and unfamiliar contexts where hesitation or evasiveness may not necessarily be a product of dishonesty, we might find a middle ground between these two positions. It may be that there are no universal indicators that show that a witness is being dishonest, but, having observed a witness on the stand for some time, judges may pick up on cues that the witness is uncomfortable, be it from their tone of voice, fidgeting in the stand, or other particular behaviours unique to this witness. Judges will then have to determine what the cause of this discomfort is. Counsel can also use cross-examination to interrogate a witness's account in a way would be impossible with documentary and other forms of evidence. We now turn to discuss those other forms of evidence.

D. The evaluation of documentary and other evidence

Evidence other than oral witness testimony covers a wide breadth of forms, including but not limited to: reports of international organisations and non-governmental organisations; media reports; official documents; minutes from meetings; diaries; personal notes; books; maps and satellite imagery; charts; statutes and laws; judgments; video recordings; audio recordings; transcripts of

[89] Ibid., 941.
[90] Ibid.
[91] Ibid.
[92] N. Combs, *Fact-Finding without Facts: The Uncertain Evidentiary Foundations of International Criminal Convictions* (CUP, 2010), 167.
[93] Ibid., 167–70.

intercepts; witness statements; testimony and transcripts from other trials; emails and other electronic correspondence; affidavits; confessions; and telecommunications data.[94] Evidence may be admitted as exhibits connected with the testimony of a witness or 'from the bar table'.[95] The tendering party bears the burden of establishing the admissibility of a piece of documentary or other real evidence.[96] This remains the case in the ICC where the submission system, as discussed in Chapter 3, is followed; the only difference is that the Chamber will consider the arguments in favour of or against admission at the close of trial, rather than making intermediate decisions on the relevance or admissibility of a piece of evidence.[97]

As with other forms of evidence, there is a tendency to err in favour of admission, leaving the Chamber the ultimate discretion as to whether to afford it any weight at the end of trial.[98] On the other hand, some have raised concerns that the wholesale admission of large masses of evidence of limited probative value risks flooding the judicial record and making cases unwieldy and inefficient.[99] To that end, some Trial Chambers of the ICTY adopted the 'best evidence rule', defined as follows:

> [T]he Trial Chamber will rely on the best evidence available in the circumstances of the case, and parties are directed to keep in mind this rule when submitting evidence to the Trial Chamber. What is considered the best evidence will depend

[94] M. Nerenberg and W. Timmermann, 'Documentary Evidence' in K.A.A. Khan, C. Buisman, and C. Gosnell (eds), *Principles of Evidence in International Criminal Justice* (OUP, 2010), 443. *Katanga* Bar Table Decision, n 45, para. 12.

[95] See Chapter 3 above; F. Gaynor, 'Documentary Evidence' in K. Ambos et al. (eds), *Evidence in International Criminal Procedure: A Commentary* (Hart/Beck, forthcoming, on file with author); *Katanga* Bar Table Decision, n 45, para. 12, noting that 'the fact that evidence is being tendered without authentication by a witness may be an important factor in the Chamber's assessment of its admissibility'.

[96] *Orić* Guidelines, n 45, para. 11, guideline (ii); *Prosecutor v Lubanga*, Decision on the Admissibility of Four Documents, ICC-01/04-01/06-1399, 16 June 2008 ('*Lubanga* Four Documents Decision'), para. 25.

[97] *Prosecutor v Abd-Al-Rahman*, Directions on the conduct of proceedings, ICC-02/05-01/20-478, 4 October 2021 ('*Al Rahman* Directions'), para. 27; *Bemba* Admissibility Appeal Decision, n 85, para. 37; *Ongwen* Trial Judgment, n 55, paras 235–6.

[98] E.g. *Gotovina* Trial Judgment, n 5, para. 38 (noting that the *Storm Over Krajina* film had been admitted but afforded little probative value); *Lubanga* Four Documents Decision, n 96, para. 33 ('any conclusions on factual issues have been reached for the purposes of this ruling on admissibility only, and they do not in any sense prejudge the eventual assessment that must be made of the evidence as a whole at the end of the case'); *Haradinaj* et al. Trial Judgment, n 7, para. 9 ('Generally, the reliability of evidence is a factor going to weight rather than admissibility'); *Prosecutor v Gbagbo and Blé Goudé*, Reasons for oral decision of 15 January 2019 on the Requête de la Défense de Laurent Gbagbo afin qu'un jugement d'acquittement portant sur toutes les charges soit prononcé en faveur de Laurent Gbagbo et que sa mise en liberté immédiate soit ordonnée, and on the Blé Goudé Defence no case to answer motion, ICC-02/11-01/15-1263, 16 July 2019 ('*Gbagbo* Reasons'), Reasons of Judge Henderson, ICC-02/11-01/15-1263-AnxB-Red, 16 July 2019, para. 37 (stating that it makes little difference whether authenticity is considered for the purposes of admission or in assessing weight at the end of the trial: if a document cannot be authenticated, it cannot be relied upon).

[99] P. Murphy, 'No Free Lunch, No Free Proof: The Indiscriminate Admission of Evidence is a Serious Flaw in International Criminal Trials' (2010) 8 *Journal of International Criminal Justice* 539, 568–9; P. Murphy and L. Baddour, 'Evidence and Selection of Judges in International Criminal Tribunals: The Need for a Harmonized Approach' in E. van Sliedregt and S. Vasiliev, *Pluralism in International Criminal Law* (OUP, 2014), 368.

> on the particular circumstances attached to each document and to the complexity of this case and the investigations that preceded it.[100]

This is distinct to the best evidence rule in some common law domestic contexts, which requires, subject to some exceptions, that the original of a document be tendered.[101] Ambos rightly sees the best evidence rule in international criminal procedure as a closer corollary to the 'immediacy principle' in civil law jurisdictions; that is to say, it expresses a 'preference of first-hand, original, direct evidence over second-hand, derivative, indirect evidence'.[102]

The best evidence rule has not been universally adopted,[103] and where it was adopted, it has not been without controversy.[104] The IMTFE, according to Judge Pal's dissent, adopted the best evidence rule after the close of the prosecution case, meaning that it only applied to defence evidence.[105] A review of the transcripts does suggest that the rule was applied more stringently to the defence than the prosecution.[106] However, it is unclear when exactly the best evidence rule was adopted by the IMTFE; Judge Pal cited the transcript from 24 March 1947,[107] as do leading scholars,[108] but a review of that transcript does not contain any ruling,

[100] *Prosecutor v Martić*, Decision Adopting Guidelines on the Standards Governing the Admission of Evidence, IT-95-11-T, 19 January 2006, para. 7. See also, *Prosecutor v Blagojević and Jokić*, Decision on the Admission into Evidence of Intercept-Related Materials, IT-02-60-T, 18 December 2003, para. 25; *Prosecutor v Perišić*, Order for Guidelines on the Admission and Presentation of Evidence and Conduct of Counsel in Court, IT-04-81-T, 29 October 2008, para. 36; *Orić* Guidelines, n 45, para. 11, guideline viii; *Prosecutor v Delalić* et al., Decision on the Tendering of Prosecution Exhibits 104–108, IT-96-21-T, 9 February 1998, para. 15.

[101] Rule 1002, Federal Rules of Evidence, as amended to 1 December 2020, available online at https://www.law.cornell.edu/rules/fre (last accessed 30 May 2023); cf. S.L. Phipson et al., *Phipson on Evidence* (20th edn, Sweet & Maxwell, 2020), para. 7-36 (arguing that 'although this maxim played a conspicuous part in the early history of the subject, today it is of little practical importance').

[102] K. Ambos, *Treatise on International Criminal Law: Vol. III: International Criminal Procedure* (OUP, 2016), 451.

[103] *Prosecutor v Bemba et al.*, Decision on Prosecution Request to Order the Disclosure of Material in Possession of the Defence, ICC-01/05-01/13-1820, 20 April 2016, para. 10 ('Further, the Single Judge is not of the view that the "best evidence rule" is a principle of international criminal law which generally applies in all cases, as asserted by the Prosecution. The jurisprudence relied on in support by the Prosecution clearly shows that it is the choice of the competent chambers to incorporate the principle in their conduct of proceedings and does not indicate the existence of a generally applicable principle. Moreover, the Prosecution itself presented evidence in its bar table motions which would have to be excluded if the principle would be applied'); see also, *Prosecutor v Ntaganda*, Decision on Defence Request for Reconsideration of Decision on Admission of Certain Documents used with Witness P-0315, ICC-01/04-02/06-1474, 8 August 2016, para. 5.

[104] The Trial Chamber's adoption of the rule was overturned by the SCSL Appeals Chamber, describing it as an 'anachronism' from a 'pre-industrial age' when copying was done by hand and the rate of errors was high: *Prosecutor v Fofana*, Appeal against Decision Refusing Bail, SCSL-04-14-AR65, 11 March 2005, para. 24.

[105] *United States of America et al. v Araki Sadao et al.*, Judgment of the International Military Tribunal for the Far East (IMTFE), 4 November 1948, Judgment of The Honorable Mr Justice Pal, Member from India, Pages 1 to 374, 308.

[106] Compare e.g. IMTFE, Transcript of Proceedings, 18 March 1947, 18585–98; IMTFE, Transcript of Proceedings, 16 May 1947, 22305 with IMTFE, Transcript of Proceedings, 17 June 1946, 765. See also N. Boister and R. Cryer, *The Tokyo International Military Tribunal—A Reappraisal* (OUP, 2008), 104.

[107] IMTFE, Transcript of Proceedings, 24 March 1947, 18975.

[108] Boister and Cryer, n 106, 106.

as such, on the best evidence rule. Instead, that transcript reveals an objection to a line of questioning insofar as it related to an unavailable telegram,[109] with the Chamber responding that it would not treat the witness's answers as proof of the contents of that document.

The earliest reference to the term 'best evidence' in the IMTFE transcripts to the rule appears to be in an (unsuccessful) objection made by defence counsel on 17 June 1946.[110] On 4 December 1946, the President noted that 'The strict rules of evidence have no application, but naturally we will look for the best evidence available'.[111] The prosecution closed its case on 24 January 1947.[112] On 19 May 1947, defence counsel Cunningham, in response to a ruling to reject an affidavit on the basis that the original document on which it relied had not been produced, submitted that 'the best evidence rule, as I understand it, does not apply in this court, it has not for the prosecution, and it does not under the Charter'.[113] The President replied that the Tribunal would not reject evidence on the basis of the best evidence rule, but insisted that the best evidence available be produced and if that evidence (for example, the original document referred to) was not available, counsel had to explain, on oath, why that was so.[114] Thus, Judge Pal's assertion that the best evidence rule was only adopted and used against the defence does not fully stand up to scrutiny.

As regards weight, a sensible general rule seems to be that the less a Trial Chamber knows 'about a document, the circumstances of its creation and usage',[115] then the less weight it is likely to give to it. In assessing the authenticity and credibility of a piece of evidence, various 'indicia of reliability'[116] will be considered, including: its source or author, including their role in events and whether they may have a particular bias or motive; the circumstances under which the document was created; whether it is an original or a copy, and whether it is sealed, stamped, or certified in any way; its legibility; its chain of custody, to the extent that it is known, and whether the information therein is consistent with other evidence on the record.[117] The absence of information on any of these factors will not lead a

[109] First raised in IMTFE, Transcript of Proceedings, 21 March 1947, 18903–25.
[110] IMTFE, Transcript of Proceedings, 17 June 1946, 762.
[111] IMTFE, Transcript of Proceedings, 4 December 1946, 11776.
[112] *United States of America et al. v Araki Sadao et al.*, Judgment of the International Military Tribunal for the Far East (IMTFE), 4 November 1948, 48425.
[113] IMTFE, Transcript of proceedings, 19 May 1947, 22445.
[114] Ibid., 22445–6.
[115] *Gotovina* Trial Judgment, n 5, para. 38.
[116] *Prosecutor v Karemera*, Decision on the Prosecution Motion for Admission into Evidence of Certain Exhibits from Other Trials, ICTR-98-44-T, 30 October 2007, paras 8–10; *Prosecutor v Bagosora et al.*, Decision on Request to Admit United Nations Documents into Evidence under Rule 89(C), ICTR-98-41-T, 25 May 2007, para. 4; *Prosecutor v Kordić and Čerkez*, Decision on Appeal Regarding Statement of a Deceased Witness, IT-95-14/2-AR73.5, 21 July 2000, paras 24–8.
[117] Outlining a range of factors considered, see *KHIEU Samphân ('Case 002/02')*, Judgment, 002/19-09-2007/ECCC/TC (E465), 16 November 2018, para. 61; *Gotovina* Trial Judgment, n 5, para. 38; *Bemba* Trial Judgment, n 16, para. 247; *Lubanga* Four Documents Decision, note 96, para. 30; *Prosecutor v Musema*, Judgment, ICTR-96-13-T, 27 January 2000, paras 66–7; *Taylor* Appeal

Chamber to automatically consider the evidence to be devoid of authenticity.[118] It is also worth noting that a document might be found to be authentic, but may nonetheless not be relied upon for the proof of its contents.[119] The Trial Chamber's ultimate decision on weight will be based on the individual characteristics of the piece of evidence and the extent to which it is corroborated by other evidence on the record. Weight is also likely to be influenced by whether the opposing party has argued against reliance on a piece of documentary evidence, and if so, the strength of those arguments.[120]

i. Prior recorded testimony

Prior recorded testimony of witnesses, in lieu of oral testimony,[121] is a central feature of international criminal trials.[122] Before the ICC, such evidence is admissible pursuant to the general admissibility criteria of Article 69(4) and further detail is set out in Rule 68 (as amended).[123] In addition, witness statements gathered in accordance with Article 56 of the Statute—where the prosecution has identified a 'unique investigative opportunity' prior to trial—may be admitted under Article 69 'and given such weight as determined by the Trial Chamber'.[124] In *Ongwen*, the Trial Chamber declared that it had no reservations in relying fully on the evidence

Judgment, n 5, para. 176 and references therein; *Prosecutor v Muvunyi*, Decision on the Prosecutor's Motion to Admit Documents Tendered During the Cross-Examination of Defence Witness Augustin Ndindiliyimana, ICTR-2000-55A-T, 28 February 2006, para. 13.

[118] See e.g. *Prosecutor v Lubanga*, Decision on the Confirmation of the Charges, ICC-01/04-01/06-803, 29 January 2007, para. 96 ('nothing in the Statute or the Rules expressly states that the absence of information about the chain of custody ... affects the admissibility or probative value of Prosecution evidence') but cf. *Prosecutor v Brđanin and Talić*, Order on the Standards Governing the Admission of Evidence, IT-99-36-T, 15 February 2002, para. 18, emphasising the importance of chain of custody.

[119] *Gotovina* Trial Judgment, n 5, para. 38 ('When the Trial Chamber was satisfied with the authenticity of a particular document, it did not automatically accept the statements contained therein to be an accurate portrayal of the facts').

[120] *Bemba* Admissibility Decision, n 10, para. 9 ('items can also be (i) self-authenticating, if they are official documents publicly available from official sources; (ii) agreed upon by the parties as authentic; (iii) *prima facie* reliable if they bear sufficient indicia of reliability such as a logo, letter head, signature, date or stamp, and appear to have been produced in the ordinary course of the activities of the persons or organisations who created them; or (iv) in case the item itself does not bear sufficient indicia of reliability, shown to be authentic and reliable by the tendering party through provision of sufficient information to enable the Chamber to verify that the documents are what they purport to be').

[121] As opposed to prior statements introduced for the purpose of cross-examination: Nerenberg and Timmermann, n 94, 460. Such statements are likely to be afforded lower probative value than the in-court testimony of the same witness: *Akayesu* Trial Judgment, n 70, para. 137.

[122] See Chapter 3, text to nn 22–4.

[123] See Chapter 1, text to nn 63–9. The Registry's Senior Legal Advisor, or any appropriate person designated by the Senior Legal Advisor, is authorised to witness declarations made pursuant to Rule 68(2)(b): *Prosecutor v. Said*, Decision on the Prosecution's First, Second and Fourth Requests Pursuant to Rule 68(2)(b) of the Rules, ICC-01/14-01/21-507-Red, 21 October 2022, para. 32.

[124] Article 56(4) ICC Statute. See further, F. Guariglia and G. Hochmayr, 'Article 56' in O. Triffterer and K. Ambos (eds), *Rome Statute of the International Criminal Court: Article-by-Article Commentary* (4th edn, Beck/Hart, 2021), 1675.

of seven Article 56 witnesses, given that the Chamber had watched the video-recordings of their testimony, and the defence had the opportunity to question the witnesses during the Article 56 proceedings.[125]

The legal frameworks differ somewhat between international criminal tribunals but broadly speaking, there are different rules applicable to the admissibility of prior recorded testimony: in lieu of oral testimony, where the parties have been given a limited opportunity to cross-examine the witness in court;[126] such testimony introduced (without cross-examination) as proof of facts other than the acts and conduct of the accused;[127] and the prior statements of witnesses who are dead or unavailable owing, for example, to witness intimidation or threats.[128] A case-by-case assessment will be undertaken on the admissibility of such statements in lieu of oral testimony, with the Chamber assessing potential prejudice to the accused, whether the statement bears sufficient indicia of reliability, good trial management, and the relative importance of the witness.[129]

When it comes to the weight to be afforded to each of these categories of prior recorded testimony, three factors will be important: whether the parties had the opportunity to examine the witness;[130] whether their testimony is corroborated

[125] *Ongwen* Trial Judgment, n 55, para. 396. This can be tricky, however, because counsel generally have not been appointed by the time of Article 56 proceedings: see F. Gerry et al., 'Forensic Archaeology, Ad Hoc Counsel and Ethics in the ICC', *Counsel*, 11 February 2022, online athttps://www.counselmagazine.co.uk/articles/forensic-archaeology-ad-hoc-counsel-ethics-in-the-icc (last accessed 30 May 2023).

[126] Rule 92 *ter*, ICTY RPE; Rule 111, IRMCT RPE; Rule 92 *ter*, SCSL RPE; Rule 156, STL RPE; Rule 154, KSC RPE; Rule 68(3), ICC RPE. This category is, of course, not strictly documentary evidence but a mixture of oral and written evidence: *Prosecutor v Milošević*, Decision on Interlocutory Appeal on the Admissibility of Evidence-in-Chief in the Form of Written Statements, IT-02-54-AR73.4, 30 September 2003, para. 16.

[127] Rule 92 *bis*, ICTY RPE; Rule 92 *bis*, ICTR RPE; Rule 92 *bis* SCSL RPE; Rule 110, IRMCT RPE; Rule 155, STL RPE; Rule 153, KSC RPE; Rule 68(2)(b), ICC RPE. See also *NUON Chea et al.* (C, Decision on Co-Prosecutors' Rule 92 Submission Regarding the Admission of Witness Statements and Other Documents before the Trial Chamber, 002/19-09-2007-ECCC/TC (E96/7), 20 June 2012, paras 21–22, finding that written statements going to acts and conduct 'shall, subjected to the limited exceptions identified below, be regarded as "not allowed under the law"' pursuant to Rule 87(3)(d), ECCC IR.

[128] Rules 92 *quater* and 92 *quinquies*, ICTY RPE; Rule 92 *quater*, SCSL RPE; Rule 158, STL RPE (referring to persons who are unavailable to testify 'for good reason'); Rule 112 IRMCT RPE (for witnesses who are dead, cannot be traced, or are unable to testify on health grounds); Rule 155, KSC RPE; Rule 68(2)(c) and (d), ICC RPE.

[129] *Prosecutor v Gbagbo and Blé Goudé*, Decision on the Prosecutor's Application to Introduce Prior Recorded Testimony under Rules 68(2)(b) and 68(3), ICC-02/11-01/15-573-Red, 9 June 2016, paras 20–3; *Bemba* Admissibility Appeal Decision, n 85, para. 78 ('In the view of the Appeals Chamber, this requires a cautious assessment. The Trial Chamber may, for example, take into account, a number of factors, including the following: (i) whether the evidence relates to issues that are not materially in dispute; (ii) whether that evidence is not central to core issues in the case, but only provides relevant background information; and (iii) whether the evidence is corroborative of other evidence'); *Prosecutor v Gbagbo and Blé Goudé*, Judgment on the Appeals of Mr Laurent Gbagbo and Mr Charles Blé Goudé against the Decision of Trial Chamber I of 9 June 2016 entitled 'Decision on the Prosecutor's Application to Introduce Prior Recorded Testimony under Rules 68(2)(b) and 68(3)', ICC-02/11-01/15-744, 1 November 2016, paras 67–84.

[130] E.g. *Prosecutor v Al Hassan*, Third Decision on the introduction of prior recorded testimonies pursuant to Rule 68(2)(b) of the Rules, ICC-01/12-01/18-1402, 26 March 2021 ('*Al Hassan* Prior Recorded Testimony Decision', Partially Dissenting Opinion of Judge Prost, ICC-01/12-01/18-1402-Anx, 14 April 2021, para. 7.

by other evidence on the record;[131] and whether the evidence is internally consistent.[132] The 'sole or decisive rule', as outlined above, applies: a person cannot be convicted solely or to a decisive extent on a statement where they have not been provided the chance to cross-examine the witness.[133] In *Martić*, the ICTY Appeals Chamber found that a witness statement admitted under Rule 92*bis* (i.e. not going to acts or conduct of the accused) was 'pivotal' to the Trial Chamber's findings in relation to the crimes in the village of Cerovljani.[134] The Trial Chamber had found the accused responsible for these crimes, which it saw as a natural and foreseeable consequence of the joint criminal enterprise (under the third category of joint criminal enterprise, or 'JCE III').[135] However, the Appeals Chamber noted that many of the findings linking the accused and the perpetrators hinged on a Rule 92*bis* statement.[136] While concluding that the evidence was so tenuous that no reasonable trier of fact could have reached the same conclusion as the Trial Chamber, the Appeals Chamber also noted that the Trial Chamber's failure to enable the accused to cross-examine this witness was a 'miscarriage of justice and accordingly his convictions for the crimes in Cerovljani would have been reversible on this ground, too'.[137]

By contrast, the Trial Chambers in *Popović* and *Stakić* both allowed untested evidence admitted under Rule 92*bis* to play a more pivotal role, and this was upheld by the Appeals Chamber. In *Stakić*, the Appeals Chamber noted that the evidence of 92*bis* witnesses 'was used to establish the context of the crimes, rather than the acts and conduct of the accused'.[138] It then went on to list 16 findings that were proven through Rule 92*bis* evidence.[139] For some of these, such as beatings in the courtyard of a detention facility and in Prijedor and the killing of 77 Bosnian Croats in Briševo in July 1992, the Rule 92*bis* account was the only supporting evidence cited.[140] This example shows the difficulty of the 'acts and conduct' distinction, where the relevant context does not speak to the actions of the accused person him or herself, but establishes a pattern of criminal behaviour by others which underpins the accused's conviction.[141]

[131] *Gotovina* Trial Judgment, n 5, para. 43.

[132] *Haradinaj et al.* Trial Judgment, n 7, para. 10.

[133] *Prosecutor v Šešelj*, Decision on Prosecution's Motion for Admission of Evidence of Mujo Džafić Pursuant to Rule 92 *quater* of the Rules of Procedure and Evidence, IT-03-67-T, 13 May 2009, para. 20; *Prosecutor v Bemba*, Decision Concerning the Prosecutor's Proposals for Redactions, ICC-01/05-01/08-48-US-Exp, 23 July 2008, para. 28; *Gucati and Haradinaj* Trial Judgment, n 29, para. 44; *Prosecutor v Ayyash et al.*, Decision on Trial Management and Reasons for Decision on Joinder, STL-11-01/T/TC, 25 February 2014, para. 93.

[134] *Prosecutor v Martić*, Judgment, IT-95-11-A, 8 October 2008 ('*Martić* Appeal Judgment'), para. 193, n 486.

[135] *Prosecutor v Martić*, Judgment, IT-95-11-T, 12 June 2007, para. 454.

[136] *Martić* Appeal Judgment, n 134, para. 192.

[137] Ibid., para. 193, note 486.

[138] *Prosecutor v Stakić*, Judgment, IT-97-24-A, 22 March 2006, para. 201.

[139] Ibid.

[140] Ibid.

[141] J.D. Jackson, 'Finding the Best Epistemic Fit for International Criminal Tribunals: Beyond the Adversarial-Inquisitorial Dichotomy' (2009) 7 *Journal of International Criminal Justice* 17.

In *Popović*, the Trial Chamber noted that it would be rare, in the specific context of the tribunal, for convictions to be based solely or decisively on Rule 92*bis* statements. It noted that 'in many cases before this Tribunal, the underlying acts which form the basis for a count in an indictment are multiple in nature, often with several layers, such that a finding with respect to one act will not form the basis for conviction' of war crimes, crimes against humanity, or genocide.[142] However, Judge Kwon in his dissent noted that the only evidence of specific beatings and killings near the Kravica supermarket was one Rule 92*bis* transcript,[143] and that the majority, based on its finding on the multi-layered and complex nature of international crimes,

> accordingly held that PW-116's uncorroborated evidence, in the context of the facts of this case, cannot be classified as evidence which could form the sole or even a decisive basis for the conviction of any of the accused and finally accepted PW-116's evidence, untested in this case, as a basis for concluding that the alleged beatings and killings have been established by the Prosecution.[144]

Judge Kwon argued that the evidence (and the sole or decisive rule) should be assessed in relation to each separate charge, not to the broader category of crimes, which are usually underpinned by several individual charges of incidents.[145] While the Appeals Chamber upheld the majority's position on this point,[146] Judge Kwon's interpretation does appear to be the correct one. The evidence underpinning each specific charge in the indictment must be examined on its own merits and cannot be proven beyond reasonable doubt by one uncorroborated witness statement that was not subject to cross-examination, even where other, similar charges were established.[147]

ii. NGO and media reports

The reports of non-governmental organisations and media reports can provide useful background information on the context and history of the alleged incidents. However, Chambers have tended to treat such reports with caution when the

[142] *Prosecutor v Popović et al.*, Judgment, IT-05-88-T, 10 June 2010 ('*Popović* Trial Judgment'), para. 63.

[143] Ibid., Dissenting and Separate Opinions of Judge Kwon, para. 40.

[144] Ibid., para. 42.

[145] Ibid., para. 43.

[146] *Popović* Appeal Judgment, n 24, paras 101–4 (acknowledging that the untested Rule 92 *bis* evidence was the only evidence on the record in relation to the Kravica supermarket killings but finding that these specific allegations in paragraph 31.3 of the indictment were not indispensable to Popović or Beara's convictions).

[147] *Popović* Trial Judgment, n 142, para. 44.

original source of the information therein is not indicated and cannot be tested; this type of report constitutes anonymous hearsay and, as such, has been found to be of limited probative value.[148] Even when applying the lower standard of proof of 'substantial grounds to believe', the majority in the *Gbagbo* confirmation decision declined to confirm the charges, expressing its concern at the prosecution's heavy reliance on evidence of this nature, concluding that it was 'not prepared to accept allegations proven solely through anonymous hearsay in documentary evidence'.[149]

Some authors have criticized this reticence to rely on the reports of UN agencies and non-governmental organisations on the basis that they are often produced following an established methodology and rigorous standards.[150] There is no doubt that investigations of international, non-governmental, or media organisations are usually carried out extremely diligently. The issue, however, is not with these bodies' reporting and investigative standards, but rather with the fact that the sources underpinning those reports are usually unknown, jeopardising the accused's right to challenge the evidence against them.

iii. Intercept evidence

Intercepted communications have proven an instrumental form of documentary evidence in numerous high-profile convictions.[151] Intercepts can be considered 'a special category of evidence in that in and of themselves, they bear no *prima facie* indicia of authenticity or reliability and as such, these requirements must generally be fulfilled by hearing from the relevant intercept operators or the participants in the intercepted conversation'.[152] In *Popović*, evidence of intercept operators was

[148] *Gbagbo* Adjournment Decision, n 31, paras 27–8; *Gotovina* Trial Judgment, n 5, para. 54.

[149] *Gbagbo* Adjournment Decision, n 31, para. 36. See also, *Ntaganda* Trial Judgment, n 29, paras 67–8; *Prosecutor v Al Hassan*, Decision on the Prosecution Motion for Authorization to File an Anonymous Summary concerning Witness MLI-OTP-P-P0113, ICC-01/12-01/18-122-Red2, 27 September 2018, para. 36; *Prosecutor v Katanga*, Decision on the Confirmation of Charges, ICC-01/04-01/07-717, 30 September 2008, para. 140.

[150] O. Triffterer and A. Kiss, 'Article 74' in O. Triffterer and K. Ambos (eds), *Rome Statute of the International Criminal Court: Article-by-Article Commentary* (4th edn, Beck/Hart, 2021), 2188, 2207; D. Robinson, 'The Other Poisoned Chalice: Unprecedented Evidentiary Standards in the Gbagbo Case? (Part 1)' (*EJIL:Talk!*, 5 November 2019). See also *Gbagbo* Adjournment Decision, n 31, Dissenting Opinion of Judge Fernández de Gurmendi, ICC-02/11-01/11-432-Anx-Corr, 3 June 2013, paras 22–7.

[151] E.g. *Prosecutor v Mladić*, Judgment, IT-09-92-T, 22 November 2017 ('*Mladić* Trial Judgment'), para. 5305; *Karadžić* Trial Judgment, n 55, para. 23; *Bemba et al.* Trial Judgment, n 29, paras 251; 403–8; 461; *Prosecutor v Krstić*, Judgment, IT-98-33-T, 2 August 2001 ('*Krstić* Trial Judgment'), paras 105–16.

[152] *Prosecutor v Tolimir*, Decision on Prosecution's Motion for Admission of 28 Intercepts from the Bar Table, IT-05-88/2-T, 20 January 2012, para. 14. See further, *Prosecutor v Blagojević and Jokić*, Decision on the Admission into Evidence of Intercept-Related Materials, IT-02-60-T, 18 December 2003, paras 21–6 (noting the supporting evidence from intercept operators and others, but excluding,

particularly important in convincing the Trial Chamber that the evidence presented was a contemporaneous record of intercepted communications.[153]

In *Ongwen*, the prosecution submitted 2,507 items of evidence related to the interception of the radio communications of the Lord's Resistance Army by the Ugandan government,[154] and the ICC Trial Chamber deemed this evidence 'highly probative'.[155] Other Trial Chambers have also viewed such communications as probative and reliable overall, provided that they are satisfied that the records have not been fabricated or tampered with.[156] However, as Diletta Marchesi has noted, technical and human factors (such as incompleteness in records or the unintentional removal of important contextual background noise, such as the sound of gunshots, through the enhancement of recordings) may introduce gaps or errors in this kind of evidence, and Chambers should be mindful of what they cannot hear in intercept records.[157]

iv. Audio-visual evidence

Audio-visual footage has played an important role in proving international crimes since Nuremberg,[158] and advances in technology and its availability mean that videos, photographs, and audio recordings are likely to only be of increasing significance over time.[159] This may include 'user-generated evidence' captured by

at para. 27, untranslated intercept notebooks for being lacking in probative value in their untranslated form); *Prosecutor v Popović* et al., Decision on Admissibility of Intercepted Communications, IT-05-88-T, 7 December 2007.

[153] *Prosecutor v Popović et al.*, Judgment, IT-05-88-T, 10 June 2010, para. 65.

[154] *Prosecutor v Ongwen*, Decision on Prosecution Request to Submit Interception Related Evidence, ICC-02/04-01/15-615, 1 December 2016.

[155] *Ongwen* Trial Judgment, n 55, para. 686. The Trial Chamber's approach was upheld by the Appeals Chamber in *Ongwen* Appeal Judgment, n 15, paras 531–82.

[156] *Popović* Trial Judgment, n 142, paras 65–6; *Bemba et al.* Trial Judgment, note 29, paras 214–27.

[157] D. Marchesi, 'Intercepted Communications in the *Ongwen* Case: Lessons to Learn on Documentary Evidence at the ICC' (2021) 22 *International Criminal Law Review* 920.

[158] See e.g. R.H. Jackson, Opening Statement before the International Military Tribunal, Second Day, 21 November 1945, in *Trial of the Major War Criminals before the International Military Tribunal: Volume II* ('We will show you these concentration camps in motion pictures, just as the Allied armies found them when they arrived, and the measures General Eisenhower had to take to clean them up'). In the *Milošević* trial, a video showing the execution of six men carried out by the 'Scorpions' paramilitary group was used to powerful effect, and this video was shown in later trials: see I. Vukušić, 'Nineteen Minutes of Horror: Insights from the Scorpions Execution Video' (2018) 12 *Genocide Studies and Prevention* 35. Audio-visual evidence also played an important role in the issuance of a warrant of arrest in *Prosecutor v Al-Werfalli*, Warrant of Arrest, ICC-01/11-01/17-2, 15 August 2017, paras 11–22 and *Prosecutor v Al-Werfalli*, Second Warrant of Arrest, ICC-01/11-01/17-13, 5 July 2018, paras 17–18, and the judgment (following a guilty plea) in *Prosecutor v Al Mahdi*, Judgment and Sentence, ICC-01/12-01/15-171, 27 September 2016. At the time of writing, such evidence had been introduced in ongoing cases including *Al Hassan*; *Said*, *Yekatom and Ngaïssona*; and *Abd-Al-Rahman*.

[159] L. Freeman and R. Vazquez-Llorente, 'Finding the Signal in the Noise: International Criminal Evidence and Procedure in the Digital Age' (2021) 19 *Journal of International Criminal Justice* 163.

individuals[160] and uploaded to the internet or shared directly with one of the parties.[161] ICC Trial Chambers have emphasised that, once the originality and integrity of such content has been established,[162] the material, 'to a significant extent, "speaks for itself"'.[163] To this end, this kind of evidence can go some way towards remedying some of the well-documented issues of witness testimony.[164] Rather than having to rely on a witness's account, the Chamber will have an additional source to examine.[165] In *Lubanga*, for example, the Chamber noted numerous internal contradictions in one witness's account, leading it to conclude that 'she is not a witness that the Chamber is able to rely on as regards many aspects of the relevant detail of her account'.[166] This witness had recognised herself in a video recording and had given comments on the content of the video shown in court.[167] The Chamber held that, despite its reservations as to the reliability of the witness's testimony, 'the video material and her comments on it ... remain essentially unaffected by these criticisms'.[168]

Trial Chambers should be wary of the alluring but incorrect proposition that audio-visual materials 'speak for themselves' and are thus free from the biases and subjectivities of human testimony.[169] In the context of police body camera footage, research has noted that such footage depicts an interaction only from the perspective of the person wearing the body camera, and as such may mislead viewers as to the broader context of the interaction.[170] Applying this insight to the context of international criminal evidence, we can imagine how a video might be recorded in such a way as to exclude relevant information that does not align with what the creator wants viewers to see. For example, in a video apparently depicting an attack on a civilian building, items suggesting that it was in fact used for military

[160] R.J. Hamilton, 'User-Generated Evidence' (2018) 57 *Columbia Journal of Transnational Law* 1; R.J. Hamilton, 'Social Media Platforms in International Criminal Investigations' (2020) 52 *Case Western Reserve Journal of International Law* 213; K. Stavrou, 'User-Generated Evidence: A Helping Hand for the ICC Investigation into the Situation in Ukraine?' (*Opinio Juris*, 14 March 2022).

[161] See e.g. *Prosecutor v Abd-Al-Rahman*, Decision on the admissibility of video (DAR-OTP-0216-0119) and records of telephone calls (DAR-OTP-0216-0127, DAR-OTP-0216-0128), ICC-02/05-01/20-876, 17 February 2023, paras 20–7 (discussing materials sent directly to a prosecution investigator via WhatsApp).

[162] *Katanga* Bar Table Decision, n 45, para. 24 (d).

[163] Ibid.; *Lubanga* Trial Judgment, n 70, para. 257.

[164] Combs, n 92.

[165] N. Combs, 'Keynote Address: Evidentiary Deficiencies in International Criminal Law: Tracing the Trajectory from Ignored to Integral to Irrelevant' (2022) 22 *International Criminal Law Review* 835.

[166] *Lubanga* Trial Judgment, n 70, para. 268.

[167] Ibid., paras 254–6.

[168] Ibid., para. 268.

[169] Clarke and Kendall, n 48; Y. McDermott et al., 'Open Source Information's Blind Spot: Human and Machine Bias in International Criminal Investigations' (2021) 19 *Journal of International Criminal Justice* 85; D. Murray et al., 'Mapping the Use of Open Source Research in UN Human Rights Investigations' (2022) 14 *Journal of Human Rights Practice* 554, 565–6.

[170] M.A. Birck, 'Do You See What I See? Problems with Juror Bias in Viewing Body-Camera Video Evidence' (2018) 24 *Michigan Journal of Race and Law* 153, 157.

purposes may have been deliberately kept out of shot.[171] Chambers should continue to exercise caution by demanding the entire recording, rather than excerpts selected by the tendering party, to gain as full a picture as possible.[172] They should also be mindful of the source of the footage; whether the person who captured the video, photograph, or audio is available to testify, and whether it is reasonable to infer facts from the audio-visual evidence itself. To be clear, this issue of perspective might not be fatal to the reliability of a piece of footage, nor should the unavailability of the individual who captured the footage in question automatically lead to it being dismissed as having limited weight. In some circumstances, the content may not be challenged by the opposing party, or the same incident may have been captured in multiple videos or images from different perspectives and/or corroborated by witness accounts, which would likely add to its evidentiary weight. As with all types of evidence, the ultimate weight to be afforded to content of this nature depends on a range of factors, including other evidence on the record.

v. Demonstrative evidence

A piece of audio-visual footage may also fall into the category of 'demonstrative' evidence.[173] In *Katanga*, the Chamber noted that photographic representations of Bogoro were introduced as a 'tool for orientation, just like a diagram or a drawing' and were of limited evidentiary weight.[174] Such orientation evidence may nevertheless be invaluable to the Chamber in drawing conclusions. In *Galić*, for example, the Trial Chamber noted that visual evidence showed that there was an unobstructed line of vision from the position of snipers to the location of two civilians who were shot at.[175]

Satellite imagery, Lindsay Freeman notes, has transformed 'from an instrument of military strategists and private corporations to an important resource for war crimes investigators and prosecutors'.[176] In a number of cases before the ICTY,

[171] See also, I. Kalpouzos, 'The Yemen Project: Open Source Investigations and the Laws of War' (*Just Security*, 23 September 2019), noting that open source evidence is open to valid counter-claims based on the attacking party's classified evidence, and that 'a direct attack on a civilian target cannot be clearly inferred from OSINT in most cases'.

[172] Kalshoven-Gieskes Forum on International Humanitarian Law, *Leiden Guidelines on the Use of Digitally Derived Evidence in International Criminal Courts and Tribunals*, available at https://leiden-guidelines.com/guidelines/ (last accessed 31 May 2023), Guideline A1 ('Instead of excerpts, videos should be submitted in their entirety'), citing *Prosecutor v Ntaganda*, Decision on Second Defence Request for Admission of Evidence from the Bar Table, ICC-01/04-02/06-2240, 21 February 2018, para. 10.

[173] See text to n 48.

[174] *Prosecutor v Katanga and Ngudjolo*, Decision on the Disclosure of Evidentiary Material relating to the Prosecutor's Site Visit to Bogoro on 28, 29, and 31 March 2009, ICC-01/04-01/07-1515-Corr, 9 October 2009, para. 39.

[175] *Prosecutor v Galić*, Judgment and Opinion, IT-98-29-T, 5 December 2003, para. 270.

[176] Freeman, n 46, 286–7.

aerial imagery taken from United States spy planes[177] was introduced to demonstrate the existence of mass graves and reburial sites.[178] In *Tolimir*, it was revealed that these images had been provided to the prosecution on condition that it was not permitted to discuss in court any information relating to the methods, tools, and personnel used to collect these images.[179] The Trial Chamber acknowledged that evidence on the method of creation of these images was lacking.[180] It dismissed the defence's challenge to their reliability and probative value, however, because prosecution investigators had testified extensively about the images, and they were corroborated by witness accounts and complemented by forensic archaeological or anthropological reports.[181]

In *Ntaganda*, satellite imagery introduced by both parties was ultimately not relied upon because the images were not contemporaneous to the events alleged. A prosecution expert witness compared satellite images of Songolo from 15 June 2002 and 22 May 2003 showing the destruction of property between those dates.[182] However, the Chamber rightly found that it could not find beyond reasonable doubt that the damage occurred in the specific attack of August 2002 charged.[183] As the expert agreed, the destruction depicted could have occurred at any time between 15 June 2002 and 22 May 2003, which was a time of ongoing conflict in the region.[184] Similarly, the defence introduced satellite imagery to counter a witness's contention that 'everything was torched in Kobu', but the Chamber concluded that this imagery apparently predated the alleged assaults in February 2003.[185] It might be expected that advances in satellite imaging technology in the intervening period would render this less of an issue today, but some regions remain under-resourced.[186] A perfunctory search of the same region of the Democratic Republic of the Congo in Google Earth Pro reveals that the satellite imagery was apparently only updated once between January 2022 and January 2023.[187] The issue of outdated satellite imagery is not limited to this region; a search for a small town in north-west Ireland revealed the imagery had last been updated almost three years previously, and the penultimate update was almost three years prior to

[177] I. Delpla, 'The ICTY Investigations: Interview with Jean-René Ruez' in I. Delpla et al. (eds), *Investigating Srebrenica: Institutions, Facts, Responsibilities* (Berghahn Books, 2012), 23, 33.

[178] E.g. *Karadžić* Trial Judgment, n 55, paras 5512–14; *Mladić* Trial Judgment, n 151, para. 2700.

[179] *Prosecutor v Tolimir*, Judgment, IT-05-88/2-T, 12 December 2012, para. 68.

[180] Ibid., para. 69.

[181] Ibid., para. 70.

[182] *Ntaganda* Trial Judgment, n 29, para. 454, note 1293.

[183] Ibid.

[184] Ibid.

[185] Ibid., para. 248, note 624.

[186] Murray et al., n 169, 565 (noting the unavailability of high-quality satellite imagery from Israel until recently owing to a piece of US legislation known as the Kyl-Bingaman amendment).

[187] Google Earth Pro imagery of Walendu-Djatsi collectivité was updated on 4 June 2022, 11 December 2020, and 15 January 2020 (last checked May 2023). Other satellite services, such as PlanetLabs and UNOSAT (the UN Satellite Centre), may be updated more frequently.

that.[188] Large urban areas are likely to be better served by high-quality satellite imagery, as we saw from the *New York Times* investigation into killings of civilians in Bucha, near Kyiv.[189] Journalists were able to compare satellite imagery from 28 February, 9 March, 11 March, and 19 March to determine that the bodies depicted in widely circulated videos were not placed there after the Russian withdrawal from the town on 30 March, as had been claimed by Russia's Ministry of Defence.[190]

Visual depictions or digital reconstructions of sites of alleged atrocities can be introduced for demonstrative purposes and may assist the Trial Chamber 'in finding context in the facts and strands of evidence'.[191] In *Al Mahdi*, for example, the prosecution introduced an 'interactive platform' to demonstrate the destruction of mausoleums in Timbuktu; this platform incorporated satellite imagery, 360-degree panoramic photographs, sketches and drawings made by experts, and audio and video recordings.[192] A similar platform, also created by SITU Research, was introduced in *Al Hassan*.[193] There is a risk, as Sarah Zarmsky has pointed out, that such platforms may fall foul of the 'seeing is believing' phenomenon, where a fact-finder finds the compelling visual presentation more convincing than the underpinning evidence upon which it is based.[194] There is also a risk to equality of arms, if the defence does not have the resources to create its own platform or challenge that submitted by the prosecution.[195] For these reasons, two safeguards are crucial: (a) the evidence upon which the reconstruction is based should be admitted to the record for examination by the parties and the judges; and (b) both parties should be given equal access to the platform (with adequate training on how to navigate it, if necessary).[196] If there is a discrepancy between the demonstrative evidence and the underlying evidence, then the former should be disregarded and only the latter should be relied upon.[197]

[188] Google Earth Pro imagery of Manorhamilton was updated on 11 April 2020 and 18 September 2017 (last checked May 2023).

[189] M. Browne et al., 'Satellite Images Show Bodies Lay in Bucha for Weeks, Despite Russian Claims', *New York Times*, 4 April 2022.

[190] Ibid. For a similar example, see Human Rights Watch, 'Burma: Satellite Images Confirm Mass Destruction', 17 October 2017, online at https://www.hrw.org/news/2017/10/17/burma-new-satellite-images-confirm-mass-destruction (last accessed 29 May 2023).

[191] *Ayyash et al.* Trial Judgment, n 24, paras 385–6.

[192] *Prosecutor v Al Mahdi*, Transcript, ICC-01/12-01/15-T-4-Red-ENG, 22 August 2016, 44 (lines 23–5) and 45 (lines 1–3).

[193] *Al Hassan* Prior Recorded Testimony Decision, n 130, paras 27–30.

[194] Zarmsky, n 48.

[195] Ibid., 221.

[196] *Al Hassan* Prior Recorded Testimony Decision, n 130, paras 28–9. This may also require hardware provision, if the platform cannot run on Court-issued computers used by one of the parties: see further, *Prosecutor v Al Hassan*, Report on further implementation of the 'Registry's Quarterly Report on Email Decisions for the months of April until June 2021', ICC-01/12-01/18-1660-Conf, 19 August 2021, Annex 2: Confidential, ICC-01/12-01/18-1660-Anx2-Red (authorising direct contact between the defence and the witnesses who created the online platform, when the defence had difficulties running the platform on their computers).

[197] *Ayyash et al.* Trial Judgment, n 24, para. 386.

vi. Forensic, ballistic, and other technical evidence

This type of real evidence, usually introduced through an expert witness report, has been seen by some Chambers as preferable to other forms of evidence,[198] likely because of its perceived objectivity and scientific nature.[199] Specialist expert evidence has played a crucial role in, *inter alia*, corroborating accounts of killings;[200] helping the Chamber in calculating the numbers of bodies buried in mass graves and the cause of death of victims,[201] and interpreting other evidence, such as information on shelling patterns,[202] or mobile phone communication and cell tower data.[203] In determining the weight to be given to such evidence, the Chamber should examine the methodology used and any assumptions made by the expert in reaching their conclusions.[204]

As with all types of expert evidence, there is a fine balance to be drawn between accepting the expertise of the witness and maintaining the Chamber's control over fact-finding.[205] On the other hand, conclusions drawn by a Trial Chamber might be legitimised by reference to expert opinion. Most notably, the Trial Chamber in *Gotovina* found a middle point between two experts' views in concluding that artillery projectiles that landed within 200 metres of a military target could be said to have been deliberately fired at that target, with impact sites outside of that 200-metre range indicating an indiscriminate attack.[206] The Appeals Chamber, in overturning the judgment, found that the Trial Chamber had not explained how it had reached the 200-metre margin of error standard, nor did the standard appear to be based on the evidence before the Chamber, and furthermore, it had disregarded important factors raised by one of the experts (such as wind speed) in uniformly applying its standard.[207] While the deference to be shown to expert accounts will hinge on a case-by-case analysis,[208] this example demonstrates that a

[198] *Gbagbo* Adjournment Decision, n 31, para. 27, noting a preference for 'as much forensic and other material evidence as possible', 'duly authenticated' and with 'clear and unbroken chains of custody' (footnotes omitted).

[199] See also text to n 163 on evidence that 'speaks for itself'.

[200] *Prosecutor v Blagojević and Jokić*, Judgment, IT-02-60-T, 17 January 2005, para. 356; *Krstić* Trial Judgment, n 151, para. 79.

[201] E.g. *Krstić* Trial Judgment, n 151, paras 71–9; *Prosecutor v Kayishema and Ruzindana*, Judgment, ICTR-95-1-T, 21 May 1999, paras 325–6; *Prosecutor v Mrkšić* et al., Judgment, IT-95-13/1-T, 27 September 2007, paras 487–98.

[202] *Prosecutor v Strugar*, Judgment, IT-01-42-T, 31 January 2005 ('*Strugar* Trial Judgment'), paras 204–12.

[203] *Ayyash et al.* Trial Judgment, n 24, paras 376–7; 1998–2145; *Bemba et al.* Trial Judgment, n 29, paras 213–23.

[204] *Ayyash et al.* Trial Judgment, n 24, paras 279–380; *Strugar* Trial Judgment, n 202, paras 209–11.

[205] See e.g. *AFRC* Trial Judgment, n 66, para. 151; *Prosecutor v Tadić*, Transcript, IT-94-1-T, 20 May 1996, 901 (objection of defence lawyer Steven Kay that the expert, Hannah Sophie Greve, would effectively be 'usurping the role of this Court, which is to make findings of fact').

[206] *Gotovina* Trial Judgment, n 5, paras 1898–1941.

[207] *Prosecutor v Gotovina and Markač*, Judgment, IT-06-90-A, 16 November 2012, paras 58–61. Judge Pocar dissented, finding that the Majority of the Appeals Chamber should have clarified what the relevant legal standard was and applied it: *Prosecutor v Gotovina and Markač*, Judgment, IT-06-90-A, 16 November 2012, Dissenting Opinion of Judge Pocar, para. 13.

[208] See also, on expert testimony, text to nn 78–79.

Chamber deciding to find a middle ground between prosecution and defence experts in drawing its own conclusions may be found to be an erroneous conclusion unsupported by the evidence.

E. Conclusion

This chapter set out some general practices derived from international criminal practice on the evaluation of evidence, before examining how different categories of evidence have been evaluated in practice. Section B outlined several key features of the framework for evidence evaluation in international criminal trials, which included flexibility, the free evaluation of evidence, the absence of a corroboration rule, the 'sole or decisive' rule for untested evidence, the duty to provide a reasoned opinion, and the principle of *in dubio pro reo*.

Section C discussed how judges evaluate the credibility and reliability of witness testimony, including special categories of witnesses such as expert witnesses and insider witnesses. Important factors in determining how much weight to afford to witness accounts include consistency, plausibility, demeanour and apparent sincerity, indications of collusion or witness interference, relationship to the accused, bias and motivation, contradictions with earlier statements or other evidence on the record, and the impact of trauma and the passage of time. Section D provided an account of how particular types of evidence, such as prior recorded testimony, NGO and media reports, demonstrative evidence, intercepts, audio-visual evidence, and technical evidence such as forensic or ballistic evidence, are weighed. This part outlined some considerations that come into play in evaluating these specific types of evidence.

An overarching conclusion that could be drawn from the detailed analysis in sections C and D could be that there is no type of evidence that is inherently more probative than any other category. The weight given to an individual item of evidence or witness account will depend on a range of factors, including the fact(s) it was introduced to prove, its perceived credibility and reliability, and whether it was corroborated by other evidence on the record. The evaluation of the evidentiary record as a whole is considered in detail in the next chapter.

For those building cases, this conclusion, and the practice of the international criminal tribunals upon which it is based, may be less than helpful. As Chlevickaitė et al. have pointed out, the flexibility afforded to judges means that it is impossible to derive a clear methodology for the (free) evaluation of the evidence, and each individual judge's subjective preferences and experiences may have as much of a bearing on the probative value of an item of evidence as the evidence's inherent qualities.[209] We see those individual preferences also play out in judges' approaches to weighing the evidence as a whole, as shall be seen in Chapter 6.

[209] Chlevickaitė et al., n 56, 187.

6

Weighing the Evidence as a Whole

A. Introduction

The previous chapter outlined how different categories of evidence are evaluated by judges in international criminal trials. This chapter builds from that discussion, by analysing how the entire record of evidence is assessed by the Trial Chamber in determining whether the prosecution has proven the guilt of the accused beyond reasonable doubt. As shall be seen, this issue has been subject to intensive judicial debate. Most, if not all, judges claim that they assess the evidentiary record in a holistic manner, considering each piece of the record in light of the entire body of evidence. However, what this means in practice seems to differ, with some judges arguing that their colleagues have scrutinised the evidence too rigorously and have failed to see the bigger picture,[1] and others opining that the weaknesses, gaps, or inconsistencies in the evidential record have been overlooked in their colleagues' analysis.[2]

Section B of this chapter presents some general remarks about the nature of fact-finding in international criminal law as an exercise in 'reasoning under uncertainty'. Section C examines the tribunals' stated approaches to the evaluation of evidence, analysing how individual pieces of evidence are assessed in the context of other evidence on the record (and any gaps in that record) to establish whether, taken as a whole, the evidence establishes material facts beyond reasonable doubt. This section explains how the debate between what have been dubbed 'atomistic'

[1] Most prominently, see *Prosecutor v Ngudjolo*, Judgment on the Prosecutor's appeal against the decision of Trial Chamber II entitled 'Judgment pursuant to article 74 of the Statute', ICC-01/04-02/12-271-Corr, 7 April 2015 ('*Ngudjolo* Appeal Judgment'), Joint Dissenting Opinion of Judge Trendafilova and Judge Tarfusser, ICC-01/04-02/12-271-AnxA, 27 February 2015, para. 31 ('The Chamber assessed in isolation individual items of evidence and failed to properly consider the evidence in its entirety'); *Prosecutor v Katanga*, Judgment pursuant to Article 74 of the Statute, ICC-01/04-01/07-3436, 7 March 2014 ('*Katanga* Trial Judgment'), Concurring Opinion of Judges Diarra and Cotte, ICC-01/04-01/07-3436-AnxII-tENG, 13 March 2014, para. 4. For a similar academic critique, see D. Robinson, 'The Other Poisoned Chalice: Unprecedented Evidentiary Standards in the Gbagbo Case? (Part 1)' (*EJIL:Talk!*, 5 November 2019), criticising what he deems the judges' 'Cartesian' approach.

[2] *Prosecutor v Bemba*, Judgment on the appeal of Mr Jean-Pierre Bemba Gombo against Trial Chamber III's 'Judgment pursuant to Article 74 of the Statute', ICC-01/05-01/08-3636-Red, 8 June 2018 ('*Bemba* Appeal Judgment'), Separate Opinion of Judge Van den Wyngaert and Judge Morrison, ICC-01/05-01/08-3636-Anx2, 8 June 2018, para. 15; *Katanga* Trial Judgment, n 1, Minority Opinion of Judge Van den Wyngaert, ICC-01/04-01/07-3436-AnxI, 7 March 2014, paras 148–54. See further, D. Guilfoyle, 'Part II—This is Not Fine: The International Criminal Court in Trouble' (*EJIL:Talk!*, 22 March 2019) ('The more devastating and fundamental disagreement which appears to run through ICC judicial decision making is the correct approach to the assessment of evidence').

Proving International Crimes. Yvonne McDermott, Oxford University Press.
DOI: 10.1093/oso/9780198842972.003.0006

and 'holistic' approaches may mask the real division between judicial approaches to the evaluation of evidence—that is, how much detail the Chamber needs to provide on precisely which evidence led it to establish which finding of fact or to find that a particular fact had not been proven. It is argued that the creation of new 'Guidelines for ICC Judgment Drafting' and 'Guidelines for ICC Judgment Structure', now incorporated into the Chambers Practice Manual, are a step in the right direction, but may not fully alleviate the clear tension between judicial preferences on the level of granularity that should be provided in the judgment in relation to the assessment of evidence, and the extent to which the evidence 'as a whole' can remedy deficiencies in individual pieces of evidence. To this end, section D argues that formal logic and tools developed from argumentation theory, decision science, and statistics may assist in structuring judgments that clearly link the factual and legal findings of the Chamber to the evidence presented.

B. Fact-finding in international criminal trials: reasoning under uncertainty

In almost all areas of human activity, people reason about information and make decisions in situations of uncertainty. For example, a doctor will be able to construct multiple hypotheses on the cause of a patient's symptoms and then will have to determine which of those causes is the most likely, often based on additional diagnostic tests.[3] Reasoning in this, and countless other daily activities, is necessarily *probabilistic* in nature: it involves thinking about the likelihood of a particular explanation or outcome in circumstances where one can never be fully certain.[4] Probability can be an off-putting concept to those with an aversion to mathematics, and in areas such as law where statistics are not a common feature.[5] However, we express likelihoods in non-mathematical terms every day, through phrases like 'it seems unlikely'; 'I am sure', and so forth. As Shafer has argued, 'Probability is more about structuring arguments than it is about numbers. All probabilities rest upon arguments.'[6] Probabilistic reasoning in international criminal trials, therefore, requires an evaluation of arguments—most importantly,

[3] A. Liefgreen, T. Pilditch, and D. Lagnado, 'Strategies for Selecting and Evaluating Information' (2020) 123 *Cognitive Psychology*, article 101332.

[4] D.A. Schum, *The Evidential Foundations of Probabilistic Reasoning* (2nd edn, Northwestern University Press, 2001), xiii.

[5] See e.g., L.H. Tribe, 'Trial by Mathematics: Precision and Ritual in the Legal Process' (1971) 84 *Harvard Law Review* 1329; A. Tversky and D. Kahneman, 'Judgment under Uncertainty: Heuristics and Biases' (1976) 185 *Science* 1124 (outlining the heuristics that are employed to assess probabilities, and their related biases); L.J. Cohen, *The Probable and the Provable* (Clarendon Press, 1977) (arguing against 'Pascalian' or mathematical probability's application to legal contexts).

[6] G. Tecuci et al., *Intelligence Analysis as Discovery of Evidence, Hypotheses, and Arguments: Connecting the Dots* (CUP, 2016), 205, citing G. Shafer, 'Combining AI and OR' (1988) *University of Kansas School of Business Working Paper No. 195*, 5–9.

the prosecution's argument that the person on trial bears criminal responsibility for the alleged crimes—against the requisite standard of proof. When probabilistic reasoning is understood in this way, as matter of evaluating competing arguments, the fierce academic debate between proponents of so-called Baconian and Pascalian approaches to probabilistic reasoning seems less important.[7]

Fact-finding in international criminal trials will always be probabilistic in nature, because the evidence is invariably incomplete, rarely conclusive, often ambiguous, frequently dissonant, and always with varying degrees of credibility and reliability.[8] It is *invariably incomplete* because no matter how much evidence is submitted in relation to a contested event or fact, it will never be all the evidence on that point. An allegation of a single international crime could potentially be supported by hundreds (if not thousands) of eyewitnesses to the alleged event, and further witnesses and potentially hundreds of documents apparently relevant to what the accused allegedly knew or did not know and the contextual elements of the crime. There is no way that a single trial can consider all of this information, nor that any investigation can capture the entirety of the relevant evidence; the parties make value judgments as to their strongest evidence and filter their information accordingly.[9] International criminal evidence is *rarely conclusive*, because there is always room for doubt.[10] As Taroni et al. have noted, because 'uncertainty is an

[7] T. Anderson, D. Schum, and W. Twining, *Analysis of Evidence* (CUP, 2009), 229 equate the Pascalian approach with a 'mathematical' theory of probability, while the Baconian theory of probability is 'nonmathematical' in nature. This is because the Baconian approach places probability on an ordinal scale: Anderson et al., 257–8. Tecuci et al., n 6, 206–7, distinguish the Pascalian approach, as asking the question 'how strong is the evidence for this proposition?', from the Baconian approach, which asks 'how much evidence do we have about this hypothesis, and how many questions about it remain unanswered?' Setting out the debate on Pascalian versus Baconian approaches, see Cohen, n 5 (coining the term 'Baconian probability'); R.O. Lempert, 'The New Evidence Scholarship: Analyzing the Process of Proof' (1986) 66 *Boston University Law Review* 439; M. Klamberg, *Evidence in International Criminal Trials: Confronting Legal Gaps and the Reconstruction of Disputed Events* (Nijhoff, 2013) 161–4; W. Twining, 'Some Scepticism about Some Scepticisms' in W. Twining, *Rethinking Evidence: Exploratory Essays* (CUP, 2009), 99. 'Inference to the best explanation' is often distinguished from probability-based theories (see e.g. R. Allen and M. Pardo, 'Relative Plausibility and Its Critics' (2019) 23 *International Journal of Evidence & Proof* 5 and R.J. Allen, 'Taming Complexity: Rationality, the Law of Evidence and the Nature of the Legal System' (2013) 12 *Law, Probability and Risk* 99, 105), insofar as it is about justified belief, not probability; but in reality the two are not so widely distinct: see e.g. H. Prakken et al., 'Editors' Review and Introduction: Models of Rational Proof in Criminal Law' (2020) 12 *Topics in Cognitive Science* 1053, 1057, noting recent attempts to develop combined approaches, such as F.J. Bex, *Arguments, Stories, and Criminal Evidence: A Formal Hybrid Theory* (Springer, 2011); F. Taroni et al., 'Statistical Interpretation of Evidence: Bayesian Analysis' in M.M. Houck (ed.), *Encyclopedia of Forensic Sciences* (3rd edn, Elsevier, 2023), 656 (framing probability as a matter of 'personal degrees of belief').

[8] This list is adopted from one drawn up by Tecuci et al. in outlining the 'five major reasons why conclusions reached in intelligence analysis based on evidence will be necessarily probabilistic in nature': Tecuci et al., n 6, 159.

[9] See X. Agirre Aranburu, 'The Contribution of Analysis to the Quality Control in Criminal Investigation' in X. Agirre et al. (eds), *Quality Control in Criminal Investigation* (TOAEP, 2020), 117.

[10] See Chapter 4, discussing the standard of proof beyond reasonable doubt; it does not mean, as is frequently emphasised, proof beyond any doubt. See e.g. *Ngudjolo* Appeals Judgment, n 1, Joint Dissenting Opinion of Judge Trendafilova and Judge Tarfusser, ICC-01/04-02/12-271-AnxA, 27 February 2015, paras 55–8.

inevitable complication' by any judge or fact-finder in legal contexts, '[i]nference, in this context, is mainly inductive and relates to the use of incomplete information, to reason about propositions of interest'.[11] Evidence in international criminal trials is *often ambiguous*, to the extent that it is unclear what it tells us. For example, in *Ongwen*, the Trial Chamber noted the use of ambiguous language in intercept evidence, and that 'none of these witnesses [whose testimony pertained to the intercepts] gave indisputably clear evidence on all points'.[12] It is *frequently dissonant* because the parties will each lead their own evidence, often in direct contradiction. This is true even for expert testimony, where two equally qualified experts may suggest quite distinct conclusions or explanations.[13] Lastly, as was clearly seen in the previous chapter, international criminal evidence bears *varying degrees of credibility and reliability*—a witness or piece of evidence may be deemed credible or reliable on some aspects but not others.[14]

Probabilistic reasoning often involves updating one's prior beliefs in light of each new piece of information as it is presented.[15] Under what is commonly called 'relative plausibility theory' or 'inference to the best explanation', a fact-finder evaluates the different likely explanations of the evidence, and considers which of these explanations is the most likely.[16] Of course, in light of the standard of proof and the presumption of innocence, even if the likely best explanation of the evidence is that the defendant is guilty, he or she must still be acquitted if another reasonable inference (that of innocence) can be drawn.[17] Considering the stated 'holistic' approach to fact-finding, as discussed at length in section C below, something akin to 'inference to the best explanation' is probably the most appropriate way of explaining how judges in international criminal trials approach their fact-finding role, rather

[11] F. Taroni et al., 'The Logic of Inference and Decision for Scientific Evidence' in C. Dahlman et al. (eds), *Philosophical Foundations of Evidence Law* (OUP, 2021), 251.

[12] *Prosecutor v Ongwen*, Trial Judgment, ICC-02/04-01/15-1762, 4 February 2021 ('*Ongwen* Trial Judgment'), para. 559; *Ongwen* Trial Judgment, para. 688 (noting the intercepts 'are replete with jargon, proverbs and ambiguous phrasing'.)

[13] See Chapter 5, section D.vi.

[14] See Chapter 5, text to n 68. See also, *Prosecutor v Simba*, Judgment, ICTR-01-76-A, 27 November 2007, para. 132 ('the probative value of a document may be assessed differently in different cases, depending on the circumstances').

[15] This is at the core of Bayesian probability theory: Bayes's theorem provides a formula for updating one's belief (or 'priors') in an ultimate hypothesis (H) given new evidence E, taking into account the likelihood of evidence E. See N. Fenton and D. Lagnado, 'Bayesianism: Objections and Rebuttals' in C. Dahlman et al. (eds) *Philosophical Foundations of Evidence Law* (OUP, 2021), 267, 271–2.

[16] See Allen and Pardo, n 7; P. Lipton, *Inference to the Best Explanation* (2nd edn, Routledge, 1991); M. Lidén, 'Confirmation Bias in Investigations of Core International Crimes: Risk Factors and Quality Control Techniques' in X. Agirre et al. (eds), *Quality Control in Criminal Investigation* (TOAEP, 2020), 461; M.S. Pardo and R.J. Allen, 'Juridical Proof and the Best Explanation' (2008) 27 *Law and Philosophy* 223; R.J. Allen, 'Nature of Juridical Proof' (1991) 13 *Cardozo Law Review* 373; R.J. Allen, 'Factual Ambiguity and a Theory of Evidence' (1994) 88 *Northwestern University Law Review* 604; F. Bex and D. Walton, 'Burdens and Standards of Proof for Inference to the Best Explanation: Three Case Studies' (2012) 11 *Law, Probability, and Risk* 113; T. Williamson, 'Abductive Philosophy' (2016) 3–4 *Philosophical Forum* 263, 267 (arguing that 'inference to the best explanation may be the closest we can get to probabilistic epistemology in practice').

[17] See Chapter 4, section C.iii.

than serially updating probabilistic judgments on the plausibility of a hypothesis.[18] Research on the 'story model' suggests that most people approach reasoning under uncertainty in this way; they consider which account is most coherent and plausible.[19] And, as shall be seen in Chapter 7, the Appeals Chamber of the ICC has said that an appellate chamber will show deference to a trial chamber's findings of fact but may overturn such findings where it considers them inconsistent with 'logic, common sense, scientific knowledge and experience',[20] which again suggests that rationality, logic, and robustness are central facets of defensible international criminal judgments. The next section examines how Trial Chambers have approached their task of weighing the evidence as a whole.

C. The structure of proof in international criminal trials

In *Ntagerura*, the ICTR Appeals Chamber set out the three 'different stages of the fact-finding process which a Trial Chamber undertakes before it can enter a conviction'.[21] The first stage involves an assessment of the credibility of the evidence presented, which cannot be undertaken in a piecemeal manner; each piece of evidence has 'to be analysed in the light of the entire body of evidence adduced'.[22] In the second stage, following the analysis of all relevant evidence, the Chamber will assess whether the evidence presented by the prosecution establishes the existence of the facts alleged, notwithstanding any evidence relied upon by the defence.[23]

[18] M. Klamberg, 'Epistemological Controversies and Evaluation of Evidence in International Criminal Trials' in K.J. Heller et al. (eds), *The Oxford Handbook of International Criminal Law* (OUP, 2020), 450; M. Klamberg, 'The Alternative Hypothesis Approach, Robustness and International Criminal Justice: A Plea for a "Combined Approach" to Evaluation of Evidence' (2015) 13 *Journal of International Criminal Justice* 535; K. Ambos, 'Introduction' in K. Ambos et al. (eds), *Evidence in International Criminal Procedure: A Commentary* (Hart/Beck, forthcoming, on file with author). Compare, however, *Prosecutor v Gbagbo and Blé Goudé*, Judgment in the appeal of the Prosecutor against Trial Chamber I's decision on the no case to answer motions, ICC-02/11-01/15-1400-Red, 31 March 2021 ('*Gbagbo and Blé Goudé* Appeal Judgment'), para. 239 ('Judges who have been conducting trials, in some cases trials lasting years, will surely have developed, and should be expected to have developed, their view of the case, based on the appropriate legal principles, over the period of time during which they are hearing that case'). The *Report of the Independent Expert Review of the International Criminal Court and the Rome Statute System*, ICC-ASP/19/16, 30 September 2020, paras 628–31, encouraged frequent deliberation, review of evidence and drafting throughout the trial, to facilitate the final judicial deliberations.

[19] N. Pennington and R. Hastie, 'The Story Model for Juror Decision Making' in R. Hastie (ed.), *Inside the Juror: The Psychology of Juror Decision Making* (CUP, 1993), 192; D. Lagnado, *Explaining the Evidence: How the Mind Investigates the World* (CUP, 2021), 186–209.

[20] *Prosecutor v Ntaganda*, Public redacted version of Judgment on the appeals of Mr Bosco Ntaganda and the Prosecutor against the decision of Trial Chamber VI of 8 July 2019 entitled 'Judgment', ICC-01/04-02/06-2666-Red, 30 March 2021 ('*Ntaganda* Appeal Judgment'), para. 39; *Gbagbo and Blé Goudé* Appeal Judgment, n 18, para. 68.

[21] *Prosecutor v Ntagerura* et al., Judgment, ICTR-99-46-A, 7 July 2006 ('*Ntagerura et al.* Appeal Judgment'), para. 174.

[22] Ibid.

[23] Ibid.

At this stage, the standard of proof is applied to all material facts (that is, the elements of the crime, the mode of liability, and the facts indispensable for entering a conviction). In the third and final stage, the Chamber must assess whether to enter a conviction, by determining whether the elements of the crime(s) charged and the mode(s) of liability have been established beyond reasonable doubt.[24] Even if some material facts pleaded in the indictment are not established beyond reasonable doubt, other material facts proven to this standard might be sufficient to underpin a conviction, if they establish the elements of the crime or mode of liability.[25] The Chamber confirmed that applying the criminal standard of proof to each piece of evidence would be erroneous.[26]

Other international criminal tribunals have similarly emphasised that each piece of evidence cannot be scrutinised individually, 'as if it existed in a hermetically sealed compartment',[27] but rather must be evaluated in the context of other evidence on the record.[28] The evidentiary weight of a piece of evidence (or lack thereof) may only become apparent when it is corroborated or contradicted by other evidence on the record.[29]

There is no doubt that the correct approach to fact-finding involves the assessment of each piece of evidence in conjunction with other relevant evidence on the record rather than in isolation. No judge would disagree with that. In recent years, however, something of a 'worn argument'[30] has emerged between ICC judges over

[24] Ibid.

[25] Ibid.

[26] Ibid.

[27] *Prosecutor v Tadić*, Judgment on Allegations of Contempt against Prior Counsel, Milan Vujin, IT-94-1-A-R77, 31 January 2000 ('*Tadić* Contempt Decision'), para. 92.

[28] Ibid.; *Prosecutor v Lubanga*, Public redacted Judgment on the appeal of Mr Thomas Lubanga Dyilo against his conviction, ICC-01/04-01/06-3121-Red, 1 December 2014 ('*Lubanga* Appeal Judgment'), para. 22 ('the Trial Chamber is required to carry out a holistic evaluation and weighing of *all the evidence taken together* in relation to the fact at issue. Indeed, it would be incorrect for a finder of fact to do otherwise'); *Prosecutor v Ayyash* et al., Judgment, STL-11-01/T/TC, 18 August 2020 ('*Ayyash et al.* Trial Judgment'), para. 232; *Prosecutor v Gbagbo and Blé Goudé*, Reasons for oral decision of 15 January 2019 on the Requête de la Défense de Laurent Gbagbo afin qu'un jugement d'acquittement portant sur toutes les charges soit prononcé en faveur de Laurent Gbagbo et que sa mise en liberté immédiate soit ordonnée, and on the Blé Goudé Defence no case to answer motion, ICC-02/11-01/15-1263, 16 July 2019 ('*Gbagbo* Reasons'), Dissenting Opinion of Judge Herrera Carbuccia, para. 5, citing *Prosecutor v Halilović*, Judgment, IT-01-48-A, 16 October 2007, para. 128.

[29] *Tadić* Contempt Decision, n 27, para. 92; see further *Ayyash et al.* Trial Judgment, n 28, para. 232; see also *Prosecutor v Kupreškić*, Judgment, IT-95-16-A, 23 October 2001 ('*Kupreškić* Appeal Judgment'), para. 334.

[30] *Prosecutor v Bemba et al.*, Public Redacted Judgment on the appeals of Mr Jean-Pierre Bemba Gombo, Mr Aimé Kilolo Musamba, Mr Jean-Jacques Mangenda Kabongo, Mr Fidèle Babala Wandu and Mr Narcisse Arido against the decision of Trial Chamber VII entitled 'Judgment pursuant to Article 74 of the Statute', ICC-01/05-01/13-2275-Red, 8 March 2018 ('*Bemba* et al. Appeal Judgment'), Separate Opinion of Judge Henderson, ICC-01/05-01/13-2275-Anx, 8 March 2018, para. 41. There is a vast body of literature on the topic of atomistic versus holistic approaches, e.g. M.S. Pardo, 'Juridical Proof, Evidence, and Pragmatic Meaning: Toward Evidentiary Holism' (2000–1) 95 *Northwestern University Law Review* 399; J.L. Mnookin, 'Atomism, Holism, and the Judicial Assessment of Evidence' (2013) 60 *UCLA Law Review* 1524; M. Schweizer, 'Comparing Holistic and Atomistic Evaluation of Evidence' (2014) 13 *Law, Probability and Risk* 65.

what have been broadly termed the 'atomistic' and 'holistic' approaches.[31] For example, Judges Van den Wyngaert and Morrison noted in *Bemba*:

> It may be considered that the above criticisms are overly 'atomistic' and that we should have appreciated that the Trial Chamber evaluated the evidence 'holistically'. If so, and with the greatest of respect, holistic fact-finding should not be an excuse or a reason for making findings beyond a reasonable doubt on the basis of a collection of weak evidence. When the Appeals Chamber says that the Trial Chamber must analyse the evidence holistically, all this means is that the evidentiary weight of individual items of evidence should not be determined in isolation, but rather in conjunction with other relevant evidence. It is also true that the credibility and evidentiary weight of specific items of evidence is not determinative. What matters is how strong and convincing the totality of the relevant evidence in relation to a particular fact is. That said, analysing evidence holistically cannot cure the weakness of individual items of evidence and a number of weak arguments for a proposition do not and cannot ever combine into a strong reason for accepting it.[32]

The approach set out by these two judges, who acknowledged that it may be criticised as being overly 'atomistic', was, however, almost identical to that of two judges in *Ngudjolo*, who criticised what they saw as an overly 'fragmentary' approach taken by the Trial Chamber.[33] Judges Tarfusser and Trendafilova also agreed that evidence should not be assessed in isolation, and expressed the need to

> adopt a holistic approach, whereby all relevant pieces of evidence are considered together as an entire body, i.e. as a system of evidence, and not merely on their own. Only when the trial chamber does not confine its assessment to each individual piece of evidence in isolation will the trier of fact be in a position to make an accurate determination on the merits of the case.[34]

The close parallels between these two pairs of judges from apparently different sides of the 'holistic versus atomistic' debate highlights how that debate poses a

[31] See e.g. *Gbagbo* Reasons, n 28, Dissenting Opinion of Judge Herrera Carbuccia, ICC-02/11-01/15-1263-AnxC-Red, 16 July 2019, para. 5.

[32] *Bemba* Appeal Judgment, n 2, Separate Opinion of Judge Van den Wyngaert and Judge Morrison, ICC-01/05-01/08-3636-Anx2, 8 June 2018, para. 15.

[33] *Ngudjolo* Appeals Judgment, n 1, Joint Dissenting Opinion of Judge Trendafilova and Judge Tarfusser, ICC-01/04-02/12-271-AnxA, 27 February 2015, paras 41–51.

[34] Ibid., para. 39. See also *Gbagbo* Reasons, n 28, Opinion of Judge Tarfusser, ICC-02/11-01/15-1263-AnxA, 16 July 2019, para. 73 ('I have looked at the evidence in its entirety, taking it all "at its highest" and "holistically"; however, I have done so in respect of the evidence tendered as a whole, irrespective of whether such evidence would or should fall under the heading and label of incriminating as opposed to exculpatory').

false dichotomy and masks the true issue at the heart of that debate. The crux of the disagreement is not, as is sometimes suggested, whether individual pieces of evidence should be assessed in the context of other relevant evidence on the record—of course they should. The main tension between the judges instead arises from two interrelated questions. First, to what extent can weaknesses in individual aspects of the evidential record be rectified by other (perhaps equally weak) pieces of evidence, taken together as part of a holistic approach? And second, how should judgments be structured, and how much detail does the Chamber need to provide on precisely which evidence led it to establish each finding of fact or to find that a particular fact had not been proven?

i. Gap-filling through a holistic approach

Some critics express an unease that references to a holistic approach may be used to paper over the cracks of an evidentiary record replete with weaknesses and inconsistencies.[35] On the other side of the debate is a concern that judges may lose sight of the bigger picture if they interrogate the individual pixels of that picture too closely.[36] But, as I have argued elsewhere, if an impressionistic overview from the evidence as a whole suggests one broad picture, but a close analysis of the underpinning evidence shows that the intuitive conclusion is not supported by that evidence, this can only be a good thing in ensuring rectitude of decision.[37] As Judge Henderson noted in *Gbagbo and Blé Goudé*:

> The Prosecutor has invited the Chamber to conduct a holistic evaluation of the evidence submitted where all the relevant items of evidence are to be considered together as an entire body of evidence and not merely on their own. While I agree that this is appropriate, such an approach is not incompatible with the need for careful scrutiny and rigorous analysis of the individual bits and pieces of evidence and the inferences that the Chamber has been invited to draw therefrom.[38]

[35] Y. McDermott, 'Strengthening the Evaluation of Evidence in International Criminal Trials' (2017) 17 *International Criminal Law Review* 682, 688; D. Guilfoyle, 'Lacking Conviction: Is the International Criminal Court Broken? An Organisational Failure Analysis' (2019) 20 *Melbourne Journal of International Law* 401.

[36] Y. McDermott, 'Inferential Reasoning and Proof in International Criminal Trials: The Potentials of Wigmorean Analysis' (2015) 13 *Journal of International Criminal Justice* 507, 528; *Bemba* Appeal Judgment, n 2, Separate Opinion of Judge Van den Wyngaert and Judge Morrison, ICC-01/05-01/08-3636-Anx2, 8 June 2018, paras 60 (on the 'wood for the trees' argument) and 67 ('The Prosecutor's appeal to the 'holistic' approach cannot counteract the absence of clear and convincing evidence').

[37] McDermott, n 36, 528. Cf. *Bemba* Appeal Judgment, n 2, Dissenting Opinion of Judge Monageng and Judge Hofmański, ICC-01/05-01/08-3636-Anx1, 8 June 2018, para. 47 (arguing that the Majority did 'not engage in any meaningful way with the factual findings entered by the Trial Chamber, or demonstrate any awareness of the evidence on which these findings were based').

[38] *Gbagbo* Reasons, n 28, Reasons of Judge Henderson, para. 31.

In carrying out that scrutiny of individual items of evidence, judges may note a gap or weakness in the evidence, but that gap may be filled by another piece of evidence, forming a sort of corroborative jigsaw.[39] For example, a document purporting to be minutes from an important meeting may be of unclear provenance, insofar as its origin and chain of custody is unclear and it bears no hallmarks of authenticity. Yet, its evidentiary weight may be strengthened by the testimony of witnesses who claim to have attended that meeting and whose accounts match those of the minutes. Alternatively, other evidence showing that the persons listed as present in the minutes could not possibly have attended the alleged meeting at that time and date, taken in conjunction with the inherent weaknesses of the document, may lead a Chamber to conclude that it bears no weight. By contrast, some evidence may be so lacking in relevance, reliability, or significance such that it is deemed inadmissible, in which case it cannot be relied upon, or, despite some weaknesses, it may be admitted with the Chamber deciding to consider its deficiencies when weighing the evidence as a whole. This piece of evidence, even if taken with other evidence, is extremely unlikely to underpin a factual finding. It seems that this is what Judges Van den Wyngaert and Morrison referred to when they said that 'analysing evidence holistically cannot cure the weakness of individual items of evidence and a number of weak arguments for a proposition do not and cannot ever combine into a strong reason for accepting it'.[40]

ii. The structure of judgments

As with other areas of judicial practice, ICC judges have recently taken some steps towards implementing shared approaches to the structure and drafting of judgments through the non-binding Chambers Practice Manual.[41] Following a judicial retreat in 2019, the judges agreed upon new 'Guidelines for ICC Judgment Drafting' and 'Guidelines for ICC Judgment Structure', now incorporated into the Chambers Practice Manual. We are told that the guidelines

> aim at establishing a unified approach to the judgment drafting process and setting out a structure for judgments on conviction or acquittal rendered by the

[39] *Ayyash et al.* Trial Judgment, n 28, paras 252 ('The combination of these pieces of evidence, even if they are individually comparatively "weaker" than others, could potentially—if examined in their totality—be used to prove a charge') and 253.

[40] *Bemba* Appeal Judgment, n 2, Separate Opinion of Judge Van den Wyngaert and Judge Morrison, ICC-01/05-01/08-3636-Anx2, 8 June 2018, para. 15. The STL took the same interpretation: *Ayyash et al.* Trial Judgment, n 28, para. 252.

[41] ICC, Chambers Practice Manual, 7th edn, Adopted following the judicial retreat of 2023 (also discussed in Chapter 3, section B). Discussed further in Y. McDermott, 'The International Criminal Court's Chambers Practice Manual: Towards a Return to Judicial Law-Making in International Criminal Procedure?' (2017) 15 *Journal of International Criminal Justice* 873.

> Court. Drawing upon best practices and lessons learned, the judges agreed on the adoption of a methodology to ensure that trial chambers commence the preparation of judgments at an early stage and follow a coherent and consistent structure, while still being appropriately adapted to the need of specific cases.[42]

These guidelines were, at the time of writing, confidential and, as such, not accessible to the public.[43] However, we might consider in the abstract what those 'best practices and lessons learned' that informed these guidelines might be, and what an optimal judgment structure might look like.

A number of factors are important in considering judgment structure. Most importantly, the judgment needs to provide adequate reasons for the Trial Chamber's decision. The European Court of Human Rights has established in several cases that Article 6(1) of the Convention includes an obligation for courts to give sufficient reasons for their decisions.[44] In *Zayidov v Azerbaijan*, the Court held that 'the right to a fair trial cannot be seen as effective unless the requests and observations of the parties are truly "heard", that is to say, properly examined by the tribunal.'[45] This does not mean that each and every argument of the parties needs to be discussed in depth, but the judgment should clearly address those arguments that are decisive to the ultimate outcome of proceedings.[46] In *Taxquet v Belgium*, a violation of Article 6 was found where the applicant could not ascertain which items of evidence and factual circumstances ultimately led to the guilty verdict against him.[47]

A clearly reasoned judgment, demonstrating how the findings reached were based on a rigorous assessment of the evidence presented, shows that the presumption of innocence has been respected. Article 74 of the ICC Statute sets out requirements for the decision, with Article 74(5) explicitly requiring that it includes 'a full and reasoned statement of the Trial Chamber's findings on the evidence and conclusions'. A fully reasoned judgment is also a prerequisite for the parties to be properly able to exercise their right of appeal under Article 81. As shall be discussed in detail in Chapter 7, the most recent explanation of the standard of review for findings of fact as set out in the *Gbagbo and Blé Goudé*, *Ongwen*, and *Ntaganda* Appeal Judgments has listed a range of errors in which the Appeals Chamber can

[42] ICC, 'ICC Judges Hold Retreat, Adopt Guidelines on the Judgment Drafting Process and on the Timeframe for Issuance of Key Judicial Decisions' ICC-CPI-20191007-PR1485, 7 October 2019. See also *Report of the Independent Expert Review*, n 18, paras 630–1.

[43] Chambers Practice Manual, n 41, para. 86.

[44] *Mazahir Jafarov v Azerbaijan*, App. No. 39331/09, 2 April 2020, paras 33–6; *Moreira Ferreira v Portugal (no. 2)*, App. No. 19867/12, 11 July 2017, paras 84–100; *Farzaliyev v Azerbaijan*, App. No. 29620/07, 28 May 2020, paras 34–6; *García Ruiz v Spain*, Case No. 30544/96, 21 January 1999, para. 26; *Orlen Lietuva Ltd. v Lithuania*, App. No. 45849/13, 29 January 2019, para. 82.

[45] *Zayidov v Azerbaijan (No. 2)*, App. No. 5386/10, 24 March 2022, para. 91.

[46] Ibid.

[47] *Taxquet v Belgium*, App. No. 926/05, 16 November 2010. See further P. Roberts, 'Does Article 6 of the European Convention on Human Rights Require Reasoned Verdicts in Criminal Trials?' (2011) 11 *Human Rights Law Review* 213.

interfere with a Trial Chamber's factual finding.[48] These include insufficient support of findings by the evidence, reliance on irrelevant evidence, a failure to take into account relevant evidentiary considerations and facts, a failure to properly appreciate the significance of the evidence on record, or a failure to evaluate and properly weigh the relevant evidence and facts.[49] Under this appellate standard, any Trial Chamber would be well advised to explicitly explain how the evidence has been evaluated, and the ways in which it was deemed to support particular factual findings, to protect its judgment from appellate review.

There is clearly a tension between ensuring that judgments are detailed enough to provide clarity to the parties on the Chamber's reasoning and making sure that the factual and legal findings are accessible. Some of the Court's multiple audiences (parties; victims; civil society; international organisations; states; scholars) will want to find what the Chamber held, but may be less interested in precisely what evidence and analysis led to this conclusion, while parties and some other interested groups will need that level of detail. The remainder of this section compares the structures of the *Ongwen* and *Ntaganda* trial judgments, as the two most recent judgments issued at the time of writing, to consider the different structures embraced by Trial Chambers, and their relative strengths and weaknesses.

1. Length

International criminal judgments are often hundreds (and sometimes thousands) of pages long and have been described as 'volumes of law that are often difficult to penetrate and explain'.[50] As well as their length, the structure of judgments, with relevant findings scattered across hundreds of pages, means that it can be rather difficult to follow the Chamber's line of reasoning.[51]

There does appear, unsurprisingly, to be a strong correlation between the complexity of the case and the length of the judgment.[52] The *Ongwen* judgment, at 1077 pages and 3116 paragraphs long, was significantly longer than the *Ntaganda* judgment, which, at 539 pages and 1206 paragraphs in length, has been praised as being 'almost light reading by international criminal law standards'.[53] The number

[48] *Ntaganda* Appeal Judgment, n 20, para. 41; *Gbagbo and Blé Goudé* Appeal Judgment, n 18, para. 70; *Prosecutor v Ongwen*, Judgment on the appeal of Mr Ongwen against the decision of Trial Chamber IX of 4 February 2021 entitled 'Trial Judgment', ICC-02/04-01/15-2022-Red, 15 December 2022 ('*Ongwen* Appeal Judgment'), para. 82.

[49] *Ntaganda* Appeal Judgment, n 20, para. 41; *Gbagbo and Blé Goudé* Appeal Judgment, n 18, para. 70; *Ongwen* Appeal Judgment, n 48, para. 82.

[50] D. Kaye, 'Archiving Justice: Conceptualizing the Archives of the United Nations International Criminal Tribunal for the Former Yugoslavia' (2014) 14 *Archival Science* 381, 393.

[51] See e.g. *Prosecutor v Šešelj*, Judgment, IT-03-67-T, 31 March 2016, Partially Dissenting Opinion of Judge Lattanzi, para. 10.

[52] S. Ford, 'Complexity and Efficiency at International Criminal Courts' (2014) 29 *Emory International Law Review* 1, 23. Ford measures 'complexity' through three proxy measures: number of trial days, number of witnesses that testify, and number of exhibits: Ford, 20. Other measures of complexity might include the number and scope (geographic/temporal) of the charges; the mode(s) of liability charged, and whether the trial is single or multi-accused.

[53] D. Guilfoyle, 'A Tale of Two Cases: Lessons for the Prosecutor of the International Criminal Court? (Part I)' (*EJIL:Talk!*, 28 August 2019).

of charges may go some way to accounting for this length: Ongwen was ultimately found guilty of 61 counts compared to Ntaganda's 18, and the *Ongwen* case had the added complexity of the affirmative defences raised. The cases were, however, otherwise broadly similar in terms of modes of liability charged and number of live witnesses heard (102 in *Ntaganda*; 130 in *Ongwen*). It may be that the structure followed in *Ongwen* added some length to the ultimate judgment, or that the structure followed in *Ntaganda* favoured brevity, especially considering that the *Ntaganda* judgment was even shorter than that in *Lubanga* (593 pages; one charge; one mode of liability).

The first substantive section ('Overview') of the *Ongwen* judgment provides a brief introduction to the historical background of the conflict, the procedural history of the case, the accused, and the charges against him.[54] The second section deals with 'defence allegations concerning the accused's right to a fair trial and "other human rights violations"'.[55] Part III of the judgment ('findings of fact') sets out the material facts and circumstances underpinning the judgment as have been established to the requisite threshold.[56] This section includes, for example, findings of fact on the accused's position, on the attacks on IDP camps, and on the commission of sexual and gender-based violence.[57] Notably, across the 100 or so paragraphs of this section, there are no footnotes linking the findings of fact to the evidence underpinning those findings. Instead, Part IV of the judgment sets out the assessment of the evidence, discussing 'the evidence which, directly or by way of inference (thus, through additional facts of a subsidiary nature), supports each of these findings on the facts and circumstances described in the charges'.[58] This section also sets out some general remarks on the Chamber's approach to evidence and the types of evidence introduced in the case, before setting out a detailed analysis of the evidence relating to the Chamber's findings of fact.[59] Throughout Part IV.C ('evidentiary analysis for findings of fact'), each of the findings of fact from Part III of the judgment are repeated in bold, followed by an analysis of the evidence underpinning each of these findings.[60] This section also discusses the defences pleaded.[61] Part V of the judgment ('legal findings') sets out the applicable law and applies it to those findings of fact discussed in the preceding sections of the judgment.[62] A concluding section is dedicated to the Chamber's verdict.[63]

In comparison, *Ntaganda* starts with two short sections on background and the scope of the charges, before moving, in Part III, to evidentiary considerations.

54 *Ongwen* Trial Judgment, n 12, paras 1–41.
55 Ibid., paras 42–120.
56 Ibid., para. 121.
57 Ibid., paras 121–225.
58 Ibid., para. 121.
59 Part IV spans ibid., paras 226–2672.
60 Ibid., paras 851–2447.
61 Ibid., paras 2448–2672.
62 Ibid., paras 2673–3115.
63 Ibid., para. 3116.

Following two short sub-sections on the burden of proof and facts requiring no evidence, Part III.C elaborates on some general principles for the evaluation of different forms of evidence, while Part III.D ('specific issues of witness credibility') contains an assessment of 16 witnesses (14 prosecution and 2 defence, including the defendant) across 72 pages,[64] as well as dealing with defence allegations regarding collusion and witness coaching. These two parts comprise approximately 100 pages. Part IV sets out 'factual findings' across 199 pages, which include detailed footnotes outlining the relevant evidence. Part V of the judgment, like the equivalent section in the *Ongwen* judgment, makes legal findings on the elements of the crimes and modes of liability charged with cross-references to the relevant paragraphs of the earlier 'factual findings' section.

There are three main differences between these two recent judgments. First, *Ongwen* contains a standalone section at the start of the judgment, setting out a list of findings of fact established, without footnotes or discussion as to the supporting evidence. Second, the 'assessment of the evidence' section of the *Ongwen* judgment is more in-depth than the *Ntaganda* judgment's equivalent, which spreads the evaluation of the evidence across two distinct sections: evidentiary considerations in Part III and factual findings in Part IV. Part IV.B of *Ongwen* comprises 228 pages and contains an assessment of each witness (grouped by type of witness), whereas *Ntaganda* singles out just 16 witnesses for credibility assessments in its Part III.D and includes credibility assessments of witnesses on particular points in very detailed footnotes to its Part IV ('factual findings'). Many of the individual witness assessments in *Ongwen* are only one or two paragraphs in length but, taken together, they certainly add some length to the trial judgment. Third, while *Ntaganda* deals with categories of evidence in general terms in its Part III, the equivalent section of *Ongwen* contains a not just detailed assessment of categories of non-testimonial forms of evidence but also, for example, an item-by-item analysis of each tape of intercept evidence presented,[65] and detailed footnotes on the authenticity of logbooks.[66]

Thus, the structure followed in *Ongwen*, and the choices made in setting out the assessment of evidence, clearly added more length (and some degree of repetition) compared to the approach taken in *Ntaganda*. For some Trial Chambers that might be seen as a good enough reason to follow the latter style, especially in view of criticisms of the lengthy nature of international criminal judgments. However, I argue that despite its length, *Ongwen* is more accessible and easier to follow than *Ntaganda*, for the reasons set out below.

[64] *Prosecutor v Ntaganda*, Trial Judgment, ICC-01/04-02/06-2359, 8 July 2019 ('*Ntaganda* Trial Judgment'), paras 89–262. The reason why these 16 witnesses were singled out for individual credibility assessments is not made explicit in the judgment.

[65] *Ongwen* Trial Judgment, n 12, paras 686–810.

[66] Ibid., para. 659.

2. Accessibility

In terms of the didactic function of international criminal judgments and the accessibility of their findings, the separate 'findings of fact' section of the *Ongwen* judgment sets out very clearly what the Chamber found. This may be all that some readers wish to know, in which case they will get a complete overview by reading Section III of the judgment, totalling 20 pages in length, grouped under 12 headings. Other readers may well wish to drill down further into the evidence underpinning each finding of fact, in which case they can cross-refer to the relevant paragraphs of the 'evidentiary analysis for findings of fact' sub-section (IV.C), where they can find the same findings of fact highlighted in bold, but with a detailed analysis of the relevant evidence underpinning each finding. The legal findings section (Part V) of *Ongwen* cross-refers to the same list of findings of fact, rigorously applying the facts set out in Part III of the judgment to a structured discussion of the contextual elements, elements of crimes, and mode of liability charged.

Some might argue that this approach is repetitive and unduly adds length to the judgment. On the other hand, the *Ongwen* judgment is perhaps more easily navigable than *Ntaganda*, given the very clear cross-references between the factual findings and the other sections of the judgment. The 12 groups of factual findings set out in Part III and justified in Part IV.C map neatly to the legal characteristics of the facts analysed in Part V.2 of the judgment. In *Ntaganda*, Part V on legal findings similarly cross-refers to relevant paragraphs of Part IV (factual findings), but it perhaps does not flow as logically as *Ongwen*, which follows the same order for findings in each of the three sections. In *Ntaganda*, many of the same 'factual findings' paragraphs are cited in different places of Part V on legal findings, while others appear to be less frequently cited. A systematic review of the footnotes found that, of the 375 paragraphs of factual findings in Part IV in *Ntaganda*, 354 of them (94%) are in fact cited in some way in Part V (either individually or by reference to a sub-section or paragraph range). However, this is not obvious from a straightforward reading of the judgment, whereas the legal findings in *Ongwen* very clearly align with the sub-headings for the factual findings and evidentiary analysis sections.

In terms of accessibility, the very large number of footnotes in *Ntaganda* may be daunting for lay readers, although it could also be argued that a 1000+ page judgment, as in *Ongwen*, is similarly off-putting. There may be alternative ways to achieve the aims of the *Ongwen* judgment in providing clarity on the Chamber's findings at the outset. For example, a relatively detailed lay summary of the factual findings could be issued simultaneously with the judgment.[67] Alternatively, some

[67] It is worth noting, however, that the separate 'factual findings' section only added 20 pages in total to the *Ongwen* judgment and is helpful in framing the rest of the judgment.

of the detailed discussion of the evaluation of different forms of evidence and the assessment of witnesses could be moved to an annex to keep the judgment at a reasonable length. A further alternative would be to discuss the assessment of the relevant witness or piece of evidence when it is first cited as supporting a finding of fact, instead of decoupling the assessment from the Chamber's reliance on it. This approach would mean effectively incorporating a lot of the type of material that falls under Part IV.B of *Ongwen* into what is Part IV.C of that judgment. However, this approach would have the disadvantage of requiring detailed footnotes, which may be seen as undesirable from a stylistic point of view.

3. Conclusions on judgment structure

Having noted three key differences between the approaches taken by the *Ongwen* and *Ntaganda* Trial Chambers, it is worth noting a couple of important similarities between the two judgments. First, both judgments are admirably restrained in re-telling the historical background to the cases. *Ntaganda* sets out the relevant background across the first 32 paragraphs of the judgment, whereas in *Ongwen* this discussion is limited to around 12 paragraphs.[68] This may not always be feasible, for example where there is dispute among the parties, but in *Ongwen* the parties apparently agreed with the broad thrust of the historical background outlined.[69]

Second, both judgments set out 'factual findings' and link those findings to an evaluation of the evidence in the case and to the legal findings. It is commonly stated that, even if a judgment does not explicitly refer to a piece of evidence, it will have been taken into account.[70] As such, it can sometimes be difficult to state with certainty which evidence led the Trial Chamber to which inference and, in turn, which inference led to which finding of fact. *Ongwen* goes further by providing an overview of the established facts before turning to the evidence underpinning each finding of fact and the legal consequences of those findings. Indeed, a reading of sections III and V.B alone, which comprise roughly 400 paragraphs of the 3116 paragraphs in the judgment, would provide readers with a good narrative of what the case was about and the Chamber's main findings.

Third, as mentioned above, the standard of appellate review for findings of fact, discussed in detail in Chapter 7, is important in considering the optimal structure

[68] Compare, for example, *Prosecutor v Karadžić*, Judgment, IT-95-5/18-T, 24 March 2016, where the historical background spans paras 32–437. Some of that material, however, pertained to command structures, which would have fallen under 'findings of fact' and 'evidentiary analysis for findings of fact' under the *Ongwen* Trial Judgment structure.

[69] *Ongwen* Trial Judgment, n 12, para. 1.

[70] E.g. *Prosecutor v Stanišić and Simatović*, Judgment, IT-03-69-T, 30 May 2013, para. 34. Cf. *Šešelj* Trial Judgment, n 51, Partially Dissenting Opinion of Judge Lattanzi, paras 10–11 ('I note that, even though the majority states in the Judgement that the evidence submitted was examined, this evidence is cited only in a disorderly manner in the footnotes, without a real analysis allowing for an understanding of how the majority arrived at such a conclusion').

for trial judgments. It is worth noting that both trial judgments were upheld on appeal, *Ongwen* unanimously,[71] which bodes well for future practice.

Nonetheless, returning to the two issues at the heart of the 'atomistic versus holistic' debate, as outlined above, the question of whether and to what extent weaknesses in the evidence can be overcome by reference to other pieces of evidence in the record is a subjective one, which cannot be answered by a judgment structure, and which may lead to disputes between individual judges in future cases.

Moreover, on the question of the level of detail the Chamber needs to provide on which evidence supports which finding of fact, there remains scope for tension between Chambers or individual judges in other cases. The *Ongwen* judgment notes that it structures its discussion of the evidence in Part IV through an 'analysis of evidence with respect to each individual finding of fact',[72] but that some evidence pertains to more than one factual finding and may not necessarily be explicitly reiterated in relation to each relevant finding, and that the Chamber has considered all the evidence holistically.[73] This is logical, and the Trial Chamber's consideration of the most relevant evidence and arguments is clear in the judgment, but future Trial Chambers may take a different approach or future Appeals Chambers may find future trial judgments to have insufficiently taken into account or weighed the relevant evidence, regardless of which approach to judgment structure is taken. The extent to which the new Guidelines for ICC Judgment Structure are instructive is unclear, because they are not publicly available, but the level of discretion afforded to individual Trial Chambers in relation to structure and choice of headings should become apparent with the issuance of further judgments.

This statement from *Ongwen* once again shows that the 'atomistic versus holistic' debate may be something of a false dichotomy. Caricatured views of common law judges as atomists and civil law judges as holists are neither helpful nor grounded in reality.[74] As I have argued elsewhere:

> Rather than seeing the two approaches as incompatible camps from which the international judge must choose one, we can develop a framework by which individual pieces of evidence, and the inferences that can be drawn therefrom, are subjected to rigorous analysis, whilst not losing sight of the bigger picture of what needs to be proven ... [A] combination of the atomistic and holistic approaches can be achieved—individual pieces of evidence can be subjected to searching

[71] *Ongwen* Appeal Judgment, n 48. As shall be seen in Chapter 7, separate and dissenting opinions have been very common in ICC Appeals Chamber judgments to date; their absence from this judgment should be seen as an endorsement of the Trial Chamber's approach.

[72] *Ongwen* Trial Judgment, n 12, para. 851.

[73] Ibid.

[74] *Gbagbo* Reasons, n 28, Reasons of Judge Henderson, para. 41 (arguing that admitted evidence in common law systems is assessed just as holistically as in Romano-Germanic legal systems.)

scrutiny, but this must take place in the context of an analysis of the evidential record as a whole.[75]

That framework can be developed by applying a systematic approach to the evaluation of evidence that incorporates both the macro- and micro- levels of assessment of evidence that need to be carried out. Given the scale and scope of international criminal cases, judges and lawyers alike may be well served by the methods and tools developed from argumentation theory and decision science.

D. A new approach to judgment structure?

I have argued at length elsewhere that lessons learned and techniques taken from argumentation theory, decision science, and probability theory could be of great assistance to both lawyers in structuring their arguments in preparation for trial, and judges in determining whether the guilt of the accused has been proven beyond reasonable doubt.[76] In relation to legal argumentation in general, many authors have recommended the use of argument mapping, to 'map out the network of inference in a given case'.[77] Lagnado's work on the psychology of assessing evidence shows that people use causal models to assess the strength, reliability, and relevance of evidence in a wide range of domains, and he argues that causal models lead to better decisions.[78] Lagnado further posits that the 'causal model framework… provides a means to quantify the strength of causal links between variables—and thus evaluate the probative force of individual items of evidence—as well as a method for integrating these individual judgments into holistic judgments for all (or any subset) of the evidence'.[79] Once again, and from a very different disciplinary perspective, this confirms a point made in the previous section, that holistic and atomistic approaches are not distinct schools of thought from which judges must select one, but rather that reasoning about evidence

[75] McDermott, n 35, 686–7.

[76] McDermott, n 35; McDermott, n 36; Y. McDermott and C. Aitken, 'Analysis of Evidence in International Criminal Trials using Bayesian Belief Networks' (2017) 16 *Law, Probability and Risk* 111; F. Cerutti and Y. McDermott, 'A Formal Argumentation Exercise on the *Karadžić* Trial Judgment' (2023) 10 *Journal of Applied Logics* 319. 'Argumentation theory' is broadly defined as the study of argument, which has disciplinary roots in mathematics (particularly around Bayesian probability), computer science, psychology, and philosophy, among many others: see F.H. van Eemeren et al., *Fundamentals of Argumentation Theory* (Laurence Erlbaum Associates, 1996), ix.

[77] D.N. Walton, *Legal Argumentation and Evidence* (Pennsylvania State University Press, 2002) 323. See further, B. Verheij, 'Automated Argument Assistance for Lawyers' (1999) *ICAIL '99: Proceedings of the 7th International Conference on Artificial Intelligence and Law* 43; S. Toulmin et al., 'Arguments, Scenarios and Probabilities: Connections between Three Normative Frameworks for Evidential Reasoning' (2016) 15 *Law, Probability and Risk* 35.

[78] D. Lagnado, *Explaining the Evidence: How the Mind Investigates the World* (CUP, 2021), Chapters 3 and 6.

[79] Ibid., 149.

requires an assessment of the weight of individual items of evidence, taken in the context of other relevant evidence.

Arguably the most prominent of the methods used to chart inference networks in a legal context is a modified version of a technique pioneered by John Henry Wigmore in the early twentieth century.[80] Thanks to authors such as William Twining, Terence Anderson, and David Schum,[81] and more recent work applying the theory and practice of Wigmore's 'chart method' to international criminal trials in particular,[82] we have developed an understanding about how this approach can structure participants' thinking about evidence and inference in complex cases such as these.

Space does not permit an in-depth explanation of the chart method and how it might be applied to international criminal law in this chapter, but readers can find a detailed overview of the underpinning theory in other published works.[83] In essence, however, the chart method encourages the creator to create an inference model, breaking down the structural elements of proof in law from the *ultimate probandum* (the essential fact in issue—i.e. the guilt of the accused), to the *penultimate probanda* (the elements of the crime/mode of liability that must be established to prove the ultimate probandum), to *intermediate probanda* (matters of fact leading to the establishment of penultimate probanda). In so doing, the chart-maker maps the evidence, inferences, and generalisations that support or disfavour each probandum. The Wigmorean approach has been praised for its ability to 'decompose our evidential reasoning task to as detailed a level as we can',[84] drilling down into to interrogate the strength of evidence in support of a proposition.[85]

As was shown in the previous section, while different Chambers may take distinct approaches to the structure of their judgments, it is common for international criminal judgments to set out a detailed factual analysis followed by a legal analysis, applying those established facts to the law to make legal findings. Yet, this decoupling of factual and legal findings may not be the best or only way of structuring judgments. In England and Wales, for example, jurors are provided with a

[80] J.H. Wigmore, *The Science of Judicial Proof: As Given by Logic, Psychology, and General Experience, and Illustrated in Judicial Trials* (3rd edn, Little, Brown & Co., 1937).

[81] Anderson et al., n 7.

[82] P. Roberts, 'The Priority of Procedure and the Neglect of Evidence and Proof: Facing Facts in International Criminal Law' (2015) 13 *Journal of International Criminal Justice* 479; McDermott, n 35; McDermott, n 36; K. McGregor Richmond and S.A. Piccolo, 'Between Fact and Opinion: The Sui Generis Approach to Expert Witness Testimony in International Criminal Trials' (2022) 22 *International Criminal Law Review* 1016; K. McGregor Richmond, 'Transforming Evidence and Proof in International Criminal Trials' (2022) 22 *International Criminal Law Review* 827; S. De Smet, 'Controlling the Quality of Reasoning About the Link Between Evidence and Factual Findings' in X. Agirre et al. (eds), *Quality Control in Criminal Investigation* (TOAEP, 2020), 611.

[83] As well as those cited in n 82, see Klamberg, n 7, 156–66; Anderson et al., n 81; Tecuci et al., n 6.

[84] Anderson et al., n 7, 60–77.

[85] McDermott, n 36, 512–13 (discussing the 'macroscopic' and 'microscopic' forms that the chart method can take).

'route to verdict', a list of key questions that the court invites the jury to answer in coming to a verdict.[86] The route to verdict essentially asks jurors to work through the elements of the crime(s) and whether they are convinced beyond reasonable doubt of each of the material facts that must be proven to satisfy those elements (where contested), rather than asking them to decide broadly what facts have been established before applying those facts to the law. Of course, domestic criminal cases tend to be much less factually complex than their international criminal law counterparts. Nevertheless, we might consider whether international criminal judgments, after some of the necessary preliminaries on the background and procedural history of the case and perhaps also the general approach to the evaluation of different categories of evidence, might also consider a structure that starts by setting out the relevant law and what needs to be proven. They could then work systematically through the contextual elements, elements of each crime, and elements of the relevant mode(s) of liability, assessing the evidence and arguments of the parties under each heading.

There are three common scepticisms about formalising the reasoning processes and fact-finding in international criminal trials in this way that need to be addressed. The first argument is that it is too time-consuming to approach proof in this way, and that judges would never draft judgments within a reasonable time[87] should they start to break down all the inferential steps that are needed to be taken in deciding whether the accused has been proven guilty beyond reasonable doubt. Two counterarguments can be raised in response to this scepticism. First, as now outlined in the Chambers Practice Manual,[88] judges are expected to deliberate on the strength of the evidence presented to them over the course of the trial, so it is not as though they are expected to leave the consideration of all the evidence until the trial has ended. Wigmorean analysis or other formalistic methods would enable judges and their legal officers to structure those interim discussions and update them in light of other relevant evidence presented over the course of trial. The chart method enables users to see where new information fits and impacts upon their confidence level in the relevant probandum. Second, following a Wigmorean approach need not involve judges or their legal officers drawing out charts—with a proper understanding of the underpinning principles, it could equally be done in narrative form, listing key propositions.[89] Even if charts were to be drawn up,

[86] Criminal Procedure Rules 2022, SI 2020 No. 759 (L. 19), Part 25, Rule 25.14(3)(b).

[87] The Chambers Practice Manual, n 41, para. 88 states that the judgment should be delivered within ten months from the close of trial.

[88] This is apparently contained in the confidential 'Guidelines for ICC Judgment Drafting', but is referred to in ICC, *Overall Response of the International Criminal Court to the 'Independent Expert Review of the International Criminal Court and Rome Statute System—Final Report': Preliminary Analysis of the Recommendations and information on relevant activities undertaken by the Court*, 14 April 2021, para. 392.

[89] Anderson et al., n 7, 152.

off-the-shelf tools now exist and can be adopted for these purposes.[90] Indeed, existing evidence management tools and techniques already used by international criminal tribunals, such as CaseMap and In-Depth Analysis Charts (the use of which, inexplicably, the judges have discouraged in the latest draft of the Chambers Practice Manual[91]), could be employed to this end.[92] Furthermore, while working through a detailed assessment of evidence in relation to each *probandum* would clearly add some length to trial judgments, these discussions would not be artificially separated from the key findings to which they relate, and that analysis needs to be included in the judgment regardless of the structure. The judicious use of headings and sub-headings could mitigate against the risk that readers could lose their way in judgments structured in this way.

A second argument arises from a position of anxiety, especially at a time of exponential developments in artificial intelligence, that such techniques could ultimately lead to the end of human judges. Such concerns perhaps overstate the intelligence of artificial intelligence agents, especially language learning models such as ChatGPT, which have been shown to 'hallucinate' and concoct false citations.[93] Moreover, as Tecuci has pointed out, there are differences between human and computer capabilities that mean that artificial intelligence can only ever complement, never replace, human reasoning.[94] While computers have benefits over humans in terms of the speed at which they can process large volumes of data, and, unlike humans, they do not suffer from forgetfulness or sloppiness, they lack humans' common sense, intuition, and ability to think creatively and see patterns and parallels in new situations, all of which are core facets of judging. Moreover, one has to be realistic about the fact that any tool or

[90] See e.g. G. Tecuci et al., 'Computational Approach and Cognitive Assistant for Evidence-Based Reasoning in Intelligence Analysis' (2014) 5 *International Journal of Intelligent Defence Support Systems* 146; G. Tecuci et al., 'Toward a Computational Theory of Evidence-Based Reasoning for Instructable Cognitive Agents' (2019) *Proceedings of the 2019 AAAI Fall Symposium 'Artificial Intelligence in Government and Public Sector'*, Arlington, VA, online at https://arxiv.org/abs/1910.03990 (last accessed 29 May 2023); H. Prakken et al., 'A Formalization of Argumentation Schemes for Legal Case-based Reasoning in ASPIC+' (2015) 25 *Journal of Logic and Computation* 1141; F. Cerutti et al., 'Cispaces.org: From Fact Extraction to Report Generation' (2018) *COMMA 2018* 269; L. Al-Abdulkarim et al., 'A Methodology for Designing Systems to Reason with Legal Cases using Abstract Dialectical Frameworks' (2016) 24 *Artificial Intelligence and Law* 1; M. Janier et al., 'OVA+: An Argument Analysis Interface' (2014) *COMMA 2014* 463; online at http://arg-tech.org/people/chris/publications/2014/comma2014-ova.pdf (last accessed 29 May 2023); Verheij, n 77.

[91] Chambers Practice Manual, n 41, paras 24 and 43. For an excellent overview of the benefits of in-depth analysis charts, see O. Bekou, 'Enhancing the Quality of Investigations: What Role Can In-Depth Analysis Charts Play' in X. Agirre et al. (eds), *Quality Control in Criminal Investigation* (TOAEP, 2020), 587.

[92] Cf. De Smet, n 82, 633–4, arguing that a new bespoke tool should be developed to allow the fact-finder to map complex arguments.

[93] S. Coen, 'Lawyer Admits Using AI for Research after Citing "Bogus" Cases from ChatGPT', *The Telegraph*, 27 May 2023.

[94] G. Tecuci, 'How Intelligent is Artificial Intelligence?', paper posted to *Evidence Dialogues*, May 2023, online at https://evidencedialogues.wordpress.com/ai-and-evidence/ (last accessed 29 May 2023).

technique to support human reasoning will only ever be just that; it is a tool to assist thinking, not a substitute to thinking.[95] As Roberts and Aitken have noted in relation to Wigmorean analysis, 'The Chart Method is sometimes measured, and predictably found wanting, against excessively inflated expectations, when all that is really required to vindicate its usefulness is some improvement in the direction of logical analysis over exclusively narrative methods or impressionistic intuitions'.[96]

The third scepticism around formalising proof is the argument that judges are professionals and know what they are doing; they do not need any further support in the judicial task of evaluating the evidence as a whole. It is worth noting, however, that other fields in which competent professionals deal with huge volumes of data, such as intelligence analysis, have moved towards an incorporation of formal techniques and tools in practice.[97] For example, a generalised form of Bayesian Network developed in decision analysis studies has been deployed in a wide range of situations, ranging from natural resource management to medicine and from economic forecasting to weather prediction.[98]

On balance, while acknowledging that a move towards incorporating lessons learned from argumentation theory, cognitive and decision science, and probability theory would likely meet with some objections from both judges and parties in international criminal cases, it is argued that the benefits for clearer judgment structures far outweigh the arguments against such practices. An incorporation of formal tools and techniques, or, at a minimum, an understanding of the principles underpinning such techniques, could lead to more logical, structured decision-making with a clearer link between evidence and inference in international criminal judgments.[99] It could also go some way to resolving the tense debate between atomistic and holistic approaches outlined above, which has dominated international criminal judging for some years.

[95] McDermott, n 36, 519.

[96] P. Roberts and C. Aitken, *The Logic of Forensic Proof: Inferential Reasoning in Criminal Evidence and Forensic Science Guidance for Judges, Lawyers, Forensic Scientists and Expert Witnesses*, Royal Statistical Society's Working Group on Statistics and the Law, Practitioner Guide No. 3 (Royal Statistical Society, 2014), available online at https://www.maths.ed.ac.uk/~cgga/Guide-3-WEB.pdf (last accessed 29 May 2023), 68.

[97] University of Dundee, 'University Helping the Real James Bonds', 17 August 2020, online at https://www.dundee.ac.uk/stories/university-helping-real-james-bonds (last accessed 29 May 2023); E.P. Nyberg et al., 'BARD: A Structured Technique for Group Elicitation of Bayesian Networks to Support Analytic Reasoning' (2022) 42 *Risk Analysis* 1155 (outlining an online platform developed to support intelligence analysts using Bayes Nets).

[98] M. Gómez, 'Real-World Applications of Influence Diagrams' in J.A. Gámez et al. (eds), *Advances in Bayesian Networks* (Springer, 2004), 161; Roberts and Aitken, n 96, 109. See also, Nyberg et al., n 97, 1150, outlining many domains that have employed Bayes Nets.

[99] See also De Smet, n 82. This chapter assumes that such techniques are not already being used in judges' deliberations, but because those deliberations are secret, one cannot be certain. It would seem (from e.g. Agirre, n 9) that the ICC's Office of the Prosecutor has made some important steps forward in its 'source evaluation' practices.

E. Conclusion

This chapter examined how Trial Chambers approach their task of weighing the evidence as a whole in the determination of the ultimate question of whether the person(s) on trial is criminally liable for the alleged acts. It showed, in section B, that fact-finding in international criminal trials is, by nature, a probabilistic exercise, because evidence is invariably incomplete, rarely conclusive, often ambiguous, frequently dissonant, and always with varying degrees of credibility and reliability. There will never be one clear and completely unambiguous conclusion, so it falls to judges to determine whether guilt has been proven to the standard of proof beyond reasonable doubt, which requires a high degree of probability.

Section C examined the courts' stated approaches to the evaluation of evidence. It showed that, despite a live debate in practice as to whether an 'atomistic' or 'holistic' approach is preferable, this debate is in fact a false dichotomy, because judges are universally in agreement that evidence needs to be examined in the context of other evidence on the record. I argued that at the heart of this debate and differences in approach are two separate but related issues: first, the extent to which other evidence on the record can 'remedy' some of the flaws in a piece of evidence on the record, and second, the level of detail that the Chamber needs to provide in showing how the evidence led to a particular finding of fact or an inference supporting a finding of fact. Section C analysed different options for the structure of trial judgments and argued that the approach followed by the Trial Chamber in *Ongwen*, while adding length to the judgment, has many benefits in terms of the clarity of the reasoning and the accessibility of the Chamber's findings to a range of audiences.

Having established that the atomistic and holistic approaches are not two divergent schools of thought from which the judges must choose, it was argued that a combined framework derived from argumentation theory could be applied to combine the necessary micro- and macro- levels of assessment in a new approach to structuring judgments. Section D addressed three likely scepticisms around this approach: that it would be too time-consuming; that it risks having judges replaced by artificial intelligence; and that it overlooks the professional nature of international criminal judges. As we saw, each of those arguments meets with strong counterarguments. Overall, an approach that is founded in logic, common sense, scientific knowledge, and experience will be necessary going forward, and Wigmore charts or other tools to assist with reasoning may be useful to that end. This degree of rigour is necessary because, as shall be seen in Chapter 7, the appellate standard of review has evolved from one of strict deference to Trial Chambers' findings of fact to a more nuanced approach that does allow Appeals Chambers to interfere if they feel errors have been made in the evaluation of evidence.

7
Proof on Appeal

A. Introduction

This chapter examines appellate review standards, with a particular focus on the standard of review for alleged errors of fact.[1] It shows that the ICC's jurisprudence on the standard of review for factual errors has evolved over the years, from an early position of deference to the Trial Chamber, to a broader standard of review in the *Bemba* Appeal Judgment, to something of a middle ground between the two positions, which may be called 'tempered deference', in more recent ICC Appeals Chamber jurisprudence. It also examines related issues, namely the distinction between factual and legal or procedural errors, the introduction of new evidence on appeal and at retrial, and the circumstances under which a final judgment can be reviewed. As with other chapters in this book, this chapter paints a picture of an evolving and at times unclear legal framework for fact-finding in international criminal trials.

B. Standard of review

i. Legal framework

The International Military Tribunal at Nuremberg and the International Military Tribunal for the Far East did not provide for a right to appeal to a judicial body.[2] The contemporary international criminal tribunals, by contrast, have allowed both the convicted person and the Prosecutor to appeal against a judgment of conviction or acquittal based on an error of law invalidating the decision, or an error of fact occasioning a miscarriage of justice.[3] Introducing the proposed text of the

[1] Given this book's focus on proving international crimes, this chapter focuses principally on appeals against decisions of acquittal or conviction and sentence and does not explore appeals of decisions on jurisdiction or admissibility; provisional release; reparations, or any other interlocutory appeal decisions. For an in-depth analysis, see V. Nerlich, 'Article 82' in O. Triffterer and K. Ambos (eds), *Rome Statute of the International Criminal Court: Article-by-Article Commentary* (4th edn, Beck/Hart, 2021), 2360–76.

[2] Article 26, IMT Charter (stating that the judgment as to guilt or innocence of the accused 'shall be final and not subject to review'). At the IMTFE, sentences were subject to review by the Supreme Commander for the Allied Powers (i.e. General MacArthur), who could amend or reduce, but not increase, their severity: Article 17, IMTFE Charter.

[3] Article 25, ICTY Statute; Article 24, ICTR Statute; Article 23, IRMCT Statute; Article 20, SCSL Statute (adding 'a procedural error' as a ground of appeal); Article 26, STL Statute. Article 46, KSC

Proving International Crimes. Yvonne McDermott, Oxford University Press. © Yvonne McDermott 2024.
DOI: 10.1093/oso/9780198842972.003.0007

ICTY Statute, the UN Secretary General noted that the right of appeal 'is a fundamental element of individual civil and political rights' and that the creation of an Appeals Chamber with the power to reverse, affirm, or revise the Trial Chamber judgment was necessary to this end.[4]

Appeals against judgments of conviction or acquittal may be brought before the ICC by a convicted person (or the Prosecutor acting on that person's behalf) under Article 81 on the grounds of procedural error, error of fact, error of law, or any other ground that affects the fairness or reliability of the proceedings or decision.[5] The Prosecutor may bring an appeal on any of the first three grounds.[6]

The appellant(s) must substantiate their arguments in their appeal brief, with reference 'to the relevant part of the record or any other document or source of information', where the alleged error is in relation to a factual finding.[7] For alleged errors of law, they must point to any relevant provision and legal authority in support of their argument. Appellants must produce 'cogent arguments',[8] and should, where possible, identify the precise page or paragraph number of the decision where the alleged error can be found.[9] For alleged errors of fact, the appellant needs to demonstrate that the Trial Chamber's finding was unreasonable, 'for example, by showing that it was contrary to logic, common sense, scientific knowledge and experience'.[10] If the appellant fails to substantiate their argument, the Appeals Chamber may dismiss it without analysing its substance.[11]

Law adds 'an error in sentencing' as a ground of appeal, and sets out the standard of review that the Court of Appeals panel shall apply in some detail. Article 36new, ECCC Law allows victims, as well as the accused and Co-Prosecutors, to appeal to the Supreme Court Chamber against the decision of the Extraordinary Chamber of the trial court on the grounds set out in Rule 104, ECCC IR. The Supreme Court Chamber is empowered to make final decisions on issues of law and fact and may not remand a case back to the trial court. The ICTY, ICTR, SCSL, and STL all later added that in exceptional circumstances, the Appeals Chamber could also consider appeals on legal issues 'of general significance for the Tribunal's jurisprudence': see *Prosecutor v Tadić*, Judgment, IT-94-1-A, 15 July 1999 ('*Tadić* Appeal Judgment'), para. 247; *Prosecutor v Akayesu*, Judgment, ICTR-96-4-A, 1 June 2001 ('*Akayesu* Appeal Judgment'), para. 19; *Prosecutor v Fofana and Kondewa*, Judgment, SCSL-04-14-A, 28 May 2008, para. 32; *Prosecutor v Merhi and Oneissi*, Appeal Judgment, STL-11-01/A-2/AC, 10 March 2022, para. 30.

4 UNSG, Report of the Secretary-General pursuant to paragraph 2 of SC Res. 808 (1993), S/25704, 3 May 1993, paras 116–18.

5 Article 81(1)(b), ICC Statute.

6 Article 81(1)(a), ICC Statute.

7 Regulation 58(2), ICC Regulations of the Court.

8 *Prosecutor v Lubanga*, Public redacted Judgment on the appeal of Mr Thomas Lubanga Dyilo against his conviction, ICC-01/04-01/06-3121-Red, 1 December 2014 ('*Lubanga* Appeal Judgment'), para. 30.

9 *Prosecutor v Ntaganda*, Public redacted version of Judgment on the appeals of Mr Bosco Ntaganda and the Prosecutor against the decision of Trial Chamber VI of 8 July 2019 entitled 'Judgment', ICC-01/04-02/06-2666-Red, 30 March 2021 ('*Ntaganda* Appeal Judgment'), para. 47; *Prosecutor v Gbagbo and Blé Goudé*, Judgment in the appeal of the Prosecutor against Trial Chamber I's decision on the no case to answer motions, ICC-02/11-01/15-1400-Red, 31 March 2021 ('*Gbagbo and Blé Goudé* Appeal Judgment'), para. 73.

10 *Gbagbo and Blé Goudé* Appeal Judgment, n 9, para. 74.

11 *Lubanga* Appeal Judgment, n 8, para. 31; *Prosecutor v Bemba* et al., Public Redacted Judgment on the appeals of Mr Jean-Pierre Bemba Gombo, Mr Aimé Kilolo Musamba, Mr Jean-Jacques Mangenda

Appellants must show not only that an error was made, but also that the error in question materially impacted the decision in question.[12] As Judge Eboe-Osuji noted in his Concurring Separate Opinion in *Bemba*, 'The Appeals Chamber will not apply its remedial powers at the instance of a trifling or harmless error (of law, fact or procedure). The error in question must be *material*.'[13] While some judges have advocated for a lower standard akin to 'reasonable likelihood',[14] materiality under the current jurisprudence requires the appellant to demonstrate a 'high likelihood' that, had it not been for the alleged error, the Trial Chamber would have reached a different judgment.[15]

ii. Errors of law

The ICC has consistently taken the position that the Appeals Chamber 'will not defer to the Trial Chamber's interpretation of the law. Rather, it will arrive at its own conclusions as to the appropriate law and determine whether or not the Trial Chamber misinterpreted the law.'[16]

Kabongo, Mr Fidèle Babala Wandu and Mr Narcisse Arido against the decision of Trial Chamber VII entitled 'Judgment pursuant to Article 74 of the Statute', ICC-01/05-01/13-2275-Red, 8 March 2018 ('*Bemba et al.* Appeal Judgment'), para. 109.

[12] *Prosecutor v Ongwen*, Judgment on the appeal of Mr Ongwen against the decision of Trial Chamber IX of 4 February 2021 entitled 'Trial Judgment', ICC-02/04-01/15-2022-Red, 15 December 2022 ('*Ongwen* Appeal Judgment'), para. 89; *Lubanga* Appeal Judgment, n 8, paras 30–1; *Prosecutor v Ngudjolo*, Judgment on the Prosecutor's appeal against the decision of Trial Chamber II entitled 'Judgment pursuant to article 74 of the Statute', ICC-01/04-02/12-271-Corr, 7 April 2015 ('*Ngudjolo* Appeal Judgment'), para. 284. For appeals under the fourth ground elucidated in Article 81(1)(b) of the ICC Statute, the standard is whether the 'other ground' of appeal impacted 'the fairness or reliability of the proceedings or decision'.

[13] *Prosecutor v Bemba*, Judgment on the appeal of Mr Jean-Pierre Bemba Gombo against Trial Chamber III's 'Judgment pursuant to Article 74 of the Statute', ICC-01/05-01/08-3636-Red, 8 June 2018 ('*Bemba* Appeal Judgment'), Concurring Separate Opinion of Judge Eboe-Osuji, ICC-01/05-01/08-3636-Anx3, 14 June 2018, para. 81.

[14] Ibid., para. 81 ('An error will qualify as *material* if it reasonably compels the view of *likelihood* that the Trial Chamber *might have* rendered a substantially different judgment had the error not occurred; or if the appellate court *could not be sure* that the trial court would have rendered the same judgment had the error not occurred') and para. 82 (noting that this formulation is a departure from earlier Appeals Chamber jurisprudence). Judge Eboe-Osuji saw a lower standard of proving materiality particularly necessary where the appellant is a convicted person: ibid., para. 85. See also, *Ngudjolo* Appeal Judgment, n 12, Joint Dissenting Opinion of Judge Trendafilova and Judge Tarfusser, ICC-01/04-02/12-271-AnxA, 27 February 2015, para. 30 (advocating that, where the Chamber's error was a failure to adopt a course of action, 'the demonstration of the erroneous nature of the inaction must be considered sufficient to substantiate the ground of appeal based on it', as it would otherwise be impossible to precisely indicate the material impact of the error).

[15] *Gbagbo and Blé Goudé* Appeal Judgment, n 9, para. 264 (noting: 'The Appeals Chamber is of the view that there is no compelling reason to depart from its jurisprudence').

[16] *Lubanga* Appeal Judgment, n 8, para. 18; *Ongwen* Appeal Judgment, n 12, para. 76; *Ntaganda* Appeal Judgment, n 9, para. 36; *Bemba* et al. Appeal Judgment, n 11, para. 99; *Bemba* Appeal Judgment, n 13, para. 36; *Gbagbo and Blé Goudé* Appeal Judgment, n 9, para. 62.

This follows from the position taken by the ICTY[17] and other international criminal tribunals[18] that the Appeals Chamber will determine whether the Trial Chamber's interpretation of the law was correct.

The line between the various forms of error that can be alleged on appeal is rarely clear cut. It is not uncommon to observe allegations of 'mixed errors of law and fact',[19] or cases where the appellant has alleged one type of error only for the Appeals Chamber to consider it as a different form of error.[20] It is perhaps unsurprising, given the appellate deference that applies to alleged errors of fact as discussed above, to see errors of fact framed as errors of law or procedure. For example, appellants may argue that the Trial Chamber committed an error of law in its approach to the assessment of the evidence or the standard of proof, rather than claim the Chamber's findings were unreasonable (i.e. an error of fact).[21] In *Gbagbo and Blé Goudé*, Judge Eboe-Osuji declared it 'singularly unimpressive ... [to] seek to overturn *factual findings*, by disguising the arguments in the terminology of "errors of law" or "procedural errors"'.[22] In reality, the fact/law distinction is blurry,[23] and appellants may not necessarily be attempting to avoid appellate deference by framing factual errors as legal or procedural errors, but may genuinely believe that a failure to properly apply or elucidate the standard of proof

[17] E.g. *Prosecutor v Furundžija*, Judgment, IT-95-17/1-A, 21 July 2000 ('*Furundžija* Appeal Judgment'), para. 35; *Prosecutor v Kupreškić*, Judgment, IT-95-16-A, 23 October 2001 ('*Kupreškić* Appeal Judgment'), paras 26–7; *Prosecutor v Krnojelac*, Judgment, IT-97-25-A, 17 September 2003, para. 10.

[18] E.g. *Prosecutor v Rutaganda*, Judgment, ICTR-96-3-A, 26 May 2003, para. 20; *Prosecutor v Merhi and Oneissi*, Appeal Judgment, STL-11-01/A-2/AC, 10 March 2022, para. 29; *KHIEU Samphân* ('*Case 002/02*'), Appeal Judgment, 002/19-09-2007-ECCC/SC (F76), 23 December 2022 ('*Case 002/02* Appeal Judgment'), para. 23; *Prosecutor v Mladić*, Judgment, IRMCT-13-56-A, 8 June 2021, para. 17.

[19] E.g. *Case 001* Appeal Judgment, n 26, para. 37; *Prosecutor v Ntaganda*, Judgment on the appeals against the decision of Trial Chamber VI of 8 March 2021 entitled 'Reparations Order', ICC-01/04-02/06-2782, 12 September 2022, para. 20; *Prosecutor v Strugar*, Judgment, IT-01-42-A, 17 July 2008, para. 252.

[20] *Lubanga* Appeal Judgment, n 8, para. 34 (noting that the defendant 'labels many of the alleged errors as factual errors, when they are actually legal errors. Other alleged errors are also categorised as legal errors, while they are procedural errors. Despite this misnomer, if substantiated, the Appeals Chamber accepts these errors as properly raised and will consider them against the relevant standard of review').

[21] *Prosecutor v Gbagbo and Blé Goudé*, Corrected Version of 'Prosecution Notice of Appeal', ICC-02/11-01/15-1270, 17 September 2019, para. 7 (arguing that 'the Majority erred in law and/or procedurally by acquitting Mr Gbagbo and Mr Blé Goudé without properly articulating and consistently applying a clearly defined standard of proof and/or approach to assessing the sufficiency of the evidence at the no case to answer ("NCTA") stage'); *Prosecutor v Ngudjolo*, Prosecution's Document in Support of Appeal against the 'Jugement rendu en application de l'article 74 du Statut', ICC-01/04-02/12-39-Red2, para. 39; *Prosecutor v Bemba*, Public Redacted Version of Appellant's document in support of the appeal, ICC-01/05-01/08-3434, 28 September 2016, para. 228; *Prosecutor v Zigiranyirazo*, Judgment, ICTR-01-73-A, 16 November 2009, para. 39 (finding that the Trial Chamber erred in law by 'misapprehending the burden of proof in the context of alibi').

[22] *Gbagbo and Blé Goudé* Appeal Judgment, Concurring Opinion of Judge Eboe-Osuji, n 71, para. 6. Cf. *Gbagbo and Blé Goudé* Appeal Judgment, n 9, Dissenting Opinion of Judge Bossa on Grounds One and Two, ICC-02/11-01/15-1400-Anx5, 31 March 2021, para. 2, finding that the failure to define, agree upon and elucidate the requisite standard of proof was an error of law.

[23] J. Frank, 'Legal Thinking in Three Dimensions' (1949–50) 1 *Syracuse Law Review* 9, at 13.

or to evaluate the evidence in a particular way is an error of law, not fact. Regardless of the appellant's framing of the error, it is open to the Appeals Chamber to review the relevant findings in accordance with the proper standard of review.[24] In other words, where it deems an alleged error to be more accurately considered an error of fact than an error of law, it can simply decide to evaluate the alleged error in accordance with the standard of review for factual errors.[25]

iii. Errors of fact

By contrast to the standard of review for errors of law, the default position in relation to alleged errors of fact has been one of appellate deference to the Trial Chamber, sometimes called the 'reasonableness standard'.[26] That is to say, appellate deference requires that the Appeals Chamber does not assess whether the Trial Chamber was *correct*, or whether the finding of fact was one that the Appeals Chamber itself would have reached, but rather whether it was *reasonable*. The Appeals Chamber will interfere with a Trial Chamber's discretion where a particular finding was one that no reasonable trier of fact could have reached.[27] This deference has been rationalised by the fact that the first instance Chamber is the forum in which the evidence is presented and tested, and therefore it is best placed to evaluate, weigh, and draw inferences from that evidence.[28] This can be closely linked to the widespread impression, as discussed in relation to the evaluation of witness testimony in Chapter 5, that judges need to observe witnesses' demeanour to determine their credibility or the truthfulness of their testimony.[29] This perception is not fully supported by the literature from psychology, which shows there are no particular 'tells' that reveal whether a person is lying.[30] Moreover, since trials are videorecorded, evidence is preserved, and detailed transcripts are created of each trial day, the impression that Appeals Chamber judges would be unable to carry out their own assessment of the evidence because they were not

[24] *Ngudjolo* Appeal Judgment, n 12, para. 44 (footnotes omitted) ('[T]he Appeals Chamber considers that to the extent that the alleged errors are based on challenges to the Trial Chamber's factual findings, her arguments under the first ground of appeal must be assessed against the standard of review for alleged factual errors since, in order to analyse the Prosecutor's arguments, the Appeals Chamber is required to review the Trial Chamber's factual findings, and it is therefore appropriate to apply the standard of review for alleged factual errors').

[25] Ibid.

[26] E.g. *Tadić* Appeal Judgment, n 3, para. 64; *Prosecutor v Karadžić*, IRMCT-13-55-A, 20 March 2019, para. 17 ('*Karadžić* Appeal Judgment'); *Akayesu* Appeal Judgment, n 3, para. 178.

[27] E.g. *Prosecutor v Mucić* et al., '*Celebici case*', Judgment, IT-96-21-A, 20 February 2001, paras 434–6; *Tadić* Appeal Judgment, n 3, para. 64; *Karadžić* Appeal Judgment, n 26, para. 17; *Furundžija* Appeal Judgment, n 17, para. 37; *Kupreškić* Appeal Judgment, n 17, para. 30.

[28] Among many others, see *Kupreškić* Appeal Judgment, n 17, 30–2 and *Bemba et al.* Appeal Judgment, n 11, paras 93–5.

[29] See Chapter 5, section C.

[30] Ibid.

present in court at the time it was presented does not seem to stand up to close scrutiny.[31]

Before turning to the evolving jurisprudence of the ICC on the standard of review for errors of fact, the practice of the ECCC warrants discussion.[32] The Supreme Court Chamber has noted that it will generally follow the standard of reasonableness, as set out by the ICTY Appeals Chamber.[33] This was challenged in Case 002/01, where the defendant Nuon Chea argued that the Supreme Court Chamber's role was 'to carry out an appellate review pursuant to Cambodian criminal procedure, which includes a *de novo* review of facts'.[34] The Supreme Court Chamber rejected this argument, finding that the *sui generis* nature of the ECCC entitled it to seek guidance from the practice of the ICTY and ICTR.[35] It further noted that it would be impracticable and inefficient for the Chamber to enter new factual findings on appeal, especially since it does not have the power to remand cases back to a trial chamber for retrial.[36]

However, the manner in which the Supreme Court Chamber has interpreted appellate deference appears to require a more searching scrutiny of the basis for the Trial Chamber's decision than the 'no reasonable trier of fact' standard followed by other international criminal tribunals.[37] The Supreme Court Chamber has noted that where the evidentiary basis for a factual conclusion is *prima facie* weak (such as where there is conflicting evidence, or where the evidence was primarily hearsay or out-of-court statements), then the Trial Chamber will need to provide more reasoning as to why it reached this conclusion on the basis of this evidence than it would when there is a strong evidence base.[38] The ECCC's approach to appellate deference proved instructive in the majority decision in *Bemba*,[39] discussed at length below.

Early ICC jurisprudence adopted the deferential standard of review and emphasised that a margin of appreciation would be afforded to the first instance Chamber in respect of its factual determinations.[40] Case law also noted

[31] *Bemba* Appeal Judgment, Concurring Separate Opinion of Judge Eboe-Osuji, n 13, paras 58–69.

[32] For an excellent overview, see S. Vasiliev, 'ECCC Appeals' (2020) 18 *Journal of International Criminal Justice* 723, at 733–7.

[33] *KAING Guek Eav* alias *Duch ('Case 001')*, Appeal Judgment, 001/18-07-2007/ECCC/SC (F28), 3 February 2012, paras 17–20.

[34] *NUON Chea and KHIEU Samphân ('Case 002/01')*, Appeal Judgment, 002/19-09-2007/ECCC/SC (F36), 23 November 2016 ('*Case 002/01* Appeal Judgment'), para. 92.

[35] Ibid., para. 94.

[36] Ibid.

[37] Vasiliev, n 25, at 734–5.

[38] *Case 002/02* Appeal Judgment, n 18, para. 28; *Case 002/01* Appeal Judgment, n 27, para. 90.

[39] *Bemba* Appeal Judgment, n 13, paras 38–46, citing *Case 002/01* Appeal Judgment, n 27, para. 90 with approval at paras 43–4. See further, Vasiliev, n 25, at 735–6.

[40] *Prosecutor v Lubanga*, Judgment on the appeal of the Prosecutor against the decision of Trial Chamber I of 8 July 2010 entitled 'Decision on the Prosecution's Urgent Request for Variation of the Time-Limit to Disclose the Identity of Intermediary 143 or Alternatively to Stay the Proceedings Pending Further Consultations with the VWU', ICC-01/04-01/06-2582, 8 October 2010, para. 56; *Prosecutor v Mbarushimana*, Judgment on the appeal of Mr Callixte Mbarushimana against the

that the Appeals Chamber would interfere with the factual findings of a first instance Chamber only where it is shown to have 'committed a clear error, namely, misappreciated the facts, took into account irrelevant facts, or failed to take into account relevant facts'.[41] The Appeals Chamber would only intervene where it was unable to 'discern how the Chamber's conclusion could have reasonably been reached from the evidence before it'.[42] In her dissenting opinion in *Lubanga*, Judge Ušacka noted that, while she agreed with her colleagues in the majority on appellate deference, she believed that 'fairness of the proceedings require[s] the Appeals Chamber to play a role in correcting fact-finding errors', particularly (i.e. but not only) where the basis for the Chamber's decision cannot be discerned.[43] She believed that the majority accepted the Trial Chamber's position that it had taken a 'cautious approach' to carrying out age determinations of alleged child soldiers on the basis of video evidence.[44] In reality, however, Judge Ušacka argued that there was a lack of reasoning in the Trial Chamber's judgment on this point, such that the Appeals Chamber should have carried out its own assessment of the relevant evidence to determine the reasonableness of the Trial Chamber's findings.[45]

Similarly, in *Ngudjolo*, the Appeals Chamber judgment reiterated the principle of appellate deference as stated in *Lubanga*,[46] but the two dissenting judges criticised their colleagues in the majority for 'regrettably not reproach[ing]' the Trial Chamber's approach to the evaluation of the evidence, which they perceived as unduly fragmentary,[47] as discussed in detail in Chapter 6. Thus, we can see disagreement among Appeals Chamber judges as to the degree to which deference should be shown.

This difference of opinion was arguably most keenly felt in the ICC Appeals Chamber's 2018 judgment in *Bemba*.[48] As Judge Eboe-Osuji noted in his separate

decision of Pre-Trial Chamber I of 19 May 2011 entitled 'Decision on the "Defence Request for Interim Release"', ICC-01/04-01/10-283, 14 July 2011; *Bemba* et al. Appeal Judgment, n 11, paras 91–2.

[41] *Ngudjolo* Appeal Judgment, n 12, para. 22; *Lubanga* Appeal Judgment, n 8, para. 21; *Bemba et al.* Appeal Judgment, n 11, para. 91.

[42] *Lubanga* Appeal Judgment, n 8, para. 21, cited in *Bemba et al.* Appeal Judgment, n 11, para. 91; *Ngudjolo* Appeal Judgment, n 12, para. 22.

[43] *Lubanga* Appeal Judgment, n 8, Dissenting opinion of Judge Ušacka, ICC-01/04-01/06-3121-Anx2, 1 December 2014, para. 48.

[44] Ibid., para. 49.

[45] Ibid., paras 49–50 (drawing parallels with the *Kupreškić* case on identification evidence).

[46] *Ngudjolo* Appeal Judgment, n 12, para. 22.

[47] *Ngudjolo* Appeal Judgment, Joint Dissenting Opinion of Judge Trendafilova and Judge Tarfusser, n 14, paras. 42, 45, 47, 53, and 68 (accusing the Majority of, *inter alia*, 'turn[ing] a blind eye' to perceived errors in the Trial Chamber's reasoning).

[48] *Bemba* Appeal Judgment, Concurring Separate Opinion of Judge Eboe-Osuji, n 13; *Bemba* Appeal Judgment, n 13, Dissenting Opinion of Judge Monageng and Judge Hofmański, ICC-01/05-01/08-3636-Anx1, 8 June 2018; Separate Opinion of Judge Van den Wyngaert and Judge Morrison, ICC-01/05-01/08-3636-Anx2, 8 June 2018. For a thorough analysis, see J. Powderly, 'Introductory Note to *Prosecutor v Jean-Pierre Bemba Gombo*: Judgment on the Appeal of Mr. Jean-Pierre Bemba Gombo against Trial Chamber III's "Judgment Pursuant to Article 74 of the Statute" (Int'l Crim. Ct.)' (2018) 57 *ILM* 1031.

concurring opinion, 'what really separates the majority and the minority is the extent to which the idea of "appellate deference" should guide the judgment of the Appeals Chamber'.[49] The majority ruled that the Appeals Chamber may interfere with the factual findings of the first instance chamber not only in circumstances where it could not discern how the conclusion could reasonably have been reached from the evidence, but also 'whenever the failure to intervene may occasion a miscarriage of justice'.[50] The majority noted that the Appeals Chamber must be careful not to 'tie its own hands against the interests of justice' in applying appellate deference, which did not appear in the Statute.[51]

Judge Eboe-Osuji emphasised the need to avoid appellate deference becoming

> a convenient subterfuge for appellate courts to escape the laborious and unglamorous work of conducting the thorough evidential review that may be necessary in the given appeal, in order to be convinced (in the face of the contrary complaint) that the trial was fair or that guilt was proved beyond reasonable doubt or that the factual finding was reasonable, as the case may be.[52]

Nevertheless, Judge Eboe-Osuji noted that an appellate chamber may not substitute its own views for that of a first instance Chamber where the factual finding of the latter is reasonable.[53] This was also emphasised in the majority judgment[54] and the joint separate opinion of Judges Van den Wyngaert and Morrison.[55] In the words of Judge Eboe-Osuji, it is only where 'the collective judicial experience of the appeals court leads it to the view (which must be clearly articulated) that the finding of the trial court was not reasonable' that the Appeals Chamber must intervene.[56] Thus, he concluded, the notion of appellate deference could be boiled down to the simple proposition that an Appeals Chamber 'should not lightly overturn the factual findings of the Trial Chamber'.[57] This does not appear to be a dramatic departure from the established position of appellate deference, but the majority judgment went somewhat further by requiring not only that the trial chamber's findings be reasonable,[58] but also that they be 'clear and unassailable':

49 *Bemba* Appeal Judgment, Concurring Separate Opinion of Judge Eboe-Osuji, n 13, para. 8.
50 *Bemba* Appeal Judgment, n 13, para. 40.
51 Ibid.
52 *Bemba* Appeal Judgment, Concurring Separate Opinion of Judge Eboe-Osuji, n 13, para. 78.
53 Ibid., para. 75.
54 *Bemba* Appeal Judgment, n 13, para. 42.
55 *Bemba* Appeal Judgment, Separate Opinion of Judge Van den Wyngaert and Judge Morrison, n 41, para. 14.
56 *Bemba* Appeal Judgment, Concurring Separate Opinion of Judge Eboe-Osuji, n 13, para. 75.
57 Ibid., paras 79–80.
58 *Bemba* Appeal Judgment, n 13, para. 42 ('When a factual error is alleged, it will not assess the evidence *de novo* with a view to determining whether it would have reached the same factual conclusion as the trial chamber … [rather] it will determine whether a reasonable trial chamber properly directing itself could have been satisfied beyond reasonable doubt as to the finding in question, based on the evidence that was before it').

> Ultimately, the Appeals Chamber must be satisfied that factual findings that are made beyond reasonable doubt are clear and unassailable, both in terms of evidence and rationale. Mere preferences or personal impressions of the appellate judges are insufficient to upset the findings of a trial chamber. However, when a reasonable and objective person can articulate serious doubts about the accuracy of a given finding, and is able to support this view with specific arguments, this is a strong indication that the trial chamber may not have respected the standard of proof and, accordingly, that an error of fact may have been made.[59]

The *Bemba* Appeals Judgment raises two important questions: first, did it represent a departure from the established standard of review? And, if so, was such a departure necessary in the context of the case?

On the first question, many commentators did see *Bemba* as a clear departure from established precedent on the standard of review for findings of fact.[60] For example, Powderly argued:

> The amended standard effectively extinguishes the notion of appellate deference, which, the majority is careful to note, is not expressly provided for in the Rome Statute. In essence, it dispenses with the established reasonableness test and replaces it with a significantly higher 'beyond reasonable doubt' standard, thereby potentially conflating the standard of review with the standard of proof. While the majority state that applying their preferred standard does not entail a de novo review, it is hard to see how that could be avoided.[61]

On the other hand, Eckelmans noted that the majority drew extensively on existing jurisprudence, concluding that 'it appears doubtful whether the majority ... had the intention to diverge from the standard of review'.[62] Eckelmans concluded that the Appeals Chamber perhaps sought to refine, rather than depart from, the established deferential standard.[63] That seems a rather optimistic reading of the judgment, given that both the majority judgment[64] and the concurring separate

[59] Ibid., para. 45.

[60] J. Trahan, 'Bemba Acquittal Rests on Erroneous Application of Appellate Review Standard' (*Opinio Juris*, 25 June 2018); A. Whiting, 'Appeals Judges Turn the ICC on Its Head with Bemba Decision' (*Just Security*, 14 June 2018); J. Powderly and N. Hayes, 'The Bemba Appeal: A Fragmented Appeals Chamber Destabilises the Law and Practice of the ICC' (*PhD Studies in Human Rights*, 26 June 2018); L.N. Sadat, 'Fiddling While Rome Burns? The Appeals Chamber's Curious Decision in Prosecutor v Jean-Pierre Bemba Gombo' (*EJIL: Talk!*, 12 June 2018); *Report of the Independent Expert Review of the International Criminal Court and the Rome Statute System*, ICC-ASP/19/16, 30 September 2020, paras 608–11; F. Bensouda, 'Statement of ICC Prosecutor, Fatou Bensouda, on the Recent Judgment of the ICC Appeals Chamber Acquitting Mr Jean-Pierre Bemba Gombo', 13 June 2018.

[61] Powderly, n 33, at 1032.

[62] F. Eckelmans, 'Article 81' in O. Triffterer and K. Ambos (eds), *Rome Statute of the International Criminal Court: Article-by-Article Commentary* (4th edn, Beck/Hart, 2021), 2311 at 2343. See further, D. Djukić, *The Right to Appeal in International Criminal Law* (Brill, 2019), at 193–6.

[63] Eckelmans, n 62, at 2343.

[64] *Bemba* Appeal Judgment, n 13, para. 40.

opinion of Judge Eboe-Osuji explicitly acknowledged that the standard adopted by the majority was a reformulation of what Judge Eboe-Osuji termed 'the older standard' (i.e. of appellate deference).[65] This departure was also noted by Judges Monageng and Hofmański in their dissenting opinion.[66] Judges Van den Wyngaert and Morrison were less explicit on this point, noting instead:

> We strongly believe that the Appeals Chamber cannot turn a blind eye to ... obvious evidentiary problems on the basis of a deferential standard of review. The deferential standard set out in the jurisprudence of the Court does not require judges of the Appeals Chamber, if they come to the conclusion that a particular finding by the Trial Chamber fails to meet the 'beyond reasonable doubt' threshold, to ignore this and to refrain from drawing the necessary conclusions. Anything less would make appellate review a pointless rubberstamping exercise, which is not what Articles 81 and 83 plainly require.[67]

While this suggests that such a review would fall within the existing boundaries of appellate deference as established by the case law, it is clear from the majority judgment and Judge Eboe-Osuji's separate opinion that the majority acknowledged their formulation to be an expansion of the existing standard of review, and that seems to be the correct interpretation of the judgment.

This leads, then, to the second question, of whether such an expansion was necessary. It is clear from the majority judgment and the two separate opinions in support thereof that all three judges in the majority believed the Trial Chamber's conclusion to be unreasonable.[68] If that was the case, the Appeals Chamber could have applied the existing appellate standard and overturned Bemba's conviction. Alex Whiting believed that they did not because the majority could not find that the Trial Chamber's findings were unreasonable.[69] This does not seem to be the case, given the findings examined by the majority by way of example of their apparent lack of solid foundation in the evidential record.[70] Instead, it appears that the judges in the majority shared a firm conviction that there was a need for the Appeals Chamber to stop 'tying its own hands', a phrase used in both the majority judgment

[65] *Bemba* Appeal Judgment, Concurring Separate Opinion of Judge Eboe-Osuji, n 13, para. 8; see further, *Bemba* Appeal Judgment, n 13, paras 42–80; *Bemba* Appeal Judgment, Dissenting Opinion of Judge Monageng and Judge Hofmański, n 41, para. 14.

[66] *Bemba* Appeal Judgment, Dissenting Opinion of Judge Monageng and Judge Hofmański, n 41, para. 47.

[67] *Bemba* Appeal Judgment, Separate Opinion of Judge Van den Wyngaert and Judge Morrison, n 41, para. 14.

[68] *Bemba* Appeal Judgment, n 13, para. 45; *Bemba* Appeal Judgment, Separate Opinion of Judge Van den Wyngaert and Judge Morrison, n 41, paras 6–14; *Bemba* Appeal Judgment, Concurring Separate Opinion of Judge Eboe-Osuji, n 13, paras 10; 18–20

[69] Whiting, n 45. See also, *Bemba* Appeal Judgment, Dissenting Opinion of Judge Monageng and Judge Hofmański, n 41, para. 47.

[70] *Bemba* Appeal Judgment, n 13, paras 166–94; *Bemba* Appeal Judgment, Separate Opinion of Judge Van den Wyngaert and Judge Morrison, n 41, paras 64–8.

and the separate opinion of Judges Van den Wyngaert and Morrison, by taking an overly deferential approach to the Trial Chamber's factual findings. While such concern is laudable, and the risk of undue deference is real, the majority's standard had the potential to be dangerously broad and subjective. It is not beyond the realms of possibility, for example, that a future Appeals Chamber might apply the standard in deeming a first instance acquittal a 'miscarriage of justice' and may seek to overturn it 'in the interests of justice', to use the terminology of the majority in *Bemba*.[71]

More recent Appeals Chamber jurisprudence has derived something of a third way between granting the Trial Chamber a very wide margin of deference and intervening in the interests of justice. The statements of the appropriate standard of review for factual findings set out in the appeal judgments in *Ntaganda*[72] and *Gbagbo and Blé Goudé*[73] are notable in three important respects. The first is that the relevant paragraphs are identical in both judgments.[74] This is hardly surprising, given that they were issued by the same Appeals Chamber just a day apart—it would be more surprising if they had changed their minds in between the two judgments. However, because the *Gbagbo and Blé Goudé* judgment does not cite the *Ntaganda* judgment,[75] later decisions adopting the identical standard of review set out in both judgments have had to cite each judgment separately.[76] The second notable aspect is the conspicuous absence of citations to ICC case law in setting out the relevant standard of review; there are only two footnotes in the relevant seven paragraphs of both decisions: one a solitary cross-reference to the *Lubanga* appeal judgment, and the other a detailed overview of national practice in relation to what evidence law from the Hispanic legal tradition refers to as the *sana crítica:* the need for findings to be consistent with 'logic, common sense, scientific knowledge and experience'.[77] The Appeals Chamber could not have been more explicit in setting its explanation of the relevant standard apart from the jurisprudence that went before it. The third fact of note is that three of the five Appeals

[71] This possibility was apparently considered by the Majority, with Judge Eboe-Osuji noting (*Bemba* Appeal Judgment, Concurring Separate Opinion of Judge Eboe-Osuji, n 13, para. 51): 'The notion of appellate deference can prove just as inconvenient for the Prosecution and the victims, given the real possibility of a case in which they may complain that the Trial Chamber's acquittal of an accused resulted from an erroneous factual finding.'

[72] *Prosecutor v Ntaganda*, Public redacted version of Judgment on the appeals of Mr Bosco Ntaganda and the Prosecutor against the decision of Trial Chamber VI of 8 July 2019 entitled 'Judgment', ICC-01/04-02/06-2666-Red, 30 March 2021 ('*Ntaganda* Appeal Judgment').

[73] *Gbagbo and Blé Goudé* Appeal Judgment, n 9.

[74] Compare *Ntaganda* Appeal Judgment, n 65, paras 37–44 with *Gbagbo and Blé Goudé* Appeal Judgment, n 9, paras 66–72.

[75] The *Ntaganda* Appeal Judgment was issued a day before the Gbagbo and Blé Goudé Appeal Judgment.

[76] *Ongwen* Appeal Judgment, n 12, paras 77–84.

[77] *Ntaganda* Appeal Judgment, n 65, para. 39; on the *sana crítica,* see F. Zubiri de Salinas, '¿Qué es la sana crítica? La valoración judicial del dictamen experto' (2004) 50 *Revista Jueces para la Democracia* 52–62; M. Taruffo, 'Rethinking the Standards of Proof' (2003) 51 *American Journal of Comparative Law* 659, at 668; J. Gonzalez Castillo, 'La Fundamentación de las Sentencias y la Sana Crítica' (2006) 33 *Revista Chilena de Derecho* 93, at 95.

Chamber judges in *Ntaganda* and *Gbagbo and Blé Goudé* were also judges on the Appeals Chamber in *Bemba*, and two of them (Morrison and Eboe-Osuji) were in the majority in *Bemba*, which makes the absence of any reference to the lengthy discussion of the requisite standard in *Bemba* even more noteworthy.

In his Separate Concurring Opinion in *Gbagbo and Blé Goudé*, Judge Eboe-Osuji helpfully provided more context to the standard of appellate review adopted in both judgments:

> In this judgment and in the *Ntaganda* merits appeal judgment, the Appeals Chamber has reformulated the standard of appellate review at the ICC—particularly as regards factual findings of Trial Chambers. The reformulation is unanimous, following a lengthy deliberation by all five judges. The effort was not by happenstance. It is a conscious jurisprudential reset, following the wake-up call of the *Bemba* Appeal Judgment.[78]

This same 'reformulation' has now been extensively cited by the Appeals Chamber in a later Article 81 judgment, which did not depart from the standard of appellate review set down in *Ntaganda* and *Gbagbo and Blé Goudé* in any way.[79] We may conclude, therefore, that for the moment at least, there appears to have been some agreement reached between ICC judges on this point.

The *Gbagbo and Blé Goudé/Ntaganda* standard of review for factual errors is composed of four key elements. First, the Appeals Chamber must be assured that the Trial Chamber correctly applied the standard of proof beyond reasonable doubt, and carried out a holistic evaluation of the evidence:

> in the sense of assessing in a connected way and weighing of all the relevant evidence taken together, in relation to the fact at issue; rather than evaluating items of evidence without regard to other related evidence. Furthermore, the Appeals Chamber must be satisfied that the trial chamber assessed all factual findings in deciding, pursuant to the applicable law, that the accused person's guilt was established beyond reasonable doubt or that he or she should be acquitted.[80]

[78] *Gbagbo and Blé Goudé* Appeal Judgment, n 9, Public Redacted Version to the Corrected Confidential Separate Concurring Opinion of Judge Eboe-Osuji, ICC-02/11-01/15-1400-Anx1-Corr-Red, 9 April 2021, para. 19. Judge Eboe-Osuji also contested, at some length, the IER's contention that the majority in the *Bemba* appeals judgment did not explain its departure from the standard of appellate deference (*Gbagbo and Blé Goudé* Appeal Judgment, Public Redacted Version to the Corrected Confidential Separate Concurring Opinion of Judge Eboe-Osuji, n 9, paras 18–52), and reiterated his position that the idea of appellate deference at the ICC should simply mean that the Appeals Chamber should not lightly overturn factual findings of the Trial Chamber (*Gbagbo and Blé Goudé* Appeal Judgment, n 9, Public Redacted Version to the Corrected Confidential Separate Concurring Opinion of Judge Eboe-Osuji, para. 82).

[79] *Ongwen* Appeal Judgment, n 12, paras 77–84.

[80] *Ntaganda* Appeal Judgment, n 65, paras 37–8; *Gbagbo and Blé Goudé* Appeal Judgment, n 9, paras 66–7.

Second, it will examine whether the findings of the Trial Chamber cohered with 'logic, common sense, scientific knowledge and experience' in considering their reasonableness in the context of the case.[81] This adoption of the *sana critíca* standard is interesting, not least because it finds legal authority not in international criminal law (although the Appeals Chamber could have referred to the case law of another international tribunal, the Inter-American Court of Human Rights, which applies the standard[82]), but through reference to domestic jurisdictions. The Chamber noted that '[t]he obligation of a trier of fact in this regard finds expression in the law and jurisprudence of various national legal systems', before citing practice from five countries (Argentina, Peru, Canada, Poland, and Spain).[83] The Chamber did not expand on whether this was sufficient evidence to establish it as a general principle of law pursuant to Article 21(1)(c) of the ICC Statute. This reference could be seen as a nod to the rationalist tradition in evidence scholarship.[84] Indeed, the full title of Wigmore's famous tome that introduced his chart method was *The Science of Judicial Proof: As Given by Logic, Psychology, and General Experience, and Illustrated in Judicial Trials*,[85] the subtitle of which bears a close resemblance to this dictum.

Third, the Appeals Chamber noted that appellate deference to factual findings is warranted by two specific features of the Court's legal framework: the specific role of the Trial Chamber in conducting the trial, and as such, to examine the evidence (the principle of immediacy), and the limited role of the Appeals Chamber in considering the trial judgment 'through the lens of the errors raised [by the parties].'[86] In other words, the Appeals Chamber cannot conduct a trial *de novo*.

Fourth, however, this deference 'is not without qualification'.[87] The Appeals Chamber provided a long list of examples of the kinds of errors of fact that an appellate chamber may interfere with, including:

- findings that are insufficiently supported by the evidence;
- findings based on irrelevant evidence;
- the Trial Chamber's failure to consider 'relevant evidentiary considerations and facts'; and

[81] *Ntaganda* Appeal Judgment, n 65, para. 39; *Gbagbo and Blé Goudé* Appeal Judgment, n 9, para. 68.

[82] Á. Paúl, '*Sana Crítica*: The System for Weighing Evidence Utilized by the Inter-American Court of Human Rights' (2012) 18 *Buffalo Human Rights Law Review* 193.

[83] *Ntaganda* Appeal Judgment, n 65, para. 39; *Gbagbo and Blé Goudé* Appeal Judgment, n 9, para. 68; *Ongwen* Appeal Judgment, n 12, para. 79.

[84] W. Twining, *Rethinking Evidence* (CUP, 2009), 35–98.

[85] J.H. Wigmore, *The Science of Judicial Proof: As Given by Logic, Psychology, and General Experience, and Illustrated in Criminal Trials* (Little, Brown & Co, 1937).

[86] *Ntaganda* Appeal Judgment, n 65, para. 40; *Gbagbo and Blé Goudé* Appeal Judgment, n 9 para. 69; *Ongwen* Appeal Judgment, n 12, para. 80.

[87] *Ntaganda* Appeal Judgment, n 65, para. 41; *Gbagbo and Blé Goudé* Appeal Judgment, n 9, para. 70; *Ongwen* Appeal Judgment, n 12, para. 82.

- its failure to properly appreciate the significance of the evidence on record, or to properly weigh and evaluate the relevant facts and evidence.[88]

The Appeals Chamber, as has been previously established in the case law, 'may interfere where it is unable to discern objectively how the trial chamber's conclusion could have reasonably been reached from the evidence on the record'.[89] Where there are 'significant contradictions in the evidence, deficiencies in the trial chamber's reasoning as to why it found that evidence persuasive may lead the Appeals Chamber to conclude that the finding in question was unreasonable'.[90]

Taken together, we can adduce a third wave of Appeals Chamber jurisprudence on the requisite appellate standard, one that might be referred to as 'tempered deference'. Tempered deference allows for appellate intervention in a wide range of situations that could render the first instance chamber's finding unreasonable, but it recognises that deference is required by the Court's statutory framework and the limited role of the Appeals Chamber. Because all three appeal judgments since the emergence of this new formulation of the standard of review upheld the relevant Trial Chamber judgments in their entirety, we are yet to observe (beyond the hypotheticals provided by the Appeals Chamber and listed above) the kind of factual findings that might lead the chamber to intervene. However, it is notable that the Appeals Chamber has emphasised that the Trial Chamber's reasoning, particularly where the underpinning evidence appears weak or where there are contradictions in the record, will be crucial in evaluating the reasonableness of its factual findings.

iv. Procedural errors

Procedural errors may be alleged based on the conduct of trial or pre-trial proceedings.[91] Procedural errors often arise in the context of an alleged abuse of discretion in relation to trial management,[92] where the Chamber's 'decision is so unfair or unreasonable as to "force the conclusion that the Chamber failed to exercise its discretion judiciously"'.[93] However, it has been emphasised that the Appeals

[88] *Ntaganda* Appeal Judgment, n 65, para. 41; *Gbagbo and Blé Goudé* Appeal Judgment, n 9, para. 70; *Ongwen* Appeal Judgment, n 12, para. 82.

[89] *Ntaganda* Appeal Judgment, n 65, para. 41; *Gbagbo and Blé Goudé* Appeal Judgment, n 9, para. 70; *Ongwen* Appeal Judgment, n 12, para. 82.

[90] *Ntaganda* Appeal Judgment, n 65, para. 42; *Gbagbo and Blé Goudé* Appeal Judgment, n 9, para. 71; *Ongwen* Appeal Judgment, n 12, para. 83.

[91] *Bemba* Appeal Judgment, n 13, para. 47; *Lubanga* Appeal Judgment, n 8, para. 20; *Ngudjolo* Appeal Judgment, n 12, para. 20.

[92] International Bar Association, *Remedying International Injustice: Appeals, Retrials and Revisions of Judgments in International Criminal Law* (2022), 30.

[93] *Bemba et al.* Appeal Judgment, n 11, para. 101, citing *Prosecutor v Kenyatta*, Judgment on the Prosecutor's appeal against Trial Chamber V(B)'s 'Decision on Prosecution's application for a finding of non-compliance under Article 87(7) of the Statute', ICC-01/09-02/11-1032, 19 August 2015, para. 25.

Chamber will not interfere with a ruling merely because it would have taken a different approach.[94] The Appeals Chamber will only intervene where the Chamber's exercise of discretion was based on an error of law or fact, or where the decision was so unfair and unreasonable as to amount to an abuse of discretion.[95] As with other errors, the material impact of the error on the judgment rendered must be demonstrated.[96]

In *Ngudjolo*, Judges Trendifilova and Tarfusser alleged that the Trial Chamber's failure to balance the rights of the accused with the rights of the Prosecutor was a 'discernible error'.[97] They considered that the Chamber abused its discretion by allowing 'flagrant detriment of one of the parties at trial and with irreparable prejudice to the establishment of the truth'.[98] The majority of the Appeals Chamber declined to consider the question of whether the Prosecutor could rightly be said to be a beneficiary of the right to a fair trial.[99] As will be recalled from the discussion in Chapter 2, it is fair to say that the dissenting judges' position that the rights of the accused need to be weighed against those of the Prosecutor is a minority view, and one that risks jeopardising the Court's core responsibility to ensure that trials are conducted fairly.[100]

Related to the discussion in Chapter 6 on the evaluation of evidence, a failure to provide 'a full and reasoned statement of the Trial Chamber's findings on the evidence and conclusions', as required by Article 74(5) of the Statute, would amount to a procedural error.[101] It has been emphasised that the Trial Chamber is obliged to indicate the factual and legal bases for its decision, in order for the Appeals Chamber to properly exercise its functions.[102] There is a presumption that the Trial Chamber assessed all the evidence before it, but that presumption may be rebutted if the appellant can show that clearly relevant evidence was not addressed by the Trial Chamber's reasoning.[103] The Appeals Chamber, in determining whether

[94] *Bemba et al.* Appeal Judgment, n 11, para. 100, citing *Kenyatta*, n 93, para. 22.
[95] *Bemba et al.* Appeal Judgment, n 11, para. 100.
[96] *Bemba* Appeal Judgment, n 13, para. 47; *Bemba et al.* Appeal Judgment, n 11, para. 107.
[97] *Ngudjolo* Appeal Judgment, Joint Dissenting Opinion of Judge Trendafilova and Judge Tarfusser, n 14, para. 15, citing *Prosecutor v Karadžić*, Decision on Appeal against the Decision on the Accused's Motion to Subpoena Zdravko Tolimir, IT-95-5/18-AR73.11, 13 November 2013, para. 29; *Prosecutor v Gotovina et al.*, Decision on Gotovina Defence Appeal Against 12 March 2010 Decision on Requests for Permanent Restraining Orders Directed to the Republic of Croatia, IT-06-90-AR73.5, 14 February 2011, para. 14; *Prosecutor v Haradinaj et al.*, Decision on Haradinaj's Appeal on Scope of Partial Retrial, IT-04-84bis-AR73.1, 31 May 2011, para. 8.
[98] *Ngudjolo* Appeal Judgment, Joint Dissenting Opinion of Judge Trendafilova and Judge Tarfusser, n 14, para. 15.
[99] *Ngudjolo* Appeal Judgment, n 12, paras 255–6.
[100] For a detailed discussion, see S. Rigney, *Fairness and Rights in International Criminal Procedure* (Edinburgh University Press, 2022), 76–90; Y. McDermott, 'Rights in Reverse: A Critical Analysis of Fair Trial Rights under International Criminal Law' in W. Schabas, Y. McDermott, and N. Hayes (eds), *The Ashgate Research Companion to International Criminal Law: Critical Perspectives* (Ashgate, 2013), 165.
[101] *Bemba et al.* Appeal Judgment, n 11, para. 102. See also, *Bemba* Appeal Judgment, n 13, paras. 49-55.
[102] *Bemba et al.* Appeal Judgment, n 11, para. 102; *Bemba* Appeal Judgment, n 13, para. 49.
[103] *Bemba et al.* Appeal Judgment, n 11, para. 105 (footnotes excluded).

there was a breach of Article 74(5) amounting to a procedural error, will examine whether pieces of *prima facie* relevant evidence were not addressed in the Trial Chamber's reasoning.[104] If so, the Appeals Chamber will determine 'whether they were of such importance that they should have been addressed'.[105]

v. Any other ground affecting the fairness or reliability of proceedings

This ground of appeal is clearly closely related to that of a procedural error, in that something may be both a procedural error and a breach of the right to a fair trial.[106] Unfairness may also constitute an error of law, as it did before the ad hoc tribunals, where the convicted person had to show, first, that their rights had been infringed, and second, that the violation caused such prejudice that it constituted an error of law invalidating the judgment.[107] However, it exists in the ICC Statute as a separate ground of appeal available only to the accused, pursuant to Article 81(1)(b)(iv), and as such has been described as a '"catch all" provision ... to ensure that any miscarriage of justice would be capable of correction on appeal'.[108] As mentioned above, before the ICC, the standard of 'materiality' appears to be different than for other forms of error—rather than having to show the error materially affected the judgment, the appellant must demonstrate that the Chamber made an error that affected 'the fairness *or* reliability of the proceedings or decision'.[109] The *Bemba* Appeals Chamber noted that this provision must be read in conjunction with Article 83(2), 'which clarifies that, for the Appeals Chamber to intervene, it must be demonstrated that the proceedings were unfair in such a way as to affect the reliability of the decision or sentence'.[110] In other words, unfairness alone will not be sufficient grounds to overturn a judgment—the impact of any unfairness, which is determined on a case-by-case basis,[111] must be assessed.

[104] Ibid., para. 106.

[105] Ibid.

[106] K. Ambos, *Treatise on International Criminal Law: Vol. III* (OUP, 2016), at 561–3. See also *Bemba* Appeal Judgment, Concurring Separate Opinion of Judge Eboe-Osuji, n 13, para. 89 ('It is obviously not always easy to construct strict compartments between appellate grievances, separating the category of material errors (of law, of fact or of procedure) from the category of unfairness amounting to miscarriage of justice').

[107] *Prosecutor v Galić*, Judgment, IT-98-29-A, 30 November 2006, para. 21; *Prosecutor v Kordić and Čerkez*, Judgment, IT-95-14/2-A, 17 December 2004, para. 119; *Prosecutor v Hadžihasanović and Kubura*, Judgment, IT-01-47-A, 22 April 2008, para. 130.

[108] Eckelmans, n 55, at 2347.

[109] Article 81(1)(b)(iv) (emphasis added); see further *Bemba* Appeal Judgment, n 13, paras. 60–1; *Lubanga* Appeal Judgment, n 8, para. 28.

[110] *Bemba* Appeal Judgment, n 13, para. 60.

[111] *Bemba* Appeal Judgment, n 13, para. 62. See further, Eckelmans, n 55, at 2347 ('The "reliability" test requires an assessment by the AC as to whether, despite the unfairness that occurred in the proceedings, the impugned decision can still be relied upon in order to convict and sentence the accused').

C. New evidence on appeal

In determining whether to permit the admission of new evidence on appeal, Appeals Chambers must strike a delicate balance between ensuring the appeal does not become a 'trial *de novo*' and avoiding miscarriages of justice. The international criminal tribunals have taken quite a restrictive approach to the admission of new evidence on appeal, requiring that the evidence was, for good reason, not available at the time of the trial, and that it is relevant, credible, and could have been decisive in the original trial.[112] Even if the evidence were available at the time of trial, in exceptional circumstances the Appeals Chamber may allow for its admission where there are compelling reasons for doing so,[113] such as where the exclusion of the evidence risks a miscarriage of justice.[114]

In *Lubanga*, the majority declined to admit additional evidence relating to the age assessments made by the Trial Chamber.[115] As Judge Ušacka noted in dissenting from the majority judgment on admissibility, the Trial Chamber (despite noting that it would treat video evidence with caution in assessing the age of people in the video) did find that some individuals in the videos were clearly under the age of 15, based solely on their appearance.[116] The defence, at appeal, sought to admit additional information in relation to two such individuals shown—D-0040 and D-0041—to attempt to show that they were not under 15 at the time the videos were created.[117] These witnesses testified before the Appeals Chamber 'without prejudice to a determination as to its [their testimony's] admissibility'.[118] Ultimately, the Appeals Chamber was unconvinced of Lubanga's arguments as to why he did not present this evidence at trial, finding it to be linked to a trial strategy to not present the evidence in his defence.[119] As such, it found the witnesses' testimony and the related items of evidence to be inadmissible.[120] It made similar determinations in relation to additional evidence on Lubanga's bodyguards, which could have rebutted the Trial Chamber's findings that children under the age of 15 formed part of the presidential guard.[121] As Judge Ušacka noted, it is difficult to square this decision with the Court's role in searching for the truth; for her, the

[112] *Lubanga* Appeal Judgment, n 8, para. 57; *Bemba et al.* Appeal Judgment, n 11, para. 515; Rule 115, ICTY RPE; Rule 115, ICTR RPE; Rule 115, SCSL RPE; Rule 142, IRMCT RPE; Rule 108(7) ECCC IR; Rule 181 KSC RPE.

[113] *Lubanga* Appeal Judgment, n 8, paras 56–9; see further, Regulation 62, ICC Regulations.

[114] *Lubanga* Appeal Judgment, n 8, para. 61.

[115] *Lubanga* Appeal Judgment, n 8, paras 74–81.

[116] *Lubanga* Appeal Judgment, Dissenting opinion of Judge Ušacka, n 36, paras 52–67.

[117] *Lubanga* Appeal Judgment, n 8, paras 65 and 67.

[118] Ibid., para. 66; *Prosecutor v Lubanga*, Further order regarding the conduct of the hearing of the Appeals Chamber, ICC-01/04-01/06-3068, 25 March 2014, at 4.

[119] *Lubanga* Appeal Judgment, n 8, para. 79.

[120] Ibid., para. 81.

[121] Ibid., paras 82–96. Other requests were found to pertain to material that would not impact upon the reliability of the verdict: ibid., paras. 105 and 113.

key criterion in considering whether to admit additional evidence is whether that evidence could have resulted in a different verdict.[122] It is difficult to argue with this. In parts, the majority's approach does come across as unnecessarily punitive of what it perceived to be a defence strategy not to present certain evidence at trial.[123] It will be recalled that each of the key witnesses who the prosecution alleged to be former child soldiers were found to be lacking in credibility by the Trial Chamber for various reasons.[124] The defence, not being aware that this would be the outcome, would have been justified in expending less effort on seemingly more tangential evidence, which ultimately transpired to be central to Lubanga's conviction.[125] For the sake of gaining a more complete picture, it would have been preferable for the Appeals Chamber to have considered the additional evidence.

Following the 'submission' system of evidence discussed in Chapter 3, the ICC Appeals Chamber may opt to rule on the admissibility of evidence in its appeal judgment when it has had the opportunity to consider all the evidence, rather than making individual decisions on admissibility at the time of each piece of evidence's submission.[126] The International Bar Association has argued that this approach should be reconsidered:

> In performing its corrective role, it is essential that the Appeals Chamber conducts a process that is logical, transparent and that the parties are able to make informed submissions on matters that will determine the final verdict in the case. Requiring parties to make their final submissions in a case without knowing whether or not additional evidence has been admitted or having to rebut evidence that may never be admitted is not conducive to a fair and transparent final determination on guilt or innocence. While ruling on admissibility during the appeal process may take additional time, an appeals chamber should be sufficiently familiar with the trial record in the early stages of an appeal to determine whether evidence *could* have led to a different verdict for the purposes of determining admissibility.[127]

[122] *Lubanga* Appeal Judgment, Dissenting opinion of Judge Ušacka, n 36, para. 58.
[123] *Lubanga* Appeal Judgment, n 8, para. 79.
[124] *Prosecutor v Lubanga*, Judgment pursuant to Article 74 of the Statute, ICC-01/04-01/06-2842, 5 April 2012, paras 479–80 and preceding discussion.
[125] *Lubanga* Appeal Judgment, Dissenting opinion of Judge Ušacka, n 36, paras 57–8.
[126] Regulation 62(2), ICC Regulations, allows either approach to be taken. The decision to decide on admissibility of additional evidence together with other issues in the appeal was taken in *Lubanga* Appeal Judgment, n 8, para. 39 and *Bemba et al.* Appeal Judgment, n 11, para. 500. A similar approach taken in some ICTY decisions, e.g. *Kupreškić* Appeal Judgment, n 17, para. 71. Cf. *Prosecutor v Ntaganda*, Public redacted version of Decision on request for the admission of additional evidence on appeal of 22 October 2020, ICC-01/04-02/06-2617, 13 November 2020, where the Appeals Chamber issued a decision rejecting Mr Ntaganda's request to file additional evidence prior to the issuance of the appeal judgment.
[127] International Bar Association, n 92, at 29.

D. Scope of retrials

Having considered the parties' submissions on the grounds of appeal, the Appeals Chamber can either confirm, reverse, or amend the judgment,[128] or it can order a retrial.[129] A retrial is rightly seen as an exceptional remedy, given the time-consuming and costly nature of conducting a new (partial or full) trial before a different Trial Chamber.[130] In view of the fact that international criminal trials are exceptionally long and defendants will, by the time of the Appeals Chamber judgment, have spent many years in custody, judges may perceive that retrials are simply not a viable option.[131] Moreover, retrials raise significant fair trial concerns, given that the accused is not obliged to present a defence case but may have done so in the original trial, thereby revealing their defence strategy to the prosecution.[132] The retrial may be seen as offering the prosecution a 'second chance' to remedy the flaws in its original case.[133]

One particularly contentious issue when it comes to the fairness of retrials is their factual scope.[134] The relevant rules are silent on the scope of retrials, and the practice of the ad hoc tribunals on this question paints a complicated picture. In *Muvunyi*, the ICTR Appeals Chamber ordered a partial retrial on one allegation of incitement to commit genocide concerning a speech given by the accused at Gikore trade centre.[135] The Appeals Chamber, in quashing the original conviction on this count, concluded that the Trial Chamber had failed to provide a reasoned opinion, especially considering inconsistencies in the evidence that were not analysed in any great detail in the judgment.[136] It recalled that the accused had already been in custody for more than eight years by the date of the appeals judgment, and that recourse to a retrial should be reserved for exceptional circumstances.[137] Nevertheless, it concluded, in light of the gravity of the alleged offence, that 'the interests of justice would not be well served if retrial were not ordered to allow the

[128] Article 25(2), ICTY Statute; Article 24(2), ICTR Statute; Article 20(2), SCSL Statute; Article 23(2), IRMCT Statute; Article 46(3), KSC Law; Article 83(2), ICC Statute; Rule 104(2) ECCC IR.

[129] Rule 117(C), ICTY RPE; Rule 118(C), ICTR RPE; Rule 118(C), SCSL RPE; Rule 144(C), IRMCT RPE; Rule 182(3) KSC RPE; Article 83(2)(b), ICC Statute.

[130] *Ngudjolo* Appeal Judgment, n 12, para. 284.

[131] See e.g., *Bemba* Appeal Judgment, Separate Opinion of Judge Van den Wyngaert and Judge Morrison, n 41, para. 73.

[132] International Bar Association, n 92, at 49.

[133] *Bemba* Appeal Judgment, Separate Opinion of Judge Van den Wyngaert and Judge Morrison, n 41, para. 73; W. Jordash, 'Merry-Go-Round Justice: The Retrial of Stanišić and Simatović' (*Opinio Juris*, 4 January 2016).

[134] See Y. McDermott, 'Double Speak and Double Standards: Does the Jurisprudence on Retrial Following Acquittal under International Criminal Law Spell the End of the Double Jeopardy Rule?' in D. Keane and Y. McDermott (eds), *The Challenge of Human Rights: Past, Present, and Future* (Edward Elgar, 2012), 176–93.

[135] *Prosecutor v Muvunyi*, Judgment, ICTR-00-55A-A, 29 August 2008, paras 148; 171 ('*Muvunyi* Appeal Judgment').

[136] Ibid., paras 142–7.

[137] Ibid., para. 148.

trier of fact the opportunity to fully assess the entirety of the relevant evidence and provide a reasoned opinion'.[138] The fact remains, however, that the trier of fact had that opportunity at first instance and, in the opinion of the Appeals Chamber, did not fully evaluate the evidence or provide a reasoned opinion. The need to give the Trial Chamber a second opportunity cannot be fully justified by the serious nature of the charge it failed to give a reasoned opinion on the first time around.

In a status conference determining the scope of the evidence to be admitted at the *Muvunyi* retrial, Judge Byron of Trial Chamber III declined the prosecution request to call new witnesses on the speech at the Gikore meeting who had not testified in the original trial.[139] He held that the retrial should 'be limited to correcting the Trial Chamber's failure, that is to say, the assessment of the evidence adduced before the first Trial Chamber, as this re-trial is not the occasion for the Prosecution to present additional evidence to strengthen its case'.[140] The Appeals Chamber, overturning this decision, held that the Trial Chamber had the discretion to hear additional evidence not presented in the original case.[141] The majority noted that the Appeals Chamber, in ordering a retrial, determined that the Trial Chamber should have an 'opportunity to fully assess *the entirety of the relevant evidence* and to provide a reasoned opinion'.[142] Judges Shahabuddeen and Meron, in their dissenting opinion, considered that this phrase needed to be considered in the broader context of the decision ordering a retrial.[143] They were troubled by the 'new, expansive trial strategy proposed by the Prosecution', including the prosecution decision not to call one of the two witnesses from the original trial whose inconsistent testimony was identified as problematic by the Appeals Chamber.[144] The judges felt that the prosecution was effectively being given a second chance to make its case, and to obscure rather than explain inconsistencies in the witnesses' accounts.[145]

In *Haradinaj et al.*, where the alleged error hinged around prosecution witness unavailability,[146] the ICTY Appeals Chamber upheld the convictions that the Trial Chamber had entered, but ordered a retrial for the acquittals on six counts of the indictment relating to cruel treatment, torture, and murder in a camp run by the Kosovo Liberation Army. As the International Bar Association noted, the Appeals Chamber declined to explain why these counts 'were specifically affected by the

[138] Ibid.

[139] *Prosecutor v Muvunyi*, Status Conference Transcript, ICTR-00-55A, 14 January 2009, at 3.

[140] Ibid.

[141] *Prosecutor v Muvunyi*, Decision on the Prosecutor's Appeal Concerning the Scope of Evidence to be Adduced in the Retrial, ICTR-2000-55A-AR73, 24 March 2009.

[142] Ibid., para. 15 (quoting *Muvunyi* Appeal Judgment, n 13, para. 148 (emphasis added by Appeals Chamber).

[143] *Prosecutor v Muvunyi*, Decision on the Prosecutor's Appeal Concerning the Scope of Evidence to be Adduced in the Retrial, n 14, Joint Dissenting Opinion of Judges Shahabuddeen and Meron, para. 3.

[144] Ibid., para. 6.

[145] Ibid.

[146] Discussed at length in McDermott, n 134.

errors identified' and did not provide instructions to the Trial Chamber on how to secure the testimony of the prosecution witnesses.[147] Despite the fact that the two 'crucial witnesses' that were unable to testify in the first trial did testify in the retrial,[148] and the prosecution was permitted to adduce additional new evidence,[149] the defendants were again acquitted following their retrial.[150]

The first full retrial on all counts of the indictment was ordered by the ICTY Appeals Chamber in the *Stanišić and Simatović* case.[151] The defence unsuccessfully sought a stay of proceedings on the basis of *ne bis in idem* and *res judicata* principles, arguing that the full retrial was broader than the errors successfully argued by the prosecution in its appeal.[152] Akin to other retrials that had raised similar points,[153] the IRMCT Trial Chamber was unpersuaded by this argument, finding that the principles only apply to final judgments, and that there is no final judgment where a retrial has been ordered.[154] However, distinct from the approaches taken in the *Muvunyi* and *Haradinaj et al.* retrials, the Trial Chamber decided to exercise its discretion to limit the prosecution's evidence primarily to evidence that was admitted in the original trial, unless there were exceptional circumstances warranting its admission.[155] As Sinclair-Blakemore notes, this decision might serve as a useful blueprint for future international criminal law retrials.[156]

E. Review or revision of final judgment

Where new evidence or new facts have been discovered that cast doubt on a final judgment, it is proper that the international criminal tribunal can reconsider that judgment. The legal frameworks of the ICTR, ICTY, IRMCT, SCSL, STL, and KSC all provided for such review in broadly similar terms.[157] Where a new fact is

[147] International Bar Association, n 92, at 50.

[148] *Prosecutor v Haradinaj et al.*, Public Judgment with Confidential Annex, IT-04-84*bis*-T, 29 November 2012, para. 689 ('*Haradinaj et al.* Appeal Judgment').

[149] *Prosecutor v Haradinaj et al.*, Decision on Haradinaj's Appeal on Scope of Partial Retrial, IT-04-84*bis*-AR73.1, 31 May 2011, paras 21–7.

[150] *Haradinaj et al.* Appeal Judgment, n 148, paras 683–5.

[151] *Prosecutor v Stanišić and Simatović*, Judgment, IT-03-69-A, 9 December 2015.

[152] *Prosecutor v Stanišić and Simatović*, Defence Request to Stay the Proceedings until the Prosecution Respects the Principle of Finality and the Appeal Chamber's Order for Retrial, with public Annex A and confidential Annex B, IRMCT-15-96-PT, 27 October 2016, paras 15-53.

[153] E.g. *Prosecutor v Muvunyi*, Decision on the Prosecutor's Appeal Concerning the Scope of Evidence to be Adduced in the Retrial, n 14, para. 16; *Prosecutor v Haradinaj et al.*, Decision on Haradinaj's Appeal on Scope of Partial Retrial, n 14, paras 24–5.

[154] *Prosecutor v Stanišić and Simatović*, Decision on Stanišić's Request for Stay of Proceedings, IRMCT-15-96, 2 February 2017, para. 13.

[155] Ibid., para. 23.

[156] A. Sinclair-Blakemore, 'The Admission of New Prosecutorial Evidence in International Criminal Retrials: An Assessment of the Exclusionary Rule in *Stanišić and Simatović*' (2023) 21 *Journal of International Criminal Justice* 903.

[157] Article 25, ICTR Statute; Article 26, ICTY Statute; Article 24, IRMCT Statute; Article 21 SCSL Statute; Article 27, STL Statute; Article 48(2) KSC Law.

discovered, which was not known at the time of the original proceedings and could not have been discovered through the exercise of due diligence, the Chamber will review the judgment and pronounce a new judgment, if it determines that the new fact could have been decisive if it were known.[158] There are subtle differences between these tribunals in the scope of permissible review—for example, most use the term 'new fact'[159] but others list 'new evidence' as a basis for review,[160] and some only allow for review to be initiated after the appeal judgment.[161] All of these tribunals allow either the convicted person or the prosecution to apply for review, although some place a one-year limit from the date of the final judgment on the Prosecutor.[162] In practice, the right of the Prosecutor to request a review of final judgment has rarely been exercised.[163]

The ICC and ECCC legal frameworks differ quite significantly from those of the aforementioned tribunals on review of conviction, sentence, or final judgment (which they call 'revision').[164] Only the convicted person (or the Prosecutor on his or her behalf, or, if the convicted person is dead, a close family member or other person who was given express written instructions from the convict) may apply for revision of the final judgment.[165] They may do so on one of three grounds:[166]

1. The discovery of new evidence, unavailable at trial for reasons not attributable to the party making the application, which would likely have resulted in a different verdict if it were available at the time of the trial.
2. The discovery that decisive evidence was false, forged, or falsified.

158 The due diligence requirement can be found in Rule 119, ICTY RPE; Rule 120, ICTR RPE; Rule 146, IRMCT RPE; Rule 190, STL RPE; Rule 112(1)(a)(i), ECCC IR; Article 84(1)(a), ICC Statute. Cf. *Prosecutor v Šljivančanin*, Review Judgment, IT-95-13/1-R/1 December 2010, para. 7 (considering that even if a new fact was discoverable through due diligence of counsel, review of the judgment was necessary where a new fact, if proven, was of such importance 'that to ignore it *would* lead to a miscarriage of justice') (emphasis in original).

159 Article 25, ICTR Statute; Article 26, ICTY Statute; Article 24, IRMCT Statute; Article 21 SCSL Statute; Article 27, STL Statute.

160 Article 48(2)(c) KSC Law. Article 27 STL Statute refers to a 'new fact', but Rule 190 STL RPE refers to the discovery of 'material new evidence'.

161 Rule 120, SCSL RPE; cf. Rule 119, ICTY RPE; Rule 120, ICTR RPE; Rule 146, IRMCT RPE; Rule 190, STL RPE.

162 This is the case before the IRMCT, ICTY, ICTR, and SCSL. No such time limit is imposed on the prosecution by the STL or KSC.

163 D. Re, 'Appeal' in L. Reydams et al., *International Prosecutors* (OUP, 2012), 797, at 863–5, noting that the prosecution initiated review proceedings in only two cases since 1994: an unsuccessful review request against the acquittal on appeal of some counts against Tihomir Blaškić (ICTY) and a successful review of an Appeals Chamber pre-trial decision dismissing the case against Jean Bosco Barayagwiza (ICTR) for an abuse of process. See further, *Prosecutor v Blaškić*, Decision on Prosecutor's Request for Review or Reconsideration, IT-95-14-R, 23 November 2006; *Barayagwiza v Prosecutor*, Decision (Prosecutor's Request for Review or Reconsideration), ICTR-97-19-AR72, 31 March 2000.

164 Article 84, ICC Statute. See further V. Nerlich, 'Article 84' in O. Triffterer and K. Ambos (eds), *Rome Statute of the International Criminal Court: Article-by-Article Commentary* (4th edn, Beck/Hart, 2021), 2405.

165 Rule 112(1) ECCC IR; Rule 84(1) ICC Statute.

166 Article 84(1) ICC Statute; Rule 112(1) ECCC IR.

3. The misconduct or serious breach of duty (of sufficient gravity to remove them from office) of a judge or judges who participated in the conviction or an earlier stage of the proceedings.[167]

The KSC similarly lists forgery or false evidence as a ground for review[168]—this would constitute a 'new fact' under the legal framework of the ICTY and other international criminal tribunals.[169] It also adds that a final judgment may be re-opened where 'it is proven that the judgment ensued from a criminal offence committed by a judge or a person who undertook investigative actions'.[170]

F. Conclusion

This chapter analysed issues of proving international crimes that arise at the appellate and review stages of proceedings. Some commentary would lead observers to believe that the majority in *Bemba* crossed a hallowed line in overturning the factual findings of the Trial Chamber, but as we discussed in relation to earlier ICC Appeals Chamber jurisprudence,[171] appeal judges' statements that the Trial Chamber erroneously evaluated the evidence are nothing new. The only aspects that were different in *Bemba* were that the judges holding this view were in the majority and that they overturned a conviction. Today, in light of more recent ICC jurisprudence and the practice of the ECCC, we can conclude that the standard of review for alleged errors of fact has evolved to what may now be called 'tempered deference'. The tempered deference approach means that the Appeals Chamber respects the role of the Trial Chamber in making findings of fact and will not disturb a factual finding just because it would have reached a different conclusion. However, it also requires the Appeals Chamber to closely scrutinise the Trial Chamber's evaluation of the evidence and whether it provided a fully reasoned opinion, particularly where the evidence is *prima facie* weak or inconsistent with other evidence on the record. This is a more rigorous and modern approach to the appellate function, in an era where recording technology and courtroom archival practices mean that the Appeals Chamber can evaluate the evidence just as closely as the Trial Chamber that first received it. While the ICC Appeals Chamber may have consciously moved away from the 'miscarriage of justice' standard set out in *Bemba*, the point of principle underpinning that dictum—that appellate judges should avoid tying their own hands

[167] I.e. confirmation of the charges for the ICC (Article 84(1)(c), ICC Statute) or judicial investigation for the ECCC (Rule 112(1)(c), ECCC IR).
[168] Article 48(2)(a), KSC Law.
[169] *Prosecutor v Ngirabatware*, Review Judgment, IRMCT-12-29-R, 27 September 2019, paras 6–7.
[170] Article 48(2)(b) KSC Law.
[171] See above, text to nn 36–40.

by accepting the outdated notion that only the Chamber that first received the evidence is in a position to evaluate it—is clearly upheld through this third wave of jurisprudence.

Relatedly, the chapter discussed the sometimes murky distinction between errors of fact, law, and procedure. Appellants' practice of occasionally presenting errors of fact as different types of error, perhaps owing to a perception that errors of fact are more difficult to prove, has clearly exercised some judges. Nevertheless, as was highlighted, errors relating to factual matters (such as, for example, a misinterpretation of the relevant standard of proof) may legitimately be framed as errors of law. Moreover, the Appeals Chamber retains the power to decide what kind of an error the appellant alleges and to evaluate that alleged error against the requisite standard of review.

This chapter also discussed the circumstances under which new evidence can be introduced on appeal. Related to the discussion in Chapter 3, it was argued that the ICC Appeals Chamber should render separate admissibility decisions where a party has sought to adduce new evidence on appeal. This is preferable to the approach taken in *Lubanga*, where the new evidence was submitted and the witnesses examined, only for the Chamber to decide in its judgment that the evidence was in fact inadmissible. Leaving parties in the dark as to whether their evidence will be duly admitted by the Chamber renders it difficult for them to present their case and closing arguments. More generally, as discussed, the approach taken in *Lubanga* was unnecessarily punitive of what the Chamber perceived to be a party's misplaced trial strategy, which appears at odds with the Court's authority under Article 69(3) to 'request the submission of all evidence that it considers necessary for the determination of the truth'.

As regards the factual scope of retrials and the submission of new evidence at retrial, it was argued that the exclusionary rule adopted by the IRMCT may provide a beneficial way forward for conducting retrials in accordance with the rights of the accused. More broadly, however, we may consider whether retrials are a satisfactory practice in proving international crimes. As discussed at length above, they pose many risks for the fairness of proceedings and may hinder the legitimacy of international criminal trials, particularly where it is perceived that judges are giving the Prosecutor a second chance to make their case. As regards the review or revision of final judgments, which remains rare in the case law, the legal frameworks of the ICC and ECCC were distinguished from those of other international criminal tribunals.

The overarching lessons learned from the law and case law discussed in this chapter are twofold. First, this chapter demonstrated that proving international crimes is by no means limited to the trial stage of proceedings. As we have seen, appellate bodies in international criminal tribunals can and do play an important role in establishing facts, be that through correcting errors committed by the Trial Chamber, considering additional evidence that was unavailable at trial, or conducting review of final judgments.[172] Second, the chapter revealed a diverse, and at times inconsistent, body of case law adducing different principles in light of particular sets of facts. Whether the law will converge around a more coherent body of practice in relation to matters such as the tempered deference standard of review for alleged factual errors remains to be seen.

172 Before the ICTY, ICTR, STL, and IRMCT, this was not limited to appellate chambers: revision could also be carried out by the Trial Chamber, where an application for revision was made before the appeals judgment was issued. Before the ICC, only the Appeals Chamber considers requests for revision.

8
Conclusion

A. Introduction

This book set out to examine how international criminal courts and tribunals have undertaken the undeniably daunting task of establishing whether core international crimes, and the responsibility of those accused of committing them or facilitating their commission, have been proven to the requisite standard of proof. It comes at a particularly timely juncture, for two reasons.

First, at the time of writing, the war following Russia's full-scale invasion of Ukraine in 2022 was ongoing, and the international community was considering avenues for bringing the perpetrators of atrocity crimes in that conflict to justice. It is likely that prosecutions will be pursued: domestically in both Ukraine and other countries; at the International Criminal Court; and perhaps also before a new hybrid or international criminal tribunal. Following the completion of this manuscript, a deadly and protracted armed conflict between Israel and Palestinian militant groups, sparked by Hamas-led attacks in Israel on 7 October 2023, broke out. The ICC Prosecutor sought arrest warrants for alleged perpetrators, and we may also see domestic prosecutions under universal jurisdiction in time.

As domestic courts grapple with the challenges of trying war crimes and crimes against humanity, and investigators rush to preserve evidence from some of the most well-documented wars in human history, questions of evidence are at the forefront of the minds of judges, lawyers, investigators, civil society organisations, and system designers. Those questions include: what kind of evidence needs to be preserved, presented, and admitted to prove international crimes; how can judges ensure a fair trial when trying these complex international crimes; how can the presumption of innocence be maintained and the standard of proof applied, and how should evidence be rigorously evaluated and marshalled towards findings of fact, to shield judgments from future criticisms that these trials were 'show trials', lacking in legitimacy? It is hoped that this book, in shedding light on how the international criminal tribunals have approached these questions, will give an insight into practices and experiences that may be instructive for future trials before domestic, hybrid, and international courts, as well as, perhaps, some of the approaches that courts may not wish to follow in the future.

Proving International Crimes. Yvonne McDermott, Oxford University Press. © Yvonne McDermott 2024.
DOI: 10.1093/oso/9780198842972.003.0008

Second, it comes at a time when the International Criminal Court, having been in operation for more than 20 years, is emerging from a period of relative crisis. In 2019, for example, the first four Presidents of the Association of States Parties issued a strongly worded statement entitled 'The International Criminal Court needs fixing', noting the need for the Court to 'clarify the legal standards it applies to its criminal proceedings, work on the basis of clear prosecutorial strategies and policies, end its endless internal squabbles, and address its management issues head-on'.[1] The Independent Expert Review of the International Criminal Court and the Rome Statute System issued a far-reaching report in 2020.[2] Some commentators have spoken of the Court emerging from its difficult teenage years and entering full maturity.[3] Many of the major controversies and notable incidents across the ICC's lifetime have been issues of evidence, ranging from the use of intermediaries in *Lubanga* (which led to a stay of proceedings owing to an abuse of process[4]), to the re-characterisation of the charges in *Katanga*,[5] to the acquittal of several accused, sometimes at an advanced stage of proceedings, owing to a lack of sufficient evidence to support a conviction.[6]

In this context, this book provided an opportunity to reflect on two key questions:

1. Whether 'international criminal evidence' could be said to exist as a body of law and practice.
2. Whether the law and practice of international criminal evidence is fit for purpose in meeting the challenges of proving international crimes.

The remainder of this chapter presents, in section B, the main findings of this book. Section C then reflects on some of the implications of the work for future practice, while section D provides some recommendations for future research.

[1] Z.R. Al Hussein, B. Stagno Ugarte, C. Wenaweser, and T. Intelman, 'The International Criminal Court Needs Fixing' (*New Atlanticist*, 24 April 2019).

[2] Independent Expert Review of the International Criminal Court and the Rome Statute System ('IER'), Final Report, 30 September 2020.

[3] L. Smith van Lin, Remarks at *International Criminal Court at 20: Reflections on the Past, Present and the Future* conference, The Hague, 1 July 2022; K. Prost, 'Keynote Address', *International Law at a Crossroads*, Bader International Study Centre, Herstmonceux Castle, UK, 30 May 2019.

[4] *Prosecutor v Lubanga*, Public Redacted Decision on the Prosecution's Urgent Request for Variation of the Time-Limit to Disclose the Identity of Intermediary 143 or Alternatively to Stay Proceedings Pending Further Consultations with the VWU, ICC-01/04-01/06-2517, 8 July 2010, para. 31.

[5] *Prosecutor v Katanga and Ngudjolo*, Decision on the implementation of Regulation 55 of the Regulations of the Court and severing the charges against the accused persons, ICC-01/04-01/07-3319-tENG, 21 November 2012.

[6] *Prosecutor v Gbagbo and Blé Goudé*, Reasons for oral decision of 15 January 2019 on the Requête de la Défense de Laurent Gbagbo afin qu'un jugement d'acquittement portant sur toutes les charges soit prononcé en faveur de Laurent Gbagbo et que sa mise en liberté immédiate soit ordonnée, and on the Blé Goudé Defence no case to answer motion, ICC-02/11-01/15-1263, 16 July 2019; *Prosecutor v. Bemba*, Judgment on the appeal of Mr Jean-Pierre Bemba Gombo against Trial Chamber III's 'Judgment pursuant to Article 74 of the Statute', ICC-01/05-01/08-3636-Red, 8 June 2018.

B. Main findings

i. International criminal evidence has not yet evolved into a coherent body of law

An overarching finding of this work is that 'international criminal evidence' cannot be said to exist as a coherent body of law, because it is still evolving and remains inconsistent, not just across courts and tribunals, but even between different Chambers of the same institution.[7] This is perhaps unsurprising: unlike domestic legal systems where the law of evidence has been shaped and developed over many centuries, international criminal tribunals have largely had to shape their own law of evidence through practice over mere decades. As can be seen, for example, from the emergence of detailed jurisprudence on situations in which the Appeals Chamber of the ICC will interfere with Trial Chambers' factual findings, as outlined in Chapter 7, it is clear that it takes time for practices to emerge.

Two key features of international criminal evidence, as identified in Chapter 1, have led to inconsistency and procedural uncertainty in practice: flexibility and the free assessment of evidence. Flexibility, particularly as it applies in the ICC's statutory framework, means that each Chamber has a large degree of discretion over issues of procedure. The Presiding Judge, under Article 64(8)(b) of the Statute, may give directions for the conduct of proceedings.[8] While the drafters built some procedural flexibility in to the Statue as part of Rome's 'unique compromise',[9] it is unlikely that they envisioned the degree of diversity set out in Chapter 3, where different Chambers of the Court were running trials taking very different forms at the same time.[10] Notably, in *Gbagbo and Blé Goudé*, the Chamber went from deciding it would rule on the admissibility of evidence on an item-by-item basis to adopting the very different 'submission model' outlined in Chapter 3 with the appointment of a new Presiding Judge.[11]

The adoption and amendment of a Chambers Practice Manual by the judges could be seen as heralding a new approach towards greater consistency and

[7] IER report, n 2, para. 474: 'Many interlocutors of the Experts were critical about the lack of consistency in the way different Chambers deal with the same issues, the failure to apply agreed procedures, delays in the delivery of decisions and judgments, fractured decisions, and the acceptance of applications through procedures not provided for under the Rome Statute. Some of these warrant particular focus.'

[8] *Prosecutor v Bemba*: 'Judgment on the appeals of Mr Jean-Pierre Bemba Gombo and the Prosecutor against the decision of Trial Chamber III entitled "Decision on the Admission into Evidence of Materials Contained in the Prosecution's List of Evidence"', ICC-01/05-01/08-1386 (OA5/OA6), 3 May 2011, para. 43.

[9] C. Kress, 'The Procedural Law of the International Criminal Court in Outline: Anatomy of a Unique Compromise' (2003) 1 *Journal of International Criminal Justice* 603.

[10] S. De Smet, 'All Roads Lead to Rome: Lifting the Veil on the ICC's Procedural Pluriformity' in P. Šturma (ed.), *The Rome Statute of the ICC at its Twentieth Anniversary* (Brill, 2019), 191.

[11] *Prosecutor v Gbagbo and Blé Goudé*, Decision on the submission and admission of evidence, ICC-02/11-01/15-405, 29 January 2016.

procedural certainty in practice. However, it was argued that certain practices now incorporated in the Manual may not be preferable in terms of ensuring rectitude of decision and the highest standards of fairness. For example, the submission approach to the admission of evidence, as discussed at length in Chapter 3, may lead to greater inefficiencies in practice, by flooding the evidentiary record with material that may later be held to be irrelevant or inadmissible, and by leaving parties uncertain about how much supporting material is needed to strengthen the chances that certain types of evidence will be admitted. It may also hinder the accused's right to a defence, because without clarity as to what prosecution evidence will ultimately be admitted, the defence's ability to shape and prepare its case can be undermined. Lastly, it was noted that the submission approach undermines the Court's standard-setting function, at a time when external bodies are looking to the Court for guidance, especially on newer forms of evidence such as user-generated evidence.

Similarly, the practices incorporated in the Chambers Practice Manual that were designed to drive the efficiency of the confirmation of charges hearing and streamline confirmation decisions were highlighted in Chapter 4 as an area of practice warranting further consideration. As noted therein, there is a risk that these measures will lead to less rigorous scrutiny of the evidence at the confirmation stage, which would be inapposite and may lead to weaker cases proceeding to trial. I argued that the lower standard of proof does not require a lesser evaluation of the evidence; rather, that evidence should be closely scrutinised to assess whether that standard of proof has been satisfied. Anything less may lead to unfairness as regards the accused's ability to prepare their case.

In other areas, such as 'no case to answer' (now known as 'motion for a judgment of acquittal') motions, there is scope for the judges to collectively solidify practice, for example through an amendment of the Regulations of the Court or a proposal to the Association of States Parties to amend the Rules of Procedure and Evidence. As Chapter 4 showed, however, this practice continues outside of the formal legal framework of the Court. Moreover, perhaps, Chapter 4 argued that the current standard of proof applied—beyond reasonable doubt—seems misplaced for this stage of proceedings. This is something that the judges could collectively deliberate on in future judicial retreats.[12] Similarly, the standard for appellate review of findings of fact, as discussed in Chapter 7, appeared, at the time of writing, to have been clarified by the most recent Appeals Chamber judgments, but only time will tell whether this standard is subject to further amendment in practice over the coming years.

[12] Such deliberations appeared, at the time of writing, to be ongoing: Press Release, *ICC judges complete assessment of IER recommendations concerning the judiciary at their annual retreat*, 5 June 2023 ('The judges discussed the Court's practice to date and agreed on the value of regulating the procedure applicable to potential motions for a judgment of acquittal. The judges will continue their discussion to develop proposals for amendments to the Court's legal texts').

The free evaluation of the evidence approach—a central feature of international criminal evidence—may also account for inconsistencies between different Chambers in practice. Trial Chambers have 'the primary responsibility to determine the reliability and credibility of the evidence and then comprehensively assess the weight of the evidence'.[13] As was shown in Chapter 5, a wide range of factors can be taken into account in the evaluation of both witness testimony and other forms of evidence. These factors might include whether the evidence was corroborated, and its perceived credibility and reliability (which, for witnesses, may include considerations such as whether the witness has a motivation to lie, whether their account has been consistent, and their demeanour on the stand). Different Chambers appear to take somewhat different approaches, so again it is difficult to say with precision which factors will be most relevant in weighing the evidence.[14] Free evaluation also leads to inconsistency between Chambers on how the evidence as a whole is weighed. As noted in Chapter 6, all judges argue that they assess the evidence 'holistically', but what this means appears to be different for different judges. Some have criticised what they see as their colleagues' overly stringent approach to the evidence,[15] while others have accused their colleagues of overlooking weaknesses in the individual components of the evidence in favour of finding a bigger picture that is not fully supported by the evidence.[16] It was argued in Chapter 6 that more structured approaches to linking the evidence presented to the inferences drawn and established facts would strengthen international criminal judgments. This could also shield judgments from later appellate review, as discussed in Chapter 7.

[13] *Prosecutor v Ongwen*, Judgment on the appeal of Mr Ongwen against the decision of Trial Chamber IX of 4 February 2021 entitled 'Trial Judgment', ICC-02/04-01/15-2022-Red, 15 December 2022, para. 17.

[14] X. Agirre Aranburu, 'The Contribution of Analysis to the Quality Control in Criminal Investigation' in X. Agirre, M. Bergsmo, S. De Smet and C. Stahn (eds), *Quality Control in Criminal Investigation* (TOAEP, 2020), 117, 231–2.

[15] Most prominently, see *Prosecutor v Ngudjolo*, Judgment on the Prosecutor's appeal against the decision of Trial Chamber II entitled 'Judgment pursuant to article 74 of the Statute', ICC-01/04-02/12-271-Corr, 7 April 2015 ('*Ngudjolo* Appeal Judgment'), Joint Dissenting Opinion of Judge Trendafilova and Judge Tarfusser, ICC-01/04-02/12-271-AnxA, 27 February 2015, para. 31 ('The Chamber assessed in isolation individual items of evidence and failed to properly consider the evidence in its entirety'); *Prosecutor v Katanga*, Judgment pursuant to Article 74 of the Statute, ICC-01/04-01/07-3436, 7 March 2014 ('*Katanga* Trial Judgment'), Concurring Opinion of Judges Diarra and Cotte, ICC-01/04-01/07-3436-AnxII-tENG, 13 March 2014, para. 4. For a similar academic critique, see D. Robinson, 'The Other Poisoned Chalice: Unprecedented Evidentiary Standards in the Gbagbo Case? (Part 1)' (*EJIL:Talk!*, 5 November 2019), criticising what he deems the judges' 'Cartesian' approach.

[16] *Prosecutor v Bemba*, Judgment on the appeal of Mr Jean-Pierre Bemba Gombo against Trial Chamber III's 'Judgment pursuant to Article 74 of the Statute', ICC-01/05-01/08-3636-Red, 8 June 2018 ('*Bemba* Appeal Judgment'), Separate Opinion of Judge Van den Wyngaert and Judge Morrison, ICC-01/05-01/08-3636-Anx2, 8 June 2018, para. 15; *Katanga* Trial Judgment, n 15, Minority Opinion of Judge Van den Wyngaert, ICC-01/04-01/07-3436-AnxI, 7 March 2014, paras 148–54. See further, D. Guilfoyle, 'Part II—This Is Not Fine: The International Criminal Court in Trouble' (*EJIL:Talk!*, 22 March 2019) ('The more devastating and fundamental disagreement which appears to run through ICC judicial decision making is the correct approach to the assessment of evidence').

ii. The principles of rectitude of decision and the highest standards of fairness should drive the development of a coherent framework for proving international crimes

As discussed in Chapter 4, to prove the culpability of the accused on trial, the prosecution must establish all material facts—these are facts that are indispensable for entering a conviction[17]—including all of the elements of the crime(s) charged, as well as the requisite mode(s) of liability, beyond reasonable doubt. The law and practice of international criminal evidence to date, while inconsistent and not always working as a coherent framework, goes some way in demonstrating what needs to be proven, and with what evidence, to meet the requisite standard of proof, and how that evidence will be evaluated. It is hoped that, by bringing this disparate practice together in the first book-length treatment of the subject, this work will provide insights from practice to date that may be informative for the future trial of international crimes, domestically, internationally, and in hybrid or regional tribunals.

International criminal evidence, in its current form, is broadly fit for the purpose of proving international crimes but could be greatly enhanced through the adoption of a coherent epistemic framework founded on the principles of rectitude of decision and the highest standards of fairness. As was noted in the previous section, practice on many key issues of proof remains unpredictable and uncertain. International criminal evidence needs a firm commitment from a wide range of actors to reflecting upon what a coherent epistemic framework for proving international crimes would look like, and what changes might need to be made to law and practice to ensure the optimal conditions for fact-finding.[18] This requires a consideration of the best structures for the admission, exclusion, and evaluation of evidence in the search for the truth.[19] It also calls for reflection on the proper marshalling of that evidence to support factual propositions,[20] and ensuring the highest standards of fairness.

The right to a fair trial (which, it was argued, is owed primarily to the accused)[21] requires a system for the admission of evidence that does not jeopardise the rights to equality of arms, to present a defence case, and to challenge the evidence against

[17] *Prosecutor v Halilović*, Judgment, IT-01-48-A, 16 October 2007, para. 129.

[18] Moving this debate beyond the civil law/common law divide, see J.D. Jackson, 'Finding the Best Epistemic Fit for International Criminal Tribunals: Beyond the Adversarial-Inquisitorial Dichotomy' (2009) 7 *Journal of International Criminal Justice* 17. See further, N.A. Combs, 'Deconstructing the Epistemic Challenges to Mass Atrocity Prosecutions' (2018) 75 *Washington & Lee Law Review* 223 (arguing that domestic fora might provide better conditions for reaching the truth). This is discussed further in Chapter 2, text to notes 12–25.

[19] See Chapters 2, 3, and 5.

[20] Chapter 6.

[21] Chapter 2. See also, Y. McDermott, *Fairness in International Criminal Trials* (OUP, 2016), 125–48.

one.[22] It also needs to ensure the exclusion of evidence that might reflect poorly on the international court.[23] Fairness also requires that the right to an appeal be effective in empowering the Appeals Chamber to overturn findings of fact that no reasonable trier of fact could have reached, while recognising the primacy of the Trial Chamber's role in this regard.[24] The presumption of innocence should be protected through a rigorous application of the burden and standard of proof throughout proceedings.[25] There are many suggestions for future practice dotted across the chapters of this book, but the next section presents three key overarching implications of these findings for future practice.

C. Implications of the study

i. The future development of international criminal evidence

As has already been outlined, there is a need to decide upon a coherent framework for proving international crimes, moving beyond the inherent flexibility of international criminal procedure to ensure greater consistency and coherence in practice. Consistency is important for the predictability of proceedings and to ensure the parties can prepare their cases to the best of their ability. The scenario where trials in the same court at the same time were conducted with very different practices on issues such as whether the 'submission' model for evidence was followed; victim participation, and witness preparation, is clearly not ideal. The latest draft of the Chambers Practice Manual, which adopts a model 'Direction for the Conduct of Proceedings' may go some way to ensuring consistency in practice,[26] although some might question whether the Manual is an exercise in judicial procedural law-making *ultra vires* the ICC's legal framework.[27] Moreover, the model direction itself is included as a confidential annex to the Manual, which means it is not publicly accessible. Furthermore, the deliberations surrounding the elements of the direction as adopted are also secret, having taken place at a 2021 judges' retreat, so there is little transparency around the justification for these procedural changes. By contrast, judge-made amendments to the Rules of Procedure and Evidence of other tribunals were sometimes accompanied by an

[22] Chapter 3.
[23] Chapter 3, section D.
[24] Chapter 7.
[25] Chapter 4.
[26] International Criminal Court, Chambers Practice Manual, 7th edition, adopted following the judicial retreat of 2023.
[27] Y. McDermott, 'The International Criminal Court's Chambers Practice Manual: Towards a Return to Judicial Law Making in International Criminal Procedure?' (2017) 15 *Journal of International Criminal Justice* 873.

explanatory note briefly setting out the amendments adopted and the reasoning behind them.[28]

Coherence requires a consideration of how different elements of a procedural model fit together as a whole system of international criminal evidence. As Damaška has argued, designing procedure is not like shopping in a boutique, where one can pick up some of the procedural elements of one system and combine it with a practice from a very different legal tradition, because each element forms part of a broader system.[29] For example, Chapter 4 noted the tension between a 'free proof' approach to the admission of evidence, with the judges bearing a duty to search for the truth, and the fact that the proceedings are party-driven and adversarial in nature when it comes to the collection and submission of that evidence.[30]

ii. Strengthening the evaluation of evidence

Chapter 6 highlighted a need to consider the evaluation of evidence and the rigorous linking of fact-finding to just legal outcomes at each stage of proceedings, in line with its standard of proof. Judges, particularly before the ICC, have found themselves drawn into a false dichotomy between 'atomistic' and 'holistic' approaches to the evaluation of evidence.[31] Chapter 6 opined that this debate 'may mask the real division between judicial approaches to the evaluation of evidence—that is, how much detail the Chamber needs to provide on precisely which evidence led it to establish which finding of fact or to find that a particular fact had not been proven'.

The atomistic/holistic debate is a false dichotomy because there is no pure version of either approach, and it can descend into caricature, with the atomists being painted as failing to see the wood for the trees while the holists are accused of allowing real weaknesses and gaps in evidence to be overlooked in favour of an impressionistic analysis.[32] Drawing from the rationalist tradition of evidence

[28] E.g. International Criminal Tribunal for the former Yugoslavia, 'Amendments to the Tribunal's Rules of Procedure and Evidence at the 22nd Plenary Session', Press Release JL/P.I.S./521-e, The Hague, 31 July 2000.

[29] M.R. Damaška, 'Epistemology and Legal Regulation of Proof' (2003) 2 *Law, Probability and Risk* 117, 121.

[30] Chapter 6, text to notes 18–21.

[31] See Chapter 6, section C.

[32] S. De Smet, 'Controlling the Quality of Reasoning About the Link Between Evidence and Factual Findings' in X. Agirre et al. (eds), *Quality Control in Criminal Investigation* (TOAEP, 2020) 611; M. Klamberg, 'Epistemological Controversies and Evaluation of Evidence in International Criminal Trials' in K.J. Heller et al. (eds), *The Oxford Handbook of International Criminal Law* (OUP, 2020), 450; *Prosecutor v Bemba*, Judgment on the appeal of Mr Jean-Pierre Bemba Gombo against Trial Chamber III's 'Judgment pursuant to Article 74 of the Statute', ICC-01/05-01/08-3636-Red, 8 June 2018, Separate Opinion of Judge Van den Wyngaert and Judge Morrison, ICC-01/05-01/08-3636-Anx2, 8 June 2018, para. 15; *Prosecutor v Ngudjolo*, Judgment on the Prosecutor's appeal against the decision of Trial Chamber II entitled 'Judgment pursuant to article 74 of the Statute', ICC-01/04-02/12-271-Corr, 7 April 2015, Joint Dissenting Opinion of Judge Trendafilova and Judge Tarfusser, ICC-01/04-02/12-271-AnxA, 27 February 2015, paras 41–51.

scholarship,[33] as well as insights from psychology,[34] intelligence analysis,[35] and argumentation theory,[36] Chapter 6 argued that an approach with rectitude of decision and the highest standards of fairness at its heart would consider a more methodical approach towards fact-finding. Such an approach could also benefit from technology that has been developed to support decision-making and the analysis of evidence in law and other domains, to formalise the processes of drawing inferences from evidence and determining whether those inferences and pieces of evidence lead to an overall conclusion.[37]

More generally, there is scope to reflect upon the role of technology in international criminal evidence. As Freeman and Vazquez Llorente have noted, the drafters of the ICC Statute in 1998 could never have envisioned that a mere two decades later, billions of people around the world would be carrying around smartphones in their pockets which hold more computing power than the NASA computers that launched Apollo 11.[38] Recent developments, such as the Office of the Prosecutor's 'OTP Link' system for the receipt of information on alleged crimes within the jurisdiction of the Court, suggest a willingness to engage with new technologies to enhance the efficiency and effectiveness of investigations.[39] Other technologies could be harnessed to improve the parties' processes of evidence management and disclosure.[40]

[33] T. Anderson, D. Schum, and W. Twining, *Analysis of Evidence* (CUP, 2009); J.H. Wigmore, *The Science of Judicial Proof: As Given by Logic, Psychology, and General Experience, and Illustrated in Judicial Trials* (3rd edn, Little, Brown & Co., 1937).

[34] D. Lagnado, *Explaining the Evidence: How the Mind Investigates the World* (CUP, 2021).

[35] G. Tecuci et al., *Intelligence Analysis as Discovery of Evidence, Hypotheses, and Arguments: Connecting the Dots* (CUP, 2016).

[36] D.N. Walton, *Legal Argumentation and Evidence* (Pennsylvania State University Press, 2002).

[37] H. Prakken et al., 'A Formalization of Argumentation Schemes for Legal Case-based Reasoning in ASPIC+' (2015) 25 *Journal of Logic and Computation* 1141; F. Cerutti et al., 'Cispaces.org: From Fact Extraction to Report Generation' (2018) *COMMA 2018* 269; L. Al-Abdulkarim et al., 'A Methodology for Designing Systems to Reason with Legal Cases Using Abstract Dialectical Frameworks' (2016) 24 *Artificial Intelligence and Law* 1; M. Janier et al., 'OVA+: An Argument Analysis Interface' (2014) *COMMA 2014* 463; online athttp://arg-tech.org/people/chris/publications/2014/comma2014-ova.pdf (last accessed 27 June 2023).

[38] L. Freeman and R. Vazquez Llorente, 'Finding the Signal in the Noise: International Criminal Evidence and Procedure in the Digital Age' (2021) 19 *Journal of International Criminal Justice* 163, 165.

[39] ICC Office of the Prosecutor, *OTP Link*, online at https://otplink.icc-cpi.int (last accessed 27 June 2023).

[40] See e.g. D. Re, 'Rethinking Disclosure: Embrace the Electronic Disclosure Suite' in X. Agirre et al. (eds), *Quality Control in Criminal Investigation* (TOAEP, 2020), 735. The Registry previously advised against the Court-wide installation of 'CaseMap' technology owing to cost and resource implications, and the risk of technical breakdowns: *Prosecutor v Bemba*, Registry Submission on the Feasability (*sic*) Study of CaseMap Installation in the Courtrooms, ICC-01/05-01/08-1004, 9 November 2010. The E-Court Protocol sets out formatting requirements for submitting documents to and evidence in electronic form, but has been criticised for its outdated authentication procedures, relying on a cryptographic hashing standard (MD5) with well-known vulnerabilities: C. Quilling, 'The Future of Digital Evidence Authentication at the International Criminal Court', *Journal of Public & International Affairs*, 20 May 2022, online at https://jpia.princeton.edu/news/future-digital-evidence-authentication-international-criminal-court (last accessed 27 June 2023).

As with the conduct of proceedings, ICC judges may be moving towards developing a more consistent approach to drafting and presenting judgments, thanks to recent innovations included in the Chambers Practice Manual. New 'Guidelines for ICC Judgment Drafting' and 'Guidelines for ICC Judgment Structure', which, like the model 'Direction for the Conduct of Proceedings', are confidential and not publicly accessible, were agreed in the 2021 amendments to the Manual. Chapter 6 analysed the structure of the *Ongwen* trial judgment, the first Article 74 judgment to be released since the judges agreed upon these guidelines, in depth and concluded that it is a positive step forward. However, it highlighted that the new judgment structure may not fully alleviate the clear tension between judicial preferences on the level of granularity that should be provided in relation to the assessment of evidence, as has been seen in case law, and the extent to which the evidence 'as a whole' can remedy deficiencies in individual pieces of evidence.

iii. Ensuring the quality of the evidence

In an era where potentially millions of pieces of evidence are generated in the context of armed conflicts, often by ordinary citizens recording on their personal devices, there is a need to have some system of quality control to ensure the efficiency of proceedings and the fairness of trials. Often this will come down to the parties selecting their best evidence to put forward; experience has shown that presenting a wide range of factual propositions and (sometimes, rather weak) evidence that support those propositions without specifically explaining how they lead to a conclusion on the individual culpability of the accused can backfire as a strategy. For example, in *Gbagbo and Blé Goudé*, Judge Henderson noted the prosecution's reliance on 'a wide range of factual allegations [that] together form a system of evidence that can only be fairly assessed as a whole.'[41] He noted:

> If it is a combination of evidence that allegedly proves a fact, then the Prosecutor must clearly identify all the pieces of the puzzle and, crucially, explain how they fit together. Simply listing a large number of individual factual claims and corresponding evidence and arguing that everything must be assessed holistically is not sufficient. A holistic assessment of evidence should not become an evidentiary black box and Chambers should not have to guess about the particulars of the Prosecutor's evidentiary arguments.[42]

[41] *Prosecutor v Gbagbo and Blé Goudé*, Reasons for oral decision of 15 January 2019 on the Requête de la Défense de Laurent Gbagbo afin qu'un jugement d'acquittement portant sur toutes les charges soit prononcé en faveur de Laurent Gbagbo et que sa mise en liberté immédiate soit ordonnée, and on the Blé Goudé Defence no case to answer motion, ICC-02/11-01/15-1263, 16 July 2019, Reasons of Judge Henderson, para. 78.

[42] Ibid., para. 87.

Chambers also have a role in ensuring the quality of evidence on the record. To this end, Chapter 3 argued for the reconsideration of the 'submission model' for evidence, whereby decisions on the admissibility and relevance of tendered evidence tend to be deferred until the end of trial (albeit with some exceptions). Although now the accepted approach (as demonstrated by its inclusion in the Chambers Practice Manual), Chapter 3 argued that the submission model gives little indication to either the parties or the wider public as to what evidence was deemed reliable and why, unless it is explicitly discussed in the final judgment. For example, in *Bemba et al.*, the parties provided competing arguments about the authenticity of screenshots of publicly available Facebook profiles.[43] The Chamber noted that its general approach was to defer its assessment of admissibility until the deliberation phase,[44] but then did not explicitly address the admissibility of these photographs found on Facebook in its judgment, which means that parties in future cases seeking to admit similar evidence were left in the dark as to what is needed to show authenticity and reliability.[45] Chapter 3 also discussed the relatively high bar that has been set for the exclusion of evidence obtained in violation of human rights, and whether that is appropriate in light of the tribunals' standard-setting role.

D. Recommendations for future research

This work gives rise to many avenues for further exploration. First, it provides an opportunity to reflect more broadly on international criminal procedure as a model, moving away from traditional adversarial/inquisitorial paradigms which are widely acknowledged to be outdated and a poor fit for contemporary international criminal law. Chapter 1 introduced different models for classifying procedural systems. Future research might build upon this introduction to examine, for example, whether the International Criminal Court is moving from what Damaška would identify as a 'co-ordinate' model to a more 'hierarchical' approach, as perhaps demonstrated by procedural features such as the submission model for evidence and the Chambers Practice Manual.[46]

43 *Prosecutor v Bemba et al.*, Public Redacted Version of Defence Response to Prosecution's Third Request for the Admission of Evidence from the Bar Table (ICC-01/05-01/13-1170), ICC-01/05-01/13-1245-Red, 9 October 2015, paras 83–6; *Prosecutor v Bemba et al.*, Public Redacted Version of the 'Prosecution's Fifth Request for the Admission of Evidence from the Bar Table', ICC-01/05-01/13-1498-Red, 30 November 2015, para. 17.

44 *Prosecutor v Bemba et al.*, Decision on 'Prosecution's Fifth Request for the Admission of Evidence from the Bar Table', ICC-01/05-01/13-1524,14 December 2015, para. 3.

45 See further J. Hak, *Image-Based Evidence in International Criminal Prosecutions* (OUP, forthcoming), Chapter 7 (on file with author).

46 Similarly, suggesting that Regulation 55 of the ICC Regulations of Court and its implementation leads to a move towards a more 'inquisitorial' approach, see D. Jacobs, 'A Shifting Scale of Power: Who is in Charge of the Charges at the International Criminal Court?' in W.A. Schabas, N. Hayes, and Y. McDermott (eds), *The Ashgate Research Companion to International Criminal Law: Critical Perspectives* (Ashgate, 2013), 205.

Second, it opens up avenues for thinking about the role of technology in the future practice of proving international crimes. Of particular interest is the rise in recent years of 'decision support' technologies, which have been used in other contexts where decision-makers weigh up large volumes of evidence, such as intelligence analysis. Chapter 6 noted the existence of some of these systems, including 'Cogent'; 'BARD', 'Ova', and 'CisSpaces.org'. There can be reticence to engage with such systems, on the basis that they are seen as potentially usurping the role of the judge. But, as I have explained elsewhere in analysing the potential utility of Wigmorean analysis and Bayes Nets in international criminal trials, these are tools to assist with the human task of weighing the evidence; they are not a replacement for the fact-finder's important thinking and deliberation on the questions before them.[47]

Lastly, Chapter 5 presented some of the leading empirical work on the factors considered in assessing witness credibility. Future socio-legal research could conduct a similar content analysis to quantitively and qualitatively assess the evaluation of other forms of evidence by international criminal tribunals. Like the work by Chlevickaitė et al. on witness assessments,[48] such research could be invaluable in establishing whether a consistent picture of the most relevant factors in the evaluation of certain forms of evidence has emerged, or whether this depends on the individual preferences of the judges on the bench conducting a free evaluation of evidence.

E. Conclusion

This book aimed to elucidate how international criminal tribunals have tackled the immense and complex task of proving international crimes such as genocide, war crimes, and crimes against humanity. The challenges posed by the scale and scope of these crimes and the distance in time and space between their commission and their prosecution cannot be gainsaid. In noting that international criminal evidence has not yet developed into a full-fledged system of law, given its flexible and still evolving nature, this book argued for the development of a coherent epistemic framework driven by two guiding principles: rectitude of decision and the highest standards of fairness.

[47] Y. McDermott, 'Inferential Reasoning and Proof in International Criminal Trials: The Potentials of Wigmorean Analysis' (2015) 13 *Journal of International Criminal Justice* 507; Y. McDermott and C. Aitken, 'Analysis of Evidence in International Criminal Trials using Bayesian Belief Networks' (2017) 16 *Law, Probability and Risk* 111.

[48] G. Chlevickaitė, B. Holá, and C. Bijleveld, 'Judicial Witness Assessments at the ICTY, ICTR and ICC: Is There "Standard Practice", in International Criminal Justice?' (2020) 18 *Journal of International Criminal Justice* 185; G. Chlevickaitė, B. Holá, and C. Bijleveld, 'Suspicious Minds? Empirical Analysis of Insider Witness Assessments at the ICTY, ICTR and ICC' (2023) 20 *European Journal of Criminology* 185.

Nevertheless, investigators, lawyers, judges, scholars, human rights advocates, and system designers often look to the law and practice of international criminal tribunals (and particularly the International Criminal Court) to establish what standards need to be met in the collection, preservation, presentation, and analysis of evidence to prove international crimes. In providing a comprehensive account of the law and practice of evidence before international criminal courts and tribunals to date, as well as some recommendations for future practice, it is hoped that this book will assist domestic, regional, and international accountability processes for atrocity crimes going forward.

Bibliography

Books

Alston, P.G., and S. Knuckey (eds), *The Transformation of Human Rights Fact-Finding* (OUP, 2016).

Ambos, K., *Treatise on International Criminal Law: Vol. III: International Criminal Procedure* (OUP, 2016).

Anderson, T., D. Schum, and W. Twining, *Analysis of Evidence* (2nd edn, CUP, 2009).

Appazov, A., *Expert Evidence and International Criminal Justice* (Springer, 2016).

Bassiouni, M.C., and W.A. Schabas, *The Legislative History of the International Criminal Court* (2nd edn, Brill Nijhoff, 2016).

Bentham, J., *Rationale of Judicial Evidence: Specially Applied to English Practice, Volume I* (Hunt and Clarke, 1827).

Bentham, J., *Rationale of Judicial Evidence: Specially Applied to English Practice, Volume VI* (Hunt and Clarke, 1827).

Bentham, J., *Rationale of Judicial Evidence: Specially Applied to English Practice, Volume X* (Hunt and Clarke, 1827).

Bergsmo, M., and C. Stahn (eds), *Quality Control in Preliminary Examination: Volumes 1 and 2* (TOAEP, 2018).

Bex, F.J., *Arguments, Stories, and Criminal Evidence: A Formal Hybrid Theory* (Springer, 2011).

Blackstone, W., *Commentaries on the Laws of England: Vol. 4* (JB Lippincott Company, 1769).

Boister, N., and R. Cryer, *The Tokyo International Military Tribunal: A Reappraisal* (OUP, 2008).

Clark, P., *Distant Justice: The Impact of the International Criminal Court on African Politics* (CUP, 2018).

Cohen, L.J., *The Probable and the Provable* (Clarendon Press, 1977).

Coleman, M., *The Presumption of Innocence in International Human Rights and Criminal Law* (Routledge, 2021).

Combs, N., *Fact-Finding without Facts: The Uncertain Evidentiary Foundations of International Criminal Convictions* (CUP, 2010).

Damaška, M.R., *The Faces of Justice and State Authority* (Yale University Press, 1986).

Dawid, P., W. Twining, and M. Vasilaki (eds), *Evidence, Inference and Enquiry* (OUP, 2011).

De Guzman, M., *Shocking the Conscience of Humanity: Gravity and the Legitimacy of International Criminal Law* (OUP, 2020).

Djukić, D., *The Right to Appeal in International Criminal Law* (Brill, 2019).

Dubberley, S., et al. (eds), *Digital Witness: Using Open Source Information for Human Rights Investigation, Documentation, and Accountability* (OUP, 2020).

Eltringham, N., *Genocide Never Sleeps: Living Law at the International Criminal Tribunal for Rwanda* (CUP, 2019).

Ferrer Beltrán, J., *Prueba y Verdad en el Derecho* (2nd edn, Marcial Pons, 2005).

Ferrer Beltrán, J., *La Valoración Racional de la Prueba* (Marcial Pons, 2007).

Ferrer Beltrán, J., *Motivación y Racionalidad de la Prueba* (Grijley, 2016).

Franck, T., *Fairness in International Law and Institutions* (OUP, 1995).

Frank, J., *Courts on Trial, Myth and Reality in American Justice* (Princeton University Press, 1973).

Fremuth, M.L., A. Sauermoser, and K. Stavrou (eds), *International Criminal Law before Domestic Courts* (MANZ Verlag Vien, 2024).

Gascón Abellán, M., *Los Hechos en el Derecho: Bases Argumentales de la Prueba* (2nd edn, Marcial Pons, 2004).

Giannoulopoulos, D., *Improperly Obtained Evidence in Anglo-American and Continental Law* (Hart, 2019).
Gillett, M., *Prosecuting Environmental Harm before the International Criminal Court* (CUP, 2022).
Goss, R., *Criminal Fair Trial Rights: Article 6 of the European Convention on Human Rights* (Hart, 2014).
Haack, S., *Evidence Matters: Science, Proof, and Truth in the Law* (CUP, 2014).
Hak, J., *Image-Based Evidence in International Criminal Prosecutions* (OUP, 2024).
Hart, H.L.A., *The Concept of Law* (3rd edn, OUP, 2012).
Henderson, C. (ed.), *Commissions of Inquiry: Problems and Prospects* (Hart, 2017).
Ho, H.L., *A Philosophy of Evidence Law: Justice in the Search for Truth* (OUP, 2008).
Hume, D., *Enquiries Concerning the Human Understanding and Concerning the Principles of Morals* (2nd edn, OUP, 1902).
Jackson, J.D., and S.J. Summers, *The Internationalisation of Criminal Evidence* (CUP, 2012).
Kahneman, D., P. Slovic, and A. Tversky (eds), *Judgment and Uncertainty: Heuristics and Biases* (CUP, 1982).
Kaufmann, W., *The Portable Nietzsche* (Viking Press, 1954).
Khan, K.A.A., C. Buisman, and C. Gosnell (eds), *Principles of Evidence in International Criminal Justice* (OUP, 2010).
Klamberg, M., *Evidence in International Criminal Trials: Confronting Legal Gaps and the Reconstruction of Disputed Events* (Martinus Nijhoff, 2013).
Labuda, P., *International Criminal Tribunals and Domestic Accountability: In the Court's Shadow* (OUP, 2023).
Lagnado, D., *Explaining the Evidence: How the Mind Investigates the World* (CUP, 2021).
Lapore, J., *The Story of America: Essays on Origins* (Princeton University Press, 2013).
Laudan, L., *Truth, Error, and Criminal Law: An Essay in Legal Epistemology* (CUP, 2006).
Lippke, R., *Taming the Presumption of Innocence* (OUP, 2016).
Lipton, P., *Inference to the Best Explanation* (2nd edn, Routledge, 1991).
May, L., and S. Fyfe, *International Criminal Tribunals: A Normative Defense* (CUP, 2017).
May, R., and M. Wierda, *International Criminal Evidence* (Transnational Publishers, 2002).
McDermott, Y., *Fairness in International Criminal Trials* (OUP, 2016).
Murphy, P. (ed.), *Evidence, Proof, and Facts: A Book of Sources* (OUP, 2003).
Nagel, T., *The View from Nowhere* (OUP, 1986).
Nicolson, D., *Evidence and Proof in Scotland: Context and Critique* (Edinburgh University Press, 2019).
Osiel, M., *Mass Atrocity, Collective Memory, and the Law* (Transaction Publishers, 1997).
Phipson, S.L., et al., *Phipson on Evidence* (20th edn, Sweet & Maxwell, 2020).
Rigney, S., *Fairness and Rights in International Criminal Procedure* (Edinburgh University Press, 2022).
Roberts, P., and A. Zuckerman, *Roberts and Zuckerman's Criminal Evidence* (3rd edn, OUP, 2022).
Röling, B.V.A., *The Tokyo Trial and Beyond: Reflections of a Peacemonger* (Polity Press, 1993).
Röling, B.V.A., and C.F. Rüter (eds), *The Tokyo Judgment: The International Military Tribunal for the Far East (IMTFE) 29 April 1946–12 November 1948, Vol II* (Amsterdam University Press, 1977).
Rorty, R., *Objectivity, Relativism, and Truth: Philosophical Papers, vol. 1* (CUP, 1991).
Safferling, C., *International Criminal Procedure* (OUP, 2012).
Sander, B., *Doing Justice to History: Confronting the Past in International Criminal Courts* (OUP, 2021).
Schabas, W.A., *The International Criminal Court: A Commentary on the Rome Statute* (OUP, 2017).
Schuon, C., *International Criminal Procedure: A Clash of Legal Cultures* (TMC Asser Press, 2010).
Schum, D.A., *The Evidential Foundations of Probabilistic Reasoning* (2nd edn, Northwestern University Press, 2001).
Sluiter, G., et al. (eds), *International Criminal Procedure: Principles and Rules* (OUP, 2013).

Stein, A., *Foundations of Evidence Law* (OUP, 2005).
Tecuci, G., et al., *Intelligence Analysis as Discovery of Evidence, Hypotheses, and Arguments: Connecting the Dots* (CUP, 2016).
Thayer, J.B., *A Preliminary Treatise on Evidence at the Common Law* (Little, Brown, and Co., 1898).
Trechsel, S., and S. Summers, *Human Rights in Criminal Proceedings* (OUP, 2006).
Twining, W., *Theories of Evidence: Bentham and Wigmore* (Weidenfeld & Nicolson, 1985).
Twining, W., *Rethinking Evidence: Exploratory Essays* (CUP, 2009).
Van Eemeren, F.H., et al., *Fundamentals of Argumentation Theory* (Laurence Erlbaum Associates, 1996).
Vázquez, C., *De la Prueba Científica a la Prueba Pericial* (Marcial Pons, 2015).
Walton, D.N., *Legal Argumentation and Evidence* (Pennsylvania State University Press, 2002).
Werle, G., and F. Jeßberger, *Principles of International Criminal Law* (3rd edn, OUP, 2014).
Wigmore, J.H., *The Principles of Judicial Proof: As Given by Logic, Psychology, and General Experience and Illustrated in Judicial Trials* (Little, Brown & Co., 1913).
Wigmore, J.H., *The Science of Judicial Proof: As Given by Logic, Psychology, and General Experience, and Illustrated in Judicial Trials* (3rd edn, Little, Brown & Co., 1937).
Williams, S., H. Woolaver, and E. Palmer, *The Amicus Curiae in International Criminal Justice* (Hart, 2020).
Wilson, R.A., *Writing History in International Criminal Trials* (CUP, 2011).
Wheeler, C., *Fairness and the Goals of International Criminal Trials* (Routledge, 2023).
Zahar, A., and G. Sluiter, *International Criminal Law: A Critical Introduction* (OUP, 2007).
Zappala, S., *Human Rights in International Criminal Proceedings* (OUP, 2003).
Zuckerman, A.A.S., *The Principles of Criminal Evidence* (OUP, 1989).

Journal articles

Accatino, D., 'Legal Evidence Theory: Are We All "Rationalists" Now?' (2020) 40 *Revus* 85.
Al-Abdulkarim, L., et al., 'A Methodology for Designing Systems to Reason with Legal Cases using Abstract Dialectical Frameworks' (2016) 24 *Artificial Intelligence and Law* 1.
Allen, R.J., 'Nature of Juridical Proof' (1991) 13 *Cardozo Law Review* 373.
Allen, R.J., 'Factual Ambiguity and a Theory of Evidence' (1994) 88 *Northwestern University Law Review* 604.
Allen, R.J., 'Taming Complexity: Rationality, the Law of Evidence and the Nature of the Legal System' (2013) 12 *Law, Probability and Risk* 99.
Allen, R., and M. Pardo, 'Relative Plausibility and Its Critics' (2019) 23 *International Journal of Evidence & Proof* 5.
Amann, D.M., 'Harmonic Convergence? Constitutional Criminal Procedure in an International Context' (2000) 75 *Indiana Law Journal* 809.
Ambos, K., 'International Criminal Procedure: "Adversarial", "Inquisitorial", or "Mixed"?' (2003) 3 *International Criminal Law Review* 1.
Ashworth, A., 'Excluding Evidence as Protecting Rights' [1977] *Criminal Law Review* 723.
Baylis, E., 'Tribunal-Hopping with the Post-Conflict Justice Junkies' (2008) 10 *Oregon Review of International Law* 361.
Behrens, P., 'Assessment of International Criminal Evidence: The Case of the Unpredictable Genocidaire' (2011) 71 *ZaöRV* 661.
Bex, F., and D. Walton, 'Burdens and Standards of Proof for Inference to the Best Explanation: Three Case Studies' (2012) 11 *Law, Probability, and Risk* 113.
Birck, M.A., 'Do You See What I See? Problems with Juror Bias in Viewing Body-Camera Video Evidence' (2018) 24 *Michigan Journal of Race and Law* 153.
Boas, G., 'Creating Laws of Evidence for International Criminal Law: The ICTY and the Principle of Flexibility' (2001) 12 *Criminal Law Forum* 41.
Bogaard, G., E.H. Meijer, A. Vrij, and H. Merckelbach, 'Strong, but Wrong: Lay People's and Police Officers' Beliefs about Verbal and Nonverbal Cues to Deception' (2016) 11 *Plos One*, available at https://doi.org/10.1371/journal.pone.0156615.

Bonomy, I., 'The Reality of Conducting a War Crimes Trial' (2007) 5 *JICJ* 348.
Buisman, C., 'The Prosecutor's Obligation to Investigate Incriminating and Exonerating Circumstances Equally: Illusion or Reality' (2014) 27 *LJIL* 205.
Byrne, R., 'The New Public International Lawyer and the Hidden Art of Trial Practice' (2010) 25 *Connecticut Journal of International Law* 243.
Caianiello, M., 'First Decisions on the Admission of Evidence at ICC Trials—A Blending of Accusatorial and Inquisitorial Models?' (2011) 9 *JICJ* 385.
Caianiello, M., 'Law of Evidence at the International Criminal Court: Blending Accusatorial and Inquisitorial Models' (2011) 36 *North Carolina Journal of International Law & Commercial Regulation* 287.
Certoma, G.L., 'The Accusatory System v the Inquisitorial System: Procedural Truth v Fact?' (1982) 56 *Australian Law Journal* 288.
Cerutti, F., et al., 'Cispaces.org: From Fact Extraction to Report Generation' (2018) *COMMA 2018* 269.
Cerutti, F., and Y. McDermott, 'A Formal Argumentation Exercise on the *Karadžić* Trial Judgment' (2023) 10 *Journal of Applied Logics* 319.
Chlevickaitė, G., and B. Holá, 'Empirical Study of Insider Witnesses' Assessments at the International Criminal Court' (2016) 16 *International Criminal Law Review* 673.
Chlevickaitė, G., B. Holá, and C. Bijleveld, 'Thousands on the Stand: Exploring Trends and Patterns of International Witnesses' (2019) 32 *LJIL* 819.
Chlevickaitė, G., B. Holá, and C. Bijleveld, 'Judicial Witness Assessments at the ICTY, ICTR and ICC: Is There 'Standard Practice', in International Criminal Justice?' (2020) 18 *JICJ* 185.
Chlevickaitė, G., B. Holá, and C. Bijleveld, 'Suspicious Minds? Empirical Analysis of Insider Witness Assessments at the ICTY, ICTR and ICC' (2023) 20 *European Journal of Criminology* 185.
Clarke, K.M., and S. Kendall, 'The Beauty… Is That It Speaks for Itself: Geospatial Materials as Evidentiary Matters' (2019) 23 *Law Text Culture* 91.
Cohen, L.J., 'Can Human Irrationality Be Experimentally Demonstrated?' (1981) 4 *The Behavioral and Brain Sciences* 317.
Combs, N., 'Grave Crimes and Weak Evidence: A Fact-Finding Evolution in International Criminal Law' (2017) 58 *Harvard International Law Journal* 47.
Combs, N.A., 'Deconstructing the Epistemic Challenges to Mass Atrocity Prosecutions' (2018) 75 *Washington & Lee Law Review* 223.
Combs, N., 'Keynote Address: Evidentiary Deficiencies in International Criminal Law: Tracing the Trajectory from Ignored to Integral to Irrelevant' (2022) 22 *International Criminal Law Review* 835.
Cryer, R., 'Witness Tampering and International Criminal Tribunals' (2014) 27 *LJIL* 191.
D'Alessandra, F., 'The Accountability Turn in Third Wave Human Rights Fact-Finding' (2017) 33 *Utrecht Journal of International and European Law* 59.
Damaška, M.R. 'Evidentiary Barriers to Conviction and Two Models of Criminal Procedure: A Comparative Study' (1973) 121 *University of Pennsylvania Law Review* 506.
Damaška, M., 'Structures of Authority and Comparative Criminal Procedure' (1975) 84 *Yale LJ* 480.
Damaška, M., 'Free Proof and Its Detractors' (1995) 43 *American Journal of Comparative Law* 343.
Damaška, M.R., 'Models of Criminal Procedure' (2001) 51 *Zbornik* 477.
Damaška, M.R., 'Epistemology and Legal Regulation of Proof' (2003) 2 *Law, Probability and Risk* 117.
Damaška, M.R., 'What Is the Point of International Criminal Justice?' (2008) 83 *Chicago-Kent Law Review* 329.
Damaška, M., 'Reflections on Fairness in International Criminal Justice' (2012) 10 *JICJ* 611.
De Brouwer, A.-M., 'The Problem of Witness Interference before International Criminal Tribunals' (2015) 15 *International Criminal Law Review* 700.

Denault, V., and L. Jupe, 'Justice at Risk! An Evaluation of a Pseudoscientific Analysis of a Witness' Nonverbal Behavior in the Courtroom' (2017) 29 *Journal of Forensic Psychiatry and Psychology* 221.

De Vos, C., 'Investigating from Afar: The ICC's Evidence Problem' (2013) 26 *LJIL* 1009.

Dixon, R., 'Developing International Rules of Evidence for the Yugoslav and Rwanda Tribunals' (1997) 7 *Transnational Law and Contemporary Problems* 81.

Doherty, T.A., 'Evidence in International Criminal Tribunals: Contrast Between Domestic and International Trials' (2013) 26 *LJIL* 937.

Douglas, L., 'The Didactic Trial: Filtering History and Memory into the Courtroom' (2006) 14 *European Review* 513.

Eltringham, N., '"We are not a Truth Commission": Fragmented Narratives and the Historical Record at the International Criminal Tribunal for Rwanda' (2009) 11 *Journal of Genocide Research* 55.

Fairlie, M., 'The Marriage of Common and Continental Law at the ICTY and Its Progeny, Due Process Deficit' (2004) 4 *International Criminal Law Review* 243.

Fairlie, M., 'Rulemaking from the Bench: A Place for Minimalism at the ICTY' (2004) 39 *Texas International Law Journal* 257.

Fairlie, M., 'The Abiding Problem of Witness Statements in International Criminal Trials' (2017) 50 *NYU Journal of International Law and Politics* 75.

Fairlie, M.A., 'Defense Issues at the International Criminal Court' (2019) 47 *Georgia Journal of International and Comparative Law* 619.

Fairlie, M.A., 'The Unlikely Prospect of Non-Adversarial Trials at the International Criminal Court' (2018) 16 *JICJ* 295.

Fernandez, J.M., 'An Exploration of the Meaning of Truth in Philosophy and Law' (2009) 11 *University of Notre Dame Australia Law Review* 53.

Ferrer Beltrán, J., 'Legal Proof and Fact Finders' Beliefs' (2006) 12 *Legal Theory* 293.

Fletcher, G.P., 'Two Kinds of Legal Rules: A Comparative Study of Burden-of-Persuasion Practices in Criminal Cases' (1968) 77 *Yale Law Journal* 880.

Ford, S., 'Complexity and Efficiency at International Criminal Courts' (2014) 29 *Emory International Law Review* 1.

Frank, J., 'Legal Thinking in Three Dimensions' (1949–50) 1 *Syracuse Law Review* 9.

Franck, T., and H. Fairley, 'Procedural Due Process in Human Rights Fact-Finding by International Agencies' (1980) 74 *AJIL* 308.

Frase, R.S., 'The Search for the Whole Truth about American and European Criminal Justice' (2000) 3 *Buffalo Criminal Law Review* 785.

Freeman, L., 'Digital Evidence and War Crimes Prosecutions: The Impact of Digital Technologies on International Criminal Investigations and Trials' (2018) 41 *Fordham International Law Journal* 283.

Freeman, L., and R. Vazquez Llorente, 'Finding the Signal in the Noise: International Criminal Evidence and Procedure in the Digital Age' (2021) 19 *JICJ* 163.

Gabriele, C., K. Matheson, and R. Vazquez Llorente, 'The Role of Mobile Technology in Documenting International Crimes: The *Affaire Castro et Kizito* in the Democratic Republic of Congo' (2021) 19 *JICJ* 107.

Gaynor, F., 'Uneasy Partners—Evidence, Truth and History in International Trials' (2012) 10 *JICJ* 1257.

Geras, N., 'Language, Truth and Justice' (1995) 1 *New Left Review*, online at https://newleftreview.org/issues/i209/articles/norman-geras-language-truth-and-justice.pdf.

Gonzalez Castillo, J., 'La Fundamentación de las Sentencias y la Sana Crítica' (2006) 33 *Revista Chilena de Derecho* 93.

Groome, D., 'No Witness, No Case: An Assessment of the Conduct and Quality of ICC Investigations' (2014) 3 *Penn State Journal of Law & International Affairs* 1.

Guariglia, F., '"Admission" *v.* "Submission" of Evidence at the International Criminal Court: Lost in Translation?' (2018) 16 *JICJ* 315.

Guilfoyle, D., 'Lacking Conviction: Is the International Criminal Court Broken? An Organisational Failure Analysis' (2019) 20 *Melbourne Journal of International Law* 401.
Hamilton, R., 'User-Generated Evidence' (2018) 57 *Columbia Journal of Transnational Law* 1.
Hamilton, R.J., 'Social Media Platforms in International Criminal Investigations' (2020) 52 *Case Western Reserve Journal of International Law* 213.
Jackson, J.D., 'Analysing the New Evidence Scholarship: Towards a New Conception of the Law of Evidence' (1996) 16 *OJLS* 309.
Jackson, J.D., 'Modern Trends in Evidence Scholarship: Is All Rosy in the Garden?' (2001–3) 21 *Quinnipiac Law Review* 893.
Jackson, J.D., 'The Effect of Human Rights on Criminal Evidentiary Processes: Towards Convergence, Divergence, or Realignment?' (2005) 68 *MLR* 737.
Jackson, J.D., 'Finding the Best Epistemic Fit for International Criminal Tribunals: Beyond the Adversarial-Inquisitorial Dichotomy' (2009) 7 *JICJ* 17.
Jackson, J.D., and Y.M. Brunger, 'Witness Preparation in the ICC: An Opportunity for Principled Pragmatism' (2015) 13 *JICJ* 601.
Janier, M., et al., 'OVA+: An Argument Analysis Interface' (2014) *COMMA 2014* 463.
Kahneman, D., and A. Tversky, 'Subjective Probability' (1972) 3 *Cognitive Psychology* 430.
Kaplow, L., 'Burden of Proof' (2012) 121 *Yale Law Journal* 738.
Karemaker, R., et al., 'Witness Proofing in International Criminal Tribunals: A Critical Analysis of Widening Procedural Divergence' (2008) 21 *LJIL* 683.
Karnavas, M., 'The Kosovo Specialist Chambers' Rules of Procedure and Evidence: More of the Same Hybridity with Added Prosecutorial Transparency' (2020) 20 *International Criminal Law Review* 77.
Kay, S., 'The Move from Oral Evidence to Written Evidence: "The Law Is Always Too Short and Too Tight for Growing Humankind"' (2004) 2 *JICJ* 495.
Kaye, D., 'Archiving Justice: Conceptualizing the Archives of the United Nations International Criminal Tribunal for the Former Yugoslavia' (2014) 14 *Archival Science* 381.
Keane, A., and P. McKeown, 'Time to Abandon "Beyond Reasonable Doubt" and "Sure": The Case for a New Direction on the Criminal Standard and How It Should be Used' (2019) 6 *Criminal Law Review* 505.
Klamberg, M., 'The Alternative Hypothesis Approach, Robustness and International Criminal Justice: A Plea for a "Combined Approach" to Evaluation of Evidence' (2015) 13 *JICJ* 535.
Kreß, C., 'The Procedural Law of the International Criminal Court in Outline: Anatomy of a Unique Compromise' (2003) 1 *JICJ* 603.
Kwon, O.G., 'The Challenge of an International Criminal Trial as Seen from the Bench' (2007) 5 *JICJ* 360.
Langer, M., 'From Legal Transplants to Legal Translations: The Globalization of Plea Bargaining and the Americanization Thesis in Criminal Procedure' (2004) 45 *Harvard International Law Journal* 1.
Langer, M., 'The Rise of Managerial Judging in International Criminal Law' (2005) 53 *American Journal of Comparative Law* 835.
Langer, M., and M. Eason, 'The Quiet Expansion of Universal Jurisdiction' (2019) 30 *EJIL* 779.
Lempert, R.O., 'The New Evidence Scholarship: Analyzing the Process of Proof' (1986) 66 *Boston University Law Review* 439.
Lev-Ari, S., and B. Keysar, 'Why Don't We Believe Non-Native Speakers? The Influence of Accent on Credibility' (2010) 46 *Journal of Experimental Social Psychology* 1093.
Liefgreen, A., T. Pilditch, and D. Lagnado, 'Strategies for Selecting and Evaluating Information' (2020) 123 *Cognitive Psychology*, article 101332.
MacLean, K., 'Interactive Digital Platforms, Human Rights Fact Production, and the International Criminal Court' (2023) 15 *JHRP* 84.
Marchesi, D., 'Intercepted Communications in the *Ongwen* Case: Lessons to Learn on Documentary Evidence at the ICC' (2021) 22 *International Criminal Law Review* 920.
Mariniello, T., 'Questioning the Standard of Proof: The Purpose of the ICC Confirmation of Charges Procedure' (2015) 13 *JICJ* 579.

McDermott, Y., 'The Admissibility and Weight of Written Witness Testimony in International Criminal Law: A Socio-Legal Analysis' (2013) 26 *LJIL* 971.

McDermott, Y., '*Prosecutor v. Karadžić* (ICTY)' (2013) 52 *International Legal Materials* 1117.

McDermott, Y., 'Inferential Reasoning and Proof in International Criminal Trials' (2015) 13 *JICJ* 507.

McDermott, Y., 'The International Criminal Court's Chambers Practice Manual: Towards a Return to Judicial Law Making in International Criminal Procedure?' (2017) 15 *JICJ* 873.

McDermott, Y., 'Strengthening the Evaluation of Evidence in International Criminal Trials' (2017) 17 *International Criminal Law Review* 682.

McDermott, Y., 'The ECCC's Approach to Evidence and Proof' (2020) 18 *JICJ* 747.

McDermott, Y., and C. Aitken, 'Analysis of Evidence in International Criminal Trials using Bayesian Belief Networks' (2017) 16 *Law, Probability and Risk* 111.

McDermott, Y., et al., 'Open Source Information's Blind Spot: Human and Machine Bias in International Criminal Investigations' (2021) 19 *JICJ* 85.

McGonigle Leyh, B., 'Using Strategic Litigation and Universal Jurisdiction to Advance Accountability for Serious International Crimes' (2022) 16 *IJTJ* 363.

McGregor Richmond, K., 'Transforming Evidence and Proof in International Criminal Trials' (2022) 22 *International Criminal Law Review* 827.

McGregor Richmond, K., and S.A. Piccolo, 'Between Fact and Opinion: The Sui Generis Approach to Expert Witness Testimony in International Criminal Trials' (2022) 22 *International Criminal Law Review* 1016.

Mégret, F., 'International Criminal Justice as a Juridical Field' (2016) 13 *Champ Pénal/Penal Field*, online at https://journals.openedition.org/champpenal/9284.

Mehandru, N., and A. Koenig, 'Open Source Evidence and the International Criminal Court' (2019) 4 *Harvard Human Rights Journal*, online at https://harvardhrj.com/2019/04/open-source-evidence-and-the-international-criminal-court/.

Miller, G.A., 'The Magical Number Seven, Plus or Minus Two: Some Limits on Our Capacity for Processing Information' (1956) 63 *Psychological Review* 81.

Miraglia, M., 'Admissibility of Evidence, Standard of Proof, and Nature of the Decision in the ICC Confirmation of Charges in *Lubanga*' (2008) 6 *JICJ* 489.

Mnookin, J.L., 'Atomism, Holism, and the Judicial Assessment of Evidence' (2013) 60 *UCLA Law Review* 1524.

Moranchek, L., 'Protecting National Security Evidence While Prosecuting War Crimes: Problems and Lessons for International Justice from the ICTY' (2006) 31 *Yale Journal of International Law* 478.

Mundis, D.A., 'From "Common Law" Towards "Civil Law": The Evolution of the ICTY Rules of Procedure and Evidence' (2001) 14 *LJIL* 367.

Mundis, D.A., Book Review of G. Boas, *The Milošević Trial: Lessons for the Conduct of Complex International Criminal Proceedings* (2008) 102 *AJIL* 691.

Murphy, P., 'No Free Lunch, No Free Proof: The Indiscriminate Admission of Evidence is a Serious Flaw in International Criminal Trials' (2010) 8 *JICJ* 539.

Murray, D., et al., 'Mapping the Use of Open Source Research in UN Human Rights Investigations' (2022) 14 *JHRP* 554.

Nerlich, V., 'Daring Diversity: Why There Is Nothing Wrong with "Fragmentation" in International Criminal Procedure' (2013) 26 *LJIL* 777.

Nicholson, J., '"Too High", "Too Low", or "Just Fair Enough"? Finding Legitimacy through the Accused's Right to a Fair Trial' (2019) 17 *JICJ* 351.

Nijboer, J.F., 'Common Law Tradition in Evidence Scholarship Observed from a Continental Perspective' (1993) 41 *American Journal of Comparative Law* 299.

Nisbett, R., and E. Borgida, 'Attribution and the Psychology of Prediction' (1975) 32 *Journal of Personality and Social Psychology* 932.

Ntanda Nsereko, D.D., 'Prosecutorial Discretion before National Courts and International Tribunals' (2005) 3 *JICJ* 124.

Nyberg, E.P., et al., 'BARD: A Structured Technique for Group Elicitation of Bayesian Networks to Support Analytic Reasoning' (2022) 42 *Risk Analysis* 1155.

O'Sullivan, E., and D. Montgomery, 'The Erosion of the Right to Confrontation under the Cloak of Fairness at the ICTY' (2010) 8 *JICJ* 511.

Pardo, M.S., 'Juridical Proof, Evidence, and Pragmatic Meaning: Toward Evidentiary Holism' (2000–1) 95 *Northwestern University Law Review* 399.

Pardo, M.S., and R.J. Allen, 'Juridical Proof and the Best Explanation' (2008) 27 *Law and Philosophy* 223.

Parlevliet, M., 'Considering Truth: Dealing with a Legacy of Gross Human Rights Violations' (1998) 16 *Netherlands Quarterly of Human Rights* 141.

Paúl, A., '*Sana Crítica*: The System for Weighing Evidence Utilized by the Inter-American Court of Human Rights' (2012) 18 *Buffalo Human Rights Law Review* 193.

Picinali, F., 'The Threshold Lies in the Method: Instructing Jurors about Reasoning Beyond Reasonable Doubt' (2015) 19 *International Journal of Evidence and Proof* 139.

Powderly, J., 'Introductory Note to *Prosecutor v. Jean-Pierre Bemba Gombo*: Judgment on the Appeal of Mr. Jean-Pierre Bemba Gombo against Trial Chamber III's "Judgment Pursuant to Article 74 of the Statute" (Int'l Crim. Ct.)' (2018) 57 *ILM* 1031.

Prakken, H., et al., 'A Formalization of Argumentation Schemes for Legal Case-based Reasoning in ASPIC+' (2015) 25 *Journal of Logic and Computation* 1141.

Prakken, H., et al., 'Editors' Review and Introduction: Models of Rational Proof in Criminal Law' (2020) 12 *Topics in Cognitive Science* 1053.

Pruitt, R.C., 'Guilt by Majority in the International Criminal Tribunal for the Former Yugoslavia: Does This Meet the Standard of Proof "Beyond Reasonable Doubt"?' (1997) 10 *LJIL* 557.

Quilling, C., 'The Future of Digital Evidence Authentication at the International Criminal Court' (2022) *Journal of Public & International Affairs*, online at https://jpia.princeton.edu/news/future-digital-evidence-authentication-international-criminal-court.

Ramsden, M., and C. Chung, '"Reasonable Grounds to Believe": An Unreasonably Unclear Evidentiary Threshold in the ICC Statute' (2015) 13 *JICJ* 555.

Ring, K.L., 'The Evolution of the Procedure for Reviewing Victim Applications at the International Criminal Court' (2023) 21 *JICJ* 29.

Roberts, A., 'The Frailties of Human Memory and the Accused's Right to Accurate Procedures' (2019) 11 *Criminal Law Review* 912.

Roberts, P., 'Does Article 6 of the European Convention on Human Rights Require Reasoned Verdicts in Criminal Trials?' (2011) 11 *HRLR* 213.

Roberts, P., 'The Priority of Procedure and the Neglect of Evidence and Proof: Facing Facts in International Criminal Law' (2015) 13 *JICJ* 479.

Roberts, R.C.E., 'The *Lubanga* Trial Chamber's Assessment of Evidence in Light of the Accused's Right to the Presumption of Innocence' (2012) 10 *JICJ* 923.

Sácouto, S., and P. Sellers, 'The Bemba Appeals Chamber Judgment: Impunity for Sexual and Gender-Based Crimes?' (2019) 27 *William & Mary Bill Rights Journal* 599.

Sander, B., 'History on Trial: Historical Narrative Pluralism Within and Beyond International Criminal Courts' (2018) 67 *ICLQ* 547.

Shafer, G., 'Combining AI and OR' (1988) *University of Kansas School of Business Working Paper No. 195*.

Schauer, F., 'In Defense of a Rule-Based Evidence Law—and Epistemology Too' (2008) 5 *Episteme* 295.

Schmitt, B., 'Legal Diversity at the International Criminal Court: Reflections of a Judge' (2021) 19 *JICJ* 485.

Schuon, C., 'The Appeals Decision in the ICC's *Jean-Pierre Bemba Gombo* Case on the Trial Chamber's "Decision on the Admission into Evidence of Materials Contained in the Prosecution's List of Evidence"' (2012) 25 *LJIL* 511.

Schweizer, M., 'Comparing Holistic and Atomistic Evaluation of Evidence' (2014) 13 *Law, Probability and Risk* 65.

Shannon, K.G., 'Passing the Poisoned Chalice: Judicial Notice of Genocide by the ICTR' (2006) 19 *Revue Québécoise de Droit International* 95.

Sinclair-Blakemore, A., 'The Admission of New Prosecutorial Evidence in International Criminal Retrials: An Assessment of the Exclusionary Rule in *Stanišić and Simatović*' (2023) 21 *JICJ* 903.

Stewart, J.G., 'Judicial Notice in International Criminal Law: A Reconciliation of Potential, Peril and Precedent' (2003) 3 *International Criminal Law Review* 245.

Stone, M., 'Instant Lie Detection? Demeanour and Credibility in Criminal Trials' [1991] *Criminal Law Review* 821.

Stoykova, R., 'The Right to a Fair Trial as a Conceptual Framework for Digital Evidence Rules in Criminal Investigations' (2023) 49 *Computer Law & Security Review*, article 105801.

Summers, R.S., 'Formal Legal Truth and Substantive Truth in Judicial Fact-Finding—Their Justified Divergence in some Particular Cases' (1999) 18 *Law & Philosophy* 497.

Taruffo, M., 'Rethinking the Standards of Proof' (2003) 51 *American Journal of Comparative Law* 659.

Toulmin, S., et al., 'Arguments, Scenarios and Probabilities: Connections Between Three Normative Frameworks for Evidential Reasoning' (2016) 15 *Law, Probability and Risk* 35.

Tecuci, G., et al., 'Computational Approach and Cognitive Assistant for Evidence-Based Reasoning in Intelligence Analysis' (2014) 5 *International Journal of Intelligent Defence Support Systems* 146.

Tecuci, G., et al., 'Toward a Computational Theory of Evidence-Based Reasoning for Instructable Cognitive Agents' (2019) *Proceedings of the 2019 AAAI Fall Symposium 'Artificial Intelligence in Government and Public Sector'*, Arlington, VA, online at https://arxiv.org/abs/1910.03990.

Tribe, L.H., 'Trial by Mathematics: Precision and Ritual in the Legal Process' (1971) 84 *Harvard Law Review* 1329.

Tversky, A., and D. Kahneman, 'Judgment under Uncertainty: Heuristics and Biases' (1976) 185 *Science* 1124.

Twining, W., 'The New Evidence Scholarship' (1991-1992) 13 *Cardozo Law Review* 295.

Vanderpuye, K., 'The International Criminal Court and Discretionary Evidential Exclusion' (2005–6) 14 *Tulane Journal of International & Comparative Law* 127.

Vasiliev, S., 'ECCC Appeals' (2020) 18 *JICJ* 723.

Verheij, B., 'Automated Argument Assistance for Lawyers' (1999) *ICAIL '99: Proceedings of the 7th International Conference on Artificial Intelligence and Law* 43.

Vrij, A., and J. Turgeon, 'Evaluating Credibility of Witnesses—Are We Instructing Jurors on Invalid Factors?' (2018) 11 *Journal of Tort Law* 231.

Vrij, A., M. Hartwig, and P.A. Granhag, 'Reading Lies: Nonverbal Communication and Deception' (2019) 70 *Annual Review of Psychology* 295.

Vukušić, I., 'Nineteen Minutes of Horror: Insights from the Scorpions Execution Video' (2018) 12 *Genocide Studies and Prevention* 35.

Wald, P., 'Judging War Crimes' (2000) 1 *Chicago Journal of International Law* 189.

Wald, P.M., 'To Establish Incredible Events by Credible Evidence: The Use of Affidavit Testimony in Yugoslavia War Crimes Tribunal Proceedings' (2001) 42 *Harvard International Law Journal* 535.

Wald, P.M., 'ICTY Judicial Proceedings: An Appraisal from Within' (2004) 2 *JICJ* 466.

Wald, P.M., 'Foreword: War Tales and War Trials' (2008) 106 *Michigan Law Review* 901.

Weigend, T., 'Is the Criminal Process About Truth? A German Perspective' (2003) 26 *Harvard Journal of Law & Public Policy* 157.

White, H., 'Response to Arthur Marwick' (1995) 30 *Journal of Contemporary History* 233.

Whiting, A., 'Dynamic Investigative Practice at the International Criminal Court' (2014) 76 *Law and Contemporary Problems* 163.

Williamson, T., 'Abductive Philosophy' (2016) 3–4 *Philosophical Forum* 263.

Zarmsky, S., 'Why Seeing Should Not Always Be Believing: Considerations Regarding the Use of Digital Reconstruction Technology in International Law' (2021) 19 *JICJ* 213.

Zubiri de Salinas, F., '¿Qué es la sana crítica? La valoración judicial del dictamen experto' (2004) 50 *Revista Jueces para la Democracia* 52.

Chapters in edited volumes

Agirre Aranburu, X., 'Methodology for the Criminal Investigation of International Crimes', in A. Smeulers, *Collective Violence and International Criminal Justice: An Interdisciplinary Approach* (Intersentia, 2010), 353.

Agirre Aranburu, X., 'The Contribution of Analysis to the Quality Control in Criminal Investigation', in X. Agirre et al. (eds), *Quality Control in Criminal Investigation* (TOAEP, 2020), 117.

Aksenova, M., 'The Role of International Criminal Tribunals in Shaping the Historical Accounts of Genocide', in U. Belavusau and A. Gliszczyńska-Grabias (eds), *Law and Memory: Towards Legal Governance of History* (CUP, 2017), 48.

Aksenova, M., and M. Bergsmo, 'Non-Criminal Justice Fact-Work in the Age of Accountability', in M. Bergsmo (ed.), *Quality Control in Fact-Finding* (TOAEP, 2013), 1.

Alamuddin, A., 'Collection of Evidence', in K.A.A. Khan et al. (eds), *Principles of Evidence in International Criminal Justice* (OUP, 2010), 231.

Ambach, P., 'A Look towards the Future—The ICC and "Lessons Learnt"', in C. Stahn (ed.), *The Law and Practice of the International Criminal Court* (OUP, 2015), 1277.

Ambos, K., 'Introduction', in K. Ambos et al. (eds), *Evidence in International Criminal Procedure: A Commentary* (Hart/Beck, forthcoming 2024, on file with author).

Ashworth, A., 'Exploring the Integrity Principle in Evidence and Procedure', in P. Mirfield and R.J. Smith (eds), *Essays for Colin Tapper* (OUP, 2005), 112.

Baddeley, A.D., and G.J. Hitch, 'Working Memory', in G.H. Bower (ed), *The Psychology of Learning and Motivation, vol. 8* (Academic Press, 1974), 47.

Bekou, O., 'Enhancing the Quality of Investigations: What Role Can In-Depth Analysis Charts Play', in X. Agirre et al. (eds), *Quality Control in Criminal Investigation* (TOAEP, 2020), 587.

Bergsmo, M., and W.H. Wiley, 'Human Rights Professionals and the Criminal Investigation and Prosecution of Core International Crimes', in S. Skåre, I. Burkey and H. Mørk (eds), *Manual on Human Rights Monitoring: An Introduction for Human Rights Field Officers* (Norwegian Centre for Human Rights, 2008), Chapter 10.

Boas, G., 'A Code of Evidence and Procedure for International Criminal Law? The Rules of the ICTY', in G. Boas and W.A. Schabas (eds), *International Criminal Law Developments in the Case Law of the ICTY* (Nijhoff, 2003), 1.

Bohlander, M., 'The International Criminal Judiciary: Problems of Judicial Selection, Independence and Ethics', in M. Bohlander (ed.), *International Criminal Justice: A Critical Analysis of Institutions and Procedures* (Cameron May, 2007), 325.

Cayley, A.T., 'Constraints and Quality Control in Preliminary Examination: Critical Lessons Learned from the ICTY, the ICC, the ECCC and the United Kingdom', in M. Bergsmo and C. Stahn, *Quality Control in Preliminary Examination: Volume 1* (TOAEP, 2018), 35.

Chau, P., 'Excluding Integrity? Revisiting Non-Consequentialist Justifications for Excluding Improperly Obtained Evidence in Criminal Trials', in J. Hunter et al. (eds), *The Integrity of the Criminal Process* (Hart, 2016), 267.

Combs, N., 'Evidence', in W.A. Schabas and N. Bernaz (eds), *The Routledge Handbook of International Criminal Law* (Routledge, 2011), 323.

Cross, M.E., 'The Standard of Proof in Preliminary Examinations', in M. Bergsmo and C. Stahn (eds), *Quality Control in Preliminary Examination: Vol. 2* (TOAEP, 2018), 213.

Davis, D., and E. Loftus, 'Inconsistencies Between Law and the Limits of Human Cognition: The Case of Eyewitness Identification', in L. Nadel and W. Sinnott-Armstrong (eds), *Memory and Law* (OUP, 2012), 47.

De Meester, K., K. Pitcher, R. Rastan, and G. Sluiter, 'Investigation, Coercive Measures, Arrest, and Surrender', in G. Sluiter et al. (eds), *International Criminal Procedure: Principles and Rules* (OUP, 2013), 171.

De Smet, S., 'The International Criminal Standard of Proof at the ICC—Beyond Reasonable Doubt or Beyond Reason?', in C. Stahn (ed.), *The Law and Practice of the International Criminal Court* (OUP, 2015), 861.

De Smet, S., 'All Roads Lead to Rome: Lifting the Veil on the ICC's Procedural Pluriformity', in P. Šturma (ed.), *The Rome Statute of the ICC at Its Twentieth Anniversary* (Brill, 2019), 191.

De Smet, S., 'Controlling the Quality of Reasoning About the Link Between Evidence and Factual Findings', in X. Agirre et al. (eds), *Quality Control in Criminal Investigation* (TOAEP, 2020), 611.

Delmas-Marty, M., 'Reflections on the "Hybridisation" of Criminal Procedure', in J. Jackson, M. Langer, and P Tillers (eds), *Crime, Procedure and Evidence in a Comparative and International Context: Essays in Honour of Professor Mirjan Damaška* (Hart, 2008), 251.

Delpla, I., 'The ICTY Investigations: Interview with Jean-René Ruez', in I. Delpla et al. (eds), *Investigating Srebrenica: Institutions, Facts, Responsibilities* (Berghahn Books, 2012), 23.

Duff, A., et al., 'Introduction: Judgment and Calling to Account', in A. Duff et al. (eds), *The Trial on Trial: Volume 2* (Hart, 2006), 1.

Eckelmans, F., 'Article 81', in O. Triffterer and K. Ambos (eds), *Rome Statute of the International Criminal Court: Article-by-Article Commentary* (4th edn, Beck/Hart, 2021), 2311.

Fenton, N., and D. Lagnado, 'Bayesianism: Objections and Rebuttals', in C. Dahlman et al. (eds) *Philosophical Foundations of Evidence Law* (OUP, 2021), 267.

Friman, H., 'Charges', in G. Sluiter et al. (eds), *International Criminal Procedure: Principles and Rules* (OUP, 2013), 381.

Gaynor, F., 'Judicial Notice and Agreed Facts', in G. Sluiter et al. (eds), *International Criminal Procedure: Principles and Rules* (OUP, 2013), 1107.

Gaynor, F., 'Documentary Evidence', in K. Ambos et al. (eds), *Evidence in International Criminal Procedure: A Commentary* (Hart/Beck, forthcoming 2024, on file with author).

Gómez, M., 'Real-World Applications of Influence Diagrams', in J.A. Gámez et al. (eds), *Advances in Bayesian Networks* (Springer, 2004), 161.

González Lagier, D., 'Tres Modos de Razonar Sobre Hechos (y Algunos Problemas Sobre la Prueba Judicial Planteados a Partir de Ellos)', in C. Vázquez (ed.), *Hechos y Razonamiento Probatorio* (Ceji, 2018), 17.

Gosnell, C., 'Admissibility of Evidence', in K.A.A. Khan et al. (eds), *Principles of Evidence in International Criminal Justice* (OUP, 2010), 375.

Guariglia, F., and G. Hochmayr, 'Article 56', in O. Triffterer and K. Ambos (eds), *Rome Statute of the International Criminal Court: Article-by-Article Commentary* (4th edn, Beck/Hart, 2021), 1675.

Heinze, A., 'Bend it Like Bentham: The Ambivalent "Civil Law" vs. "Common Law" Dichotomy within International Criminal Adjudication', in M Bergsmo et al. (eds), *Power in International Criminal Justice* (TOAEP, 2020), 155.

Ho, H.L., 'The Legal Concept of Evidence', in E.N. Zalta (ed.), *The Stanford Encyclopaedia of Philosophy* (Stanford University, 2015), online at https://plato.stanford.edu/entries/evidence-legal/.

Ho, H.L., 'The Fair Trial Rationale for Excluding Wrongfully Obtained Evidence', in S. Gless (ed.), *Do Exclusionary Rules Ensure a Fair Trial?* (Springer, 2019), 283.

Ho, H.L., 'Evidence and Truth', in C. Dahlman, A. Stein, and G. Tuzet, *Philosophical Foundations of Evidence Law* (OUP, 2021), 11.

Hunt, D., 'The Meaning of a *Prima Facie* Case', in R. May et al. (eds), *Essays on ICTY Procedure and Evidence—In Honour of Gabrielle Kirk McDonald* (Kluwer, 2001), 137.

Jackson, J., 'Taking Comparative Evidence Seriously', in P. Roberts and M. Redmayne (eds), *Innovations in Evidence and Proof: Integrating Theory, Research and Teaching* (Hart, 2007), 291.

Jackson, J.D., and Y.M. Brunger, 'Fragmentation and Harmonization in the Development of Evidentiary Practices in International Criminal Tribunals', in E. van Sliedregt and S. Vasiliev, *Pluralism in International Criminal Law* (OUP, 2014), 159.

Jackson, J., and P. Roberts, 'Beyond Common Law Evidence: Reimagining, and Reinvigorating, Evidence Law as Forensic Science', in D.K. Brown, J.I. Turner, and B. Weisser (eds), *The Oxford Handbook of Criminal Process* (OUP, 2019), 787.

Jacobs, D., and C. Harwood, 'International Criminal Law Outside the Courtroom: The Impact of Focusing on International Crimes for the Quality of Fact-Finding', in M. Bergsmo (ed.), *Quality Control in Fact-Finding* (TOAEP, 2013), 325.

Jacobs, D., 'A Shifting Scale of Power: Who is in Charge of the Charges at the International Criminal Court?', in W.A. Schabas, N. Hayes, and Y. McDermott (eds), *The Ashgate Research Companion to International Criminal Law: Critical Perspectives* (Ashgate, 2013), 205.

Jacobs, D., 'Standard of Proof and Burden of Proof', in G. Sluiter et al. (eds), *International Criminal Procedure: Principles and Rules* (OUP, 2013), 1128.

Jørgensen, N.H.B., 'Judicial Notice', in K.A.A. Khan et al. (eds), *Principles of Evidence in International Criminal Justice* (OUP, 2010), 695.

Klamberg, M., 'General Requirements for the Admission of Evidence', in G. Sluiter et al., *International Criminal Procedure: Principles and Rules* (OUP, 2013), 1016.

Klamberg, M., 'Epistemological Controversies and Evaluation of Evidence in International Criminal Trials', in K.J. Heller et al. (eds), *The Oxford Handbook of International Criminal Law* (OUP, 2020), 450.

Koh, H.H., 'Mirjan Damaška: A Bridge Between Two Legal Cultures', in J. Jackson, M. Langer, and P. Tillers (eds), *Crime, Procedure and Evidence in a Comparative and International Context: Essays in Honour of Professor Mirjan Damaška* (Hart, 2008), 29.

Lidén, M., 'Confirmation Bias in Investigations of Core International Crimes: Risk Factors and Quality Control Techniques', in X. Agirre et al. (eds), *Quality Control in Criminal Investigation* (TOAEP, 2020), 461.

Longobardo, M., and D. Fleck, 'Means of Combat', in D. Fleck (ed.), *The Handbook of International Humanitarian Law* (4th edn, OUP, 2021), 129.

Mariniello, T., 'The Impact of International Commissions of Inquiry on the Proceedings before the International Criminal Court', in C. Henderson (ed.), *Commissions of Inquiry: Problems and Prospects* (Hart, 2017), 171.

Mariniello, T., and N. Pons, 'The Confirmation of Charges at the International Criminal Court: A Tale of Two Models', in T. Mariniello (ed.) *The International Criminal Court in Search of Its Purpose and Identity* (Routledge, 2015), 217.

McDermott, Y., 'Double Speak and Double Standards: Does the Jurisprudence on Retrial Following Acquittal under International Criminal Law Spell the End of the Double Jeopardy Rule?', in D. Keane and Y. McDermott (eds), *The Challenge of Human Rights: Past, Present, and Future* (Edward Elgar, 2012), 176.

McDermott, Y., 'Rights in Reverse: A Critical Analysis of Fair Trial Rights under International Criminal Law', in W.A. Schabas et al. (eds), *The Ashgate Research Companion to International Criminal Law: Critical Perspectives* (Ashgate, 2013), 165.

McDermott, Y., 'Absent Witnesses and the Right to Confrontation: The Influence of the Jurisprudence of the European Court of Human Rights on International Criminal Law', in P. Lobba and T. Mariniello (eds), *Judicial Dialogue on Human Rights: The Practice of International Criminal Tribunals* (Brill, 2017), 225.

Mekki, M., 'Preuve et Vérité en France', in Association Henri Capitant (ed.), *La Preuve: Journées internationales 2013 d'Amsterdam, Pays-Bas et Liège, Belgique, Vol. LXIII* (Bruylant, 2015), 813.

Morrison, H., 'Judging in International Criminal Cases: Challenges, Aspirations and Duties', in M. Böse et al. (eds), *Justice Without Borders: Essays in Honour of Wolfgang Schomburg* (Brill, 2018), 299.

Murphy, P., and L. Baddour, 'Evidence and Selection of Judges in International Criminal Tribunals: The Need for a Harmonized Approach', in E. van Sliedregt and S. Vasiliev, *Pluralism in International Criminal Law* (OUP, 2014), 368.

Nerenberg, M., and W. Timmermann, 'Documentary Evidence', in K.A.A. Khan, C. Buisman, and C. Gosnell (eds), *Principles of Evidence in International Criminal Justice* (OUP, 2010), 443.

Nerlich, V., 'Article 82', in O. Triffterer and K. Ambos (eds), *Rome Statute of the International Criminal Court: Article-by-Article Commentary* (4th edn, Beck/Hart, 2021), 2360.

Nerlich, V., 'Article 84', in O. Triffterer and K. Ambos (eds), *Rome Statute of the International Criminal Court: Article-by-Article Commentary* (4th edn, Beck/Hart, 2021), 2405.

Nicolson, D., 'Gender, Epistemology, and Ethics: Feminist Perspectives on Evidence Theory', in M. Childs and L. Ellison (eds), *Feminist Perspectives on Evidence* (Taylor & Francis, 2000), 13.

Oeter, S., 'Methods of Combat', in D. Fleck (ed.), *The Handbook of International Humanitarian Law* (4th edn, OUP, 2021), 129.

Orie, A.M.M., 'Accusatorial v. Inquisitorial Approach in International Criminal Proceedings', in A. Cassese, P. Gaeta, and J.R.W.D. Jones (eds), *The Rome Statute of the International Criminal Court: A Commentary, Volume 2* (OUP, 2002), 1439.

Peirce, C.S., 'The Objectivity of Truth', in C. Hartshorne and P. Weiss (eds), *The Collected Papers of Charles Sanders Peirce, Volume II: Elements of Logic* (Harvard University Press, 1932), 135.

Pennington, N., and R. Hastie, 'The Story Model for Juror Decision Making', in R. Hastie (ed.), *Inside the Juror: The Psychology of Juror Decision Making* (CUP, 1993), 192.

Piragoff, D., and P. Clarke, 'Article 69', in O. Triffterer and K. Ambos (eds), *Rome Statute of the International Criminal Court: Article-by-Article Commentary* (4th edn., Beck/Hart, 2021), 2035.

Pocar, F., 'Common and Civil Law Traditions in the ICTY Criminal Procedure: Does Oil Blend with Water?', in J. Walker and O.G. Chase (eds), *Common Law, Civil Law and the Future of Categories* (LexisNexis, 2010), 437.

Prosperi, L., and A.Z. Borda, 'A Partial View of History: ICTY Judgments as "Judicial Truths"', in C. Stahn et al. (eds), *Legacies of the International Criminal Tribunal for the Former Yugoslavia: A Multidisciplinary Approach* (OUP, 2020), 174.

Re, D., 'Appeal', in L. Reydams et al, *International Prosecutors* (OUP, 2012), 797.

Re, D., 'Rethinking Disclosure: Embrace the Electronic Disclosure Suite', in X. Agirre et al. (eds), *Quality Control in Criminal Investigation* (TOAEP, 2020), 735.

Roberts, P., 'Why International Criminal Evidence', in P. Roberts and M. Redmayne (eds), *Innovations in Evidence and Proof: Integrating Theory, Research and Teaching* (Hart, 2007), 347.

Roberts, P., 'Groundwork for a Jurisprudence of Criminal Procedure', in R.A. Duff and S.P. Green (eds), *Philosophical Foundations of Criminal Law* (OUP, 2011), 379.

Rohan, C., 'The Hybrid System of International Criminal Law: A Work in Progress or Just a Noble Experiment?', in M. Aksenova et al., *Breaking the Cycle of Mass Atrocities* (Hart, 2019), 95.

Ryngaert, C., 'Article 58', in O. Triffterer and K. Ambos (eds), *Rome Statute of the International Criminal Court: Article-by-Article Commentary* (4th edn, Beck/Hart, 2021), 1708.

Schabas, W.A., E. Chaitidou, and M. El Zeidy, 'Article 61', in O. Triffterer and K. Ambos (eds), *Rome Statute of the International Criminal Court: Article-by-Article Commentary* (4th edn, Beck/Hart, 2021), 1759.

Schabas, W.A., and Y. McDermott, 'Article 66', in O. Triffterer and K. Ambos (eds), *Rome Statute of the International Criminal Court: Article-by-Article Commentary* (4th edn, Beck/Hart, 2021), 1947.

Schwöbel-Patel, C., 'Commissions of Inquiry: Courting International Criminal Courts and Tribunals', in C. Henderson (ed.), *Commissions of Inquiry: Problems and Prospects* (Hart, 2017), 145.

Schuppli, S., 'Entering Evidence: Cross-Examining the Court Records of the ICTY', in E. Weizman (ed.), *Forensis: The Architecture of Public Truth* (Sternberg Press/Forensic Architecture, 2014), 279.

Schwikkard, P.J., 'Convergence, Appropriate Fit and Values in Criminal Process', in P. Roberts and M. Redmayne (eds), *Innovations in Evidence and Proof: Integrating Theory, Research and Teaching* (Hart, 2007), 331.

Sluiter, G., et al., 'Introduction', in G. Sluiter et al. (eds), *International Criminal Procedure: Principles and Rules* (OUP, 2013), 21.

Smith, E., 'Trauma in the Witness Stand: Effective Evaluation of Trauma-Impacted Testimony at the International Criminal Court', in A. Heinze and V.E. Dittrich (eds), *The Past, Present and Future of the International Criminal Court* (TOAEP, 2021), 439.

Stahn, C., and D. Jacobs, 'The Interaction Between Human Rights Fact-Finding and International Criminal Proceedings: Toward a (New) Typology', in P. Alston and S. Knuckey (eds), *The Transformation of Human Rights Fact-Finding* (OUP, 2016), 255.

Stahn, C., and L. van den Herik, '"Fragmentation", Diversification and "3D" Legal Pluralism: International Criminal Law as the Jack-in-the-Box?', in L. van den Herik and C. Stahn (eds), *The Diversification and Fragmentation of International Criminal Law* (Martinus Nijhoff, 2012), 21.

Taroni, F., et al., 'The Logic of Inference and Decision for Scientific Evidence', in C. Dahlman et al. (eds) *Philosophical Foundations of Evidence Law* (OUP, 2021), 251.

Taroni, F., et al., 'Statistical Interpretation of Evidence: Bayesian Analysis', in M.M. Houck (ed.), *Encyclopedia of Forensic Sciences* (3rd edn, Elsevier, 2023), 656.

Triffterer, O., and A. Kiss, 'Article 74', in O. Triffterer and K. Ambos (eds), *Rome Statute of the International Criminal Court: Article-by-Article Commentary* (4th edn, Beck/Hart, 2021), 2188.

Twining, W., 'Moving Beyond Law: Interdisciplinarity and the Study of Evidence', in P. Dawid, W. Twining, and M. Vasilaki (eds), *Evidence, Inference and Enquiry* (OUP, 2011), 73.

Van den Herik, L., and C. Harwood, 'Commissions of Inquiry and the Charm of International Criminal Law: Between Transactional and Authoritative Approaches', in P. Alston and S. Knuckey (eds), *The Transformation of Human Rights Fact-Finding* (OUP, 2016), 233.

Van Lent, L., and I. Braam, 'The Dutch *Unus Testis, Nullus Testis* Rule', in J. Chalmers, F. Leverick, and A. Shaw (eds), *Post-Corroboration Safeguards Review Report of the Academic Expert Group* (Scottish Government, 2014), 250.

Van Sliedregt, E., and S. Vasiliev, 'Pluralism: A New Framework for International Criminal Justice', in E. van Sliedregt and S. Vasiliev, *Pluralism in International Criminal Law* (OUP, 2014), 3.

Vasiliev, S., 'General Rules and Principles of International Criminal Procedure: Definition, Legal Nature and Identification', in G. Sluiter and S. Vasiliev (eds), *International Criminal Procedure: Towards a Coherent Body of Law* (Cameron May, 2009), 19.

Vasiliev, S., et al., 'Introduction', in G. Sluiter et al. (eds), *International Criminal Procedure: Principles and Rules* (OUP, 2013), 8.

Whiting, A., 'The ICTY as a Laboratory of International Criminal Procedure', in B. Swart et al. (eds), *The Legacy of the International Criminal Tribunal for the Former Yugoslavia* (OUP, 2011), 83.

Reports

Cassese, A., *Annual Report of the International Tribunal for the Prosecution of Persons Responsible for Serious Violations of International Humanitarian Law Committed in the Territory of the Former Yugoslavia since 1991*, A/49/342, S/1994/1007, 29 August 1994.

Corten, O., and V. Koutroulis, *Tribunal for the Crime of Aggression against Ukraine—A Legal Assessment* (Policy Department, Directorate-General for External Policies, European Parliament), December 2022.

Council of Europe, *Annual Report 2022 of the European Court of Human Rights* (Council of Europe, 2023).

Ferro Ribeiro, S., and D. van der Straten Ponthoz, *International Protocol on the Documentation and Investigation of Sexual Violence in Conflict* (2nd edn, UK Foreign and Commonwealth Office, 2017).

Human Rights Center, University of California, Berkeley and Office of the United Nations High Commissioner for Human Rights, *Berkeley Protocol on Digital Open Source Investigations* (OHCHR, 2020).

Independent Expert Panel for the Legal Definition of Ecocide, *Commentary and Core Text*, June 2021.

Independent Expert Review of the International Criminal Court and the Rome Statute System, Final Report of the Group of Independent Experts, ICC-ASP/19/16, 30 September 2020.

International Bar Association, *Witnesses before the International Criminal Court* (2013).

International Bar Association, *Remedying International Injustice: Appeals, Retrials and Revisions of Judgments in International Criminal Law* (2022).

International Criminal Court, *Overall Response of the International Criminal Court to the 'Independent Expert Review of the International Criminal Court and Rome Statute*

System—Final Report': Preliminary Analysis of the Recommendations and Information on Relevant Activities Undertaken by the Court (April 2021).
International Criminal Court Office of the Prosecutor, Eurojust, and EU Genocide Network, *Documenting International Crimes and Human Rights Violations for Accountability Purposes: Guidelines for Civil Society Organisations* (September 2022).
Kalshoven-Gieskes Forum on International Humanitarian Law, *Leiden Guidelines on the Use of Digitally Derived Evidence in International Criminal Courts and Tribunals*, online at https://leiden-guidelines.com.
Roberts, P., and C. Aitken, *The Logic of Forensic Proof: Inferential Reasoning in Criminal Evidence and Forensic Science Guidance for Judges, Lawyers, Forensic Scientists and Expert Witnesses*, Royal Statistical Society's Working Group on Statistics and the Law, Practitioner Guide No. 3 (Royal Statistical Society, 2014).
Wald, P.M., *Tyrants on Trial: Keeping Order in the Courtroom* (Open Society Justice Initiative, 2009).

PhD theses

Aksamitowska, K., *Justice at Home, Justice Abroad: The Accountability Efforts Relating to the Conflicts in Eastern Ukraine, Northern Iraq, and Syria* (PhD thesis, Swansea University, 2023).
Buisman, C., *Ascertainment of the Truth in International Criminal Justice* (PhD thesis, Brunel University London, 2012).
Egan, U., *A Socio-Legal Intersectional Analysis of the Role of Technology in the Investigation of Conflict-Related Sexual and Gender-Based Violence* (PhD thesis, Swansea University, 2023).

Journalistic and online publications

Al Hussein, Z.R., B. Stagno Ugarte, C. Wenaweser, and T. Intelman, 'The International Criminal Court Needs Fixing' (*New Atlanticist*, 24 April 2019).
Amann, D.M., 'In *Bemba* and Beyond, Crimes Adjudged to Commit Themselves' (*EJIL Talk!*, 13 June 2018).
Bensouda, F., 'Statement of ICC Prosecutor, Fatou Bensouda, on the Recent Judgment of the ICC Appeals Chamber Acquitting Mr Jean-Pierre Bemba Gombo', 13 June 2018.
Bradfield, P., 'No Case to Answer? Show Me the (Standard of) Proof!' (*Opinio Juris*, 20 January 2019).
Browne, M., et al., 'Satellite Images Show Bodies Lay in Bucha for Weeks, Despite Russian Claims' (*New York Times*, 4 April 2022).
Chiarini, G., 'Can We Return to the Law, Please? Rethinking the Judicial Interpretation of Procedural Rules in the ICC—A Conversation with Judge Tarfusser after the *Gbagbo-Blé Goude* Appeal Judgment' (*Opinio Juris*, 13 April 2021).
Coen, S., 'Lawyer Admits Using AI for Research after Citing "Bogus" Cases from ChatGPT' (*The Telegraph*, 27 May 2023).
Council of Europe, 'Secretary General Joins the Summit of Leaders for Creation of Special Tribunal on the Crime of Aggression against Ukraine', Strasbourg, 9 May 2023.
De Smet, S., 'Enhancing the Quality of Reasoning about the Link Between Evidence and Factual Propositions', Indian Law Institute, New Delhi, 22 February 2019, online at www.cilrap.org/cilrap-film/190222-smet/.
Gerry, F., et al., 'Forensic Archaeology, Ad Hoc Counsel and Ethics in the ICC' (*Counsel*, 11 February 2022).
Guilfoyle, D., 'Part I—This Is Not Fine: The International Criminal Court In Trouble' (*EJIL:Talk!*, 21 March 2019).
Guilfoyle, D., 'Part II—This is Not Fine: The International Criminal Court in Trouble' (*EJIL:Talk!*, 22 March 2019).
Guilfoyle, D., 'A Tale of Two Cases: Lessons for the Prosecutor of the International Criminal Court? (Part I)' (*EJIL:Talk!*, 28 August 2019).
Hayes, N., and Powderly, J., 'The Bemba Appeal: A Fragmented Appeals Chamber Destabilises the Law and Practice of the ICC' (*PhD Studies in Human Rights*, 26 June 2018).

Heinze, A., 'Some Reflections on the *Bemba* Appeals Chamber Judgment' (*Opinio Juris*, 18 June 2018).

Human Rights Watch, 'Burma: Satellite Images Confirm Mass Destruction', 17 October 2017, online at https://www.hrw.org/news/2017/10/17/burma-new-satellite-images-confirm-mass-destruction.

International Criminal Court, 'ICC Judges Hold Retreat, Adopt Guidelines on the Judgment Drafting Process and on the Timeframe for Issuance of Key Judicial Decisions', ICC-CPI-20191007-PR1485, 7 October 2019.

International Criminal Court, 'ICC Judges Agree on Reforms in Response to Independent Expert Review at Annual Retreat', Press Release, ICC-CPI-20211121-PR1627, 22 November 2021.

International Criminal Court, 'ICC Judges Complete Assessment of IER Recommendations Concerning the Judiciary at Their Annual Retreat', Press Release, 5 June 2023.

International Criminal Court, Chambers Practice Manual, 7th edn., adopted following the judicial retreat of 2023, online at https://www.icc-cpi.int/about/judicial-divisions/chambers-practice-manual.

International Criminal Tribunal for the former Yugoslavia, 'Amendments to the Tribunal's Rules of Procedure and Evidence at the 22nd Plenary Session', Press Release JL/P.I.S./521-e, The Hague, 31 July 2000.

Jacobs, D., 'The ICC Katanga Judgment: A Commentary (part 2): Regulation 55 and the Modes of Liability', *Spreading the Jam*, 11 March 2014, online at https://dovjacobs.com/2014/03/11/the-icc-katanga-judgment-a-commentary-part-2-regulation-55-and-the-modes-of-liability/.

Jordash, W., 'Merry-Go-Round Justice: The Retrial of Stanišić and Simatović' (*Opinio Juris*, 4 January 2016).

Kalpouzos, I., 'The Yemen Project: Open Source Investigations and the Laws of War' (*Just Security*, 23 September 2019).

Karnavas, M.G., 'Making Sense of the Standard & Burden of Proof in Hybrid Courts: Reflections on the Common Law & Civil Law Approaches to Proof—Part IV', 5 July 2016, online at https://michaelgkarnavas.net/blog/2016/07/05/standard-burden-of-proof-hybrid-courts-part-iv/.

Labuda, P., 'The ICC's "Evidence Problem"' (*Völkerrechtsblog*, 18 January 2019).

Luban, D., 'Torture Evidence and the Guantanamo Military Commissions' (*Just Security*, 26 May 2021).

McIntyre, G., 'ICTR—Assessment of Evidence', *Symposium on the Legacy of The International Criminal Tribunal for Rwanda*, Arusha, Tanzania, 6–7 November 2014.

Niv, A., 'Revisiting the "No Case to Answer" Procedure—the First Step in the Right Direction' (*Opinio Juris*, 28 May 2021).

Powderly, J., and N. Hayes, 'The Bemba Appeal: A Fragmented Appeals Chamber Destabilizes the Law and Practice of the ICC' (*PhD Studies in Human Rights*, 26 June 2018).

Robinson, D., 'The Other Poisoned Chalice: Unprecedented Evidentiary Standards in the Gbagbo Case? (Part 1)' (*EJIL:Talk!*, 5 November 2019).

Sadat, L.N., 'Fiddling While Rome Burns? The Appeals Chamber's Curious Decision in *Prosecutor v Jean-Pierre Bemba Gombo* (*EJIL Talk!*, 12 June 2018).

Schabas, W.A., 'Thoughts on the Kenya Confirmation Decisions' (*PhD Studies in Human Rights*, 30 January 2012).

Stavrou, K., 'User-Generated Evidence: A Helping Hand for the ICC Investigation into the Situation in Ukraine?' (*Opinio Juris*, 14 March 2022).

Tecuci, G., 'How Intelligent is Artificial Intelligence?' (*Evidence Dialogues*, May 2023).

Trahan, J., 'Bemba Acquittal Rests on Erroneous Application of Appellate Review Standard' (*Opinio Juris*, 25 June 2018).

University of Dundee, 'University Helping the Real James Bonds', 17 August 2020, online at https://www.dundee.ac.uk/stories/university-helping-real-james-bonds.

Van Schaak, B., 'Witness Proofing and International Criminal Law' (*Int Law Grrls*, 26 November 2008)

Whiting, A., 'Appeals Judges Turn the ICC on Its Head with Bemba Decision' (*Just Security*, 14 June 2018).

Index

For the benefit of digital users, indexed terms that span two pages (e.g., 52–53) may, on occasion, appear on only one of those pages.